THE LATER MIDDLE AGES IN ENGLAND 1216—1485

by

B. WILKINSON

LONGMAN

LONGMAN GROUP LIMITED
London

Associated companies, branches and representatives
throughout the world

© Longman Group Limited (formerly Longmans, Green and Co. Ltd) 1969

First published 1969
Second impression 1970
First issued in paperback 1977
Second impression 1978
ISBN 0 582 48032 9 (paper)

ACKNOWLEDGEMENTS

We are grateful to Edward Arnold (Publishers)
Ltd for permission to reproduce the maps on
pages 268 and 269 from *The Later Plantagenets*
by V. H. Green.

Printed in Great Britain by
Lowe & Brydone Printers Limited, Thetford

To Edith

INTRODUCTORY NOTE

ONE of the effects of two world wars and of fifty years of ever-accelerating industrial and social revolution has been the growing interest of the citizen in the story of his land. From this story he seeks to learn the secret of his country's greatness and a way to better living in the future.

There seems, therefore, to be room for a rewriting of the history of England which will hold the interest of the general reader while it appeals at the same time to the student. This new presentation takes account of the recent discoveries of the archaeologist and the historian, without losing sight of the claims of history to take its place among the mental recreations of intelligent people for whom it has no professional concern.

The history will be completed in a series of eleven volumes. The volumes are of medium length, and are intended to provide a readable narrative of the whole course of the history of England and give proper weight to the different strands which form the pattern of the story. No attempt has been made to secure general uniformity of style or treatment. Each period has its special problems, each author his individual technique and mental approach; each volume is meant to stand by itself not only as an expression of the author's methods, tastes, and experience, but as a coherent picture of a phase in the history of the country.

There is, nevertheless, a unity of purpose in the series; the authors have been asked, while avoiding excessive detail, to give particular attention to the interaction of the various aspects of national life and achievement, so that each volume may present a convincing integration of those developments—political, constitutional, economic, social, religious, military, foreign, or cultural—which happen to be dominant at each period. Although considerations of space prevent minute investigation it should still be possible in a series of this length to deal fully with the essential themes.

A short bibliographical note is attached to each volume. This is not intended to supersede existing lists, but rather to call attention to recent works and to the standard bibliographies.

W. N. MEDLICOTT

CONTENTS

MAPS

PREFACE

The preparation of this volume has been greatly helped by grants from the Canada Council and from the A.C.L.S. My colleague Professor Brieger has generously read through my discussion of architecture and art. Professor Medlicott, the general editor of this series, and Longmans' reader have given me valuable advice. As ever, my wife has been called upon to bear a heavy burden, albeit in a happy common enterprise. She has contributed not only an unfailing judgement but also a full measure of forbearance. Any virtues which may appear below are the product of our conjoint effort: for the errors which remain I must take the responsibility alone.

Toronto.
25 October 1968   *B. Wilkinson*

INTRODUCTION

IN the pages below some general assumptions have been made which cannot be discussed at length but whose importance is beyond question. The interplay of the idea of the *Respublica Christiana* and an emerging national order in England is a commonplace, but it represents a complex and comprehensive development. The assumption that the whole civilization of the West was still, towards the end of the Middle Ages, strong and viable is perhaps more controversial;[1] but it is largely a matter of semantics. No one can fail to regard the three centuries before 1500 as part of a continuous evolution which began long before and still continues, though there may be debate as to the best way to describe the effect of this process on various aspects of medieval society. Whatever our judgment in regard to particular problems, there seems to be little doubt that emphasis on an antithesis between 'medieval' and 'modern' is essentially misleading. We are not dealing in the pages that follow with a transition from one civilization to another, except in a very limited sense. The date chosen for the end of this survey, as for the beginning, has no great significance; it was adopted on grounds of convenience alone.

A good deal of attention has been given below to non-political aspects of history. Indeed, an attempt has been made to discern, however inadequately, the essence of various periods, reflected in the infinite variety of life. This gives rise to many problems, but offers compensation by a greater insight into the processes of change. The same is true of the recurring complexities of history generated by the interaction of forces and personalities. We shall never agree as to the precise contribution of the many factors of historic change: we do not need to. The historian's craft does not become less, but more, exciting by virtue of our inability to be comprehensive, and by virtue of the differences of interpretation which, for this and other reasons, will always persist.

English history between 1216 and 1485 has a special excitement because of its wealth of records and chronicles, its great issues, and

[1] I have discussed this problem in a chapter, 'English Historians and the late Middle Ages in England', in *The Medieval World*, edited by Vaclav Mudroch and G. S. Couse (McGill University Press).

its equally great personalities. Its many failures were paralleled by equally striking achievements in many aspects of life, by great challenges and by great responses. I have tried to make it clear in the pages that follow that the company of great men grappling with such challenges is one of the privileges of the student of history. The company of great ideas is perhaps an even greater privilege; though it must never be forgotten that ideas are never created in a vacuum. They are the product of individuals working on the heritage, and in the environment, of their times.

I

ENGLISH SOCIETY AT THE BEGINNING OF THE LATER MIDDLE AGES

1. Manor and Vill

At the beginning of the thirteenth century, England was still overwhelmingly rural. Towns were small, forests and open fields predominated outside the wide areas of mountains or moors. Most of the population still lived in manors or vills, strong in community life but weak in resources. Society was hierarchic, dominated by a French-speaking, militaristic aristocracy supported by an illiterate English-speaking peasantry. Life was meagre and insecure, but society was astonishingly creative. The thirteenth century ranks high in the history of the progressive social order of the West.

The dominant idea was of order and gradation, the pattern on earth reflecting the pattern of heaven. Lords were at the apex, securely marked off by rank, power, distinctive speech, wealth and knightly accomplishments. At the bottom were the peasants, free and unfree, looked on by their superiors, laity and clergy alike, without obvious sympathy and sometimes with contempt. In between was a middle class, if we may use this term, consisting of merchants, administrators, and some clergy, which was still too feeble to act either as a buffer or as a link.

The lord's castle was still essentially a place of defence; the manor and vill were a means of community life in which private enterprise was subordinated to the imperative needs of survival. Despite the harsh terms used above, it would be utterly wrong to conceive of this society as entirely organized for exploitation or oppression by the aristocracy, or as quite lacking in the good life. On the contrary, it was the best that men knew under the stringent needs of the age, and it was generally accepted. Mixed in with its brutalities were the warmth and strength of a co-operative existence. Society was mostly poverty-stricken and the span of life was short (so that medieval generations were dominated by young men); but the common outlook was brightened by proximity to nature and harmony with the environment; and most men were comforted, however crass their materialism, by a simple faith in the rightness of the judgment of God. The strong religious sanction did not mean fatalistic acceptance, and the sharply hierarchic order did not prevent individualism at all levels. All estates had obligations as well as rights, though in very different degrees. There is no evidence of widespread unrest in the thirteenth century, and no threat of a Peasants' Revolt. Strange though it may seem, happiness was one of the precious products of what to most moderns seems to be a cruel and illogical ordering of affairs.

This society might have been, but was not, rigid and unprogressive. In fact its very strength created the conditions of change. The thirteenth century had the advantage of the important commercial revolution of the eleventh and twelfth, when a primitive agrarian society had accumulated surplus wealth; and a money economy had made possible the emergence of merchants and towns, and had provided the conditions for a demographic expansion which had a profound influence on every aspect of life.

Throughout the century, agriculture was the staple occupation. There were many kinds, in different parts of England, with agrarian predominating in the flat lands and pastoral in the hilly country of the north and west. In every part, the village or hamlet provided the environment in which most men spent their lives. The society of the southern midlands is much the most familiar to students of history. Here, the 'typical' village was nucleated. The houses were grouped together and surrounded by large open fields cultivated on either a two-field or a three-field system, and by the all-important woodland, meadow and waste. In the former system, one field was ploughed and one lay fallow each year: in the latter, one field lay fallow every third year. Beasts were fed in the meadows and forests, and were folded for manure. There was little understanding of the science of agriculture and for many centuries there had been only negligible technological progress. The system only worked in its poverty through common effort: the fields were divided into strips, the proceeds of which were privately owned, but were cultivated co-operatively. The average peasant was either a freeman with access to the king's courts and the protection of the king's law, or a villein who was, in theory at least, a chattel of his lord.

Alongside and frequently coinciding with the village was the manor, the unit through which the lord organized his lands and the cultivation of his demesnes. The manor did not destroy the village community but, rather, used it. But smaller manors, which we may arbitrarily define as those with less than five hundred acres of arable land, did not usually coincide with the village; they represented only a part of it, or perhaps even the sum of several parts of different villages.[1] Though much of the agrarian life was organized through manor courts, presided over by the lord's steward, this was not universal. In the Danelaw, for example, the village community normally filled this important role.

By means of the labour which the peasants owed, aided by his own *famuli* or servants, the lord cultivated his demesne. The proportion of free and villein holdings varied from manor to manor, as did every other feature of manorial life, including the relations between the freeman and the villein. According to strict legal theory, the latter held at the will of the lord; and the statute of Merton gave the lords extensive rights to enclose common lands, protecting only the freeholder's rights. The villein was liable to have his services increased arbitrarily. Bracton laid it down that he was distinguished by the fact that he did not know at night what service his lord might require of him in the morning. The land of the freeman usually carried no labour dues, or only light ones, whilst that of the villein usually carried dues that were moderate to heavy. However, in some instances these may have been due to more extensive holdings.[2] In any case, labour services frequently had a money value, entered on the records, so that if the lord was agreeable they could be rendered in cash.

Other differences between the freeman and the villein were probably much more resented. The villein was liable to various payments such as the *heriot* on the death of the head of the household, *merchet* for permission to marry, and *leyrwite* for the incontinence of a daughter. The fact that the villein was tied to the soil did not normally seem irksome, for he wanted to keep his land and his local

[1] E. A. Kosminsky, *Studies in the Agrarian History of England in the Thirteenth Century*, edited by R. H. Hilton (Oxford 1956), p. 73; Sir Frederick Pollock and F. W. Maitland, *The History of English Law Before the Time of Edward I* (Cambridge 1923), vol. I, pp. 361–83.

[2] E. Miller, *The Abbey and Bishopric of Ely* (Cambridge 1951), pp. 113–53.

attachment; but it was another sign of his inferiority. According to a thirteenth-century abbot of Burton, the villeins owned nothing but 'their own bellies'. They could be bought and sold together with the land they held. Bracton equated them with the Roman slaves.

The stigma which resulted is unmistakable. In October 1300 Robert, the son of Christine of Illey, was amerced because he called his neighbours villeins. In 1391 the Commons in parliament petitioned that no bondman be suffered to send his sons to school 'in order to advance them by clergy'. As late as the end of the fifteenth century, when villeinage was losing its significance in men's eyes, a bondman of the Abbot of Malmesbury could still say, 'If I might bring [my freedom] about, it would be more joyful to me than any worldly good.'

Villeinage, like the destitution and drudgery which were the lot of all the poorer peasants, was inherited from the dark days when Europe struggled for the very rudiments of an ordered life. Fixity of tenure and hierarchic organization of society both served their purpose, but the more they succeeded the more they were likely to be resented. Much has been made of them as a means of exploitation by the favoured few, but there is a modern reaction which emphasizes the strong and sustaining bonds which united the village community, the tenacity with which most peasants strove to enter or remain part of it, and the sense in all ranks, however tenuous it was in some, that they were united, despite many prophets of gloom, in a successful way of life.[1] On the whole, freemen and villeins lived and worked in one community, and not infrequently intermarried.[2] In some areas, the freemen and not the villeins might be the poorest people in a village.

The actions of the village community were on a very modest level an exercise in self-government. The manorial court met in theory every three weeks to dispose of the problems of the manor. The lord's steward presided, but he was not a judge in the modern sense, except in the case of offences against the lord. He gave effect to the judgment of the court, arrived at by the suitors who might

---

[1] J. A. Raftis, 'Social Structures in Five East Midland Villages' in *Econ. Hist. Rev.*, vol. XVIII (1965), pp. 83–100; G. C. Homans, *English Villagers of the Thirteenth Century* (Cambridge, Mass. 1942), p. 348.

[2] H. M. Cam, 'Pedigrees of Villeins and Freemen in the Thirteenth Century' in *Liberties and Communities in Medieval England* (Cambridge 1944). For poor freemen, see R. H. Hilton, *A Medieval Society* (London 1966), pp. 131, 137–9. For village by-laws, see the work of W. O. Ault and other references in my *Constitutional History of Medieval England, 1216–1399*, vol. III (London 1958), p. 188.

include villeins as well as freemen. By-laws were a common feature of the life of a manor or vill; they were enacted by the villagers 'by common consent'. They not only ensured the services exacted by the lord; they were also intended to serve the common interest. They expressed the will of the *vicinitas*, the whole community of the vill. That this was a force to be reckoned with, humble though it was, is shown by the actions of the villagers of Peatling Magna in 1265. They sided with Simon de Montfort, making a decision on high political matters, and attacked the marshal of the king's household as he was passing through the village. The peasants of a village community, Sir Maurice Powicke has observed, had grasped the idea of the community of the realm; and they had acted as a body in this matter as they were wont to act in other affairs.

Despite the rigidity of his legal bonds, the villein did, in fact, make the beginnings of progress in the thirteenth century. The forces making for change were cumulative and in the end would be irresistible. Towns exercised an ever-increasing attraction; and in England, as in Germany, *Stadtluft macht frei*. Cultivation for profit and exchange, rather than for subsistence, encouraged a more scientific exploitation of estates; and this could increase the prosperity of peasants as well as of landlords. Both were aided by rising prices. Advantage could be gained from expanding cultivation, including *assarts* (the clearing of woodland), the draining of marshes like Romney and the Fenland, and the creation of new towns (the bishop of Winchester created six new ones between 1200-55). All this expansion gave opportunity for greater freedom and the acquisition of new land. An example of this is provided by a certain Stephen Puttock at the turn of the century, villein of the prior of Ely on his manor of Sutton, and a great buyer of land. We have records of his purchases in 1300, 1303, 1304, and 1305, 1307, and 1310. He became an important man in the village, holding offices and serving on juries. And what could be achieved by a villein could obviously be achieved by a freeman.

There were other forces working in the peasant's favour. The government began to broaden its claims upon the villein and gave him a certain recognition in return. In a writ of 1225, he was exempted from taxation on the arms to which he had been sworn. In 1230 he was again assessed to arms along with other owners of property. Even though many villeins were stick-armed and fit for little but the hue and cry, it was important that the basis of selection for military service in the local levies was wealth and not status. Similarly the Statute of Winchester of 1285 enacted that guard was to be kept by any six or four men of a vill, and armour was to be maintained for keeping the peace according to wealth and not legal estate. In general it may be said that changing conditions made the peasant more important in warfare and weakened the distinction between the free and unfree. Similarly, the villein was assessed for the new tax on movables in 1225, 1232, and 1237.[1] His possessions, as well as his arms, were becoming important to the community; and it was natural that he acquired some of the rights to property appertaining to the freeman.

The increasing importance of the villein may even, despite Bracton, have been reflected in the Common Law. He was allowed to make and enforce a contract. If he purchased freehold land he could protect it against a third person by use of the assize of Novel Disseisin. The law excluded the villein from the royal courts, but it did not tolerate an arbitrary extension of villeinage. When a dispute was brought before the judges concerning the status of an individual, the judges usually placed the onus of proof not upon the alleged villein but upon the lord. Adam, son of Reginald Stenwith, was able successfully to defend his freedom at Lincoln in 1219 by appeal to a jury, which declared that his father had been free although his own status was in doubt. By Bracton's day it was argued that the child of a mixed marriage was free unless he had been born in the villein tenement of the villein partner; but in practice, the courts seem to have favoured the rule that the child followed the condition of the father.

On the whole, however, the balance of profit and loss seems somewhat surprisingly to have been against the peasant, both freeman and villein, at least on a short term view. Demographic growth was to be an abiding source of strength; but by the end of the thirteenth century it seemed to present itself as a weakness to the poorest of the poor, who were least able to grapple with the problems it created. It gave rise to a great land hunger which enabled a number of lords to maintain and even to revive the traditional labour dues, especially those owed by the villeins, wherever they considered this to be profitable. In the process they not infrequently attempted to depress free tenants into villeinage. Hence increasing general prosperity did not necessarily result in any general benefit

[1] J. A. Raftis, *The Estates of Ramsey Abbey* (Toronto 1957), pp. 232–8.

to those who held the smallest holdings or were otherwise not well defended. Labour services remained important. They were retained most, not in the backward areas of the north and west where manorialization was only just spreading, but in the south and east where it had long been established with the exception of Kent. The Essex men were still demanding the abolition of villeinage and labour dues in 1381, though by this time such dues were everywhere visibly in decline.

Demographic increase also brought about a density of cultivation which in some areas was greater than it was to be again before the eighteenth century. Marginal lands were ploughed. Agricultural techniques were improving, especially in the exploitation of demesnes; but they did not keep pace with the growing need for productivity, even though there is evidence of change from the two-field to the three-field system. Hence, whilst in general the thirteenth century was unquestionably a time of remarkable economic advance, and this strengthened liberalizing forces in the agrarian society, this society was neither as prosperous nor as stable as might be expected at first sight. Changes were in fact beginning to occur which, aided by famine and plague, would lead to far-reaching dislocations in the fourteenth century.

2. TRADE AND TOWNS

A more unmistakable progress, but with some problems not dissimilar, occurred in the cities and towns. Here, also, there was a hierarchical order of society. Trade and town privileges were the creation of the wealthy, organized into gild merchants. Corresponding to the lower strata of the vill were the unenfranchized of the cities, who bore no special burdens but who also had no voice in civic affairs and few chances of profit. But the city, nevertheless, was more democratic than the countryside and enclosed the most vital and progressive part of society. Citizens were fiercely self-conscious, hostile to the outer world, and loyal to their own community. Their way of life was far richer, more varied and more stimulating, than anything in the agrarian areas outside great feudal households or important religious centres. Humble though the towns were at the beginning of the thirteenth century, they stood for a new way of living and for new potentialities of advance. Their wealth and number both increased. They had begun as humble enclaves in a feudal world, but gradually began to assume the proportions of a challenger and a competitor, helping to sustain governments and competing in their interests with the feudal lords. Gradually and imperceptibility they began to change the basis of the whole medieval society from agrarian to urban, from one dominated by a military aristocracy to one dominated by an aristocracy of wealth.

In the thirteenth century the greatest factor making for change was the export of wool, which affected both the city and the countryside. The original impetus came mainly with the development of weaving in Flanders. Already before the thirteenth century began fifteen towns led by Bruges had formed the 'Hanse of London' which handled much of the trade that developed from the Flemish need of English wool, a commodity better than that even of Spain and obviously much nearer. 'From England', a book written in Bruges about 1200 explained, 'come wool, hides, lead, tin, coal and cheese.' Of course, wool export in the thirteenth century was the result of expansion, not innovation. The manors of the Abbey of Ely had stocked over 13,000 sheep, as recorded in Domesday Book. In the twelfth century the Cistercians, followed by some other Orders, gave the rearing of sheep a great impetus. But expansion in the thirteenth century was much more spectacular. By the end of the century England could export eight million fleeces a year.

At the same time there developed a cloth industry in England, with famous centres at towns like Beverley, Lincoln, Stamford and Northampton. York and Leicester were also well known, but produced somewhat cheaper cloth. Much of all this was for export, but with the growth of population and wealth there also developed an increasing domestic market. The most conspicuous craftsmen to organize the industry were the dyers. A good many of them, like Philip Tinctor who became mayor of Exeter in 1259, acquired considerable wealth. In contrast, weavers and fullers were generally excluded from the ranks of the burgesses. By the mid-thirteenth century a class of entrepreneurs had emerged in Leicester employing weavers and fullers, controlling the production of cloth, and selling it at the great fairs of Boston, Stamford, and St. Ives. The products were sought by merchants as far away as Italy and Spain. The scarlet cloth of Lincoln was highly priced in a tariff made at Venice in 1265. The sale of such cloth promoted the glory of the great East Anglian clothmaking towns.

The industry was aided by the harnessing of water power to the strenuous process of fulling. Fulling mills may just possibly have been introduced by the Templars as early as the twelfth century, but the evidence is scarce. It becomes abundant after the middle of the thirteenth century. There was a royal mill at Elcot near Marlborough as early as John's reign: it was rebuilt in 1237 at a cost of £4 17s 4d.[1] By the end of the century, fulling mills were mentioned in the records in many parts of England, though their spread was accompanied by strong opposition in some towns. The new development had wide repercussions, including a tendency for the broadcloth industry to find new centres in the valleys of the west riding of Yorkshire, the Lake District and the West of England. Changes such as this are hard to reconcile with the once popular insistence on the static nature of medieval society.

As the consequences of varied economic growth both at home and abroad made themselves felt, credit expanded and banking was organized, including branches and central management, efficient bookkeeping and a division of profits according to capital investment. Italians gradually replaced older lending agents like the papacy and the Jews; this was, indeed, the main reason why the latter were expelled from the country in 1290, though increasing anti-semitism played a part. The Riccardi and Frescobaldi started their great career as receivers of moneys for the papacy and as international bankers on their own; and they became especially active in support of the finances of the Crown. Representatives of Italian banking houses were recorded in England as early as 1220. Henry III permitted Sienese and Florentines to stay for three years at a time, and it shocked Matthew Paris that they could live in London like any respectable citizens. Meanwhile foreign merchants helped to increase English trade. Genoa and Florence began organizing the direct sea route between England and Italy. A Genoese fleet was in English ports in 1278, and a Venetian state fleet appeared in 1319. Their two great centres were London and Southampton, the one for finance and the other as the great port of call for the galley fleets. The London merchants often cordially disliked their Italian counterparts, who were in competition with them; but they were welcomed in Southampton, despite the turbulence of the galley crews, on account of the profits they brought.

Without trade and credit, some of the most striking activities

---

[1] E. M. Carus-Wilson, 'An Industrial Revolution of the Thirteenth Century' in *Econ. Hist. Rev.,* vol. XI (1941), pp. 39–60; also, 'The English Cloth Industry in the late Twelfth and early Thirteenth Centuries', *ibid.,* vol. XIV (1944), pp. 32–50.

of the territorial state could not have developed. Henry III at first borrowed from many sources, particularly from his brother Richard, earl of Cornwall; but after 1254 he obtained huge sums from Italian companies. Henry's policy of heavy borrowing ended in disaster, but the system was successfully used by Edward I, backed by new taxation. The Italians were frequently granted the receipt of part of the custom on wool from which to recoup their loans; the whole customs were in the hands of the Riccardi from 1275 to 1294, and in those of the shipowners and wine merchants of Bayonne between 1299 and 1302.

Population increase was both a cause and a consequence of this complex movement. It has been calculated that the number of Londoners grew from some 20,000 in 1200 to some 40,000 in 1340. The population of York may have nearly doubled between 1086 and the second quarter of the fourteenth century.[1] This is reflected in the naval strength of some ports. The Cinque Ports, not yet a confederation, had usually supplied Henry II with twenty-five ships for an expedition overseas. During Henry III's reign the number was raised to fifty-seven. The exceptional fleet which Henry gathered for his French expedition of 1230 contained in all about 290 ships, mostly from English ports.

Old towns began to burst at the seams and new towns appeared. The earl of Derby made Higham Ferrers a borough in 1251 and Bolton in Lancashire a borough in 1253. Stratford-on-Avon had eighteen peasant tenants in 1182, but was a borough community of some 300 tenants by 1252.[2] Urban areas were built up, filling what had once been ample empty spaces, and their suburbs spread out into the countryside. Bristol developed four different sets of walls where it was not bounded and protected by the Avon and the Frome. There is similar evidence of building and expansion in York. In London, the building was continuous; in the Bridge ward there was apparently no vacant site left to develop by 1279. Houses filled the gap between London and Westminster.

Other consequences of expansion are to be seen. English merchants were able to increase their share in the export of wool. The early

---

[1] E. Miller in the *V.C.H., The City of York* (Oxford 1961), pp. 52–3; G. A. Williams, *Medieval London* (London 1963), p. 317. Cf. J. C. Russell, *British Medieval Population* (Albuquerque 1948).

[2] R. H. Hilton on the West Midlands in *A Medieval Society*, pp. 185–6; E. Carus-Wilson, 'The First Half-Century of the Borough of Stratford-upon-Avon' in *Econ. Hist. Rev.* series 2, vol. XVIII (1965), pp. 46–63.

domination by foreigners is shown by the fact that even at the end of the thirteenth century Italian, German, Flemish, and French merchants were buying wool in York and paying a toll of 1*s* a sack. In 1275 only four merchants from York were engaged in the export of wool from Hull. But in the 1290s there were from six to twelve, and in 1303–4 more like twenty. Rivalry was strong, and in the early fourteenth century citizens of York petitioned that foreign traders should not be allowed to stay more than forty days on one visit. On the national scene the progress of English merchants was the same. By 1273 they shipped about a third of the 32,743 sacks which were licensed by the government for export abroad. Statistics of taxation tell a similar story. Already in 1204–5 London contributed £836 12*s* 10*d* to a tax on movables. Boston contributed £780 15*s* 3*d* and Southampton £712 3*s* 7*d*. These contributions steadily increased. Finally, a sure sign of the times though not a complete novelty, the names of wealthy merchants begin to find a place in the records, men like William of Doncaster and Laurence of Ludlow, following in the footsteps of the twelfth-century financier William Cade.

Along with increasing population and wealth, the towns acquired new forms of government in the shape of the mayor and council or some similar instruments of common action. These were a happy product of medieval creative genius and have lasted down to the present day. It was a piece of good fortune that they were instituted to be a focus of local patriotism and self-expression before the growth of the national order, economic as well as political, diminished the need for any important measure of self-government.

The emergence of the mayor and council was probably a deliberate act of creation rather than the result of gradual evolution from an existing municipal court. The new council was an advisory as well as judicial body, with functions which were broad and elastic enough to enable it to meet the rapidly expanding needs of the towns. As early as John's reign, twelve Chief Portmen had been appointed in Ipswich, 'as there are in other free boroughs in England', to govern and maintain the borough; but in general the council began as an aid to the mayor. It was appointed by the community of the town. Later government of towns tended to be by mayor and council acting together, just as the supreme authority in the realm tended to become the king-in-parliament.

Oxford obtained the royal licence to elect a mayor as early as 1199 'and there seems to have been a general impression that to have a mayor would bring the millennium'. The first mayor of Northampton to be recorded was William Tilly in 1215. He and the *probi homines*, who were the substantial men, possibly the freemen, were to expedite the affairs of the town. Leicester, not far away, set up a body of twenty-four by 1225; they were to help and counsel the alderman in the affairs of, and to give counsel to, the town. In or before 1250 this alderman had become a mayor. In 1217 William nephew of Warner was confirmed as mayor of Lincoln, as he had been in the time of John; and in 1218 the citizens elected a successor by common consent. From 1212 or soon afterwards York was headed by a mayor assisted by three bailiffs. A council also emerged, though the date of its origin is uncertain.[1]

The moving element in the growth of the towns was the merchant gild, filled with traditions of both individual enterprise and mutual aid. Such gilds had first taken shape in an age of weak government and predatory neighbours when the dominant motive of merchant groups had to be exclusive self-interest; though particular towns did, in fact, often admit merchants of the neighbourhood to their fellowship, and Ipswich even accepted the earl of Norfolk. In these circumstances, the gild's primary interest in trade was inseparable from its interest in town government. Their Piepowder courts administered Merchant Law, and they had their own privileges; but they actively promoted the growth of civic institutions and the obtaining of charters, the former of which helped to establish a new element in the English practice of self-government under the Crown. But in England there was never a degree of self-government in any way comparable to that gained by the continental commune. The mayor, for example, was the king's servant as well as chief officer of the municipality. The king's authority was not greatly limited by most city walls. He reserved for himself an interest in all matters of trade and commerce throughout the land, inside the towns as well as outside. In 1266 (probably), for example, Henry III fixed the price of ale and the weight of a farthing loaf of bread. In 1283 Edward I enacted laws for the recovery of debts in the great Statute of Acton Burnell. His lawyers worked out a concordat between Common Law and Merchant Law in the Statute of Merchants (1285) and the *Carta Mercatoria* of 1303. He was praised by a chronicler because he

[1] H. M. Cam in *V.C.H. Northamptonshire*, vol. III (London 1930), pp. 4–5; J. W. F. Hill, *Medieval Lincoln* (Cambridge 1948), p. 200; James Tait, *The Medieval English Borough* (Manchester 1936), especially pp. 265–96; B. Wilkinson, *The Medieval Council of Exeter* (Manchester 1931).

'redressed many enormities, and especially the false dealings of bakers and millers'.

Whilst the merchants were fighting for the privileges of the city and defending them against many hostile forces, their leadership was rarely challenged; but increasing prosperity and security within the towns tended to undermine rather than strengthen their ascendancy. This is not surprising since, like other medieval groups, they could be both grasping and tyrannical. Thus, to quote an extreme case, a jury reported in Derby in 1330 that

> by reason of this Gild [Merchant] the custom has prevailed among them that, if anyone bring neats' leather, wool, or wool-fells into the said town to sell, and one of the said Gild places his foot upon the thing brought, and sets a price for which he would like to buy it, no one but a member of the said society will dare buy it, nor will he to whom it belongs dare sell it to anyone save a member of the said society.[1]

Nor have we much reason to think that the Merchant Gild changed greatly when, as often happened, it became merged w th the evolving government of the town.

As aristocratic leadership appeared less vital to progress than in the early heroic days, popular ambitions expanded. Increasing prosperity underlined the rewards of office and power. Memories remained of London's *commune* and of similar movements abroad. In London itself, described in 1326 as the 'mirror to all England', the unrest of Richard I's reign clearly continued. The *populus* of London opposed the king in 1258–65. In 1262 the mayor Thomas Fitz Thomas encouraged the poor to proclaim a '*commune* of the city'. In regard to 1263 it was said 'in this year, Thomas Fitz Thomas was again elected mayor by the populace, the aldermen and principal men of the city being little consulted'. In 1272, it was claimed, 'we are the commons of the city and to us belongs the election of the mayor'.

In Northampton an inquest of 1274–75 made by the lesser folk complained bitterly that the wealthier burgesses evaded the burdens of the town, and similar complaints were made in King's Lynn, Carlisle, Norwich, Stamford, Gloucester and Winchester. In 1253 the 'lesser commune' of Oxford petitioned the king about their treatment by the greater burgesses. There was unrest in Bury St. Edmunds. As Sir Maurice Powicke has observed, the whole subject needs further investigation; though it is unlikely, he believed, that this will confirm vague generalizations that have been made about

---

[1] G. G. Coulton, *Medieval Panorama*, vol. I, pp. 332–3. A neat is an animal of the ox-kind: an ox, bullock, cow, or heifer.

movements in towns especially in the time of the Barons' Revolt.[1] Nevertheless, some friction was almost certainly inevitable and is, in fact, plainly to be discerned.

Here again, as in the countryside, progress brought its own peculiar problems. But great unrest as opposed to friction is not really to be expected. The thirteenth-century towns were lively and gregarious, bustling and growing, with something to offer to all. They gave most people a chance of a deeply satisfying way of life, above all the enjoyment of personal liberty. This priceless boon compensated for many shortcomings and helped to create great vitality. Hence, injustice and the abuse of authority were often balanced by intense loyalties and a care for the common weal. The power and glory of England still resided in the magnates and the countryside; but we can see, with the hindsight of history, that the future belonged to the towns.

3. ARISTOCRACY AND WAR

The increase of prosperity and of a comparative measure of peace had no less important effects on the aristocracy. The magnate class retained many of its old characteristics, including its aristocratic exclusiveness and pride; but it became more sophisticated and civilized. There were the beginnings, if only the beginnings, of a movement which in the end brought lords and commoners closer together. This affected many aspects of aristocratic society; but its first and perhaps most important appearance was in the field of military service, the central and essential function of the feudal lord and the ultimate basis of all his privilege and power.

Basically, the changes in military service were a result of the growth of the territorial state, whose government made wider demands for support, in war as well as in peace. There were more limited causes such as the clause against mercenaries in Magna Carta, and the development of archery in warfare which enhanced the role of the common soldier. Most changes tended to diminish the importance of individual military service on the part of the magnates, further lessened perhaps by the king's reliance on a core of household knights and sergeants. These were highly expert and reflected an increase in organizational efficiency and centralization which was generated by the growth of government. But perhaps the most important single cause of changes in the military service of the aristo-

[1] *King Henry III and the Lord Edward* (Oxford 1947), vol. II, p. 446.

cracy was a tendency towards 'rustication' of the nobility, a product of more settled conditions after the wars of Stephen and John.

This resulted in a marked tendency towards the commutation of the feudal military obligation. Tenants-in-chief brought less than their *servicium debitum* to the royal standard, and they expected to serve only forty days. The number of magnates and knights who gave personal service diminished; the payments of scutage, or fine for non-attendance, increased. The king was compelled to encourage the status of knighthood by ceremonial inauguration of young aspirants (the *adoubement*), with the gift of equipment (*arma militaria*). The status remained the honourable status of a warrior; but knights were more and more used for administrative and peaceful duties, such as service on juries or royal commissions.

Henry III and Edward I were also compelled by their needs to enforce the acceptance of knighthood by those who could afford it, regardless of any other consideration. The first general distraint to knighthood was in 1224, and applied to every layman who held one or more knight's fees. In 1240 only one knight's fee or even less was required, as long as the individual had enough land to support the knightly condition. The normal income stipulated came to be £20. The effort to enforce knighthood was long and on the whole unsuccessfully persisted in by Henry III. Edward was somewhat more successful. He wanted to create a reservoir of knights in order to strengthen, not undermine, the feudal methods of recruiting an army. He did not need money for exemptions as much as he needed the *arma militaria*, especially the heavy horse.

But enforcement of knighthood was not enough to meet the needs caused by rustication and the changing conditions of war. New demands had to be made on those below the status of knights. The *jurati* of neighbouring counties had been summoned in 1220 to help in the siege of Rockingham castle; they carried arms according to their wealth, as had been decreed in 1181. In 1242 classes of mounted men-at-arms and of archers were recognized beneath the £20 landowners. These classes gradually became a very important element in the English armies, especially under Edward I. The obligations of the local levies to keep arms commensurate with their wealth was restated in the Statute of Winchester of 1285; and though this statute was more concerned with police duties than war, it provided some assurance that if local levies were summoned to the king's armies they would already be equipped with some arms.

The combination of dismounted men-at-arms with archers was the great development of warfare under Edward I; lords played a large part in the commissions of array by which the local levies, including footmen and archers, were recruited; and their leadership in war was not obviously diminished. The service of the levies was compulsory; each township or town had to supply its quota. Nevertheless, Edward found it wise to supplement his commands by appeals to patriotism and the duty of all subjects to defend England from her enemies. The obligation he stressed fell outside the scope of feudal loyalty, and was based on the idea of a general obligation to the king and the *respublica*. Such a system of military service and such an appeal could not fail, in the long run, to have important social and political results.

Finally, Edward was led to attack, though not directly or intentionally, the whole system of territorial feudalism which was fast becoming anachronistic. He helped the aristocracy to move towards a more elastic system of military service which would allow for the effect of social and economic change. One element of elasticity was the fact that he began to 'request' military service from his tenants-in-chief, rather than 'command' it as Henry had done. He allowed individuals a greater freedom of choice by more and more recruiting from the nobility on a basis of agreement with certain magnates to serve for pay, with a stipulated retinue. The use of such agreements (indentures) and of pay (even to tenants-in-chief after their forty days' service) changed the complexion of the Edwardian armies and undermined the territorial basis of feudal service. Regional loyalty to great lords was still extremely powerful; but it was fostered not so much by knight-service owed from knight's fees, as by relationships which had no territorial basis.

The tenant-in-chief could recruit his following by the same methods of indenture and pay that were employed by the king. One of the earliest indentures known was between two magnates, Edmund Mortimer and Lord Peter de Maulay; it was dated 27 July 1287. A landmark in the use of such agreements by the lords actually came in 1290 when the Statute of *Quia Emptores* put an end to sub-infeudation, so that a lord could no longer reward his servants by making them his feudal tenants, though the effect of the statute has been overstressed.[1]

[1] J. M. W. Bean, *The Decline of English Feudalism 1215–1540* (Manchester, 1968), pp. 306–9.

The new Bastard Feudalism, as modern historians have called it, was a boon both to the ruler and the magnate. It met the king's need for a more flexible service from the aristocracy to fight his long campaigns and his 'national' wars. It helped the lords to accommodate themselves to the increasing importance of money; and it allowed both king and magnate a greater use of patronage and favour and a greater exploitation of the new organizational power. Incidentally, it helped to break down the rigidity of the feudal hierarchy by giving greater freedom to the enterprising individual, one more sign of the loosening ties of society which constituted a widespread feature of this age.

The changing outlook of the aristocracy is perhaps nowhere more clearly illustrated than in the tournament, first legalized by Richard I in 1194. It had been popular as early as Henry II's reign, when Gerald of Wales had lamented that tournaments had put literary pursuits quite out of fashion. Richard I's motive had been to improve the skill of English knights in fighting. His tournaments were rough and bloody with no rules and no holds barred. Landless and impoverished knights like William Marshall could make their fortunes by prizes and ransoms. There was no intent to kill, but there were many casualties. Hence the denunciations by the Church; in 1220 for example, those partaking and those who aided and abetted were excommunicated.

During the thirteenth century some of this roughness and bloodshed began to disappear. Tournaments became increasingly popular, at least for the barons; but this was probably a sign of diminishing, not increasing, fighting and war. Unlike Richard, Henry III distrusted tournaments as facilitating the spread of political discontent. Strict limitations were imposed in 1267, a time of bitter opposition to Henry, on the holding of tournaments and particularly on the bearing of arms by squires and spectators. Edward I encouraged them for the same reasons as Richard I; but statutes of his reign forbade pointed swords, reduced the number of esquires, and limited the arming of attendants. Tournaments where there was danger of a *mêlée* were forbidden.[1]

A revival of Arthurian romance introduced a conspicuous note of chivalry. Round tables began to be fashionable as early as 1252

[1] N. Denholm-Young, 'The Tournament in the Thirteenth Century', in *Studies in Medieval History Presented to F. M. Powicke*, edited by R. W. Hunt, W. A. Pantin, R. W. Southern (Oxford 1948), pp. 240–68.

(the first mentioned in the Public Records was in 1232). In 1284 Edward I held a round table at Nevin on the Carnarvonshire coast to celebrate his victory over Llywelyn of Wales; and the festivities included dancing in an upper chamber, which collapsed, throwing everybody to the floor. Nobody, as far as we know, duplicated the famous feat of St. Dunstan in 978, who 'alone stood upon a beam'.

The tournament reflects an aristocracy still wedded to military pursuits but moving towards greater refinement and *courtoisie*. The change can be discerned also elsewhere. As V. H. Galbraith has observed, the steps by which first in Glanville and then in Bracton we trace the rise of a working alternative to fighting are momentous advances in civilization.[1] Cumulative influences were operating to make the typical magnate tend to become as much politician and administrator as warrior. Simon de Monfort was exceptional in his combination of qualities; but others, like the young Gilbert de Clare, for instance, followed his example if on a lower plane. The hero of the thirteenth-century *Florance et Blancheflor* was taught as a child to read Latin and write on parchment. Simon de Montfort was a sound Latinist and something of a scholar; his elder brother had been the pupil of a mathematician highly praised by Roger Bacon; and his children were taught by the great Robert Grosseteste. The normal education for a nobleman's son was still obtained in some aristocratic household, where he was taught military skill and social accomplishments; but it was not necessarily quite lacking in letters. Grosseteste's household, for example, was crowded with *domicelli*. Both Henry III and Richard de Clare asked Robert what was in effect the same question: how one of such humble birth could teach the nobility so well.

Alongside this training the universities began to offer an education. Both Bogo de Clare, who was intended for the Church, and his younger brother Thomas who was not, received gifts from Henry III whilst they were in Oxford from 1257 to 1259. Since Bogo was only eleven or twelve when he left, he cannot have been at the university as an ordinary student, but his education under its shadow remains significant. In any case, whether attending a university or not the average noblemen in this century achieved an increasing education in public affairs. Versed in the management of broad estates, well supplied with expert advisers, proud of their

[1] V. H. Galbraith, 'The Death of a Champion', in *ibid.*, p. 289.

ancestry and traditions and secure in their strongholds, they stood on the steps of the throne and expected to aid in the government of the realm. Tough and hard and shrewd, they were secure at the apex of society and, along with the bishops, held much of the destiny of England in their hands.

4. The Middle Classes and The Pursuits of Peace

Nevertheless, the aristocracy had now for the first time to reckon seriously with what we may for convenience call the middle classes, who were preoccupied with the arts of peace rather than of war. The term 'middle class' is notoriously difficult to explain as applied to any period of the Middle Ages;[1] and by almost any definition the importance of such a class in the thirteenth century was still small. It goes without saying that it included the merchants, but its most important members were still in the countryside, consisting of the smaller gentry who filled the offices of sheriff and escheator and were appointed on judicial commissions by the king. It has been claimed that under Henry III the knight was already a landed proprietor, with an essentially civilian mode of life and a predominantly administrative occupation. We get a glimpse of his activities in the Statute of Westminster II in 1285, and the law *De illis qui debent poni in Juratis* of 1293, by which only those who had 40*s* a year in rents were to be put on assizes, juries, and recognitions. Other duties, particularly those of Justice of the Peace which came later, gave the knights vast administrative experience and not inconsiderable power. Indeed, such experiences may well have contributed greatly to their success in parliament.

However, the ascendancy of the country gentry in the middle class was steadily diminishing. One rival who was now becoming significant in the political and social hierarchy was the managerial expert without whom the complex ordering of thirteenth-century society would have been impossible. Such experts now acted as stewards, bailiffs and councillors not only to the king but also to prelates and magnates; and they had a rapidly increasing influence on the community. In March 1284 Archbishop Pecham wrote to Earl Gilbert of Gloucester suggesting that disputes between them might best be settled by a meeting between the archbishop and his council and the earl and his council, in or near London. The earl of

[1] See my 'Fact and Fancy in Fifteenth-Century English History', in *Speculum*, vol. XLII (Oct. 1967), pp. 673–92.

Glouecster probably had eleven councillors in 1299, consisting of seven household knights and four clerics, most of whom had had valuable experience in administration.[1] The royal service was increasingly dependent on the contribution of permanent officials; many of them were very highly skilled and an increasing number of them were university trained.

Such men had absorbed the subtleties of scholasticism, and some had also studied Civil and Canon law. They helped to bind the increasingly complex society of the century together, including its hierarchical order and its group organizations. The broadest distinctions in the society between men of prayer, men of war, and men of work were as old as the time of King Alfred and would outlast the Middle Ages. They still evoked strong loyalties and mutual obligations which permeated all ranks. But they were derived from a time when men's outlook was in the main regional and bounded by the relationships of a still primitive agrarian society, when the needs of survival seemed to justify the subordination of the individual to the group, and when men perforce tolerated a violence and brutality increasingly incompatible with the refinements of the age. All men, even the merchant, habitually wore sword or dagger. Violence was endemic and brutality common. But, like modern violence, it had a disproportionate place in the records. Alongside it were a great sensitivity to beauty and suffering, and a gradual amelioration of the brutalities of life.

5. RELIGION

One all-pervading and powerful element in society was religion; indeed, in some ways medieval Christianity was at its apogee in this century. It had gained by social and intellectual progress, and it was not yet appreciably weakened by scholastic speculations on the one hand or by a growing secularism on the other. The Church showed serious and growing weaknesses; but it produced a fine devotional literature and some eminent bishop-scholars. Its contribution to a gradual refinement of manners and lessening of cruelties may be impossible to assess; but it kept a light of idealism burning brightly

[1] R. F. Treharne, 'The Knights in the Period of Reform and Rebellion, 1258–1267: A Critical Study in the Rise of a New Class', *Bulletin of the Inst. Hist. Res.*, vol. XXI (May–Nov., 1946), pp. 1–12; N. Denholm-Young, 'Feudal Society in the Thirteenth Century: the Knights', in *History*, vol. XXIX (Sept. 1944), pp. 107–19; Michael Altschul *A Baronial Family in Medieval England: The Clares: 1217–1314* (Baltimore: Johns Hopkins Press 1965), p. 225.

in spite of its own deficiencies. It was a potent, if incalculable, factor in a vast and complicated process of change.

The dominant note for the Church in this century was set by Innocent III's not unsuccessful efforts, in politics and councils, and in legislation and institutional organization, to give expression to his ideal of a united and centralized *Respublica Christiana* under a pope to whom all men owed obedience *ratione peccati*. His successors carried on his work by crushing heresy and defeating the political challenge of the Hohenstauffen emperors. Finally, the friars carried the influence of the Church to new heights in the market place, and by their efforts brought the new urban centres securely into the Christian fold.

The Church in England was still an integral part of the Church Universal and shared its strength and its weakness. The monks, with the oldest Order going back to St. Benedict, stood for an ordered life and withdrawal from lay society; the secular clergy had the cure of souls; and some monks, like the Premonstratensians, shared the outlook and duty of both. As always, the monkish orders through their ideals of asceticism and withdrawal from the world called for greater sacrifice and testified more to the Christian inspiration, but fell away more, in consequence, from their ideals. In the twelfth century they had been reinforced by the Cistercians with stark rules of labour, poverty, and seclusion in inaccessible places; but at the beginning of the thirteenth there was need for a new testimony of faith in the monastic ideal of renunciation and sacrifice if the bright vision which had inspired St. Benedict and a long line of successors was not to be almost completely obscured.

This was provided by the Franciscans and Dominicans who in the early years of the century epitomized the finest idealism in the Church. The Franciscans patterned their lives on the model of Christ himself, pushing the renunciation of worldly goods and ambitions to the uttermost. The Dominicans, scarcely behindhand in austerity, exemplified the Christian union of intellectual and religious experience. The popularity of both orders showed the strength of idealism in the community and of the Christian belief. Both, in their own way, brought new skills and new zeal in the unending battle to keep the allegiance of the laity and to maintain and enlarge the vitality of the Church.

Arriving in England in 1221 and 1224 in the persons of thirteen Dominicans and nine Franciscans, both Orders had a generous reception. Oxford became a citadel of both; the former went there as to a centre of learning, the latter in search not so much of scholars as of bright young men who might be atttracted by their ideals. They produced eminent intellectuals like Roger Bacon and William of Ockham; but the early inspiration of both was their founders' visions of upholding and disseminating the Christian truth. They were peripatetic and mendicant, at least in the beginning; they made the sermon a formidable means of instruction; and they brought new skill to the confession. Their humility and zeal earned widespread admiration. Three things, according to Albert of Pisa, distinguished the Franciscans of England: they went barefoot; they wore shabby clothes; and they refused money. Henry III made them his confessors. Townsmen welcomed them warmly. Only the older orders of monks showed them hostility; though to these must later be added many a parish priest. To the monks they appeared as rivals; at Bury St. Edmunds the hostility was so strong that they only lodged there in 1257 under cover of darkness, and even so they were shortly driven away. But nothing could stop their progress. By 1300 both orders had more than fifty houses. Their recruits included two bishops. Robert Grosseteste himself almost joined them. They had become a familiar and vital element in religious life.

Their brilliant start was followed by an equally conspicuous failure; but nothing can destroy the significance of their struggles and achievements in the century after 1221. Their decline may almost be regarded as inevitable. Wealth was the greatest single enemy of the ascetic Christian ideal; and the friars' way of life, like that of the Cistercians, brought the speedy accumulation of wealth. In such a movement, which was vowed to poverty and renunciation, it may be claimed paradoxically that nothing fails like success. Gifts, payments and influence obscured St. Francis's ideals of humility and mendicancy. There were rewards for preaching, confessions and burials; there were elegant churches and impressive houses. Matthew Paris said that these last were as grand as royal palaces. The mendicants even, in time, farmed out the right to beg. Such an arrangement was behind the description much later of the friar in Chaucer's *Canterbury Tales:*

> He was the beste beggere in his hous
> For thogh a widwe hadde noght a schoo
> So plesaunt was his *In principio*
> Yet wolde he have a ferthing er he wente
> His purchas was wel bettre than his rente.

On the continent, already in the thirteenth century, Bonaventura declared that the people were as much afraid to meet a friar as a highway robber, for he was certain to take some of their money from them. In England, Matthew Paris lamented that 'during the last three or four centuries or more the monastic Order has not fallen so rapidly downward as their Order [of the Friars]'.

What the friars could not accomplish could not now be achieved by the older monastic orders. These still reflected some of the idealism which had long before moved St. Benedict, but they had much less to offer than the friars. Of the Benedictines themselves it has been said:

> The old simplicity has gone: and the picture [at Monte Cassino in the sixth century] of a group of men supporting themselves by the labours of their hands, cut off from the sights and sounds of the world, conforming to the standards of living appropriate to peasants, has changed to one of a flourishing community, owning vast estates and employing large numbers of men, involved in all the anxieties and excitements of the business world, and enjoying a standard of living which was shared only by their richer neighbours.[1]

Even the comparatively new order of the Cistercians had lost much of the original inspiration. Their earliest foundation in England was at Waverley in 1128. By 1200 they had sixty-two houses in the country. They were free from episcopal control, but had their own system of visitation. During the twelfth century they had made a tremendous impact on public opinion; but by the beginning of the thirteenth they differed little from the Benedictines. In particular, their sheep-farming had brought them wealth. Work in their fields came to be done by the *conversi* or lay-brothers.

Among the Cistercians and Augustinians this term was applied to men living according to a rule, but one not as strict as that of a monk or canon. The *conversi* lived in their own quarters, had their own part of the church, and carried out the manual work. In the early days, they outnumbered the monks. They were illiterate, turbulent, and hard to discipline. All the orders of monks had their *conversi*; but, because of the difficulties they created, they tended to be superseded by paid servants, especially among the older orders. There were at one time thirty servants to fourteen canons in the Priory of Austen Canons at Bolton in Wharfedale; whilst at Nostell there were seventy-seven servants for twenty-six canons. When

[1] J. R. H. Moorman, *Church Life in England in the Thirteenth Century* (Cambridge 1945), p. 243.

Evesham was mismanaged by its abbot, the monks went without food in order to feed the servants, 'since without them we cannot live'. Servants helped monasteries to bear their great burden of hospitality, but at a very heavy cost.

The keeping of many servants did not mean that a monastery was wealthy; indeed, servants were part of an all too prevalent waste that led inevitably to debt. They were one sign that the old monkish ideals of austerity had almost disappeared. Grosseteste's three essentials of well-being — food, sleep, and laughter—were all provided in full measure; but 'the plain fare envisaged by St. Benedict had been considerably modified by the addition of flesh-meat and numerous pittances (special allowances of food); the rough once sombre clothing of the early days had been embellished by warmer and softer garments; manual labour had been replaced by reading or administration, and the tedium of the cloister was constantly interrupted by entertainments, holidays and expeditions into the towns or into the woods'.[1] The management of the monastic estates and the performance of public duties often absorbed most of an Abbot's time. The monks themselves had become a greatly favoured minority among hard-working agrarian communities, and gave comparatively little for what they received.

To meet their financial needs they had developed many sources of income besides the rents and profits from their estates, though it is interesting that the rich flow of legacies and bequests which they had once enjoyed was drying up. Among other sources was one that was not easy to justify; this was the system of appropriation by which the monasteries took to themselves the income of a living in the church and appointed a vicar at a pittance (or failed to appoint one at all). To gain further income many monasteries indulged in trade and farming for profit. Bolton Priory had over 2,000 sheep in 1301, and the size of the Cistercian flocks is very well known. But balancing these profits there were losses which came to most of them at one time or another. They had to face the vicissitudes of inexpert administration, the improvidence of abbots, the burden of taxation, hospitality, and extravagance. These could, and did, reduce particular monasteries to poverty. In 1275 the monks of Faversham were almost starving, so badly had their finances been mismanaged.

---

[1] J. R. H. Moorman, *Church Life in England in the Thirteenth Century* (Cambridge 1945), p. 349.

Bright though some of the achievements of thirteenth-century monasticism were, the ultimate well-being of Christianity lay with the secular clergy, organized in hierarchical order from the two archbishops at the apex to the humble parish clergy at the bottom. Here, too, the century witnessed a mixture of successes and failures. Signs of expanding horizons and a more resolute effort to promote Christian ideals can be seen in the work of reforming councils in England, like those held at different times in Oxford, Lambeth and Reading. Homiletic literature was a conspicuous feature of the century. Brilliant scholar-bishops, notably Robert Grosseteste, John Pecham, and Robert Kilwardby, led the attack on the weaknesses of the clergy. Their devotion and zeal matched that of any century.

Pluralism was attacked repeatedly, by the council of Oxford in 1222, by Grosseteste in 1238, by the papal legates Otto and Ottobuono, and by Pecham immediately after his consecration. Nonresidence was equally condemned. Great efforts were made to ensure that rectors and vicars were ordained priests who could perform the duties of their office, with Grosseteste and Pecham again taking the lead. Richard le Poore, successively bishop of Chichester, Salisbury, and Durham, set an example in his statutes by carefully stating the faith that a parish priest was expected to teach. Others taught him how to perform his duties, including the celebration of the Mass. The morals of the clergy were not neglected. They were harried for their concubines, condemned for their greed, assailed for their laziness. Their inner life and thought were harder to penetrate, though statutes demanded that every parish priest should know the Ten Commandments, the Creed, the Seven Sacraments, and the Seven Deadly Sins. There was a considerable process of organization throughout all levels of the clergy, including an important movement to increase the activities of the laity by developing the office of churchwarden. Archbishop Gray, in his injunctions of 1250, made the lay congregation responsible for providing ornaments, vestments, and books. Aided by the friars, reformers improved the practice of preaching and the quality of the sermon. They gave learning a new importance in the Church.

Robert Grosseteste himself was not only a scholar of towering capacity, he was also a reformer of courage and pertinacity. He was a great preacher, in both Latin and English, and two or three hundred of his sermons have survived. He was of humble origin, born in Suffolk about 1168. He taught in Oxford after 1190, and studied in Paris between 1209 and 1214. Bishop of the wealthy diocese of Lincoln from 1235 to 1253, he became a leading statesman of the Church. He began his pastoral exhortations at Lincoln by denouncing drunkenness which 'deprives man, made in the image of God, of the use of his reason', and he continued to be unsparing in his castigation of weaknesses in both laity and clergy. He was unwearying in episcopal visitations, and wrote admirable Constitutions to educate 'rectors, vicars, and parish priests' in their duties. According to Matthew Paris, he 'came down on the monks like a hammer', and he particularly denounced appropriations. Yet he defended the rights of the clergy against both king and pope: obedience, he claimed, was only owed to the king as long as he acted rightly, and to the pope as long as his commands were in harmony with Holy Writ. He is famous for his subtle, perhaps over-subtle, justification of opposition to the Vicar of Christ: 'It is out of filial reverence and obedience that I disobey, resist, and rebel.'

Grosseteste inevitably made many enemies, including his own Dean and Chapter, and engaged in many controversies; but in most of these he was right. His episcopal career was one of *Sturm und Drang*; but it made him almost the real, if not the formal, head of the English Church. And he had warm friendships—with Queen Eleanor, with the king's sister who was Montfort's wife, with the great Franciscan scholar Adam Marsh, and with Simon de Montfort himself.

In 1250, towards the end of his long life, he paid a fruitless visit to the Papal Curia at Lyons. He is reputed to have said in shame 'O money, money, how much power you have, especially at the Roman Court!' He departed, Matthew Paris wrote, 'amid the insulting cries of all present', and returned to England with empty hands and a sad countenance. But he had had the courage to read before the pope and cardinals a denunciation of ecclesiastical abuses as forthright as any that has ever been penned, rarely surpassed in the vigour of its invective even in the writings of the sixteenth century. In particular, he argued that reform of abuses in the central administration was an essential condition of a general improvement of the Church.

He died on (probably) 9 October 1253, bequeathing his precious books to the Franciscan library at Oxford. Roger Bacon constantly spoke of him as Saint Robert. Matthew Paris warmly praised his virtues. Wyclif ranked him above Aristotle. Attempts were made later to canonize him. 'God knows', a Canon of Lincoln wrote about 1330, 'why the attempts did not succeed.' Besides praising his unrivalled scholarship, his admirers stressed most of all his humility, simplicity, and sanctity.

John Pecham, born about 1230 and made archbishop of Canterbury in 1279, was a lesser figure, but still outstanding. He began his public career as a great scholar and ended as a distinguished reformer. He spent thirteen years in Paris, achieved fame for his lectures at Oxford, and in 1277 was made lector in theology at the papal Curia. He also became provincial of the Franciscan Order. As archbishop he was famous for his extreme severity and austerity. In 1276 he walked all the way across Europe to attend the chapter general of his order at Padua. His nomination to Canterbury by Nicholas III was unexpected, almost certainly unsought, and probably unwelcome. It was here, however, that he left his greatest mark on history.

He had been made archbishop especially to apply the reforming decrees of the Second Council of Lyons and he began his task early, in Provincial Councils at Lambeth (1261). His 'application of the surgeon's cautery', as he called it, was comprehensive but most of all directed against the evils of pluralism. His refusals to compromise made him many enemies, including the king, and contributed to some spectacular failures, such as the public humiliation he received in the parliament of 1279. The opposition he met seldom failed to surprise him, for he was warm-hearted and well-intentioned; but his zeal had a habit of outrunning his discretion, as when he talked of the 'mass of immorality, inefficiency, and indifference' he saw around him, or told the monks of Christ Church, Canterbury, that he had shunned their society because of their persistent and malicious attacks upon his rights. Nor can we altogether justify his excommunication of bishops, in the name of God, the Virgin, and St. Thomas of Canterbury, for opposition to his methods of rule.

But all this must not be allowed to obscure his real stature, or his contribution to reform. His decree *Ignorantia Sacerdotum*, instructing the clergy in the performance of their duties, was influential for generations. It was used in the fourteenth century by John Stratford and by John Thoresby, archbishop of York, and by Archbishop Arundel in the fifteenth. He rivalled Grosseteste in his visitations: in his first eight years as archbishop, he visited every diocese of his province, including Wales, a feat never accomplished before. The thirteen years of his archiepiscopal office may have seemed largely a failure, but they illustrate the nature of the problems which beset the Church in the thirteenth century and the heroic struggles that were made to achieve a significant measure of reform.

The struggles for reform did, indeed, lead to better organization in the Church and to a more effective exercise of the priestly office. Unfortunately some of the gains were more than offset by increasing weaknesses. Many of these flowed from the influence of wealth and power on the clergy. Others can be seen stemming from the growing identity of interest between the Church and the secular State, and the tendency of the clergy to become the instruments of the ruler, resulting in an almost complete abandonment of the Hildebrandine ideal. Clerics took over much of the complex administration at the centre of government and were rewarded by livings in the Church, frequently becoming noted pluralists. Ministerial bishops owed a divided loyalty to matters spiritual and matters temporal. The whole structure of the Church suffered. Nor was its spiritual zeal kindled by the papacy, busy organizing on the lines set out by Innocent III, or by the conflict between the pope as vicar of Christ and the lay ruler as Emperor in his realm.

The unity of the *Respublica Christiana* was not yet threatened. Nevertheless, Robert Grosseteste who had been a stout defender of it had himself revealed a process of erosion. He was perhaps the first great prelate since the Anglo-Saxon Wulfstan of Worcester who can be claimed, with all due reservations, as an Englishman, much more so than the cosmopolitan Londoner Thomas Becket of the century before. Similarly, King Edward I may perhaps be claimed as the first ruler to claim from his bishops a loyalty to England which at times outweighed that which they owed to the pope. But though Edward forsook his father's dependence on the papacy, this did not mean any diminution of the injurious policies followed by the king and pope in conjointly exploiting the resources of the Church.

Both pope and king were responsible for the failure to reform; each supported the other in the abuse of pluralism, one of the greatest evils. Nor were the lay magnates quite innocent: they wanted church appointments for their clerical helpers and for their younger sons. The scandalous pluralism of Bogo de Clare, younger son of the rich and powerful earl of Gloucester, is a well-known example. Pluralism of course often meant underpaid vicars or outright neglect; Robert Grosseteste testified to the consequences in eloquent terms.

But the greatest single obstacle to reform was probably the papal Curia. Roger Bacon traced to this source the 'immeasurable corruption' which he saw in the Church. The pope could get his nominees (often absentee) appointed to English benefices; and by the use of his *plenitudo potestatis* he could grant dispensations from prohibitions, such as those at Oxford in 1222, by which the leaders of the Church in England tried to curb the abuse.

One result of the increased papal activity was an outburst of anti-papalism in England. In what have been called the Anti-Roman tumults of 1231, a secret society was organized by laymen who declared themselves to be 'the whole community of those who would rather die than be put to shame by the Romans'. Their aim was 'to rescue the Church as well as the king and the kingdom from the yoke of such oppressive slavery'; and to achieve this they plundered the barns and seized the property of foreign clergy who held English benefices. Some time later magnates and clergy joined hands to complain to Rome. The clergy were, indeed, as the English abbots put it in 1245, ground between the upper and nether mill-stones, oppressed by the exactions of the king as well as of the pope.

A milestone in the growth of anti-papalism came with the famous quarrel between Edward I and Boniface VIII. Edward was trying to tax the clergy and thus put them on a level with the laity in subjection to the demands of the state; Boniface was attempting to protect them from the sovereign's demands. But, deeper than this, the quarrel was not so much concerned with the attack on, and defence of, the liberty of the Church in England as with the rival claims of two 'monarchies', papal and 'national'. On the whole it was the secular ruler who won; but there was in fact a concordat in which both 'monarchs' combined to dispose of livings and nominate to benefices. This worked reasonably well for a good many years; but it did nothing to promote the spiritual life of the Church.

Thus, in spite of a higher general level of civilization in England, and in spite of some inspiring efforts at reform, progress was disappointing. The Church made an unprecedented attempt to influence the lives of the laity. It made new and vital contacts with the people, especially through homilies and sermons in their mother tongue. If it failed to make any notable improvements, this was not so much through lack of effort as because of the magnitude of the problems involved. These were both inside and outside the Church itself;

but perhaps the deepest of all were within, accentuated by wealth, institutional development and power. The Church has always been confronted with a broad gulf between unattainable Christian ideals and the defects arising from original sin. At no time was this gulf more apparent than in the days of the fast waning inspiration of the friars. At no time was the zeal and idealism of reformers more inspiring or less effective in lasting results.

6. INTELLECTUAL LIFE

The learning of the century was closely allied to religion but it was perhaps freer from the limitations imposed by human imperfection. It had great vitality and inspiring traditions, and limitless worlds of darkness to explore. It profited abundantly from its historical and cultural dependence on France. It was also stimulated by the energies of a conspicuously successful way of life. The result was a remarkable process of advance, helped by the fact that the world of learning was now, for the first time, bound up with the newly emerged phenomenon of the university, one of the many creative medieval groups.

The first Oxford teacher recorded was Theobaldus Stampensis, from Étamps in Normandy, who came to the city about 1100; it was said that he taught a hundred scholars, more or less. By 1214, there was a Chancellor, and presumably a university, which had been depleted in 1209 by a migration of scholars to Cambridge. The Chancellor was probably selected by the masters from among themselves, though until 1368 the election had to be confirmed by the bishop of Lincoln, in whose diocese Oxford lay. The evolution of the university followed that of Paris, though local circumstances created important differences.

Oxford and Cambridge, like Paris, were *universitates* or associations of teachers. They were *Studia Generalia*, recognized as centres of learning throughout Europe, whose masters could teach anywhere. Great universities in Europe specialized in different aspects of knowledge. The English, like most of the French, specialized in theology and philosophy. The students were drawn from all classes. Most of them received their preliminary education from parish priests, or later from grammar schools. Poor men's sons were sent to the university by wealthy patrons or religious Orders. A student might enter at an early age, no more than 14 years old, with meagre attainments but some knowledge of Latin. It would take him at least five or six years to become a master, studying the *trivium* (Grammar, Rhetoric and Logic) and *quadrivium* (Arithmetic, Astronomy, Music and Geometry). After that he would become expert in the subject of his choice, philosophy, theology or law, leading to a doctorate which might take up to twelve or thirteen years, though uninterrupted residence was not insisted on. Law was probably the most favoured and lucrative course to take. The long courses were not as broad and deep as at first sight might appear, but they were nevertheless arduous. Lectures began at 6 a.m. Books were scarce. The well-known words in the biography of St. Richard Wych, bishop of Chichester, are worth repeating[1]:

> Richard therefore hastily left both [his father's] lands and the lady [marked out to be his bride], and all his friends, and he took himself to the university of Oxford and then to Paris where he learned logic. Such was his love of learning that he cared little or nothing for food or raiment. For, as he was wont to relate, he and two companions who lodged in the same chamber had only their tunics, and one gown between them, and each of them had a miserable pallet. When one, therefore, went out with the gown to hear a lecture the others sat in their room, and so they went forth alternately. Bread and a little wine and pottage sufficed for their food. Their poverty never allowed them to eat meat or fish except on a Sunday or some solemn holy day, or else in the presence of companions or friends. Yet he has often told me how he never afterwards, in all his days, led such a pleasant and enjoyable life.

The universities developed traditions and organization. Smaller groups were established within the larger societies, the best known of which are the well known colleges for scholars. These in general followed the pattern set by St. Louis's chaplain Robert de Sorbon at Paris in 1258. The oldest such foundation at Oxford was created by William of Durham in 1249, by a bequest to provide for the support of ten or more masters of arts who were studying theology. In 1264 Walter de Merton began the long and illustrious career of the college called after him, providing for eight original scholars. Balliol College had a *de facto* existence before June 1266. The early colleges were largely independent and self-governing like any medieval gild. Many students without Richard Wych's devotion to learning never obtained a degree, but they had been given a great opportunity. The system of lectures and disputations they encountered was the outcome of a chronic scarcity of books and writing

[1] They refer to what G. G. Coulton called 'the golden days of the thirteenth century'; *Medieval Panorama* (Cambridge 1938: reissued London, 1961), vol. II, p. 24.

equipment, but it was nevertheless effective. Lectures, literally the reading of authoritative books with the master's glosses, encouraged an undue dependence on authority, whilst disputations encouraged extravagance and mere verbal dexterity. But, properly used, the methods produced some remarkable scholars. The pursuit of knowledge, as at all times, had very mixed motives; but it has seldom been more admirably practised than in this remarkable age.

The fact that in the thirteenth and fourteenth centuries students were normally in minor orders at least did not prevent those who had brains and energy from entering and obtaining the highest rank in every profession, religious and secular. They adorned the bench of bishops and filled many lesser positions of administration in the expanding organization of the Church. They were the pillars of the rapidly developing administration of kings and nobles, and they contributed to the spread of the Common Law. They acted as confessors and advisers to kings, prelates, and nobles. They gave to the growing universities their distinguished scholars and teachers. They wrote innumerable books, treatises and works of devotion, and influenced profoundly the whole outlook of their times. There was nothing quite like the universities in any previous generation in Europe, perhaps not anywhere.

At the beginning of the thirteenth century Oxford was still in its infancy, and the great impact of the two English universities on the life of the community had not really begun. One dynamic event, the advent of Dominican and Franciscan scholars, had yet to occur. English scholarship was still overshadowed by that of France. Even during the course of a century of advance, it failed to obtain the allegiance of most European scholars, but it nevertheless had an abiding influence on medieval thought.

The nearest counterpart to Thomas Aquinas in England was Robert Grosseteste, who has already been discussed in relation to religion. This many-sided man of genius became Oxford's most distinguished teacher, rising to become its Chancellor. Only the fact that he lived just before the full integration of Aristotle into Christian learning prevented him from rivalling Bonaventura and Aquinas as an enduring architect of European thought. The time seemed propitious for such a scholar. For half a century before Grosseteste's birth the foundations for his great intellectual work had been laid by translators and encyclopaedists. Many scholars during this period observed things for themselves, but they could not generalize problems or establish general proofs and explanations. Nevertheless a genuine scientific method had become possible; some scholars could even regard mathematics as the model science. Speculation seemed to hover on the threshold of a revolutionary advance.

Grosseteste himself injected a new and potent element into scholastic thinking. He showed the strength and versatility of scholasticism in its greatest period and its capacity to develop new attitudes without discarding old and fundamental beliefs. That he did not change the broad lines of intellectual development is not a sign of his limitations; it merely suggests that there was no short cut from the preoccupations of scholasticism to those of modern science.

With the aid of Aristotle, Grosseteste worked out fruitful methods and principles of scientific enquiry.[1] Among his principles was a belief in the uniformity of nature. 'Things', he said, 'of the same nature are productive of the same operations'; and 'the same cause, provided it remains in the same condition, cannot but produce the same effect'. He also taught a principle of economy, asserting that 'nature operates in the shortest possible way'. He worked out a system of experimental verification and falsification to separate true theories from false. Among the means of achieving knowledge he gave special importance to mathematics. By his scientific methods he was able to realize the contradictions between Ptolemy and Aristotle in astronomy; in fact he pointed the way to the reform of the whole subject which was much later effected by Copernicus and Newton.

To Grosseteste there was no gulf between metaphysics and physics and no conflict between neo-Platonic scholasticism and his own. He was a great if not original theologian; and he betrays no sense of an antagonism between his understanding through religion and that arrived at by science. Indeed, one characteristic of his teaching was a close attention to the Bible, read textually and critically together with a study of languages, especially Greek; though he himself, if we may trust Bacon, was no great translator. His philosophy, theology, and science were all harmoniously related and indeed inseparable. His Augustinian view of knowledge as the illumination of the intellect by the divine ideas led naturally to his

[1] E.g. the phenomenon of the rainbow: see 'Grosseteste's Position in the History of Science', by A. C. Crombie, in *Robert Grosseteste Scholar and Bishop*, edited by D. A. Callus (Oxford 1955), pp. 98–120.

concept of the importance of light; and with him, as with Bacon later, sciences such as optics and astronomy were an essential part of philosophy, along with the traditional logic and metaphysics. The whole complex system of his thought was one of the most remarkable products of his age.

The same is partly true of Roger Bacon, his successor as a leading English scholar, though Roger was so much out of tune with his age that he spent about fourteen years in an episcopal prison. In the first part of his life Roger followed the beaten path, as he himself declared[1]; in the second he struck out on a line of his own. In the first period, argument was the principal guide, in the second, experience; but there was no simple break. He protested against the excessive importance attached to logic and metaphysics; but he also valued his own philosophical training, and denounced those who ventured on theology without a similar background. He was not, in any case, as original a thinker as has sometimes been thought. He developed ideas, with great learning and ingenuity, but he did not often originate them. He searched for the laws of nature, but he did not allow this to conflict with his acceptance of religious tradition; and he denied strongly that such laws obscured the handiwork of God. Nature, he believed, was the instrument of this handiwork. By knowledge of created things we reach a knowledge of the Creator. It is true that he believed, contrary to most contemporary thinkers, though not against Grosseteste, that the two principal keys to knowledge were languages and mathematics, not logic. Indeed, he believed this so strongly that he produced a Greek and a Hebrew grammar. Geography, too, was important in his eyes; and here he had some very original ideas. His suggestion that it might be possible to reach the Indies by sailing westward was later quoted by Columbus. He had a remarkable vision of far-off future things, like the prototype of the modern tank, or of burning glasses that could destroy whole fortresses; but, more important, he was probably nearer the conception of general laws harmoniously combining to form an ordered system than any thinker before the eighteenth century.[2]

Nevertheless, he was no revolutionary; indeed, in some ways he was not ultra-modern but rather ultra-medieval. He did not reject

[1] A. G. Little, 'Roger Bacon' in *Proceedings of the British Academy*, vol. XIV (1928), pp. 265–96.

[2] *The Universities of Europe in the Middle Ages*, by Hastings Rashdall, edited by F. M. Powicke and A. B. Emden, vol. III (Oxford 1936), p. 246.

current beliefs but rather pressed them more vigorously than other scholars to their logical conclusions. Thus, he believed that all knowledge was contained in the Bible; but he did not deduce from this that the Bible alone should be studied. He merely believed that in order to understand the Bible *oportet theologium scire omnia*. He believed in the imminent coming of Antichrist; but he used the belief to urge the study of the secret powers of art and nature in order to confound the enemy of mankind. Similarly, like everybody else, he believed in astrology; but he argued, more logically than his contemporaries, that, since all believed in it, men should study it more deeply and use it to regulate their lives. He also believed in experience; but since he was acutely aware of its limitations he arrived at an advocacy also of the need for revelation. However, this did not prevent him from insisting that facts should be ascertained before theories were produced. Nor did it prevent him from questioning the prevailing scholastic methods and preaching the value of observation and experiment. On the one hand he condemned undue deference to authority and he believed that theology and philosophy should be studied differently from science; but on the other he still did not accept the notion of a conflict between reason and revelation.

Bacon was not without honour in his own generation. If he was imprisoned and out of favour in later years, he was renowned in his lifetime. He wrote his greatest works by command of Pope Clement IV, even though Clement could have no idea of some of the disconcerting observations these works were to contain. Bacon's later troubles may have been the result of his highly individualistic approach to truth, but they were also the result of a good measure of scholarly arrogance: at the very end of his life he could refer to a seeker after knowledge of forty years earlier as that 'utter fool'. But this might have brought him nothing worse than unpopularity except that he was involved in a fierce scholastic dispute between Franciscans and Dominicans which threatened to split Christian learning asunder. There were investigations at Paris in 1277 into heretical teaching, and these led to Roger and ended in his imprisonment. He died immediately after his release from prison in 1292. Bacon and Robert Grosseteste together represented an English movement of thought which was unique in its anticipation of the scientific enquiry that was to come. The 'school' inspired by them never emerged. Nevertheless, with them Oxford may be said to have begun a tradition of originality and independence in scholarship which it was to sustain brilliantly for another hundred years.

The great system of Thomas Aquinas which Bacon, like Bonaventura, had attacked gained many adherents; whilst Bacon himself only had one really famous, and not very grateful, pupil in Archbishop Pecham. Aquinas was canonized in 1323; but whilst his teaching immensely broadened scholastic thought, it tended to lead to a cul-de-sac. It elevated Aristotle to the rank of a purveyor of absolute truth, and his writing almost to the level of Holy Script, though the great philosopher's system of thought was only one of deductive reasoning from certain premises. Thus the cult of authority was strengthened, as well as the emphasis on logic and metaphysics, all of which Bacon had deplored.

Thomas's reliance on logic and metaphysics is understandable. The materials simply did not yet exist for quantification of nature, despite the thirteenth-century emphasis on mathematics. There was a dearth of both classification and of precise instruments. Bacon himself declared that he was quite impoverished by the effort to provide what must have been elementary tools. But the reliance on logic and metaphysics did not prevent a growing divergence between reason and revelation which even St. Thomas had not been able to avoid. One result of this was an increasing acerbity of scholastic disputation. Archbishop Pecham declared that his academic life had been one long struggle to defend the truth against two erroneous interpretations of Aristotle which were undermining the foundations of faith.[1] Many scholars were deeply shocked by the signs of deep cleavages of opinion which multiplied after 1277.

The greatest English (or, more precisely, Scottish) opponent of Thomist philosophy, vying in stature with St. Bonaventura, was Duns Scotus, possibly born about 1265 at Maxton in Roxburghshire. He became a Franciscan and was trained in the Oxford Schools. He died at Cologne in 1308. For a century and a half his work enriched and at times dominated the English scene. To his contemporaries he was the *Doctor Subtilis*. He was, indeed, a very great scholar; but he tended to abuse the syllogism, to employ an unintelligible jargon, and to create fine-spun theories which, in modern eyes, have no real substance.

His formidable reasoning was a powerful dissolvent of the system Aquinas had constructed, and led unmistakably towards the diverg-

[1] D. L. Douie, *Archbishop Pecham* (Oxford 1952), p. 18.

ence between reason and faith which St. Thomas had denied. Scotus asserted the real existence of universal essences common to all members of a given genus or species. The essence of the human nature which all men share could be comprehended by the intellect through a process of abstraction: this was a universal. Its perfect existence was in the mind of God. Without participating in it a man would not be a man. But the individual man also possessed an individuality which made him what he was, distinct from other men: this Scotus called his *haeccitas*, his *thisness* (the universal he called the *quidditas*, the *whatness*). The importance of his thinking lay in the fact that it represented a move from preoccupation with universal essences to a concern with individual things. Allied to a new stress on the individual was an insistence on the absolute freedom and omnipotence of God. Human knowledge depended not on ideas present in God but on His will. Such an insistence tended to make God inaccessible to human reason, and His ways incomprehensible. Scotus made a clear distinction between metaphysics, the study of being, and theology, the study of God. The first is known by reason. The second may be deduced from God's work, but only indirectly: strictly speaking, it is only intelligible by revelation.

Thus Scotus, as Hastings Rashdall unsympathetically said of him, was content for the most part to let theology rest on an emotional prostration before authority, popularly called Faith; his theological energies, and those of the Franciscan order, were devoted to fastening on the Church, in the teeth of patristic authority and Dominican orthodoxy, the baseless fancy of the Immaculate Conception of the mother of Christ. Thus when the urgency went out of the problems which faced him, Scotus's subtleties became slightly ridiculous. As is well known, his name came to be bestowed in derision on backward scholars. During the suppression of the monasteries, one of Cromwell's visitors wrote of the wanton destruction of his books at Oxford:

> We have . . . utterly banisshede hym Oxforde for ever, with all his blind glosses, and is nowe made a comon servant to everye man, faste nailede upon postes in all comon houses of easment, *id quod oculis meis vidi*. And the seconde tyme wee came to New College affter we had declarede your injunctions we fownde all the gret quadrant court full of the leiffes of Dunce, the wynde blowyng them into evere corner.[1]

This was what time and extremism did to one aspect of the great

[1] Hastings Rashdall, in *The Universities of Europe in the Middle Ages*, as above, vol. III, pp. 259, n. 1, and p. 261.

philosophical ferment of the thirteenth century. Fortunately, by then the scholasticism so derided and misunderstood had helped to create the intellectual basis for a new more quantitative and less metaphysical approach to the problem of truth.

7. LITERATURE

The literature of the thirteenth century was dominated by the French language, and inherited a rich legacy from the writing of Henry II's reign, inspired both in the royal court and in baronial halls. Indeed, so difficult is it to determine the chronology of much of this writing that a line of demarcation between twelfth and thirteenth centuries is almost meaningless. The bulk of the literature, apart from works of scholasticism and of devotion, was 'courtly' and romantic verse, appealing to a European aristocracy whose tastes and interests were very much the same from the Mediterranean to the Baltic. Important works of history were produced in England, especially in the great school of St. Albans, but their popularity was comparatively limited. The nature and quality of English literature in the thirteenth century may be assessed, though with serious reservations, largely from the writings in the 'courtly' and romantic tradition alone. These writings were created to entertain the nobility. There is ample evidence that they were normally intended to be recited before a large audience of lords. The *Boeve de Haumtone*, for example, whose form was that of the old *chanson de geste*, began with the words: 'Seingnurs barons, ore entendez a mei.' Its origins went back to the twelfth century but it was very popular in the thirteenth.

Such literature was a product of feudalism, increasingly dominated by the traditions of chivalry. As such, it was in essence not English but European, not even Anglo-Norman but French. Nevertheless, as in architecture, so in literature, we very soon encounter the beginnings of an English accent. This was not merely a matter of linguistic difference; though as early as 1163–69 a nun of Barking confessed that she knew a false French of England; and as early as 1180 French courtiers could make fun of Canon de Bethune's use of dialect after he had spent some time in England. It was also a matter of content and of feeling. The change was, indeed, very gradual. The last great Anglo-Norman poet, Gower, wrote as late as the end of the fourteenth century. Nevertheless, long before that, influences were at work to make the English accent noticeable if as yet not very pronounced.

England followed the French change from the old national epics, the *chansons de geste*, which had been designed for the hall, to the new romantic verse intended to be read in my lady's bower. The new romances, like the old *chansons*, met the same simple desire for entertainment, in a world where men and women had few resources outside minstrels and their own social activities. Thus, not unnaturally, the 'courtly' literature was an acceptable mirror of the *mores* of an aristocratic society, suitably idealized. It brought pleasure to the listeners and renown to the patrons. Despite its freshness, skill, and imagination, its merits are now not easy to appreciate. It is starkly out of tune with the twentieth century. Its language is difficult. Its copious detail, much appreciated in its day, is now tedious. How far men believed it is a moot question. It was probably not sharply criticized in respect to its general truth, because it reflected the kind of life men wanted to hear about, portraying virtues and faults they were familiar with, made larger than life. It was also, and this was not unimportant, a powerful instrument for creating the kind of atmosphere with which kings and princes wanted to be associated. Like all literature, it was the product of a particular society. More than most it depended on its own peculiar social and political environment which was, in fact, in process of rapid and radical change.

Part of this new verse, the 'ancestral' romance, has been explained by a desire of the Norman-French aristocracy, who were isolated in their castles among a people who did not even speak their own language, to overcome their loneliness; but it is hard to attribute such sentiments to the tough Norman-French nobility. They were more likely to be influenced by political arguments than by sentiment; though they had no doubt begun to become acclimatized in their new environment and to feel an affinity with the famous figures of its past. The courtly romances, in England as well as in France, had their locale all over Europe and in the East; but they were readily applicable to the English scene, and some had Viking or Anglo-Saxon origins. Though they may have been written for an Anglo-Norman audience, or a king like Henry II who was more French than Anglo-Norman or English, they sprang from the English soil. *Horn* was a Viking story adapted to romantic ends, and was first told, perhaps, by people of Norwegian descent in western England. *Gui de Warewic* may have been written to flatter the Earl of Warwick some time between 1232 and 1242. It has been said that this tedious romance, which had enormous popularity, provided an *exemplum* of loyalty which the age needed.[1] William Marshal, who had served England well, not least by helping in 1217 to defeat the French Dauphin Louis at the Fair of Lincoln, may have provided a model. In general, as one would expect, there is an absence of English patriotism, though the absence is not complete. French material was adapted without re-colouring; but the English accent is there.

Other 'courtly' literature had affinities with England, though these are less evident. *Kyng Alisaunder* and *Richard Coeur de Lion* set forth heroic virtues in rulers and their aristocratic companions which would be highly regarded at the court of a ruler like Henry III. Nor would it be unnoticed that Richard was depicted as being on the side of the angels, or at least having a bevy of them giving him moral support, and as getting the better of Philip Augustus. Even the universally popular Arthurian legends, as for example that of Arthur and Merlin, had a wide appeal in England, ancient foe though Arthur had been of the Anglo-Saxons. Arthur's qualities were the universal virtues of knighthood. He was not so much a Roman or a Briton as a courteous knight, defender of law and order, preserver of harmony in the kingdom. He and his knights only met with disaster when they fell away from their ideals and lost their unity.

Thus depicted, Arthur and his knights could provide heroes for both Anglo-Normans and English, and even a basis for increasing unity. This was, indeed, how they were portrayed by Layamon, a priest of Arley Regis Worcester, on the right bank of the Severn, not far from the uncertain boundary between the English and the Welsh. Layamon wrote the *Brut* in English, early in the thirteenth century, to tell the story of Britain from the Flood, and to honour the ancient heroes who had held Britain. The fact that he chose to write in English proves beyond question that he was not addressing himself primarily to the Anglo-Norman aristocracy. His work has been regarded as a silent witness to a literary revolt in which the claims of legend and fancy were advanced anew for recognition in a field where religion had held the monopoly; but even more significant, perhaps, was his appropriation of the Celtic tradition for the people whose tongue was English, as well as for the Anglo-Norman *élite*.

[1] M. Dominica Legge, *Anglo-Norman Literature and its Background* (Oxford 1963), p. 169.

Beneath the literature of the aristocracy there was a vast outpouring of writing in English for entertainment and edification. For literary purposes Old English had become a submerged language. But it had a great tradition, immense vitality, and as we now know, the promise of the future. An example of such writing, directed specifically for those who 'na Frenche kan' was the *Ancren Riwle* (Anchoresses' Rule), a book of guidance which was written in, or translated into, English early in the century. It was fine devotional writing and has been called the greatest prose work of the time.[1] In a similar tradition, Orm, a Mercian canon of the Augustinian order, translated the lessons prescribed by the Church's calender into unrhymed verse, adding his own comments for the benefit of simple folk. In 1303, Robert Mannyng of Brunne, Canon of Sixhill, translated an aid to confession into English, under the title of *Handlyng Synne*. He told how

> For lewed men I undertoke
> In English tonge to make this boke;
> For many beyn of such manere
> That talys and rymys will blithely here
> In gamys and festys at the ale.

But English prose and verse was not confined to legends and homiletics. *The Owl and the Nightingale*, the early MS. of which comes from the first half of the century, has been hailed as a herald of the later love-theme. And an enormous volume of more popular writings must have been lost. A fragment of a thirteenth-century bilingual play has been recovered, containing twenty-two lines in Anglo-Norman, followed by the same number in English. The English is a paraphrase, not a translation of the French. This was possibly done so that the play could be performed in whichever language was most suitable for the occasion.[2] Such a bilingual fragment teaches us not to put the language of the conquered Anglo-Saxons on too low a plane. Its growth as a vehicle for literature was encouraged by the decrees of the Fourth Lateran Council, which encouraged the use of the vernacular in the ministrations of the parish priest. The loss of Normandy by John also contributed, though perhaps less than used to be thought.

Of course Latin was still vigorous as the language of history, literature, scholarship, religion, and government. This was an

---

[1] J. W. H. Atkins in *The Cambridge History of English Literature*, edited by A. W. Ward and A. R. Waller (1920), vol. I, p. 230.
[2] M. D. Legge, *Anglo-Norman Literature and its Background*, pp. 329–30.

important factor contributing to the European unity of culture, religion, and traditions of law and order. In the early fourteenth century a writer who was called Sir John Maundeville and was probably English, wrote a book of travels which appears to have been first composed in French, then translated into Latin, and lastly into English. Gower would use Latin as a medium of literature as late as the end of the fourteenth century, and its use by scholars and publicists was still common in the seventeenth century. There was as yet no obvious challenge to its supremacy in its own spheres. Thus England continued to be enriched by three languages, slowly and subtly changing in their relative importance. English was submerged but gaining in vitality. French was dominant, but was exposed to strong influences operating on the English soil. The English accent became unmistakable. As the French poet Philippe de Reimes said of his English heroine, cultured though she was:

> Un peu parroit à son language
> Que ne fu pas née à Pontoise.

It was only a matter of time before the converging forces at work would strongly affect the relations of the Anglo-Norman and the English languages. They would even undermine the use of Latin, solidly entrenched though it was.

8. Architecture

The dominant artistic expression of the later Middle Ages was that of architecture, especially ecclesiastical. Domestic building was also impressive and the development of the castle was remarkable, but the cathedral summed up the achievement of the age. It was inspired by the deep and universal force of religion. It owed some of its symmetry and design to scholasticism. It was a *summa theologica* in glass and stone, dominated by symbolism and abstraction. Every cathedral reflected and was intended to reflect the eternal City of God. Each one was the product of a great collective effort by kings, nobles, clergy, and people and reflected in some measure the underlying unity of medieval society which is to be discerned beneath its divisions and strife. Finally, the great Gothic tradition, in spite of its universality in an agrarian world, was closely linked in its most impressive expression with urban life. It was the product of a successful way of living which had its latest and in some ways most striking manifestation in the expanding communities organized for manufacture and trade.

Gothic architecture had its origin in the Île de France, with the building of the Abbey Church of St. Denis, begun in 1137. It was thus a creation of the twelfth century. But its complete dominance in Europe north of the Alps came from the prolific building of the thirteenth.

> The Thirteenth century [it has been said] was a time which could neither be retained nor recalled; its very greatness lies rather in its struggles than in its immobility. It was like that wonderful moment in a summer dawn, when the first light of day grows and broadens upon a world still fresh with all the dews of night; no power on earth could have kept it in that same freshness until noonday; and no power in heaven would wish to keep it so . . . .[1]

It covered England with gleaming white churches, of which the outstanding example, perhaps, was at Salisbury, erected on a new site unprejudiced by an earlier work, where building progressed steadily for forty years. The result was a pure creation with a near-uniformity of style which was unique. It had all the hallmarks of English thirteenth-century Gothic; the ribbed vaulting and the pointed arch; the flying buttress and the grouping of the lancet windows or their replacement by large traceried windows in order to give more spaciousness and light; the slender shafting of Purbeck marble to take advantage of the extra light that was given.[2] It was religious architecture secure in its mastery over material, unspoiled by extravagance, clear in its expression of faith. On a mundane level, it was the product of a more perfect science of architecture and a more skilful support of stresses and weight.

But the tranquil and serene beauty of Salisbury[3] was not alone. It was shared by that of Wells, whose famous west front was built in the 1230s, and by that of Lincoln, equally impressive in the eyes of many, though not so uniform in style. Its roof, said a contemporary poet, looked as if it were conversing with the winged birds, spreading out broad wings and, like a flying creature, striking against the clouds. Greatly influenced by Lincoln was the beautiful Beverley Minster, in the second quarter of the century; and the new style was also reflected in the great transept on the south side of the cathedral at York.

Whilst the twelfth-century origins of English Gothic are to be

[1] G. G. Coulton, *Art and the Reformation* (Cambridge 1928), p. 7.
[2] Geoffrey Webb, *Architecture in Britain: The Middle Ages* (London 1956), Plates, p. 90.
[3] P. Brieger, *English Art 1216–1307* (Oxford 1957), p. 25. I also owe to Professor Brieger the quotation from the contemporary poet.

traced largely to the cathedral of Christchurch, Canterbury, later development owed most to Westminster. This shift in the centre of gravity, so to speak, was of very great importance. It was part of a process which made Westminster the capital of England, a capital which was dominated not by the clergy as was Canterbury, but by the royal court.

The rebuilding of Westminster Abbey was not begun by Henry III, but it was taken over by him in 1244 and finished in 1269. The pope himself wrote to commend Henry for assuming the cost of the new building; but his reason, namely that one of the richest abbeys in England had begun a project which was beyond its means, is not in itself very convincing.[1] The king's act of generosity has the appearance of being part of a wider design and there is little doubt that of this Innocent IV strongly approved. Part of such a design may have been the artistic portrayal of the activities of famous kings, as in the 'Antioch chamber' at Westminster and Clarendon, whose paintings depicted the feats of Richard Coeur de Lion. Similarly, Henry caused the story of Alexander the Great to be set forth in Nottingham castle, and that of Edward the Confessor in Clarendon chapel. The choice of such topics may have been without significance: most of the scenes were a commonplace in the literature of the time. But this hardly applies to Edward the Confessor who was the subject of what may fairly be called a deliberate cult by Henry III.[2]

It is probable that royal and courtly architecture and paintings reflected political influences as well as personal taste. On the other hand it must not be thought that the new architecture was nothing more than a royal creation. It was the expression of a great flowering of culture, piety, and wealth. Henry's efforts were rivalled by those of bishops like Robert Grosseteste and Richard le Poore who planned the Gothic architecture of both Salisbury and Durham. Architecture was still dominated by French influence, but it was increasingly English. Even the flying buttress, the product of French architectural practice, showed traces of English influence. More important was the cumulative effect of this influence on many details of building. The example of Westminster brought together features of English Gothic which had earlier been found only occasionally, but which henceforth became part of English design.

[1] Geoffrey Webb, *op. cit.*, p. 110.
[2] See Chapter 2 below.

Towards the end of the century English Gothic developed an exuberance and prolific ornamentation which has earned for it the title of Decorated. The change in spirit and style, first shown on a large scale in the choir of Westminster, was fully displayed in two great enterprises, the Angel choir at Lincoln (finished about 1280) and Exeter (begun at about the same time). In the latter, there was developed an outstanding treatment of surface texture and colour, and especially a bold emphasis on the ribs of the vaults. The wide adoption of the new style can be dated with some precision about 1292, in the influence exercised by the crosses which Edward I built to mark the resting places of his wife Eleanor's body on the way from Harley near Lincoln, where she died in November 1290, to Westminster. The crosses were beautiful examples of stonework, with complex Gothic curves and elaborate traceries. Their mood helped to inspire the new kind of vaulting, with a multiplicity of ribs. This in turn led to the sacrifice of the triforium, prominent earlier in thirteenth-century building, to allow for the building of great traceried windows, a superb example of which is the great west window of York, begun in 1291 but not glazed until 1338. Another common feature of the new fashion was an elaboration of the piers, moving still further from the solidity of the romanesque, as in the central pillar of the Chapter House at Wells, begun about 1290. From these sprang beautiful fan-like ribs.

The new freedom and love of decoration which inspired builders can be seen also in sculpture and illumination. The Luttrell Psalter (*c.* 1335–40) is one of the latest of a group of highly decorated manuscripts of an East Anglican school of illumination, with endlessly elaborate borders. Its grotesques and large and ludicrous monsters are crudely drawn, almost crossing the line between fantasy and buffoonery, though the Psalter also contains charming scenes of everyday agricultural life.[1] The use of the monkey in realistic and often quite irrelevant decoration, made *babewyns* (baboons) a hallmark of the new style. Typical of the spirit it betrays is the well-known monkey waggoner of the Luttrell Psalter, and the delightful funeral procession by rabbits in the Gorleston Psalter of about 1305. Windows at York, dating between 1306 and 1338, depict a monkey's funeral complete with knights and ladies and canons in their stalls. The new spirit of decoration may perhaps be seen also

---

[1] *Medieval England*, edited by A. L. Poole (Oxford 1958), vol. II, p. 502; cf. another example, Plate 103.

in wall-hangings embroidered with children chasing butterflies, or in a plate belonging to Edward III which was decorated with a monkey playing a harp. Heraldic designs and tournaments appear in spandrels and vaults of churches and in misericords. An ewer in King Edward III's treasury was enamelled with knights of the Round Table. In the book of psalms, Sir Geoffrey Luttrell is depicted as being armed by his wife and daughter, in preparation for the lists.

Architecture and art were the supreme expression of the culture and atmosphere of the thirteenth century, even though literature, scholarship, the royal court or the baronial hall, and the merchant gild all had their claims. No one aspect of society could be all-embracing, and no creation could reflect its many-sided life; but the cathedral of this century was no mean monument to the inner harmony and strength of the community, still sure of its foundations, proud of its achievements, and confident of its future. Its social progress had, indeed, been remarkable; and signs of weakness and discord were still comparatively rare. One of the outstanding features of the century was man's adaptability to new conditions, his capacity to reconcile massive change with the unbroken heritage of the past. This capacity was soon to be severely tested, but in the great age of the first Edward, at the end of the century, England still, in spite of some reverses and darkening clouds of domestic discord, seemed to be poised on the verge of yet another period of apparently limitless advance.

2

HENRY III

1. The Minority

IN spite of conflicts at home and reverses abroad, England under
Henry III enjoyed many advantages. She was fortunate in both
her geography and her history. Her geography made her not too
large for unity, but large enough to become a major state; part of
the *Respublica Christiana* yet defended from aggression by the Narrow
Sea; absorbing European notions of political order but tenacious
of unique political traditions of her own. Her history gave her both
a strong monarchy and exceptionally vigorous traditions of limited
monarchical power. Like all their neighbours, the English people,
now beginning to achieve a self-conscious identity, were faced with
the complex problems which arose from the growth of a dynamic
and successful society.

The prolonged effort in the thirteenth century to meet the challenge of politics had a spectacular beginning in the resistance to
John, but it entered into a hardly less critical phase with his death
in 1216 and the accession of his son Henry, a boy nine years old.
Henry had not only to be concerned with the great humiliation which
had been inflicted on his father by the successful rebellion of his
barons and by the loss of Normandy, he had also to reckon with the
adverse effects on the monarchy of his own minority.

When Henry was crowned king on 28 October 1216 by Peter
des Roches, bishop of Winchester, he was very much alone. He
did not have the crown or the regalia or the jewels; he had no
exchequer with him and no royal seal. Half his kingdom was held
by Louis of France with English support. He depended almost
entirely on a limited group of magnates, and on the papal legate
Guala who brought the assistance and protection of the Church.

He might never have survived but for two great lords in particular: William, earl marshal, who became *rector regis et regni*, and Ranulf de Blundevill, earl of Chester, who fortunately happened to be the greatest magnate in the land. His dependence on his counsellors and protectors continued for some years, and upon them fell the heavy burden of safeguarding the future of the Crown.

The Minority was a period of great danger for England, but in the end it continued the developments of 1191–94 and 1215–16 and enlarged the baronial responsibility for the welfare of the realm. One of the first and most decisive acts of the Council of Regency was a reissue of Magna Carta in 1216, giving John's charter the character of the coronation charter of Henry I and Stephen, and solemnly endorsing the chief result of the opposition to John. Some clauses were omitted, notably one which had provided for a baronial committee to harass the king if he failed to keep his promises; but the essence of the royal concession remained.

By this act, it has been said, the king's advisers not only made an effective appeal for the support of moderates who were loyal to both the young king and the Charter; they also made the Charter, which could now evoke the loyalty of both the king and his subjects, a symbol of liberty and a safeguard against the excesses of personal rule. As such it was reissued again and again. The king's advisers may have taken an oath not to allow his lands to be diminished; and the king's vassals shortly assumed a responsibility to maintain the 'state' of the Crown. The implied distinction between the king and his crown was potentially of great significance. As has been observed, the fact that Henry's interests were thus protected gives the lie to the view that there was natural enmity between the king and the barons.[1]

For a time, England was divided. London and the south-east supported Louis and the baronial rebels, and they had allies in the north, where opposition to John had been strong. The midlands and the west were royalist. Sporadic warfare was the order of the day, with notable efforts by both sides to control Louis's lifeline across the Channel. This led to a spectacular sea fight in August 1217, when the French made a last effort to bring reinforcements to England. Hubert de Burgh and Philip Daubeny, titular warden of the Cinque Ports, intercepted the French fleet near the mouth of the Thames. The French were led by Robert de Courtenai, a kinsman

[1] F. M. Powicke, *The Thirteenth Century* 1216–1307 (Oxford 1962), p. 6.

of Prince Louis, and by Eustace, nicknamed the Monk, a French adventurer of good birth who had made himself a scourge to the English in the Narrow Sea. The engagement was short and sharp. Sailing to the windward of the great ship which carried the two French leaders, the English threw powdered lime into the breeze and blinded their opponents. They boarded the vessel and killed or captured its sailors and thirty-six knights. Eustace the Monk was found below, apparently in hiding, though this goes ill with his record. He was immediately beheaded, in keeping with the savagery of war at sea. The other troopships in the French fleet fled back to France, and the English played havoc with the smaller vessels which had carried the stores. It was not a great battle, but it sealed the fate of Louis's effort to dispossess Henry III.

Meanwhile a similar engagement had been fought on land in the previous May, almost equally decisive. Louis had unwisely divided his forces, part besieging the great castle of Dover, heroically defended by Hubert de Burgh, part slipping off to the north where it eventually helped a rebel force to besiege the castle of Lincoln. The castle was built on a high bluff overlooking the city, where much of it still survives as a great historic landmark. It was held by Nicolaa de la Hay, one of the heroic women the High Middle Ages knew well how to produce; and the earl marshal, seeing his opponents divided, hurried to its relief. He penned in the beseigers between the castle and the cathedral and broke them in confusion. The French were pursued into the narrow streets of the town; and a force of only 406 knights, 317 crossbowmen, and their attendants defeated a superior force of 600 knights, and captured half of them, with such small loss that men called the battle the Fair of Lincoln. This double defeat, on land and sea, led Louis to seek terms of an honourable peace.

These were immediately forthcoming, for their own needs as well as statesmanlike moderation moved the royalists to generosity. Even if they had not been generous, Louis had little choice, for his English allies began to change sides with remarkable alacrity, once the tide of war had plainly turned. As it was, the earl marshal offered a general amnesty, including restoration of all confiscated lands, and freedom from all ransoms except those already agreed to before the peace. Louis on his part promised never to renew his alliance with the English rebels. It was a statesmanlike and as it proved a lasting peace, followed by a speedy pacification of the whole country. It enabled the Council to turn immediately to the task of restoring efficiency to the government and prosperity to the realm.

The struggle had been bitter, and England had been deeply divided; but the scars were not so deep as appeared at first sight. The king had been humiliated and the succession to the throne had been endangered; but though some barons had wanted to change monarchs they had not made a direct attack on the monarchy. No one imagined that the institution had not suffered a setback in the events of 1214–16; but once Henry's succession was assured he was free to strive for a full restoration of his traditional powers and of the rightful prerogatives which still belonged to an English king.

It is true that the Minority continued for some time, and that the papal influence and protection remained. One Legate, Guala, departed in November 1218, but another, Pandulf, arrived. However, the earl marshal, aged and full of honour, died with dignity in May 1219, and he had no successor either as *rector regis et regni* or in his own personal pre-eminence in the state. Moreover, Henry became thirteen in May 1220; he was crowned at Westminster; and there was some talk of declaring him of age. In 1223 he obtained the personal use of his seal. He got Pope Honorius III to advise the English prelates that their king was of full age, and should now ordain the business of the kingdom 'principally by the counsel of his own servants'; and it was probably deeply significant for the future that his action was based rather on the support of the pope than on the co-operation of the *universitas* of the realm.[1] One reason for the action was the need to bring about a surrender of royal castles, still held throughout England by mercenaries and magnates who had been loyal to John and Henry, but whose power was now an obstruction to order and good government. By the end of April 1224 nearly all had been restored to the king or to bishops who acted as temporary wardens. The whole movement immensely strengthened the hand of the ambitious and able justiciar Hubert de Burgh by whom, in part, it had been inspired.

The king, the justiciar, and Stephen Langton, archbishop of Canterbury, combined to overcome the only serious open defiance,

---

[1] My *Constitutional History of England 1216–1399*, vol. I, *Politics and the Constitution 1216–1307* (London 1948), pp. 83–4; cf. F. M. Powicke, *The Thirteenth Century*, p. 19, where there is a slightly different interpretation.

that of Fawkes de Breauté in the summer of 1224. Fawkes was outlawed, his great castle of Bedford besieged, and for good measure he and his associates were excommunicated. After a siege of eight weeks the castle surrendered and the garrison, including Fawkes's brother William, were hanged.[1] Fawkes himself died in exile two years later. The supremacy of the royal centralized government was vindicated, as also apparently was the policy of Henry III.

Henry himself, who thus began to grasp the reins of power, had the bearing and spirit of a prince, and in less difficult times might have made a respectable ruler. He was not hostile to the liberties of his subjects; he was merely a stubborn and sometimes a misguided defender of his royal rights. Many of his critics have ignored the peculiar difficulties of his reign.[2] Few English kings have begun to rule under less auspicious circumstances; few have weathered so many storms to come out at last, if not triumphant, at least retaining and even adding to the substance of royal power. Henry's personal gifts, if not striking, were considerable. He was of middle height, muscular and well built. One of his eyelids drooped over the eye, but this was his only defect. His forehead in middle age became deeply lined, but his spirits remained buoyant, his mind clear, and his tastes refined. He was interested in scholars, enjoying, for example, the society of Matthew Paris, and he encouraged building and art. He was generous, affable, and religious, regularly attending three masses a day. He made a great ceremony of receiving the relic of the Holy Blood in England in 1247, carrying it himself from St. Paul's to Westminster. But he was extravagant and suspicious of his magnates, delighting in French tastes and French intimates. In his dealings with his subjects he mixed pertinacity with weakness; in his politics vision was combined with inability to be realistic. His difficulties were by no means all of his own making; many were the outcome of forces which neither he nor his subjects understood; but he certainly added to them his own lack of good sense and moderation. Despite this, he retained to his death the loyalty of many of his subjects. At the darkest moment there was no serious thought of removing Henry from his throne.

Yet he came near it on occasions, and he encountered many

---

[1] Three knights were cut down from the gallows before they died, and later served with the Templars in the Holy Land.

[2] See my *Constitutional History 1216–1399*, vol. I, p. 3; F. M. Powicke, *The Thirteenth Century*, p. 19.

failures. In truth, his abilities were incommensurate with his ambitions; he was for ever trying more than he could achieve. He stooped to tricks and evasions, and more than once, by his failure to understand the changing world around him, built up an opposition as unanimous and formidable as that of his father's reign. Dante placed him in the region of purgatory reserved for simpletons; but his 'simplicity' was, it has been said, a kind of innocence which remained in him all his life and gave him an appeal to both contemporaries and posterity, even when he was at his worst.

In 1227 he produced another letter, this time from Gregory IX, which advised that he be able to order the business of the kingdom for himself.[1] Before that, in 1225, he had made a momentous reissue of Magna Carta, 'voluntarily and of our own good will'; in return, all the people of the realm granted a fifteenth of their personal property. He thus marked the closing period of his minority by recognizing his obligation to the Charter, but also by emphasizing his royal authority. But the grant of 1225, made by all the people of the realm, had a deeper significance. It was a recognition that taxation was a common business, affecting all the community. It signified a movement away from the idea that consent to a tax was a personal affair, so that one man could agree and another refuse. Lurking behind this development was the idea of a *universitas* of the realm which had the right to speak with one voice on certain matters. At bottom, this was to prove irreconcilable with an important aspect of the feudal practice of personal monarchy, a rough and *ad hoc* agreement by individual tenants-in-chief.

2. Experiment in Personal Rule

The existence of a spirit of common action, at least among the magnates, was quickly shown during a minor dispute in 1227 between Henry and his brother Richard, who had been made earl of Cornwall in 1225, and in 1225–27 had been nominal leader of an expedition to Gascony, acquitting himself well though still only a boy. The quarrel began over the disposal of a manor which Richard claimed belonged to his earldom, but which had been granted by King John to one of his followers named Waleran the German. In a stormy meeting between the brothers, Richard refused to

---

[1] It was addressed to the magnates of England, translated in my *Constitutional History 1216–1399*, pp. 91–93. But cf. P. Chaplais, *Diplomatic Documents Preserved in the Public Record Office* (H.M.S.O., 1964), pp, 163–4.

surrender the manor and demanded the judgment of the magnates. Henry bade him resign the manor or quit the country. The dispute was hardly more than a family quarrel between two very young men, but it served to raise important issues. Henry had just been declared fully of age and did not welcome the appeal to the *universitas* of lords. Richard got unexpected support; a gathering which included eight earls met at Stamford to maintain his cause. In the end, Henry got the manor but paid for it much more than it was worth. He was reconciled to his brother but must have found it hard to reconcile himself to the action of the lords.

Nevertheless, the *universitas* had come to stay, as a permanent feature of English political life. It soon showed itself again, this time in opposition to Hubert de Burgh who had been made justiciar by King John at Runnymede, and was Henry's adviser who had helped to bring about the reconciliation between the king and his brother. Hubert had won great fame by his courage and skill as a royalist during the civil wars, but he lost much of it in the complexities and difficulties of the peace. He was justiciar and chief adviser to the king after 1227, but he soon united many interests against him. He loyally supported Henry but at the same time looked well after his own interests. He built up a great position in south Wales and the Marches, and began to do the same for his nephew in Ireland. He offended the lords by his royalism, but he did not carry it far enough to satisfy his king. His power in Wales and the Marches was strong enough to offend the barons, but not strong enough to overawe them. Even there, he had one great opponent he could neither placate nor subdue; Llywelyn ab Iorwerth was in process of becoming the great prince of Aberffraw and lord of Snowdonia, strong enough to wage a most successful war against Henry himself in 1231. He frustrated Hubert in Wales and diminished his stature in England, and he promised the rise of a new Welsh unity.

Above all, Hubert could not restrain Henry's unrealistic ambition to regain the French territories lost by his father. This was for many years one of the young king's consuming ambitions; and it was both fruitless and costly. In France, England was faced by a state which was evolving as rapidly and successfully as she was herself, and which was even richer and greater. It is true that the French monarchy was in difficulties after the death of Louis VIII in 1226. The young king Louis IX who now ascended the throne was only twelve years old, just three years older than Henry himself had been in 1216.

There was an opportunity for English aggression which was tempting indeed. Unfortunately for Henry, his young neighbour's fortunes were very ably defended by his mother, Blanche of Castile.

By the end of 1227 the opportunity for the English ruler to attack Louis and his mother had passed. Nevertheless, Henry entered into intermittent negotiations with an ambitious and unreliable scion of the royal house, Peter of Dreux, lord of Brittany by virtue of his wife's inheritance, who in 1229 got himself involved in open war with the redoubtable regent. Henry immediately prepared for a great expedition to help his ally. Peter crossed to England and did homage for Brittany; Henry gathered a great army to go to his aid. His discovery at Portsmouth in October 1229 that his army was not ready, and that the sailing would have to be deferred, was a major cause of his estrangement from Hubert. Henry even accused his justiciar of treachery.

Hubert was almost certainly lukewarm about the whole adventure, but it is equally certain that he was not responsible for the fact that it failed. In the end Henry had enough troops to have made a serious campaign; but though he made a foray from Nantes to Bordeaux, his lords behaved 'as though they were at a Christmas party' whilst the common soldier starved, and nothing whatever was achieved. Henry's great adventure petered out in a temporary truce, but he was not the man to indulge in self-examination or reproach, and he had a convenient whipping boy in Hubert. Undoubtedly the failures of 1229 and 1230 paved the way for Hubert's dismissal in 1232.

The immediate cause of this, however, was probably the advice and influence of the versatile and ambitious Peter des Roches, old supporter of John and recent adviser and companion to Frederick II. He had gone crusading with Frederick because of his estrangement from Henry in 1227, but had returned to England and to the king's favour in 1231. One result of Peter's influence with the king was a series of new appointments in administration, especially the promotion of his son or nephew Peter de Rivaux. The bestowal of many offices on the bishop's relative was to some extent balanced by a grant that Hubert and his chief administrative colleagues should hold office for life, backed by a curious mutual oath between king and justiciar. The king swore on the gospels to observe all the charters he had granted to the justiciar and to his wife, and also to other high officers. The justiciar swore that he would do all in his power to preserve the charters inviolate and to impede any attempt by the king or by others to violate them. But what all this signifies it is difficult to say.

In spite of it, Hubert found himself on the way to dismissal. A new justiciar, Stephen Segrave, was appointed in August 1232. Hubert was defended by the community of the barons, but somewhat unaccountably he fled. No serious charge had been made against him, though he was accused of countenancing a popular movement against papal provisions to benefices in the Church in England. Flight did not save him. He was pursued and captured at Brentwood in Essex, where he was dragged out of sanctuary; and he was thrust into the Tower. Restored to the sanctuary by the agitation of the bishop of London, he surrendered himself voluntarily and was again thrust into prison. By throwing himself on the king's mercy, he evaded trial in the king's court; but he lost all his offices and was removed from public life to the seclusion of the castle of Devizes. It was a curious and devious process of degradation and a sorry termination to an honourable public career. We shall never know the inner truth of this struggle, but what we do know does no great credit to king Henry, who could be very unmindful of services rendered and devotion to the royal cause.

A new group of administrators gathered around Henry, and worked with the two Peters. It included men like Stephen Segrave and Robert Passelewe. Their enthusiasm for the royal prerogative was only matched by their ability. They were, indeed, conservative reformers of a high order, such as have often been encountered in English history. As such, they were more dangerous to traditional liberties than any mere purveyor of a narrow loyalty to the privileges of the Crown. Their monopoly of the king's ear earned them the deep distrust of the lords, despite their good intentions, and they quickly proved to be far more unpopular than the moderate Hubert de Burgh.

Peter de Rivaux was made sheriff of twenty-one shires, besides holding other posts and being made treasurer of the exchequer in January 1233. He was able to institute a far-reaching overhaul of government, both central and local. Hubert had already begun this task, but it was now far more energetically pursued. The old office of justiciar was deprived of its importance, and the king's council became the core of the administration. As a result, the council rapidly developed as the pivotal body in government, beginning to add executive functions to its primary and essential duty of advice.

Its personnel became clearly marked by an oath of office, and it included both magnates and ministers; but it remained, in the nature of things, a restricted body in which the expert professional administrator tended to exercise a preponderant influence. Hence, suspicion and distrust were quickly engendered in the minds of the magnates; and their resentment quickly led to the first of many serious conflicts between Henry and his barons in which both sides learned valuable lessons about the conduct of public affairs.

In 1233 Henry planned a great expedition to conquer the whole of Connaught in Ireland for the Crown. His expedition was complicated by a quarrel with Richard the earl marshal, earl of Pembroke, younger son of the great William. Like Richard of Cornwall six years earlier, Pembroke found strong support among the English lords. The Dominican scholar Robert Bacon is said to have told Henry that peace in the land was impossible as long as Peter des Roches was in power. War did, indeed, break out in the Marches of Wales. However, there was no general conflagration and negotiations for peace were begun. Henry promised to remove his evil advisers, and reconciliation was in sight when news arrived that Richard, who had gone to defend his estates in Ireland, had been slain at a meeting with the supporters of the king. A crisis immediately arose which threatened to revive the worst days of the reign of King John.[1]

The 'assassination' seemed to confirm all the worst fears that had been held about the spirit and methods of Henry's rule since 1227 and especially since 1232. The bishops, who had great influence, had only recently declared that, since scarcely any great business was done in the realm by his seal or command, but only by the seal or command of Peter de Rivaux, the country did not seem to have Henry for a king.[2] At a great gathering at Gloucester in May 1234 they compelled the king to disavow the methods of his councillors. He professed, rightly or wrongly, not to have known the contents of a letter he had sealed which had led to the death of the earl marshal.[3] To the admiration of all present, he was overcome with

[1] See my *Constitutional History 1216–1399*, vol. I, pp. 99–116. Sir Maurice Powicke's latest view may be seen in *The Thirteenth Century*, pp. 58–9.

[2] My *Constitutional History, 1216–1399*, vol. I, p. 106.

[3] In this letter, his councillors had claimed that it was by their counsel the king and kingdom were ruled. Such a claim, if made, would have been derogatory to both magnates and king; see *ibid.*, p. 101.

emotion and burst into tears. There was a general reconciliation in which all was forgiven except to the councillors. These were forbidden the royal presence and new members of the council were appointed, including Hubert de Burgh, again restored to favour after more adventures in and out of prison. Peter des Roches, Peter de Rivaux, Stephen Segrave and others were summoned to answer for moneys received and for their evil use of the royal seal. But they were never punished for their alleged misdeeds.

It has been argued that Henry had, indeed, been tricked by his advisers,[1] and that this accounts for his rage against them; but Henry not only did not punish his councillors, he also soon reinstated at least some of them. Peter de Rivaux was banished on 2 January 1236, but four months later Henry 'remitted his rancour' against him. The king had no doubt had a great shock and henceforth would be more discreet, but his goal was unaltered and his temperament unchanged.[2]

In any case, circumstances were widening the gap between Henry and his barons. Bureaucracy was weakening the personal contact that had once united them, and secluding the ruler behind a circle of experts entrusted with all the secrets of the king. When the king asked his barons for agreement to taxation in 1237, they moved to confer apart from the king. Gilbert Basset thereupon advised Henry to send 'one of your own people' to attend their discussion, which led Richard Percy to enquire 'Are we aliens and not also the king's friends?'. The problem this underlines was not made easier by Henry's marriage in January 1236 to Eleanor of Provence, the sister of the French queen. Henry's court became a place of welcome to his wife's relatives, their numbers swollen by countrymen from both Provence and Savoy, where Eleanor's grandfather had produced a numerous progeny. Among the latter, the most famous were Peter, who became Count of Savoy but spent much time in England, and Boniface of Savoy, another uncle of the queen.

Henry's council was said to be organized under William of Savoy, brother of Peter and Boniface and bishop-elect of Valence. Simon de Montfort, son of a famous French Crusader, came to England as a foreign 'favourite' and was secretly married to the king's sister in 1238. Peter of Savoy obtained the earldom of

[1] F. M. Powicke, *The Thirteenth Century*, p. 58.
[2] T. F. Tout, *Chapters in the Administrative History of Medieval England* (Manchester 1920–33), vol. I, p. 281; Powicke, *loc. cit.*, p. 59; my *Constitutional History 1216–1399*, vol. I, p. 106.

Richmond in 1240 as a gift from the king. Boniface became arch-bishop of Canterbury in 1245, the only foreign prelate to hold the position in the thirteeenth century and said to be the most hated man in England.[1] Aymer of Lusignan, the king's half-brother, became bishop of Winchester in 1250. Such advisers were too highly born to be regarded as upstarts, but had too shallow roots in Eng-land to speak for the magnates whom they supplanted at the side of the king.

His intimates encouraged Henry to adopt high views of his royal dignity, and to demand from all his advisers and ministers a befitting loyalty and obedience. On one famous occasion he deprived the Keeper of the Great Seal of his office, because of a lack of complete readiness to obey. Out of loyalty to his office rather than to his ruler, the Keeper had refused to seal a writ which conceded to Thomas of Savoy, titular Count of Flanders, a payment on each sack of English wool carried through his land. Probably Henry's lofty notion of his dignity was one reason why he dispensed for some years with the office of Chancellor and appointed only Keepers of his seal.

In any case, the mere presence of such foreign servants and advisers between the magnates and the king was an affront. It deprived the lords of what they considered to be their inalienable right to have a voice in important matters pertaining to the govern-ment of the realm. In 1236 they were alarmed by the rumour that the king had created a sworn council of twelve headed by William of Savoy, and had taken an oath to be obedient to their advice; but they had no proposals to make in face of a development which was quite beyond their previous experience and for which a remedy was difficult indeed to conceive. Early in 1237, sensitive to their growing anger, Henry 'gave himself to the counsel of the faithful men of his realm' and added three magnates to his council; but what he had conceded of his own will and grace he could as easily with-draw. And though he also confirmed Magna Carta, this provided no adequate remedy for what his subjects were beginning to regard as his misinterpretation of the very essence of his duty as their king. Within a year (in 1238) they were so angry at the news of Simon de Montfort's marriage to the king's sister that Henry found it expedient to take refuge in the Tower.

Their basic complaint was succinctly expressed in 1237: 'all these things he [the king] had done without the counsel of his faithful

[1] *Constitutional History 1216–1399*, vol. I, p. 23–4.

subjects; nor ought they to share the penalty who had not shared the crime'. Against this, the best that Henry could do, somewhat later, was to claim that the magnates denied him what each of them demanded for himself—the right of choosing his own advisers. Beneath the clash of personalities there was a debate about a problem which went to the roots of political liberty. The magnates were handicapped because they were not able to evolve a programme of reform commensurate with the gravity of the problem. They had not even developed as yet, their own corporate unity as a *universitas*, together with a sense of responsibility for the kingdom. Nevertheless, they learned quickly, and probably put forward more than one tentative proposal; in 1244, indeed, they produced a very remarkable plan of reform.

This is known as the 'Paper Constitution' because it came to nothing; but the courage and insight it showed should not be ignored.[1] In it, the barons made a resolute effort to grapple with the problem of the council and gave a new stature to the collective community of the realm. 'Let four', they said, 'be elected by common assent . . . who shall be of the king's council and shall be sworn that they will faithfully "treat" concerning the business of the lord king and of the realm. . . . And they shall be conservators of liberties. And . . . none can be removed without common assent. . . . And the *universitas* shall not meet again without them, but shall meet when it shall be necessary and at their instance.' For the first time in history, the magnates put forward a definite plan of constitutional reform to enable them to share in all major decisions of government which affected their interests as well as those of the king. These decisions included the appointment of the king's chief ministers, whose loyalty Henry had jealously preserved for himself.

It is clear that the *universitas* had, indeed, learned to go to the heart of the problem of government, and that a great issue had been raised which was not likely to be settled without bitter political conflict and even the threat of civil war. It has been suggested that the proposals were no more than the ideas of a particular group of magnates; but this seems on the whole unlikely. Matthew Paris said that both the lay magnates and the prelates had agreed some time

---

[1] For the varied opinions on this document, see Sir Maurice Powicke, *The Thirteenth Century*, p. 78; my *Constitutional History 1216–1399*, vol. I, pp. 117–26; and C. R. Cheney, 'The "Paper Constitution" preserved by Matthew Paris', in *E.H.R.*, vol. LXV (April 1950), pp. 213–21. The alternative date of 1238 has been put forward by N. Denholm-Young and (at one time) by Sir Maurice Powicke.

earlier to act only as a general *universitas*. The most important measures proposed in the plan of reform were to be taken by 'common assent'.

The friction of these years did not involve only the secular lords; it involved also the clergy. The developing English monarchy was brought into ever more critical relations with the evolving monarchy of the popes. The traditional view of the *Respublica Christiana* was still dominant in England though modified by the claims of the English monarchy. As set forth by Robert Grosseteste, the sacerdotal power was greater and more dignified than the secular, and kings must not try to make ecclesiastical persons accountable to them. Nor did Grosseteste find it possible ever to deny his episcopal duty of obedience to the pope. He was quite consistent in his attitude. In 1236 he defended the special rights and responsibilities of the clergy and their courts against a decision by the secular barons and judges, who refused to agree that subsequent marriage of the parents might legitimize a bastard. In this, he opposed those who maintained the Common Law of England against the Canon Law of the Church.

The increasingly conflicting claims of monarchy and Church, as Grosseteste himself found, could only be reconciled by a policy of co-operation between the temporal and spiritual rulers, which was increasingly difficult to maintain. Only Henry's personal piety and political need for papal support made it possible at all. No English ruler, indeed, was ever so conscious of his debt to the pope and his need to co-operate with him as was Henry; and no English ruler in the end paid a higher political price for papal support. Ultra-Papalism was as necessary, in the final analysis, and as fatal, to Henry III, as High Anglicanism was later to Charles I.

The English bishops played an uncomplicated and highly successful role in Henry's early years as mediators and exponents of moderation; but friction was aroused in 1237 when the king requested the pope to send a legate to England. Gregory IX sent Cardinal Otto, deacon of S. Nicola in Carcere, despite the fact that the English bishops, including the archbishop of Canterbury, had no enthusiasm for the legate, even though his conduct was conciliatory. Reformers and recalcitrants joined hands in suspicion of his intentions. He soon became so unpopular that he thought it prudent to make his own brother his master cook. During a fruitful council of reform at St. Paul's in 1237, he had to have a military escort to and from the place of meeting; and he was said to be in fear of his life. In 1238 his brother involved him in a bitter dispute with the scholars at Oxford, one of whom, a poor Irish chaplain who begged at the cardinal's kitchen for food, had received a pot of scalding broth in his face. English opinion favoured the scholars against the prelate; much feeling was aroused; and the age of Pandulf and Guala had plainly departed, never fully to return.

During the conflict between Gregory IX and Frederick II, the papal need for funds led to a vast increase in demands for taxes and fees. In his search for Italian support, the pope even ordered that 300 clerks of Roman families be 'provided' to English benefices. Such exactions and unpopularity redounded on Henry, who had accepted Otto and, in any case, did not use the royal power against him: 'I neither wish nor dare', he is reported to have said, 'to oppose the lord pope in anything.'

Others were not so inhibited. The clergy of Berkshire, for example, drew up a remonstrance which must have expressed a widespread opinion. Indeed, Henry was blamed for evils emanating from the Curia for which he had no responsibility whatever; and he had a delicate balance to preserve between the pope and his great adversary Frederick II, who had married Henry's sister Isabella in 1235. He even permitted Peter of Savoy to lead an English contingent in the Emperor's war against the Milanese. On the other hand, he permitted the Legate Otto to proclaim Frederick's excommunication. However, when the Emperor protested against Otto's residence at the royal court, Henry urged Otto to leave. He thus kept some sort of balance with both adversaries; but it was his relations with the pope which had the important repercussions in England and which in the end were to cost him very dear.

In order to impose further levies on the clergy, Master Martin was sent as a special envoy to England, but was received most inhospitably. The magnates told him in 1245 that he would be torn to pieces if he did not depart, and when he asked Henry for a safe-conduct all he got in reply was: 'May the devil give you a safe-conduct to Hell.'[1] The clergy probably found themselves in warm agreement with Henry's sentiments at this moment, even if they did

[1] Matthew Paris, *Chronica Majora* (edited by H. R. Luard, R.S., 1877), vol. IV, p. 421. Cf. the famous letter Henry wrote to Master Martin in August 1244 (translated by Powicke, *King Henry III and the Lord Edward* (Oxford 1947), vol. I, p. 354) beginning '. . . Your stony heart is too hard to receive our words. We will soften it and have you make a virtue of necessity, for we cannot tolerate your attempt to upset our realm.'

not enjoy the same freedom of language. Henry himself was, indeed, not indifferent to their plight; in 1246, at a great council in London, he presented articles against papal exactions, backed by declarations from his subjects. But by this time the clergy had begun a momentous political reorientation which was to have far-reaching results. The abbots warned that the people of England might withdraw their fealty unless Henry did something about the abuses permitted by the Curia; but, more important, the bishops began to make common cause with the magnates in opposition to the exploitation of the clergy, and to find a place in the emerging *universitas* of the realm.

3. FOREIGN AFFAIRS

Internal friction was enhanced by the effects of foreign policy. This policy was on the whole unfortunate, not only because of Henry's frequent ineptness, as in his relations with St. Louis, but also because the development of the territorial state involved him in ever closer and potentially more explosive relationships with neighbouring states and even with the purely political designs and conflicts of the pope.

The consequences of outward expansion, affecting most thirteenth-century politics, are particularly noticeable in the case of the Welsh, the most vulnerable of the neighbours of England, and the most likely to suffer from English aggression. After its great promise in the twelfth century, the old Welsh kingdom of Deheubarth in the south had dissolved. In the thirteenth century, hope of political unity came to be pinned on the princes of Gwynedd, supported by the lawyers and the poetry of the bards. At the same time, one basic condition of a territorial state began slowly to emerge: notions derived from the possession of, or lordship over, land began to transcend age-long tribal relationships. These had produced passionate loyalties but had kept the Welsh divided. The embryonic state thus evolving in the thirteenth century seemed destined one day to a path not dissimilar from that travelled by Scotland in the north.

At the beginning of the century, Welsh strength and independence were being ably maintained by Llywelyn the Great, who had married a natural daughter of King John and ruled over Snowdonia or Gwynedd. He developed his court and his administration; he acquired a treasurer, a chancellor, and seals of government. Thus equipped, he extended his influence over the princes; and he received their submission in his high court, which became the seat of government attended by kinsmen and officials, bishops and lords. His power was greatly increased by both the civil war of John's reign and the minority of Henry III. Hubert de Burgh laboured hard to restrain him, as well as to enhance his own position. Among Hubert's measures was the building of Montgomery castle. But in spite of all such efforts, Llywelyn continued to flourish. He changed his title from Prince of Gwynedd to Prince of Aberffraw and Lord of Snowdon, beat off a strong attack in 1231, and wrested a truce from the English in 1234. From that time until his death in 1241 he was able to rule his territories in peace.

After his death, however, English pressure revived. Cardigan and Carmarthen were organized as English shires, and Henry took advantage of the initial weakness of Llywelyn's successor David to overrun a considerable portion of north Wales. He followed this in 1244 by an ambitious campaign, complete with provisions and troops from Ireland, which anticipated in some respects his son's more famous and decisive expeditions and was fought by both sides with great ferocity. By 1247 Welsh resistance had been so far worn down that Henry gained, in a treaty at Woodstock, all the land between the county of Chester and the Conway valley, and 'the homage and services of all the barons and nobles of Wales'.

There was to be an important respite in this long process by reason of the great quarrel between Henry and his barons, but it did not change the broad balance of forces. Welsh fears of England, and Welsh hostility, were both increased when in 1254 Prince Edward was given the rule over Chester and the Four Cantrefs of Wales, the latter consisting of the lands between the Conway and the Dee. Prince Edward was as yet an untried and inexperienced young man with little to indicate the great future that lay before him. His officials roused Welsh anger by their harshness and hostility to Welsh custom, and strengthened the position of Llywelyn ap Gruffydd who succeeded to Snowdonia in 1246 and assumed the title of Prince of Wales in 1258. In the same year he had entered into an alliance with the Scots. Between 1256 and 1263 Llywelyn went far towards uniting all the princes of north and south Wales under his leadership, greatly extending his direct authority. His power moved the Welsh tenants of the Marchers to revolt, and brought the Welsh lords of the south to unite on his side; whilst many of Prince

Edward's castles in north Wales were subdued. In 1264-65 Llywelyn compelled Simon de Montfort's government to recognize his title and lordship over the magnates of Wales; and after the battle of Evesham he pursued the same end with Prince Edward and gained the same recognition in the treaty of Montgomery in 1267, which acknowledged Llywelyn as Prince of Wales and lord of all the Welsh princes except Mareddud of Dryslwyn on the Tywi.

In spite of all this the gains he made were to some extent illusory. They depended on English disunion, and they taught the Marcher lords a new spirit of co-operation with the central government and a new readiness to abate their jealousy of its advance into Wales. The Welsh Marchers strongly supported the royalists at Lewes and Evesham, and their new loyalty presaged ill for Welsh independence once English domestic unity was restored. Nothing was more certain than that, under Henry's strong and able son Edward, English pressure against Wales would soon be strongly resumed.

Meanwhile, Anglo-Scottish relations moved even more inexorably towards a climax. Scotland was a sparsely inhabited land (it is said to have had only 400,000 inhabitants in 1300), and it had even more extensive mountains than Wales. It offered the same potentiality of development into a territorial state, though the obstacles were just as formidable and initial progress hardly as great. Celtic and Norwegian tribesmen were predominant in the north and Anglo-Norman aristocracy in the south. The clan, with its personal relations, was dominant in the sparsely settled highlands, whilst the lowlands had accepted the methods of more centralized rule. The clansmen were as much a threat to the lowlanders as were the English. With the latter, indeed, relations had been friendly and close since the reign of Henry II. Even the currencies of England and Scotland were interchangeable, and many lowland magnates held possessions in England and were hard to distinguish from English lords.

The unification of Scotland entered a new phase in 1266 with the king of Norway's surrender of his hold on the mainland and the Western Isles. The growth of centralization and the extension of kingly power were conspicuous in the reigns of Alexander II (1214-49) and III (1249-86), though they did not yet affect the highlands of the north.

At the same time there was increasing intercourse with the south. Scottish magnates were often in England; they took an active part in English politics, and found English brides among the aristocracy. In 1221 Alexander II married Joan, Henry III's sister. In 1251 Alexander III who was ten, was married to Henry's daughter Margaret, who was eleven. Under the terms of the treaty of 1237, when Alexander II renounced the ancient Scottish claim to Northumbria, he received important lands in Northumberland and Cumberland. There was, indeed, friction between the two countries when in 1239 Alexander took Marie de Coucy of France as his second wife. Relations with England became so strained that both the English and the Scots committed unfriendly acts. But war was in the end averted, and Alexander bound himself not to make an alliance with an enemy of the English king. The whole minor crisis showed how sensitive the English were to the measure of encirclement threatened by an alliance between Scotland and France.

The minority of Alexander III from 1249–62 made Anglo-Scottish relations comparatively simple. Henry III was able to intervene effectively in Scottish affairs on the friendly basis of a family relationship. Alexander had done homage to Henry in York and was knighted there when he married Henry's daughter; and Henry regarded himself as having a responsibility for both him and his wife. In 1254, in return, Henry sought for Scottish help through a mutual consideration of his difficulties abroad. In 1255 he organized a great assembly of Anglo-Scottish magnates at Wark-on-Tweed, in which the Scottish council of regency was changed. Such intervention provoked a Scottish reaction; in 1257 a group led by the Comyns seized Alexander; and when Henry gathered an army together the 'rebels' significantly made a convention with Llywelyn of Wales. In 1262 Alexander came of age; and this, together with domestic troubles south of the border, brought an end to English interference. But a pattern had been set for the future. Scotland, like Wales, had everything to fear if the expanding state of England should ever fall into the hands of an able and popular king.

But the most prolonged and destructive clash of expanding kingdoms was in the end to be that between England and France. This was almost inevitable in spite of the fact that Henry was more French in many ways than English, the magnates of both countries were closely united in culture and blood, and a serious conflict was deferred by the statesmanship and moderation of the French king Louis IX. It was likely to be stubborn and prolonged because in

France Henry had to deal with a territorial state as large and almost as well-organized as his own. He had failed dismally in his invasion of 1230; but he thought that a better opportunity for fulfilling his long dream of recovering English power presented itself in 1241. In that year French influence in the south had been both extended and advertised by the investment of Louis IX's brother Alphonse as count of Poitou in succession to Raymond of Toulouse. Louis's action was opposed by Hugh de Lusignan, count of La Marche, and his wife Isabella of Angoulême, former widow of King John, together with the lords and cities of Gascony. Against the wishes of his barons Henry supported this revolt. It came to nothing: the rebels never achieved unity by their own efforts; and Henry had not the personality to impose it, though he took a considerable army to France. Louis defeated him at the bridge over the Charente at Taillebourg and compelled him to retreat to Saintes. His allies deserted him and he was lucky to obtain lenient terms of peace in 1243.

Henry had sense enough not to repeat this form of attack on the rising power of France; in any case, no favourable opportunity occurred. Hence, after long negotiations, outstanding differences between England and France were settled by the treaty of Paris in 1259: Henry surrendered his claim to Normandy, Maine, Anjou, and Poitou: Louis acknowledged Henry's lordship over Gascony. Henry's claims to some lands formerly possessed by Henry II were recognized; on the other hand, Henry became a vassal of Louis and one of the peers of France. The negotiations and the treaty kept the two countries at peace during a period of English weakness, and enabled St. Louis to act as mediator in the dispute between Henry and his barons. They could not end the friction between the expanding monarchies of England and France, which arose now not so much from memories of John's lost 'Empire' as from French designs on the duchy of Gascony, last remaining possession of the English ruler in France.

In the later years of his reign the relations between Henry and the pope did not resemble those between a secular ruler and the vicar of Christ. The two acted towards each other much more like two secular powers whose relationship was complicated but not dominated by the religious authority and attributes of the pope. This relationship deteriorated rather than improved after Henry took the cross on 6 March 1250, an act which helped to reconcile him to the crusading St. Louis but brought many complications later on. He was to start on his crusade on 24 June 1256, but, as we should expect, he was unable to go. On the other hand his new and close relations with the pope led him in 1254 to accept from Innocent IV the crown of Sicily which was offered to his second son Edmund. It was a glittering prize but had to be won from the descendants of Frederick II.

The Sicilian agreement did more harm to the reputation of Henry III and to his relations with his subjects than any other single action that he took. This, and perhaps this alone, seemed quite indefensible to the vast majority of his subjects. Sicily, as the barons themselves pointed out, could not be conquered from a country as far away as England: Manfred, Frederick's illegitimate son, was crowned king at Palermo in August 1258, and was quite impervious to anything Henry could do. All that Henry got by the agreement was responsibility for the vast papal debt of 135,541 marks which he had to meet before Michaelmas 1256, under penalty of excommunication and the laying of England under interdict. He received nothing, absolutely nothing, in return. When Pope Innocent IV in 1252 had first sought effective action against Manfred he had offered the crown to Richard of Cornwall, Henry's brother; but Richard had observed that the pope might as well have asked him to climb into the skies and capture the moon. Richard's estimate of the situation would seem to be nearer the mark than those of a modern historian who has argued that Henry's prospects were fair until the end of 1254.[1] It is no excuse for Henry to point out that he later empowered Simon de Montfort and Peter of Savoy to 'settle the whole business', and that he was prepared to surrender Edmund's rights in Sicily altogether. The more hopeless his prospects became, the more the pope was likely to keep him to his obligations as well as to his illusory rights. The more his debts multiplied, the less likely was he to find anything but opposition from his magnates, who had never approved his adventure from the start.

The Sicilian affair in its sequel was largely a matter of secular politics, even though the pope kept Henry faithful to his obligations by a flagrant abuse of his spiritual powers. Henry's subjects, if not their ruler, were dominated by the needs of the *regnum*; and in defence of these they were prepared for open defiance of the pope. The interests of monarch and pope were kept in a semblance of

---

[1] Sir F. M. Powicke, in *The Thirteenth Century*, p. 122.

harmony by the mutual sympathies of two régimes which were authoritarian in their tendencies, and by Henry's supposed need of papal support in pursuance of his political aims; but it is easy to see the extent to which circumstances were tending to drive them apart.

4. BARONIAL OPPOSITION

Thus, external affairs pointed the way to bitter 'national' conflicts. It seems a mistake to interpret them simply in terms of personalities, though personal ambitions played an important part. If this is true of foreign relations, it seems similarly true and even more important in the case of domestic politics, in the later as in the earlier period of the reign. These were a continuation and expansion of the discords of the early years, culminating in the tragedy of civil war. But they showed the same signs of high endeavour and constructive statesmanship, and ended with a contribution of lasting importance to English constitutional advance.

In the parliament of 1257 Henry led his son, in Apulian dress, before the magnates and begged for supplies to meet his debts; but 'the ears of all men tingled' when they heard this request, and from the lay magnates he got nothing except unpalatable advice. They had known of Henry's obligations to the pope since October 1255, but were unshakable in their opposition. The pope, on his part, would not abate his pact. Henry must make peace with France, and he must reach Sicily with 8,500 armed men by 1 March 1259.

To rescue the king from his commitments and to prevent such folly in the future, the magnates, by April 1258, had probably produced a sworn confederacy. It was headed by Richard of Clare, earl of Gloucester, Roger Bigod, earl of Norfolk, and Simon de Montfort; and it was designed for mutual aid in the cause of right, save the faith all owed to king and crown. The confederates obtained strong support from the general body of magnates, and this same month went in arms to Westminster where, leaving their swords at the door, they entered the hall of the king. They demanded that Henry accept their advice; and Henry, together with Prince Edward, swore on the gospels to submit himself to their counsel and to consent to all they wished to be done.

Such a promise went directly against the king's conception of his office. Even if nothing further had resulted, his submission to such compulsion would have been a deep humiliation for Henry III. But the magnates also presented a definite proposal to reform the realm to which Henry agreed in a letter of 2 May, 1258, promising the reforms before the following Christmas;[1] and in another letter of the same date he specifically conceded that a council of twenty-four should reform the state of the kingdom, though he did not agree that the king, as well as the kingdom should be reformed, and his letter was far from a complete surrender of his royal rights. On the other hand, there was no disposition on the part of the magnates to destroy the royal power. They did not feel that they were mere rebels, but had a feeling of dedication to a noble cause, to betray which would be a dishonour. 'Our magnates', Henry wrote, 'setting our affairs before their own . . . devote all their might to our interests and those of our realm.' They were, the lords believed, the *universitas regni* standing for the good of all. The commonwealth was a body nourished by the gift of God, moved by equity and controlled by reason. It could not allow the separate working of its members; it demanded the loyalty of all.

These views and this unity may have been inspired in part by Simon de Montfort, not yet dominating the opposition to Henry but active within it. He was a man of great vision and fine intelligence. He had long left the ranks of Henry's friends and supporters, and had given his outstanding abilities to the opposition. The decisive experience which determined this was probably his recall from Gascony, doubly important because it revealed both the weakness and instability of Henry and the pride and obstinacy of Simon, ingredients in both their characters which contributed to the tragedy of 1258–65.

After the war of 1242, Gascony had continued to be in great disorder and Earl Simon was asked to pacify it in the spring of 1248. He was given wide powers, guaranteed for seven years. His strong rule secured a measure of peace but infuriated the Gascons; and in 1252 Simon was summoned home to defend himself against many complaints. He did so with much success, amid scenes of bitter recrimination by him and his Gascon enemies; on the other hand it became clear that he had lacked both understanding and sympathy. He returned to his Gascon appointment in June 1252; but Henry shortly superseded him, despite earlier promises of support. The duchy was handed to Prince Edward as its future lord. Henry had

---

[1] Modern differences of opinion are discussed in my *Constitutional History, 1216–1399*, vol. I, pp. 131–71, and there is also a discussion of the main problems of the period 1258–65.

shown himself excitable and vituperative as well as ungrateful. Simon had shown qualities of violence and pride. His enemies were reminded by his bearing and actions of 'the bad ways of his race'. He returned from Gascony to France where he later helped Anglo-French negotiations. Constant in his behaviour, he supported his ungrateful king loyally, but imperilled the settlement by insisting on the payment of his wife Eleanor's dowry, stubbornly refusing to renounce any of his claims even those that might conflict with the terms of peace. From this point his path began clearly to diverge from that of his king. He had been shocked in the campaign of 1242 by Henry's incompetence and that of his advisers, and now his personal friendship was undermined. He became one of the leading opponents of Henry in 1258; later he was to be the main prop of the whole movement of reform.

What part he played in shaping the Provisions is uncertain. These were only a preliminary set of proposals for a far-reaching effort of reform. They provided for the committee of 24 who were to make further detailed proposals, and arranged for a council of fifteen with wide and dangerously vague powers of advising the king and redressing all wrongs. Twelve magnates, elected by the barons, and representing the whole community of the land, were to treat about the common needs along with the council of fifteen, at parliaments to be held three times a year. The king's position in such activities was not defined. The Provisions were a courageous attempt to launch a great programme of reform. They inevitably suffered from a lack of precision but, partly in consequence, both contained the seeds of bitter disputes over interpretation and posed a formidable threat to the supremacy of the king.

Some of the idealism which Simon contributed to this movement may have been the baronial appeal to, and trust in, the smaller gentry. At every meeting of the shire court, they decreed, four knights elected by the shire were to attend in order to hear and record all complaints of injuries and trespasses. The plaints they received were to be brought before the justices of the king. At a later point knights were similarly given wide powers to help survey all defects of local administration. In October 1258 all freemen were formally enrolled in support of the reforming movement; they were to take an oath of loyalty to it, in the same manner as the greater lords. Knights of the shire were summoned to those parliaments which were under the control of the barons. There are many indications that with the great reforming movement of 1258 a new age for the knight of the shire and a broader concept of the *universitas* had arrived.

The broadening interest of the gentry in public affairs is probably to be seen in the protest made in 1259 by the community of the Bachelors of England at the delay in completing reforms. The Bachelors were probably the knights and lesser landowners in the households of the magnates. The chronicler who used the term probably picked it up from a Westminster source but did not explain what he meant by it. It may well have described knights and local gentry attending at Westminster in time of parliament. The spontaneous if informal organization of the Bachelors into a 'community' shows how endemic the idea of the *universitas* was in this society; and their protest shows how keen was the interest roused by the reformers in many ranks of society.

The Bachelors addressed Prince Edward and the earl of Gloucester. They claimed that the king had performed all that the barons had constrained him to do, but that the barons had done nothing of what they had promised for the good of the realm; they had acted only for their own good and the harm of the king. Unless a remedy was provided, the agreement (of Oxford?) would be restored in another way. Despite the reluctance of many historians to take this protest at its face value, and despite the problems it raises, it seems clear that the Bachelors had been bitterly disappointed at the protracted and apparently sterile dominance of the reforming magnates long after Christmas 1258.[1] It is hard not to credit those who made the protest with a double purpose: the ending of the system of controls over the king set up by the Provisions of Oxford, and the completion of the baronial programme of reform. The second purpose was, in fact, largely accomplished by a further instalment of regulations, the so-called Provisions of Westminster: the first, if it was indeed an aim of the protest, was not conceded; and it is probable that this failure on the part of the barons to end their attempt to control Henry was a basic cause of the mounting bitterness and suspicion which persisted throughout the realm.

Whether or not there was any connection between this protest and a pact between Prince Edward and Simon de Montfort on 15 October we have no means of knowing. Edward swore to give the

---

[1] For a discussion, with a translation of evidence, see my *Constitutional History 1216-1399*, vol. I, pp. 141–3, 171–2.

earl aid and counsel against all men except his father, to whom both men reserved their fealty, and not to make war on any of the confederates. Thus the 'common enterprise', as Simon called it, was strengthened against opposition. The pact did not last very long, but like the Bachelors' protest it reflects something of the tensions created by the reformers' clinging to power.

At the end of 1259 both Henry and Simon de Montfort were in France, and in their absence foreign affairs took a turn for the worse when Llywelyn of Wales attacked the English in Wales. Henry increased the domestic tension by writing from St. Omer to put off indefinitely a parliament which was to have been held at Candlemas, an action which Simon called into question as being against the Provisions. On 27 March Henry, for his part, summoned a great council of lords, to meet on 25 April, from which Simon de Montfort was to be excluded. Edward and Earl Simon proposed, in reply, to hold a parliament or *colloquium* at London. Both sides recruited extra forces. When Henry at length hurried home, cured of the illness which had kept him at St. Omer, he found nobody to deny his royal honours, but he knew that civil war had been very close. At first he refused to see his son Edward, for he was sure that if he did, his love would overcome his anger, and that he would not be able to withhold his embrace. Edward was, indeed, reconciled to his father, and took part in great festivities in October. It was then arranged that he should leave England and work off some of his youthful energies (he was, in fact, twenty years old) not in the dangerous arena of domestic politics but in the congenial adventure of tournaments in France.

As for Simon de Montfort, Henry planned to bring him to trial; but Simon defended himself so ably in the preliminary investigation that the plan was abandoned. Simon was even chosen to lead a royal army from Chester against Llywelyn of Wales. Nevertheless, the king's policy had strengthened the royalist position and threatened the unity of the baronial opposition. It has been claimed that only one thing now saved the 'common endeavour'. This was the oath which had been taken by all the lords and others, which made every opponent of the Provisions of Oxford an enemy of all, exposed to a common attack.

Henry was not content with these important gains. He sought papal absolution from his oath to maintain the Provisions. In the spring and summer of 1261 he issued proclamations in the shires in which he denounced his detractors and attacked the whole plan of reform. He demanded freedom from restraints. He obtained the papal bull he sought, on 14 April, and he began to dismiss baronial sheriffs and ministers. He thus once more brought England to the very brink of war. In the crisis which followed, he issued a powerful manifesto to his *populus* defending his position, which anticipates in some ways the famous proclamations of the Wars of the Roses. Further, both Henry and his opponents summoned knights of the shire to rival 'parliaments', whilst he called to his side many magnates and their retinues. In spite of all this, peace was again patched up; but it was so favourable to Henry that Simon felt deserted. He left England in anger, to meditate on the instability of Englishmen. By May 1262 the king's position seemed to have been peacefully and completely restored.

Outstanding features of the struggle had been the reluctance of Englishmen to proceed to extremes against their ruler, and the growing interest and influence of the knights, and even of a wider *populus*. The mood of Englishmen matched the hour as it did many centuries later in 1940; and there was such a search for novel measures to meet new needs as would reflect credit on any community at any period of time. The inner harmony of society was strong, and this was a creative age. Up to the tragic year of 1263 it seemed as if the efforts of the idealists and the moderates would be successful in the end.

But in 1263 the war which all dreaded and which many had tried to avert, broke over the kingdom. The failure of peace was the product of many causes. The intractability of the political problem of government was enhanced by defects of personality and mutual suspicion. A group of 'young sparks'[1] headed by Roger Clifford clung to the Provisions, organized tournaments, and in April 1263 invited Simon de Montfort to return to England from France. An illness of Henry in Paris in September 1263, together with rumours that he had died, added to uncertainty. The malcontents, under Simon de Montfort and Roger Clifford, gathered at Oxford. They demanded that the Provisions be kept, and denounced as public enemies all those who opposed them, only the king, the queen and their children being excepted. When Henry refused their demands, they at long last broke into open rebellion. In the west they seized Gloucester and the passage of the Severn. In the south they secured

[1] Sir Maurice Powicke, *The Thirteenth Century*, p. 172.

the Cinque Ports and the countryside of Kent. The Londoners rose against Henry, and the queen took refuge in St. Paul's. The king, surprised and bewildered, could make no headway and in July accepted the rebels' terms.

In September an assembly of bishops and magnates heard the king's renewed acceptance of the Provisions; and Earl Simon took charge of the realm in the name of the incomplete reforms. The movement had succeeded without any major engagement because it expressed the will of all the 'community of England'; but in itself it offered no solution to the deep problems of 1258; indeed, it divided England more deeply than ever and brought one step nearer the tragedy of a major civil war.

Despite their appearance of strength, Simon and his allies were actually on the horns of a dilemma. The whole political structure still depended in the final analysis upon the king. The barons could not work with Henry and they could not do without him. They stood for the welfare of England, but they could never determine exactly where the welfare of England ended and that of the monarch began. Many magnates had supported a great movement of protest, but not so many could escape from the old and strong loyalties which bound them to the Crown. Henry could not be prevented, sooner or later, from recapturing his royal authority even whilst professing his allegiance to the Provisions. 'We are,' he declared, 'and always will be ready firmly to observe the oath we made at Oxford'; but between his interpretation and Simon's lay a gulf wide enough to wreck all the peace of the realm.

This was shown dramatically by the mediation of Louis IX in the famous Mise of Amiens of January 1264. Both sides had agreed to submit to this arbitration, and both sides had equal opportunity to present their complaints. There seems to be no evidence that Simon offered to accept Louis's arbitration only on the details of the Provisions, whilst keeping the principles intact.[1] The argument that the wording of the letters of agreement was deliberately vague seems to have little to commend it. Even the more specific accusation that Louis 'extended himself beyond the power conceded to him' is far from conclusive. The French king may have taken a very liberal view of his responsibilities in arbitration; but he had certainly

---

[1] P. Walne 'The Barons' Agreement at Amiens, January 1264' in *E.H.R.*, vol. LXIX (July 1954), p. 418; R. F. Treharne, in 'The Mise of Amiens, 23 January 1264' in *Studies in Medieval History Presented to F.M. Powicke* (Oxford 1948), pp. 236-7.

been given wide powers. He could hardly avoid a judgment on the Provisions of Oxford, for they had proved to be the very pith and marrow of the whole dispute. Thus, Louis felt compelled to restore to the king all that he had held before May 1258, and to sweep the Provisions of Oxford entirely away. His judgment 'shows that a ruler who was famous throughout Christendom precisely for the virtues of honesty and love of justice believed that right was overwhelmingly on the side of the king'. The result was a final and irrevocable appeal by Simon and his allies to the arbitrament of war. By so doing, whatever their motives, they laid themselves open to a charge of bad faith, and probably turned a good many waverers away from their cause.

The war thus began auspiciously for the royalists, but it ended in disaster. Despite their broken oaths, the reformers still had widespread support and in Simon they had an inspired leader. The royalists had a more impressive army, including Prince Edward, but their opponents had the greater skill. Edward showed his mettle by clever policy and tactics in the Severn valley. Henry gathered the royal forces at Oxford. Bishops worked feverishly as mediators. But Simon adorned his followers with the white cross of the crusader, and claimed, like the rebels of 1215, to be leading the army of God. At the little town of Lewes he surprised the king by the rapidity of his movement and gained a tactical advantage. On the morning of 14 May 1264 his forces were already deployed on the downs above Lewes whilst the royal army was still in the town. The Londoners, strong in enthusiasm but weak in discipline, were on his left; the might of his army was in the centre and on the right. King Henry himself commanded the royalist centre, Edward his right flank and Richard of Cornwall his left. Outnumbering the rebels and led by great princes, the royalists were confident in attack and ready to take the adverse slope in their stride. Edward did, indeed, break and mercilessly pursue the Londoners; but Earl Simon kept his main forces intact and gained an almost bloodless victory over Henry and Earl Richard, weakened by the absence of the prince. He won the military struggle by one impressive victory: it remained to be seen if he could also triumph in the peace.[1]

Even with Henry prisoner in his hands, and Prince Edward making an involuntary submission, Simon was still faced with an insoluble problem. He did, indeed, obtain an agreement, known

[1] R. F. Treharne, *The Battle of Lewes, 1264: its place in English History* (Lewes 1964).

as the Mise of Lewes, sealed on the field of battle. As far as we know, though this contained many useful provisions, it did not aspire to be anything so ambitious as a final settlement. It provided for a council to be elected by certain arbitrators, whose counsels Henry promised to use. Another attempt at settlement was made in the parliament of June 1264, to which four knights for each shire were summoned.[1] This was the famous 'form of government' which set up three electors to nominate the royal council and reform the state of the kingdom. The council had nine members, and was to advise the king in some of his most important acts, including the disposal of castles (a matter of supreme interest to all) and the affairs of the realm; or else (presumably if Henry did not co-operate) they were to act in place of the king.

Neither scheme of government was intended to be more than provisional; despite sincere efforts nothing more permanent could be agreed upon. The precise limits of the king's authority and that of the reformers were never clearly defined. The reason seems clear. Neither side would yield to the other the substance of royal power. Yet this was something which could not be divided; it could not be taken only in part out of the hands of the king. Thus Simon was still faced with his old dilemma. He could not, and probably did not wish to, usurp the essence of kingship; yet on the other hand to divide authority would sooner or later cause it all to revert to the ruler, whose possession was sanctified by coronation and upheld by tradition. The situation may be illustrated by the fact that the rebels of 1264 had renounced Henry before the battle of Lewes by an act of *diffidatio*, but when they had won the battle they at once issued writs from the king's chancery in his name. Hence, despite Simon's victory in the field, he could not devise a form of government satisfactory to himself, and the balance of power after 1264 tilted once again in favour of the king.

When the country was threatened by invasion by royalist exiles and their allies, shortly after Lewes, most men still rallied to Simon's cause. But the Marcher lords were irreconcilably against his government; a group of his young supporters even made an unsuccessful attempt to rescue Prince Edward from Wallingford Castle. Simon, did indeed, pacify most of the west by December

---

[1] This difficult question is discussed in my *Constitutional History, 1216–1399*, vol. I, p. 158); Sir Maurice Powicke in *The Thirteenth Century*, p. 194; *Diplomatic Documents Preserved in the Public Record Office*, edited by Pierre Chaplais (H.M.S.O. 1964), reviewed in the *A.H.R.*, vol. LXXI (Oct. 1965), pp. 141–2.

1264, but his success was more apparent than real. He tried hard, in a famous parliament of January 1265, to obtain a settlement and an expression of general support; but he did not get more than a limited agreement to accept the government as it stood; and this offered no permanent solution. Prince Edward and Henry of Almain, son of Richard of Cornwall, were surrendered to the king, though required to swear an oath to maintain the provisional government; but this gesture achieved little except to add to Simon's active foes. A letter by Pope Clement on 19 July reveals the bitterness of the hostility towards Simon: the pope warned his new legate in England 'not to admit a treaty of false peace until the pestilent man with all his progeny be plucked out of the realm.' What Clement put in his letter many Englishmen began to feel in their hearts.

A great movement of defection from Simon began, fomented by Prince Edward, who had finally escaped from all restraint whilst he was out riding during the week of Whitsuntide. Gilbert of Clare, the young Earl of Gloucester, headed the list of turncoats; he had come to suspect Simon's motives as much as he hated his sons. Roger Mortimer provided another famous name; it was to his castle at Wigmore that Edward rode when he made his escape. Undermined by this general exodus, Simon's cause suddenly collapsed. His son Simon was caught in isolation with part of the baronial forces and defeated at Kenilworth by Prince Edward; and Simon himself and his main army were then penned in at Evesham by the superior forces of the prince.

The battle of Evesham, on 4 August 1265, was short. Though Simon had possession of the king and was strong in the passionate loyalty of his remaining supporters, he knew that his cause was lost, and he advised his justiciar and Ralph Basset of Drayton to flee and wait for a better day. His Welsh footmen soon fled, broken by the power of Prince Edward's cavalry; but his knights and barons formed a circle around him and fought until all was lost. Many of them, including Ralph Basset, were slain as were Simon and his son. King Henry, who had been kept by Simon's side, was wounded. The reformer's body was dismembered by a knight who had fought at his side at the battle of Lewes. Such changes of heart had not been uncommon in the rapidly changing circumstances of the civil war, and mutilation was not unknown; but in this case it is a grim reminder of the passions and fears which the reforming experiments of 1258–65 had aroused.

More lasting than such passions was the memory of a gallant fight for an inspiring cause. It does not detract from such a memory that the cause may well be said to have been hopeless from the start. The monarchical power was mishandled by Henry; but it could not be subjected to a permanent bridle by any procedures or institutions known to the men of the age. Nevertheless, Simon had a great vision which was destined to endure. He conceived a government set on broader foundations and supported by a clearer purpose than had yet been achieved in any medieval kingdom; and his vision and his sacrifice fired the imagination of Englishmen. Miracles adorned his memory, and songs were sung about him, such as those Edward II heard later, when travelling in the north in 1323.

5. THE LAST YEARS

The pacification of England which followed his death would in any case have been difficult. It was made more so by an ordinance of 17 September by which the lands of all his accomplices were declared forfeit to the king, and all Simon's acts since Lewes were undone. Not only were his supporters threatened with loss of all their possessions, but no man knew exactly how a supporter of Simon was to be defined. The citizens of London were collectively fined, and the city was ruled from the Tower by the seneschals of the king. A desperate resistance of surviving rebel leaders at the Isle of Axholme by the Trent was suppressed. The Cinque Ports were subdued, and Prince Edward became their warden and castellan of Dover. But the rebels were hard to destroy; they were too large a section of the community, too much in its life and heart. One focal point of their obstinate resistance became the Isle of Ely, besieged by both Edward and his father. Foreign invasion was feared.

At length, however, the efforts of the papal legate, Cardinal Ottobuono, began to bear fruit. A plan of pacification and agreement called the Dictum of Kenilworth was finally published on 31 October 1266. By this the accomplices of Earl Simon were given a chance to redeem their lands. On the other hand, the king, it was said, 'shall . . . exercise his dominion, authority, and royal power without impediment or contradiction'.[1] His precepts were to be obeyed, and his subjects were to seek justice, as of wont, in his courts (not by violence and rebellion). For this end, the king would nominate men who would respect the laws and customs of the kingdom; and he was

[1] My *Constitutional History 1216–1399*, vol. I, p. 184.

urged to observe all the liberties granted in the past to his subjects and to the Church. These terms of settlement did not ensure the triumph of peace overnight; but the Dictum was nevertheless a great constitutional document. It restored the monarchy and ended baronial reform; but it did not merely establish royalist reaction. It restored the old monarchical structure of government, but it could not destroy the memory of resistance to absolute power, and of the ideals of 1258.

There was one final and dramatic action by the young Gilbert of Gloucester. In April 1267 he suddenly marched with his followers to London, encamped at Southwark, and shortly entered the city. He was joined by men from the Isle of Ely; he restored the commune of London; and for two months he held the city, heart of the kingdom. It looked as if the civil war would start all over again but wiser counsels prevailed, and a final settlement was reached by which the main principles of the Dictum of Kenilworth were strengthened and confirmed. The Statute of Marlborough, issued in November, reasserted the Charter of 1225 and the main clauses of the Provision of Westminster of 1259. The Charter was put on the same footing as a statute, enforceable by appropriate chancery writs; though this could not be put into full effect. A little later the full liberties of London were restored.

The exact reasons for Gloucester's action are uncertain, but he seems to have stood for a moderate opinion, widely held, which earnestly desired an end to conflict through conciliation, compromise, and reason. He was supported, or inspired, by Cardinal Ottobuono, who stood above the conflict and used his fine talents to procure peace and preach a crusade. Largely as a result, Prince Edward and other important magnates took the cross at Northampton, an act which eventually resulted in Edward's long absence in the Holy Land and in France. On 20 August 1270 the prince and his wife left England for Aigues Mortes.

The settlement was followed by taxation to repair the damages of war and to meet the cost of the proposed Crusade. In order to pay the debts incurred by Queen Eleanor on behalf of her husband while she was in France, Clement IV granted a tenth for three years, the first mandatory tax levied by the pope on the clergy in England not for a crusade but for the use of the king. The clergy themselves in 1267 granted one twentieth of their revenues for a year to aid the disinherited. The king tallaged the cities and his demesne; and, for this and other matters, he summoned representatives of cities as well as magnates. The former were 'to do in the aforesaid matters what we shall be led to provide by the common counsel of our realm'.[1] Eventually, a subsidy of a twentieth of personal property was obtained by the agreement of a great Hoketide parliament of 1270, to which knights and free tenants were summoned along with the great men of the realm. A great and united effort was thus made to repair the ravages of war; though it should perhaps be recorded that the lower clergy objected to being taxed by the king, and would not be bound by the consent of the bishops.

Henry died on 16 November 1272. His last hours were troubled by the cries of the Londoners, busy about their civic quarrels. His son was absent on his crusade. Henry was very much alone. But he died as he had lived, not without dignity and most assuredly with the consolation of his faith. He had lived long enough to see the dedication of Westminster Abbey, child of his piety and love of beauty, in 1269; and he had translated the bones of St. Edward, his patron saint, to their new shrine behind the high altar. He had come with honour and a measure of success to an end of his secular quarrels. Though they had cost blood and sacrifice and the destruction of a very gallant opponent, they had kept his throne secure and his monarchy intact. He was, indeed, fortunate in his times and in his son. He lived in a creative age in which problems could be resolutely dealt with and progress made in spite of bitter struggles. Though defeated at times, he never ran a real risk of destruction. This was not, like the fourteenth century, a time of extremes. It was an age of experiment and the broadening of old institutions; and both the king and the opposition to him learned much, achieved much, and left an inspiring political legacy to future times.

[1] My *Constitutional History 1216–1399*, vol. III, p. 272; G. O. Sayles, 'Representation of Cities and Boroughs in 1268' in *E.H.R.* vol. XL (October 1925), p. 585.

3

EDWARD I

KING EDWARD I was much nearer the ideal of a medieval ruler than his father had been. He embodied many of the heroic virtues his subjects deeply admired. When he was born in 1239, Henry III had insisted that the presents his subjects made to celebrate the occasion should be costly, so that it was said of him 'God gave us this infant, but our lord the king sells him to us'. Nevertheless, Edward was well worth the high price. He stood head and shoulders above most of his subjects, with the body of an athlete and the brow of a student. His abundant hair, which was yellow in childhood, turned snowy white in old age. His left eyelid drooped like his father's, but apart from this his only blemish was a slight stammer, not enough to spoil his eloquence.

He loved war and tournaments, but he was at home in the law courts and familiar with all the intricacies of government. He was reckless of dangers but could be tortuous and subtle in policy. He was hot and impulsive, but learned to value moderation and restraint. Despite his father's well-founded reference to his boyish wantonness and lack of discipline, he developed to meet his responsibilities as later did Henry V. He proved to be a devoted husband and a long-suffering father. He was pious and conventional in religion, but no slave of his priests. T. F. Tout believed that a true sympathy bound him closely to his nobles and people, and despite misunderstandings and quarrels between him and his magnates in his later years he kept their admiration to the end. He was born to great endeavours and notable achievements, and he came at a time in English history which was propitious for both.

Like the great Saint Edward, after whom he was named, he had a lofty concept of his duties and his powers.[1] Like Philip the Fair of France and Alfonso the Wise of Castile, he both symbolized and contributed towards the rise of a new monarchy, product of the territorial state. He combined in his royal estate both the attributes of personal kingship and those of the impersonal Crown, the latter forged by expanding bureaucracy. In addition, he became a centre for Arthurian romance; as part of the cult, he opened Arthur's alleged tomb at Glastonbury. He anticipated his grandson in the chivalric custom of the round table. He gathered to himself what was left of feudal loyalties and the friendship which was the product of the old rough familiarity between the feudal king and his great lords; but he was also the lawmaker and administrator, taking into his hands new resources and demanding new loyalties from all the subjects of the *Respublica Anglicana*. Out of both old and new elements of his kingship he created a synthesis which became a pattern for English monarchs for many generations to come.

Edward succeeded to his father's throne during his crusade which had begun in 1270. He had joined Charles of Anjou at Carthage in November 1270, spending the winter in Sicily, and arriving at Acre in May 1271. Things were going ill for the Christian remnants in Palestine. The great city of Antioch had recently been stormed by the Mamluks. Jaffa had been taken by surprise. The fortresses of Krak and Montfort had been lost. Edward had far too small a force to have much influence on this situation. All he could win was a breathing-space. He made a small raid; but he was not strong enough even to capture one unimportant castle which stood in his way (Qâqun beyond Mount Carmel). As Bibars, ruler of Egypt and most of Palestine observed, if they cannot take a house, they are unlikely to conquer the kingdom of Jerusalem. Hostilities ended in April 1272, when the titular ruler of Jerusalem and the citizens of Acre combined to negotiate a treaty with Bibars which was to last ten years, ten months, ten days and ten minutes. In spite of Edward's lack of success, the Sultan thought well enough of him to send an assassin against him. Though Edward nearly died of his wounds, he had so far recovered as to set sail from Acre on 22 September. Whilst at Sicily on his way home he heard of his father's death. He did not hurry back. By July 1273 he was in Paris and did homage to his cousin Philip III. He delayed his return for nearly a year whilst he

---

[1] D. C. Douglas, *William the Conqueror* (University of California Press 1964), p. 253. Edward the Confessor, it was said, had worn 'the crown of the kingdom of Christ'.

straightened out affairs in Gascony; and he only landed at Dover on 2 August 1274.

He had been recognized as king in his absence, as soon as his father died. Immediately after the funeral service, the magnates, clergy and people who were in the church went up to the high altar and took an oath of fealty to him. Nearly two years later, on 19 August 1274, he was crowned king at Westminster amid general rejoicing. Unfortunately no copy of his coronation *ordo*, which would be of extraordinary interest, has survived.

2. FOREIGN POLICY: WALES

Just like his father's early reign, Edward's was in one sense a rehabilitation of the monarchy after a period of royal failure; it was marked by a vigilant defence of both his rights and his claims. But his policies at home and abroad were not always compatible with each other. Foreign policy involved him in undertakings beyond his planning and resources, and in the end undermined his position at home. Hence, in spite of his ability, his achievement finally fell short of his designs, and probably of his deserts. Nevertheless, he launched his country nobly into a new current of history.

English involvements abroad, it may be argued, entered on a new phase with the beginning of a long and costly attack on the independence of Wales, different in scope and persistence from anything which had been attempted before. In one sense this was merely an effort to wrest from the Welsh gains that they had made during the English civil war; in another, it was an expression of new aggressiveness and power by the expanding English state.

In the later years of Henry III, the great Welsh prince Llywelyn ap Gruffydd, lord of Snowdonia, had given some signs of providing a nexus for Welsh political unity; but after 1274 the opportunity for Welsh consolidation and aggression came to an end. A quarrel between Llywelyn and his brother David gave occasion for English intervention, but if this opportunity had not been provided no doubt some other would have occurred. The Welsh magnates mistakenly encouraged Llywelyn to refuse homage. Amauri, the youngest son of Simon de Montfort, helped to promote a crisis in 1275 by attempting to take his sister Eleanor to Wales to marry her to Llywelyn, to whom she had been betrothed when her father Simon was in power. Edward was not unnaturally deeply suspicious of such an alliance. He intercepted the two Montforts in the Channel, sent Eleanor to honourable captivity at Windsor, and thrust Amauri into prison. The projected marriage came to naught; but it contributed towards a grave deterioration of relations between England and Wales.

War actually began in 1276, though Edward did not summon his feudal host until June 1277. It cost the Welsh their independence and cast a dark shadow over English life, but it was not quite a total loss. The Welsh lost their chance to create a polity of their own, but they kept their pride and their culture. Nor could anything ever destroy their courage. They made a contribution to the conjoint history of England and Wales, and perhaps got something in return —for example, English law and administration. The English gained a province, which they administered both wisely and unwisely; and for the most part they had Welsh assistance, instead of enmity, in their future wars. But before that they had to face prolonged fighting, and this, though it cost much blood and treasure, added to the efficiency and complexity of their government. It gave them new visions of military organization, logistics, and tactics; and it made them in due course the most redoubtable warriors of their age.

By the spring of 1277 Edward's captains had already recovered the lands which Llywelyn had conquered in the Marches. By July the king himself arrived at Chester in the north, and assembled an imposing army in which there were probably 800 knights and 15,000 footmen, besides 370 archers and crossbowmen. Added to these were labourers and craftsmen for road-building and supplies, and thirty vessels in the estuary of the Dee. The army has been called the best controlled and best led to be gathered in Britain since 1066.[1]

Llywelyn was hemmed in and confined to Snowdonia. English soldiers and Welsh 'friendlies' gathered the crops in Anglesey, without which the mainland Welsh of the north were likely to starve. Confronted with this massive and skilful use of force the Welsh leader surrendered. The treaty of Conway in November 1277 saw him shorn of his powers outside Snowdonia and Anglesey and reinstated as Edward's vassal. He did homage to Edward at Westminster but retained his title of Prince of Wales and kept his rule over his restricted lands under Welsh laws and customs. The reconciliation between him and Edward seemed to be sincere and

[1] F. M. Powicke, *The Thirteenth Century*, p. 411.

promised to be lasting; and in October 1278 he was at length permitted to marry Eleanor of Montfort at Worcester, with much ceremony and at Edward's expense.

The failure of the settlement was not due to the actions of Llywelyn but to those of his restless brother; but David was sustained and encouraged by Welsh resentment at the expansion of English rule and by the extension of English law. In 1282, frustrated by the restricted size of his lordship in Dyffryn and Rufoniog, David rose against his lord and former benefactor, Edward; and he dragged his somewhat unwilling and very distrustful brother in his wake. All Wales blazed into revolt. Many successes were achieved, including the capture of much-hated English castles, and the defeat in the open field of Gilbert de Clare, earl of Gloucester. The revolt had taken Edward completely by surprise.

A Welsh rising seemed like nothing more than a distraction from Scottish and French affairs, but the king reacted with vigour and despatch. Whilst the situation in South Wales was restored by the Marcher lords, he himself concentrated in the north a large force of 750 knights, 8000 footmen, and 1000 archers, supported by sixty ships from the Cinque Ports. Luke de Tany, former seneschal of Gascony, occupied Anglesey and built a bridge of boats over the Menai strait to Bangor. Meanwhile, Edward and his lieutenants conquered all the lands and castles north of the Dee. The time for a combined attack on Snowdonia from Anglesey and the north had arrived, but Luke spoiled everything by a premature advance into Snowdonia on 6 November. His forces were defeated and he himself was drowned in the Menai strait.

However, nothing could deflect Edward, and his unceasing pressure soon brought dramatic results. Llywelyn made a foray into South Wales and his forces were defeated at Orewin Bridge in December 1282 by an English mixed contingent of heavy cavalry and archers, fighting together as one body. The engagement was little more than a skirmish; but the tactics employed paved the way for the famous combination of bowmen and dismounted knights of the future; and the immediate consequences were decisive. Llywelyn, who had been absent from the battle itself, was run through the body by a Shropshire soldier, Stephen of Frankton, who did not know whom he had slain. Deprived of its leader, Welsh resistance suddenly collapsed. Though Llywelyn's brother David tried to hold out in the wild hills of mid-Wales, he was finally handed over to Edward 'by men of his own tongue'. He was tried before the English magnates at Shrewsbury and hanged, drawn and quartered. For the time being, the Welsh surrendered; but the memory of their stubborn fight for freedom lived on down the years.

After the war came the settlement. Its main form was laid down in the famous Statute of Wales issued from Rhuddlan in 1284; but this was supplemented by the building of castles and towns and the setting up of a whole administrative system on the pattern of the county of Chester. The Edwardian castles in Wales are one of the most striking and enduring monuments of the age; at one castle alone, that of Beaumaris, 400 masons were at work. The administrative settlement was no less impressive. Snowdonia was divided into shires. An administration, with an exchequer of its own, was set up in Caernarvon. In 1301, the princedom of Wales was created and joined to Chester the control of the future Edward II. The conquest proved to be lasting, despite two Welsh revolts, one in 1287 whilst Edward was in Gascony, and another in 1294–95 whilst he was again preoccupied with France. The latter, which was sudden and dangerous, was stamped out with exemplary speed and efficiency, as noticeable as the lightning-like fury of the rebellion itself. The main Welsh forces were defeated at the battle of Maes Moydog, marked by a further development of English tactics based on the use of cavalry interlinked by crossbowmen and archers. This was on 5 March 1295.

The order which the English set up must be regarded in the main as enlightened, but it had its grave shortcomings. It was efficient, but it was also unsympathetic. Welsh law and custom were maintained, but they did not include those features which the English considered to be bad or outmoded. Criminal law, for example, became anglicized: and though it was no doubt an improvement, it was not what Welshmen desired. In any case, nothing could compensate the Welsh for the surrender of liberty, the endangering of their native culture, and the decline of their native tongue.

3. Foreign Policy: Scotland

If Edward's relations with Wales were a mixture of success and failure, so also were his relations with Scotland; though in this case the success was more limited and the failure, in the end, much more pronounced. Unlike Wales, Scotland was large enough and her geography was favourable enough to enable her with French help to survive English attack. Chronology as well as geography helped, for she profited by English entanglement with France and Wales. Welsh and Scottish courage and pride must be reckoned as equal; but a larger stage and a better outcome have given greater fame to the Scottish fight for freedom in the days of William Wallace and Robert Bruce.

Before the accession of Edward, Anglo-Scottish relations had followed the Welsh pattern. Long periods of peace and friendly intercourse were intermixed with war, or threat of war, generally created by English pressure, direct or indirect. The Scottish nobility was even more at home in England than the Welsh: John Comyn, to cite but one example, held fiefs from Henry III in Northumberland, and fought for him at Northampton and Lewes. The Scots, like the Welsh, made tentative steps towards unity during the long reign of Henry, despite this busybody's intervention and claims to paternal influence. In 1266, Magnus IV, king of Norway, ceded to Alexander III the Isle of Man and all the Western Isles.

But English claims to overlordship, set forth in the treaty of Norham in 1212 (though the record of this was later destroyed), were never abrogated. They were in Edward I's mind in 1279 when Alexander III did homage to him in England, becoming his liege man against all men, and when Edward reserved the right to talk about the homage for the kingdom of Scotland when he should wish. Homage for Scotland had not been specifically mentioned; but Edward had grounds for arguing, if the occasion ever arose, that it had been implied.[1] The occasion, it may be argued, was probably only delayed by Edward's preoccupation with Wales; it lay in the logic of the political situation at any moment after 1279.

King Alexander III died in 1286, his horse stumbling during a night ride in wild weather from Edinburgh to Kinghorn in Fife to visit his young second wife. He left as his heir his grand-daughter Margaret, the 'Maid of Norway', daughter of his daughter Margaret and Eric, king of Norway. In the crisis which followed, Scotland was dominated by King Edward, 'superior lord of Scotland', who made use of all his feudal rights. He obtained an agreement, made in his presence in 1289, that the Maid, who was six years old, should return to Scotland to be queen. She would be free of any contract

[1] See F. M. Powicke, *The Thirteenth Century* p. 595, n. 3.

of marriage and would not be married without Edward's consent. If disputes arose in Scotland during her minority, the mediation and counsel of Edward would be sought. This agreement, it was arranged, should be confirmed by the people of Scotland; and this was done at Brigham in March 1290. At the same time the Scots approved of a marriage between Margaret and Edward, son of Edward I; though it was set forth in a formal agreement in the following August that Scotland was to maintain her separate existence and her freedom. Nevertheless, a notable step towards the union of the two kingdoms had clearly been achieved.

Unfortunately Margaret died on 26 September 1290 on her way from Norway to Scotland. Rival claimants to the Scottish throne immediately appeared. As a result Edward was given a great chance, if not to unite England and Scotland, at least to exercise his authority as overlord and make his influence supreme. He searched the chronicles and records for evidence of his rights. He caused all the claimants to recognize him formally as superior lord of Scotland; and he prepared to receive temporary custody of Scotland pending the installation of a new ruler, who should be chosen by his award.

Edward's counsellors finally advised in favour of John Baliol, the grandson of the eldest daughter of King William the Lion's brother David. Two other strong claimants had a similar descent from David: Robert Bruce, lord of Annandale, and John Hastings of Abergavenny were the son and grandson of the second and third daughters. Eighty assessors failed to agree on an opinion, but they subsequently came round to the counsellors' advice. There is little doubt that this was offered in good faith and was reasonable; and Edward pronounced accordingly through his justice Roger Brabazon. John Baliol was installed as ruler on the Stone of Scone, and did homage at Newcastle on 26 December 1292 after the Christmas feast.

Edward had acted with constitutional propriety; but nevertheless he had advanced far-reaching claims to intervention in Scottish affairs. It may be argued in his favour that all along he did no more than maintain rights which had been freely recognized in the past; that he would have tarnished his reputation and weakened his throne had he acted otherwise. The Scottish nobles, not he, ruined a settlement he had imposed with great restraint and against his own narrow interests. If he had really wished to weaken and dominate the rising kingdom of Scotland, he would have divided it between the three main claimants instead of uniting it under one. This is true, but it does not entirely exonerate him from a charge of expansionism. He must share with the Scottish claimants and nobility responsibility for a tragic drift into a war which was to be both heroic and at the same time disastrous for both countries involved. It is idle to argue that if Edward had lived a little longer much of the subsequent tragedy might have been averted. He continued to be active to what was considered to be a ripe old age by medieval standards, yet he left a problem which could not be solved by any English ruler for the next 300 years.

Much of the friction which began immediately after 1292 arose from Edward's insistence that he had the right to hear appeals from Baliol's judgments, and even to summon the king of Scotland before him to answer for his actions in the royal court. Against this, Baliol argued that he was king of Scotland and dared not answer, in any matter concerning his kingdom, without the counsel of the good men of his realm. He even stated his case in the English parliament at Westminster, only to have it rejected by the king's council. His weak actions caused him to forfeit the esteem of the Scots; but Scottish stock suddenly stood very high in France, and in 1295 a treaty of mutual aid was negotiated with Philip the Fair.

It is not easy to blame Edward for reacting violently against such an alliance, even though he himself had done much to provoke it. In the period between December 1295 and March 1296 he made preparations for war against a vassal who had, he claimed, broken his sworn obligations. There was, indeed, an air of crisis in England in the late summer of 1295, for the French reached an agreement with the Norwegians so as to obtain a fleet which could transport an invading army across the Channel. King Eric of Norway promised in return for the payment of £50,000 a year, to equip 100 great ships, to serve for four months every year, as long as there was war between England and France. The Welsh might be expected to rise, and England had thus to prepare for a war on three fronts. Accordingly, Edward made elaborate and effective preparations for the defence of the shores, extending and improving similar measures taken by John and Henry III.[1]

The atmosphere of the time is reflected in the capture and trial of Thomas de Turberville, an English knight who acted as a spy in

[1] A. Z. Freeman, 'A Moat Defensive: the Coast Defence Scheme of 1295', in *Speculum*, vol. XLII (July 1967), pp. 442–62.

the service of King Philip the Fair. Thomas belongs to a genre almost unknown in medieval England. His execution was a public event. He was led across London from the Tower to Westminster, secured on the back of a sorry mount by a rope under its belly. His hands were tied in front of him. Six 'tormentors' dressed like devils escorted him, and the hangman guided his steed. At Westminster he was sentenced to a traitor's death and was drawn on an ox-hide by six horses to the gallows. On the way he was insulted and beaten by his tormentors. He was hanged and left to rot 'as long as anything of him should remain'.[1]

In March 1296 Edward crossed the Tweed and stormed Berwick, where he received Baliol's formal *diffidatio*. Berwick itself was rebuilt to become a great English fortress. Lothian was next overrun and Edinburgh captured. Most of the Scottish leaders were taken after a defeat at Dunbar. By August, Edward had 'perambulated' the Scottish realm. John Baliol made his submission to him, surrendered his kingdom, and left Scotland for ever. Edward held a parliament at Berwick and received the homage of all the Scots. He appointed John de Warenne, earl of Surrey, to be guardian of their country, aided by a chancellor and treasurer. The alliance with France and the independence of Scotland seemed both to be at an end, but in both cases the appearance was illusory. Edward was, in fact, at the beginning, not the end, of a bitter struggle with Scotland which was to outlast his own lifetime by very many years.

In 1297 William Wallace, a free tenant of the king's steward in Renfrew, was involved in a dispute arising in the court of the English sheriff of Lanark. As a result he murdered the sheriff, and after some forays against the English agents established himself in Ettrick forest. Andrew of Moray led another revolt in the north. Great magnates like Robert Bruce, earl of Carrick, joined the insurrection, and soon all Scotland was ablaze, the flames fanned by Robert of Wishart, bishop of Glasgow. But the first revolt had no success, and most of the leaders submitted: among them was William Douglas, an old offender, who was imprisoned in Berwick castle and was described as 'very savage and abusive'. However, William Wallace remained at large, fighting in John Baliol's name. The loss of other leaders was tragic but not fatal; the core of the opposition came, in the end, not from the Anglo-Scottish magnates but from

---

[1] J. G. Edwards, 'The Treason of Thomas Turberville, 1295', in *Studies in Medieval History Presented to Frederick Maurice Powicke* (Oxford 1948), pp. 296–309.

the small-holders of Scotland. With their help Wallace kept the cause of Scottish independence alive and made himself beloved for his courage and enterprise.

Faced with this kind of opposition Warenne's attempt to stamp out the revolt met with disaster at the battle of Stirling Bridge on 11 September 1297. We know little about the battle, except that the English forgot all the lessons they had learned in the Welsh wars. They encountered the Scots led by Moray and Wallace on the banks of the Forth just south of Stirling. Under the command of Earl Warenne and Cressingham, an exchequer clerk, the English army attempted to attack by crossing the river over a narrow bridge, in face of the enemy, though they could have crossed by a shallow ford only a few miles away. It was a simple matter for the Scots to bear down upon them when only half the army was across. Warenne threw away every advantage he had. The cavalry were cut down or drowned in retreat; only the unencumbered Welsh footmen could swim to safety on the southern bank. Cressingham was slain: his skin was stripped from his body and pieces of it were sent throughout Scotland as tokens of the English defeat. Wallace and the Scots were now able to attack England herself, and they worked havoc in Northumberland and Cumberland. The battle and its sequel brought about a temporary political truce in England, but it nevertheless helped to make possible a war of independence by the Scots. It marked a minor turning point in the history of England but a major turning point in that of the kingdom to the north.

The English did, indeed, make a great effort to retrieve their defeat. Edward summoned the feudal host to serve at pay, as well as local levies from northern shires and footmen from Wales. He moved the whole headquarters of his government to York, where it remained until 1304, and he organized an army which included about 2,400 knights of whom more than half received pay, and 10,500 paid Welsh archers, apparently preferring these to the northern foot. How many he led into battle we cannot say; but it is clear that the effort he made was quite comparable with any he made in Wales. He himself arrived at Roxburgh in June 1298. His strategy nearly failed through lack of supplies and through quarrels between Welsh and English soldiers; but Wallace fortunately gave him a chance to fight the set battle he desired.

The Scots were over-confident in the strength of their *schiltrons* or circles of footmen bristling with long spears, which seemed able

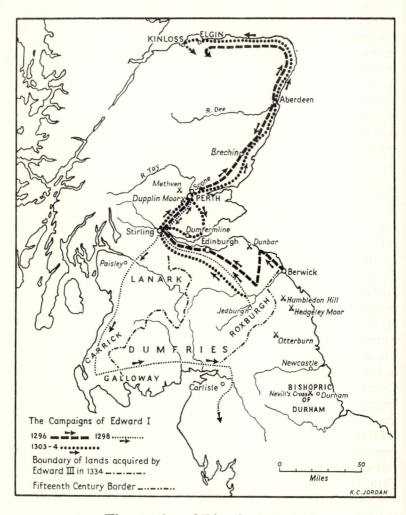

The Campaigns of Edward I

1296 ━━━▶━━ 1298 ·············

1303–4 ●●●●●●●●●

Boundary of lands acquired by
Edward III in 1334 ─··─··─··─

Fifteenth Century Border ─···─···─··

0   50

Miles

K.C.JORDAN

1. The campaigns of Edward 1 in Scotland

to beat off any cavalry attack. Wallace set up four of these near the tiny village of Falkirk, protected by marshland and girded with stakes and rope. He filled the gaps between with archers from Ettrick Forest, and he awaited the English attack. Edward arranged his cavalry in four squadrons, the first two of which, though held up by the marsh, scattered both the weak Scottish cavalry and the protective archers. The Scottish cavalry are said to have fled without striking a blow, but the English fared badly against the serried ranks of footman. Apparently their archers, who were mainly Welshmen, at first refused to advance. When they did, they easily decimated the ranks of the Scots who had no means of retaliation or defence. After this, the English cavalry was irresistible. Once inside the schiltrons it won an easy and a bloody victory.

The battle of Falkirk, fought on 22 July 1298, was a triumph for Edward's generalship and for the longbow, which was gradually becoming a decisive instrument of war. Edward had spent the night before the battle in the open field along with the lowliest of his soldiers, and had received a kick from a horse which broke two of his ribs. He led his troops despite his injury, but he was in no condition to follow up his victory, though he advanced north as far as Stirling where he rested for a while. Meanwhile, his soldiers fearfully ravaged the country as far north as Perth. But all the south-west of Scotland was now in revolt. Despite its ravaging, Edward's army wearied of fighting in a harsh country which offered little reward. There were many desertions: the contingent from Durham is said to have deserted in a body. On 8 September the king was back in Carlisle, where he was forced to dismiss most of his troops. In the beginning of 1299 he returned to the south, feeling that he had lost the fruits of victory by lack of support from his lords.

Edward did not lead another expedition against the Scots until June 1300. The army he then gathered was comparable with that at Falkirk, and he had fifty-eight ships to carry supplies into the Solway Firth. But though he continued the monotonous task of ravaging and intimidation, he achieved no important result. In August the archbishop of Canterbury presented him at Sweetheart Abbey with Pope Boniface's exhortation to desist from harming Scotland, which was a fief of the Holy See. In October he granted the Scots a truce until 1301.

There was another repetition of these kingly raids in 1301, shared by the young prince of Wales. Truces and campaigns alternated for the rest of the reign. However, on 20 May 1303 an event occurred which seemed to presage the final subjection of Scotland: Edward I and Philip the Fair patched up their differences in the definitive Treaty of Paris. Edward was now in a position to concentrate his efforts. He beat down all Scottish resistance. In 1303–4 he was able to winter at Dunfermline. On 24 July 1304 he captured Stirling castle, the only great fortress in which he was still defied. In the previous February most of the Scottish earls had made their submission. The conquest of Scotland seemed to be achieved.

As a sign of his confidence in peace, Edward moved the law courts from York back to Westminster. In 1305 William Wallace, hero of the resistance to Edward, was captured through the help of a Scot in Edward's service and was executed in London for treason, sedition, sacrilege and murder. He was tried and condemned in Westminster Hall, dragged by a horse to the Tower and thence to Tyburn, and there hanged and quartered. His head was impaled on London Bridge for all Englishmen to see. As T. F. Tout wrote, the full measure of William's fame belongs to a later age, but it was a sure instinct which made the Scottish people celebrate him as a popular hero in their struggle for independence. It was Wallace's glory that he fought a great fight and paid a full penalty for it; but with his death the struggle must have seemed to many to have been finally lost.

In a full assembly of parliament from 28 February to 21 March 1305, Edward decreed the 'establishment of our realm of Scotland'. He was aided by twenty councillors of his own and ten Scottish delegates. His enactments were reasonable, if his lordship be regarded as now accepted, and looked like being successful. He created a lieutenant and warden of Scotland, and a chancellor, chamberlain and controller, The country was divided into districts for judicial purposes.[1] Sheriffs, 'natives of either England or Scotland', were set up throughout the country, and most of those appointed were Scots. Celtic wergilds were abolished. The people of Scotland were to determine for themselves those laws of King David and the amendments to them which were to be kept, doubtful matters being referred to King Edward. The parliament of the Scots was to be retained; it was to deal with all matters referred to it from

---

[1] There were to be four pairs of justiciars, one each for Lothian, Galloway, and Scotland south and north of the Mounth, each pair consisting of an Englishman and a Scotsman. On the other hand, the key castles were to be under English control. For the abolition of the wergilds see G. W. S. Barrow, *Robert Bruce* (Berkeley Calif., 1965), p. 192.

England. Petitions from Scotland were to be received and answered in the English parliament.

The whole scheme was a worthy counterpart of the Statute of Wales. If the Scots were to be ruled by Edward, they could not have hoped for a much wiser or more liberal settlement. It had, indeed, only one major flaw, but this was fatal: it was the gift of a conqueror to a people whose love of freedom was obstinate and enduring, not to be quenched even by Edward's thoroughness and determination. Scotland, despite all appearances to the contrary, had still to be conquered. The contrast between the strength of English order and discipline and the weakness revealed by the wild individualism of the Scots can be very misleading; it is apt to obscure the intangibles of courage and pride, and love of liberty. Nor does it bring out the war-weariness of the English, fighting in a cause which lost some of its inspiration as the weary years of savage warfare dragged out their interminable course.

The English magnates, it is true, were in the main obedient to their king; but they were distrustful of him, as shown by demands for the confirmation and extension of the Charter and the perambulation of the forests; and England was disillusioned and impoverished. There were doubts in some quarters about the king's rights in Scotland, as we may see by the wording of royal writs which had been issued on 26 September 1300. Contrary to what might have seemed to be the dictates of common sense, it was England and not Scotland which had the deepest misgivings about the war, and it was Scotland which began the last and decisive struggle by an obscure act of 10 February 1306 which once again set all the northern country ablaze.

The act was not a great patriotic gesture and appeal to Scottish love of freedom, but it was nevertheless a spark to fire the smouldering discontent of a people and, as it proved, to provide a turning point in Scottish history. On 10 February 1306 Robert Bruce, grandson of the claimant of 1296, murdered John Comyn in a private quarrel at Dumfries. With nothing to lose and everything to gain, he proceeded to harness Scottish patriotism to support his own claim to the Scottish throne. The old Bishop Wishart of Glasgow produced the royal standard from its hiding place, and on 25 March a new king of Scotland was crowned at Scone, his head encircled by a golden circlet made by a local smith. Edward's unending task of subduing the stubborn Scots had to begin all over again.

The final revolt occurred when Edward was already in failing health, but the English organization in Scotland proved its worth. In June Robert Bruce was defeated by Edward's lieutenants in two minor engagements, one at Methven near Perth and the other probably at Dalry in Ayr; his small forces were scattered by Scottish allies rather than by the English themselves. The captured Scots were treated brutally. Scottish knights were hanged. Bruce's brothers were executed; though he himself eluded capture and was ultimately to take a terrible revenge. His sister Mary and the countess of Buchan who had seated Bruce on his royal throne, were penned up for a time in wooden cages in the turrets of Roxburgh and Berwick Castles. Eminent clerics were imprisoned in chains. From September 1306 to March 1307 Edward made preparations for a final crushing of all opposition. But he was confined to bed by sickness near Carlisle, sustained now mainly by his indomitable will. In February he learned that Bruce had reappeared in Carrick, still supported by Scottish freemen and still formidable and full of fight.

The old king was carried as far as Burgh-on-the-Sands on the Solway, and died on 7 July 1307 aged sixty-eight, his face towards the still unconquered north. Not without cause had he been called the Hammer of the Scots. He had pursued with high intelligence and great skill what seemed the destiny of his country; but the spirit of Scotsmen and the leagues of their barren moors had been too much for him. Altogether, he was driven by ambition and circumstances to attempt too much in too many places; and in Scotland, in the end, his failure was complete. It was the coincidence of his wars that finally defeated Edward. The strength of his country, at times beset by enemies, was remarkable; but it was not adequate when to his enemies in Wales and Scotland was added the formidable power of France.

4. Foreign Policy: France

For twenty years, between 1273 and 1293, there was an uneasy peace between England and France during which friction was constantly engendered over Gascony by the aggressive designs of the French king and his lawyers. The friction was great and growing, but peace was supported by close family connections. Edward himself was a cousin of the French king. His mother and the widow of Louis IX were sisters. Many of his ancestors came from Aquitaine.

Though his beloved wife was half a Spaniard, in 1279 she inherited Ponthieu in the north of France. He and Philip the Fair of France were good friends and had many interests in common. It has been argued, indeed, that the expansion of French power in the south, especially in Navarre, did not alarm Edward, and need not have caused a deterioration in Anglo-French relations. What was really responsible for this, it is suggested, was the triumph at the court of King Philip of a group actively hostile to English rule in Gascony. They supported a return to the expansionist policy of Philip Augustus and indulged in a bellicose revival of a pseudo-Carolingian tradition. There is much to be said for this view, but it should not be allowed to obscure the deeper forces at work. What mattered most of all in Anglo-French relations was the growing power and expansiveness of the French monarchy, parallelling in its consequences for England the results of English development for Scotland and Wales.

The potentially explosive Gascon situation may be discerned in the homage Edward rendered to Philip in 1285 after the latter's accession to the throne. He performed it 'for the lands I hold on this side of the sea according to the form of peace made between our ancestors', thus leaving himself free to reclaim any territory which he deemed to have been usurped. It is true that hostilities were slow to develop, and that Edward played a prominent part as peacemaker in French and European affairs. He was partly engaged in such friendly offices during his long stay in Paris and Gascony from the summer of 1286 to 1289. He helped to reconcile Philip with Peter of Aragon, after the disastrous Crusade of 1285. But his long stay was also made necessary by the need to strengthen his position in a Gascony which was exposed to growing pressure from both Aragon and France.

The French pressure on the duchy had been greatly increased by the death of Alphonse of Poitiers in 1271. His lands had encircled Gascony from the Bay of Biscay to the Pyrenees and, within two years of his death, they were all surveyed by the assiduous officers of the French monarch and transferred to the Crown. King Philip III himself had made a royal perambulation of his new acquisition and ensured the submission of its lords. For the whole period from 1272 to 1286, Edward and his officials were busy preventing this great transfer of land, and the judgments it involved, from weakening the English king's rights. In this they more than held their own. They were able to consolidate the work of Henry III and attach Gascony firmly to the English Crown. Henry had added the title *Dux Aquitanie* to his seal, and some years before his death had given Edward full control over the duchy. The English position was helped by the lucrative trade in wine, and by the natural preference of the Gascons for a distant rather than a neighbouring lord. They willingly helped Edward in his Welsh and Scottish wars, and rallied to his support when Gascony was threatened by absorption into the realm of France.

However, the French pressure, exerted in many ways, finally produced a conflagration. The occasion was an obscure conflict off Cap Saint-Mathieu in Brittany between the sailors of the Cinque Ports helped by ships from Bayonne, and those of Normandy, on 15 May 1293. The English were victorious and proceeded to sack La Rochelle. Philip IV chose to retaliate, not in the Channel but in Gascony. He required the punishment of the Gascons who had been involved, and restitution for damages; and he sent troops to the frontiers of the English possessions. He refused Edward's suggestion for a judicial settlement, ordered the dignitaries of Bayonne to be delivered to him for imprisonment, and even commanded the surrender of Bordeaux. Finally, he ordered Edward to appear in person to answer charges against him. In order to obtain a withdrawal of this citation, and a restoration of friendly relations, Edward allowed a formal seizing of the duchy by Philip, on a secret but clear understanding that this was only a gesture to satisfy Philip's outraged dignity, and that within a decent interval the duchy would be restored. Philip flagrantly broke this agreement; he cited Edward before him, and when Edward did not appear he confiscated the duchy altogether on 19 May 1294. This humiliating and disastrous failure in Edward's diplomacy was the work of his brother Edmund and Edmund's wife, who was the mother of the French queen.

Philip's dishonesty was matched by his initial success. He only made one miscalculation, but this was very important: he underestimated the rapidly growing power of England, keeping pace with and even surpassing his own. Edward was able to fight a war on two fronts and organize military operations far more formidable than those of Henry III or King John. In June 1294 he formally renounced his homage to Philip, and in October 1294 he was able to send some reinforcements to Gascony in spite of a rebellion in Wales and increasing dangers from the disputed succession to the

Scottish throne. Other troops were sent in 1295 and 1296, and meanwhile Edward planned an attack on Philip from Flanders. As a result of these efforts he was able to obtain a truce in October 1297, though this left most of Gascony still under the control of the French. Edward had lost nearly all its revenues, and had incurred an enormous debt for military expenses and for compensation to Gascon allies.

During the truce both kings submitted the quarrel to Boniface VIII, who agreed to arbitrate, not as pope but in his private capacity of Benedetto Gaetani. He made fruitful suggestions for reconciliation, including a marriage between Edward and Philip's sister Margaret. An award to this effect was proclaimed by the pope in June 1299. For the settlement, such as it was, Edward paid a high price. He deserted his ally the count of Flanders, and he allowed his alliances with Rhenish princes to lapse; though he did manage, in return, to isolate the Scots. But he failed to obtain the return of his Gascon lands, which he only acquired eventually, after Philip's defeat by the Flemings at Courtrai in 1302. In 1303, a treaty paved the way towards a full restoration of Edward's authority. He did fealty for the Gascon duchy through Henry Lacy, Earl of Lincoln; and his son Edward was formally affianced to the French princess Isabella, daughter of Philip the Fair. Commissioners began the task of returning his lost authority. But peace was harder to restore than it had been to destroy. There were too many old problems and new complications. The betrothal of the prince and princess did not, in the end, bring England and France any closer; rather it ultimately added a new and formidable obstacle to peace in the shape of the English monarch's claim to the crown of France.

Edward had been prevented by circumstances from bringing more than a fraction of his strength to bear in Gascony; though it must be added that the same was true of Philip the Fair. But the war revealed the two strongest territorial states of the West coming closer to grips and beginning to bridge the Channel more effectively. Both kings took important steps towards dominance over the Narrow Sea. Philip early made plans to build a great fleet of galleys in the Mediterranean and blockade the English ports. Edward ordered the building of two hundred new ships, and he created for a time a unified command of English seamen in the shape of a new captain or admiral, first heard of in 1295. William Leyburn was 'admiral of the sea of the king of England' in 1297. If Edward's hands had been free, he might well have begun a new age in naval warfare and anticipated the spectacular achievements in France of his grandson Edward III.

What defeated him finally was the growing disaffection of his own subjects. His foreign wars were not only a matter of logistics and manpower; they also involved the willingness and endurance of the whole community. And though Edward made immense efforts to instruct and persuade his subjects, in the end their enthusiasm flagged as it did against the Scots. The old political opposition of his father's reign began to revive, though his own high reputation and good intentions ensured that it never reached the dimensions of that which Henry III's demands had provoked.

5. DOMESTIC POLITICS

The deterioration in domestic affairs is not to be explained only by the growing strain of Edward's wars. One of the factors which caused it was provided by defects in his own temperament and political ideas. He began as an idealist and as an inspiring reformer; he ended as a paternalistic king who was in danger of becoming despotic and bequeathing to posterity a memory, not of progressive legislation, and high endeavour in co-operation with his subjects, but of political struggles which involved the same disturbing problems of authority as those which had troubled the later years of Henry III.

Edward showed his stature as king in the first general parliament of his reign, that of 1275, where he obtained the *custuma magna et antiqua*. He began a great age of statutes with Westminster I, by which he made comprehensive reforms in the whole field of law and administration. In the Statute of Gloucester of 1278 he resumed investigations, interrupted by the first Welsh war, into the working of franchises held by his subjects. He did not wish to abolish such liberties; he merely wished to know what they were, and by what warrant they were claimed. His main purpose, it has been said, was 'to respect all rights and overthrow all usurpations'. The enquiries he renewed continued for the remainder of his reign and were extraordinarily thorough. They are famous as the *Quo Warranto* inquisitions whose records fill more than eight hundred pages of the *Placita de Quo Warranto* published by the Record Commission in 1818. They undoubtedly irritated the barons, but we must not attach too much significance to the famous alleged reply of Earl

Warenne to the commissioners: 'Here is my warrant. My ancestors won their lands with the sword. With my sword I will defend them against all usurpers', even though the earl did offer some fairly strong opposition to the activities of the commissioners in respect to his liberties.

The Statute of Gloucester reveals Edward's zeal for good government combined with a care for his own royal interests, and this combination runs through all his legislation. Two great enactments came immediately after his conquest of Wales—the Statute of Westminster II and the Statute of Winchester, both in 1285. In the former, according to a well-known description by the contemporary Canon of Osney, Edward 'revived the ancient laws which had slumbered through the disturbance of the realm. Some, corrupted by abuse, he restored to their proper form. Some, less evident and apparent, he declared. Some new ones he added, useful and honourable.' In the latter, he made comprehensive regulations for the bearing of appropriate arms by all who had property in his realm.

It used to be believed that in this and other remarkable legislation Edward was anti-feudal in intention; but such a view is no longer accepted. The spirit of his legislation may be illustrated from the Statute of Mortmain or *De Religiosis* of November 1279,[1] prohibiting the alienation of lands or tenements whereby these came into mortmain, that is into the hands of the Church which did not die, did not pay the feudal dues which were owed at the succession of an heir, and could not perform some of the feudal services which lay tenants performed. The act was restrictive, but it was not aimed deliberately against either feudal lordship or the privileges of the Church, though both were affected. It seems to have been based mainly on simple considerations of efficiency. In point of fact licences to alienate lands to the Church were freely granted or sold by the Crown in the years after 1279.

The same is true of the *De Donis Conditionalibus*, part of Westminster II, by which Edward facilitated the creation of entailed estates by providing that in such estates the rights of the heir should not be barred on account of the alienation of land by the previous tenant. Thus were created the great landed holdings of the English aristocracy, passing down from generation to generation, protected from disintegration. The king's enactment has been regarded on the one hand as a subtle long-term attack on the feudal nobility;

---

[1] Translated in my *Constitutional History 1216–1399*, vol. III, pp. 316–7.

the king, it is argued, profited most from such entailments since the estates escheated to the Crown on the failure of heirs. On the other hand, the law has been described as 'a monument of colossal family pride and feudal arrogance'. It seems, indeed, to have been the result of pressure from the magnates, and to have represented a royal boon to them which was a natural outcome of Edward's intimacy with his great lords. In this, as in a good many other matters, the interests of the king and his greater subjects were essentially the same.

The same is also true of the *Quia Emptores*, or Westminster III, of 1290. Edward decreed that when part of an estate was alienated by its lord, the grantee should not become the subtenant of the grantor, but should hold from the ultimate lord of the fief in the same manner as the grantor himself. Though the law was enacted at the request of the magnates themselves, it has been regarded as more helpful to the king than to his vassals. Yet both suffered from sub-infeudation. This robbed the king of services which could no longer be properly performed, but it also robbed the lords of services owed by their vassals. The intention was to preserve the rights of lords great and small.[1] That it prevented lords from making new grants to followers, on a basis of tenure by knight service, and that this would in due course change the feudal structure of society, was something which neither Edward nor his advisers may have clearly foreseen.

Edward's prolonged activity in the making of statutes began a new age in the history of law and government and entitles him to rank as the English Justinian. The statutes were not the product of his genius alone, any more than the codifications of Tribonian and others had been the work of Justinian. They were also the product of his times, of a fortunate period of development which was conducive to the definition and recording of law. But they were nevertheless an expression of a singularly harmonious co-operation between a highly intelligent ruler and his subjects. They were not concerned only with feudal land-holding. The Statute of Merchants of 1285 ordered the imprisonment of a defaulting debtor until his debts had been paid.[2] If the jailer refused to accept the prisoner or let him

---

[1] F. M. Powicke, *The Thirteenth Century*, p. 379; my *Constitutional History 1216–1399*, vol. I, p. 42. See also p. 18 above.

[2] This was a modification of the Statute of Acton Burnell which had decreed execution in the first place only against the debtor's chattels and burgages; see T. F. T. Plucknett, *Legislation of Edward I* (Oxford 1949), p. 140.

escape, he himself had to pay the debt. Other details of the statute were businesslike and enlightened. The statute was rigorous, but the merchants wanted it so. Edward did not impose these enactments on unwilling subjects, though they were largely the work of his council. They were the fruits of two decades of highly successful co-operation between him and his subjects in the happiest and most constructive period of his reign.

In spite of such fruitful co-operation, the relations between Edward and his subjects were complicated and disturbed, not only by his paternalism and wars but also by the whole complex expansion of government which was a conspicuous feature of his reign. At the core of this expansion was the growth of bureaucracy with its counterpart of impersonal monarchy.[1] The former not only took the shape of an expansion of old offices like chancery and exchequer, and a growth of the king's courts of law, but also of a development of the council to become the central office of government, next to the monarch himself. Its function of serving the king's interests had already complicated the problem of politics under Henry, and continued to do so under his son. By the middle years of his reign Edward had gone a long way towards a temporary solution of the problem of advice; but he found it harder to solve that which arose from the rise of impersonal rule which, despite his good intentions, cut him off, as it had his father, from the magnates and created conditions of political revolt.

Bureaucracy and impersonal monarchy affected adversely even the question of taxation, which might have seemed to have been satisfactorily solved by 1275. Edward's taxes were broader and heavier than those of any preceding ruler; and, despite his use of parliamentary consent, they not only proved to be unpopular, but also by the opposition they evoked showed that he had lost touch with public opinion in his realm. He received the grant of a fifteenth of movables in 1275, a thirteenth in 1283, and a fifteenth in 1290. There were nine such taxes in the reign, two before 1290, and seven between 1290 and 1307. The comparison shows the increase in frequency: indeed, it has been said that Edward turned what had been no more than financial expedients in 1225, 1237, and 1269 into a normal method of raising revenue. The acceptance of such subsidies

---

[1] See a discussion of origins in H. G. Richardson and G. O. Sayles, *The Governance of Medieval England from the Conquest to Magna Carta* (Edinburgh 1963); but cf. *A.H.R.* (January 1964), pp. 427–9.

as an unavoidable penalty of progress (like the modern income tax) caused them to be placed in 1290 under the direct control of the exchequer, the king's most important office of finance. The fifteenth of 1290 was assessed by twelve men of each hundred, and brought in £117,000; the ninth of 1297, which theoretically ought to have produced much more, yielded only £34,419; it was assessed by sworn men of each vill who seem to have had a high regard for the goodwill of their neighbours. Perhaps partly in consequence the taxes came to be calculated on a fixed assessment after 1334.

Edward recognized that his magnates had a right to consent to extraordinary impositions; but this was not clear in the case of the burgesses and knights. In 1282 he got the consent of burgesses, but he asked for it in terms of command rather than request. In 1294 and 1297 the king got some consent to taxes, but not that of the Lords and Commons in parliament; the burgesses may not have been represented in the Michaelmas parliament of 1275, or when some other subsidies were granted.

Much propaganda accompanied such taxes, and did something to diminish the opposition to them. Historians debate whether knights and burgesses can have had the vaguest ideas about the constitutional niceties in matters of taxation which perplex the historian. Nevertheless, when an eighth had been granted only by the *plebs* in 1297, the Earl Marshal and the Earl of Hereford, speaking on behalf of all those present at the bar of the exchequer and of all the commonalty of the realm, declared that taxes should be granted with the consent of the earls, barons, knights, and community.[1]

Besides imposing heavy subsidies on movable property, Edward extended his demands by taxing the merchants and others who were interested in the rising export of wool. In 1275 he levied an export duty of half a mark on each sack (364 lb) of wool and on each 300 wool-fells or skins, plus a mark (13/4) on each last of hides. It was to be a permanent imposition; and the average return for the first years was £8,800, rising to £13,000 in later years. It was known, and accepted, as the *Magna et Antiqua Custuma*; it was the greatest contribution of that generation to governmental finance; and it remained a cardinal feature of taxation for the next two hundred years.

The tax was imposed in parliament, with the consent of magnates

---

[1] My *Constitutional History 1216–1399*, vol. III, 294; F. M. Powicke, *Thirteenth Century*, pp. 524, 526, 532.

and merchants; indeed, Edward claimed that it was by the request of the latter.[1] But it is doubtful how far the king believed that parliamentary consent was necessary for future increases which were, in fact, very heavy. In any case, the new revenue greatly increased the power of government, not only by providing much needed ready cash, but even more through the credit which could be developed through Italian bankers and merchants. These now displaced the Jews, whose position was, in any case, subject to increasing attack.[2] In 1275 Edward had forbidden them to lend money at interest and encouraged them, without success, to broaden their activities. In 1290 he expelled them from England altogether. For many important years, both before and after this date, the rapidly expanding trade of England was dominated by Italian merchants and papal agents. In June 1277 seven societies of Italian merchants helped to receive the proceeds of the papal tenth imposed at the Council of Lyons in 1274. The Italian firm of the Riccardi became collectors of the customs on wool and made heavy loans to the king. They were succeeded as agents and creditors by the Frescobaldi whose pre-eminence lasted through the reigns of Edward I and Edward II. These developments earned for the Italians an unpopularity similar to, if much less bigoted and dangerous than, that of the Jews. In financial matters the king seemed to adopt a policy of *divide et impera*, and his ideas and those of his subjects on consent to taxation became dangerously wide apart.

This was also true in his dealings with the clergy; but here Edward had to deal not only with his own subjects but also with the pope. Secular taxation of clerics helped to destroy the unity of the *Respublica Christiana* and underlined the expanding claims of secular rulers. It probably made inescapable a sharp reaction by the pope to the steadily increasing encroachments of the secular power on the privileges of the clergy, and brought into prominence again the problem of their twofold loyalty to the secular ruler and to the Vicar of Christ. A conflict between the king and the clergy may have been delayed by Edward's early popularity and by his zeal as a crusader. His second crusade was to be made in 1293, and until then he had favoured treatment from all clergy up to and including the pope. But long before that date there were signs that his reign

---

[1] My *Studies in the Constitutional History of the Thirteenth and Fourteenth Centuries* (Manchester 1937), p. 59.

[2] Gavin I. Langmuir, 'The Jews and the Archives of Angevin England: Reflections on Medieval Anti-Semitism', in *Traditio*, vol. XIX (1963), pp. 183–244.

had begun a new era. He did not need the same support from the pope as his father had received, and he had strong views of his powers as king and the loyalty owed to him by every subject in his realm.

The Act of Mortmain or *De Religiosis* had been well justified by the needs of his kingdom, but it put these needs first and those of the clergy second. In 1285 the writ of *Circumspecte agatis* in effect extended the jurisdiction of royal as against ecclesiastical courts. Disputes over such jurisdiction had led, the clergy had complained, to 'new oppressions of the Church', especially in the parts of Norwich. Edward accordingly directed his judges not to punish the clergy if they held pleas on purely spiritual matters; but his definition of what should be left to the courts christian diminished rather than increased their activities. Such actions despite the protests of the clergy are evidence of a steady and significant expansion of the claims of the secular ruler against the liberties of the Church. Even more offensive was Edward's heavy taxation of the clergy in 1294 without permission or agreement of the pope, and his summons of clerics to the parliament of 1295, probably with a similar aim. The tax of 1294 met with much opposition in a convocation called by the king at Westminster; the dean of St. Paul's was said to have fallen dead at Edward's feet though doubt has been cast upon this colourful story; and the summons of 1295 played an important part in contributing to the famous bull *Clericis Laicos* of 1296.

By this pronouncement, Boniface bade the rulers of both England and France to respect the liberties of the Church. In point of fact the bull was a general pronouncement, and all that the pope did was to give added though provocative definition to the law of the Church as it had been defined in 1215. He declared that taxation of the clergy by the laity was a matter requiring the authority of the Holy See. All who took part in an unauthorized imposition were automatically excommunicated. Later, when he was faced with strong opposition in both England and France, Boniface modified his position; he admitted in the bull *Etsi de Statu* of July 1297 that his prohibition did not apply to a period of admitted emergency, and that the secular ruler could decide when such an emergency had arisen. But this was too late to prevent a bitter conflict with both Philip of France and Edward I.

As a result of this conflict, the clergy in England found themselves standing exposed between two great protagonists. Their loyalties had been harmonized in the past by the pragmatic co-operation of king and pope; this had caused them to suffer materially, but spiritually they could remain in tolerable peace. Such a *modus vivendi* had worked as long as neither of the controlling powers made excessive claims. It was now destroyed by the increasing demands of the secular ruler, not by the seeming aggression of the pope.

Faced with this situation Archbishop Winchelsey, who had only just returned to England in January 1295 after his consecration, summoned no fewer than four assemblies of the clergy for anguished consultation. The clergy agreed that they were unable to obey their monarch in defiance of the pope. Edward retaliated by withdrawing from them the protection of his government, by which act they were thrust from the shelter of the state and exposed to outlawry. The result was a bleakness and deprivation which revealed cruelly how much they normally owed to the secular society. Very soon, Winchelsey was compelled to leave to each individual, guided by his conscience, the decision whether or not to surrender to Edward. Meanwhile, in France the bishops showed a way of honourable surrender by petitioning Boniface to allow them to grant a subsidy to their king, and the English bishops prepared to follow suit. The way to a general reconciliation was eased by Edward's offer to confirm the Charters with their promise that the Church should be free. His gesture enabled the clergy to make an honourable compromise even though the king forbade them to excommunicate those who had infringed the papal prohibitions, and he gave orders that they should be taxed without waiting for their assent. They were to pay a third of their temporalities or, if they wished, a fifth of their assessed revenues. The tax was never actually collected, but others were substituted; and Winchelsey was finally compelled to agree, with some qualification, that the plea of necessity might be adopted in such cases, to justify a contribution without waiting for the approval of the pope.

Thus, on the whole, Edward and Philip came out as victors in the struggle, and Boniface has been greatly blamed for his rashness in challenging the secular powers; but there was much to be said in favour of his resolute stand. Nothing less seemed adequate to the occasion. In point of fact, his challenge did not entirely fail. Edward did not again try to tax the clergy by royal decree. In April 1298 Winchelsey was still able to tell the king that he should not hope for any further subsidy without papal consent; and the archbishop could still threaten excommunication of all those who invaded the rights of the Church.

Whether or not it was either wise or ably conducted, the pope's challenge made the clergy for a brief period an important ingredient in a hostile coalition which suddenly confronted Edward in 1296 and 1297. They were not, indeed, foremost in this coalition. The laity led the opposition, especially those who were being continually called upon to support Edward's wars. The core of the king's armies was provided by the household retainers, and by the tenants-in-chief with their retainers; but others were deeply involved. The household knights were committed by their special status and ,training; but Edward had made heavy demands for aid in his wars on all the community. All felt increasingly alienated by the burdens imposed upon them and by Edward's tendency to assume that they would respond to any call he made upon them by reason of his imperative needs.

This alienation specially affected the great lords, who had a responsibility for the welfare of the kingdom to complement their loyalty to their ruler; but it also extended to the lesser knights, both those who held their lands by knight service and those whom the king 'distrained' to accept the status and assume the obligations of a znight. The practice of distraint had begun under Henry III as early as 1224, and from 1241 had been applied to all who held lands to the annual value of £20. Hereafter the demands for their attendance in the king's armies steadily increased. They were particularly heavy in the years when Edward was involved in wars and troubles on three fronts. In 1282 he summoned to Northampton or York all who held more than £20 of land who were fit and suitable for war; in 1295 all who had £40 of land were commanded to be ready to serve in Scotland at the wages of the king; in 1297 all £20 landowners were ordered to be ready to accompany the magnates overseas. Edward seemed to be establishing a formidable obligation of the smaller tenants to serve the king at his summons by virtue solely of their loyalty to the Crown.

The needs of his wars led the king to develop also the service of other able-bodied subjects in the shires and towns. The equipment which they should possess, primarily for the suppression of disorder, was set forth, graded according to wealth, in the Statute of Winchester in 1285. With this equipment assured, Edward increasingly summoned local levies to provide footmen for his armies. In 1282, for example, he issued Commissions of Array to William Wyther to select three hundred foot soldiers in the shires of Nottingham and Derby, from those more capable and fit to bear arms, to help him in his Welsh campaign.[1] Such contingents were becoming steadily more important, and though Edward bore most of the expense the service became a considerable burden on the countryside.

Edward's armies were, in fact, becoming 'national', based increasingly on loyalty, or agreement, between individuals and the 'national' king. This could not fail to create a special uneasiness in the minds of the great magnates, who saw their ancient importance in warfare diminished and feared the ultimate political consequence of the new developments. Common interests in military service, as well as in taxation, brought the great lords and the middling classes together, and linked them with the clergy. Thus the 'national' monarch evoked a 'national' opposition. It was of course, as it had to be, led by the great magnates. In March 1297, Bohun and Bigod, earls of Hereford and Norfolk, and constable and marshal of England, refused to lead an army to Gascony unless under the king's own banner and to serve abroad in the following July. They argued that they had only been affectionately requested to serve, not commanded, and were thus at liberty to refuse.

In a sharp exchange, Edward is said to have perpetrated an early historic pun ('By God, sir Earl, you shall either go or hang') but he could not fulfil his threat because the earls were part of a very widespread opposition to his demands. They had already met together in a 'parliament' in the forest of Wyre in the Welsh March where their strength lay; and they had aims for which most could unite.

In face of this movement Edward effected a reconciliation with Winchelsey—just when or how is uncertain—and on 14 July the two appeared together on a platform which had been set up in front of Westminster Hall. The king made a moving speech seeking pardon for any wrongs he or his ministers had committed, and asking for the loyalty of his subjects against his enemies, thirsty for English blood. 'Behold,' he said, 'I go to expose myself to danger on your behalf. I beg of you, if I return, receive me as you have met me at present, and I will return to you all that I have taken. If I do not come back, crown my son as your king.'[2]

[1] My *Constitutional History 1216–1399*, vol. III, p. 223.
[2] Stubbs *C. H.* vol. II, p. 141; *S.C.*, p. 433. Edward himself recorded his speech a little differently; my *Constitutional History 1216–1399*, vol. I, p. 217.

But even this could not move the hearts of the earls, or of all the clergy, despite Winchelsey's example. Edward sailed for Flanders, as he had planned; but instead of taking some two thousand cavalry as he had hoped, including £20 landowners as well as tenants-in-chief, he had with him only a hundred knights and bannerets, along with 570 squires.

The king fully realized the gravity of the crisis. He got an aid, before he sailed, from a body of *plebs* assembled in his Chamber; but he left the barons and their supporters virtually masters of England (they promptly cancelled the aid in the Exchequer after he had embarked); and he knew that they would present him with far-reaching demands.[1] Indeed, he had received a foretaste of these before he left, in a document known as the *Monstraunces*, coming from the commonalty of England who included or were supported by the lords. His penultimate act in England was to have a brush with death while riding along the rampart of Winchelsea. His horse shied at a windmill and leapt down an embankment on to a road far below. Luckily it lighted on its feet and Edward was unhurt. As a final act before he embarked, he wrote a letter on 12 August, explaining and justifying his policy, and reminding his subjects of the horrors of his father's civil war: 'Let each one consider', he wrote, 'what great discord arose formerly in this kingdom, from one end to the other . . . and the harm that resulted.' But it is doubtful if he ever believed that the danger was quite as imminent as he portrayed. And it seemed likely that Oliver Sutton, the venerable bishop of Lincoln, for one, had slight reservations in his response. He publicly prayed God to grant that the king 'would devise with prudent mind, and perform with strenuous labour, only those things which are pleasing to Thy Majesty'.

In point of fact the opposition was both moderate and constructive. It consisted essentially of a demand for the reissue of Magna Carta with certain additional clauses to bring it up to date. All that the magnates and their supporters wanted was an end to arbitrary exactions, both financial and military; they did not seek to place the king under any far-reaching restraint. They asserted the principle of consent; they did not seek control. This is what appears in a famous list of demands, called the *De Tallagio non Concedendo*, which was sent to Edward in Flanders. These demands

[1] My *Constitutional History 1216–1399*, vol. I, p. 213. A slightly different account is in Sir Maurice Powicke's *Thirteenth Century*, p. 680.

were substantially conceded by the king in a solemn charter, the *Confirmatio Cartarum*, which was sealed at Ghent on 5 November 1297. In this Edward accepted the principle of consent to taxation; the question of military service was settled in his absence by discussion in parliament.[1]

The whole episode deeply wounded Edward's pride, and embittered politics for the remainder of his reign; but apart from personalities the opposition reflected the authentic political tradition of England, which Edward himself had often proclaimed. It was a great step forward to bring major problems of war and taxation within the purview of the expanding parliament, and the whole crisis reminded one of the strongest medieval kings of the limitations which existed on the exercise of his royal powers.

But despite its moderation the crisis inevitably left an aftermath of distrust. In January 1298 the magnates insisted on a public proclamation of the Charters before they joined in the Scottish expedition. They interrupted the winter campaign of 1299, it was said, not only because of the bad weather but also because they did not wish to labour in vain unless the king observed his promises. After the campaign they reminded Edward in a great council of 8 March 1299 that he had promised to confirm the Charters on his return, only to be met with open trickery by the king. Edward finally agreed to give the barons an answer the following day, but he silently departed from the council during the night. Their suspicions aroused, the lords rode after him, only to be told that he was seeking fresher air than that of Westminster and that they should go to the king's council for an answer. This flagrantly evasive action was unworthy of any ruler who wished to retain the confidence of his subjects. Even when Edward's council did produce a confirmation of the Charters, this strengthened rather than allayed the growing suspicions of bad faith by containing a reservation safeguarding the rights of his crown. When the confirmation was published at the cross of St. Paul's, the reservation was reported to have changed into curses the gratification of those who heard it read.[2]

Once more, in the parliament of March 1300, the lords returned to their major point. They wanted a reissue of the Charters with new

[1] My *Studies in the Constitutional History of the Thirteenth and Fourteenth Centuries*, pp. 61–6; Sir Maurice Powicke, *The Thirteenth Century*, pp. 678–83. The crisis of 1297 is discussed with reference to recent differences of opinion in my *Constitutional History of England, 1216–1399*, vol. I, pp. 187–232.

[2] A contemporary account of these events is translated in *ibid.*, vol. I, pp. 229–30.

additions, to remedy the sufferings of the people caused by the wars. In reply Edward finally granted them a most solemn reissue of the Charters of 1225 conceded by Henry III, to be published henceforth in the county court four times a year; and he added articles intended to remedy complaints. Perambulations of the forests were to be hurried along, and three good men were to be elected in the county court to hear cases in which the Charters were infringed. The concessions of 1300 were probably a genuine act of conciliation on the part of the king and a gesture towards the lesser gentry, whose political support had been given to the magnates; but Edward still included a clause which reserved the rights and prerogative of his crown, and there is no doubt that he felt that these had been attacked.

The king and his subjects were brought closer together in June 1299 by Boniface VIII's denunciation of English aggression against the Scots. 'It is the custom of the realm of England', Edward declared, with the full support of seven earls and ninety-seven barons, 'that in all things touching the state of the realm there should be asked the counsel of all whom the matter concerns'; and accordingly he and they, acting for themselves and all the community of the land, rejected Boniface's claims. But the united front which was thus offered against papal presumption did not provide any solution to the domestic problems. How intractable these were was shown when, in 1301, a knight of the shire, Henry of Keighley, put forward a bill in parliament which was supported there. The bill was said to be on behalf of all the community, a procedure hitherto unknown. In the main, it did no more than add details to the *Articuli Super Cartas* of 1300, and was conceded by the ruler though the original idea of a reissue of the Charter fortified by the seals of the barons as well as that of the king had been regarded by Edward as a great affront. Even in the form they took, the king thought the new concessions were dangerous and objectionable because they inaugurated a process by which the subjects, not the king, could initiate enactments in parliament. They united the parliamentary Lords and Commons in opposition to the ruler. Five years later Edward sent Henry of Keighley into honourable captivity in the Tower, to be released on an oath not to offend against the king or the crown. It was one thing for a knight to use parliament to petition for redress of a grievance by the grace of the king; it was another thing to attempt to move the king in parliament by a conjoint action of Commons and Lords.

Edward's own attitude is shown by a papal bull of 1305 in which Clement V revoked the royal concessions of 1297. Even though the king had sworn to keep these, it was said, he had also taken an oath to preserve the honour and rights of his crown. Edward had no wish to go back on all his concessions; but he condemned both the spirit and the methods of the opposition since 1297. He never made use of the papal bull to withdraw any major concession, but its issue shows how far he and his subjects had drifted apart. If their conflicting claims and ideas could trouble the last years of a great and conscientious ruler beset by war, how would these affect the destinies of England in the reign of Edward's mediocre and often very misguided son?

Edward died a lonely, difficult and disappointed man, with his great glories far behind him and few trusted friends left at his side. He had never quite recovered from the death of Queen Eleanor in 1290, not yet forty-five years old. She had borne him thirteen children, of whom six survived her, but only one of whom reached the age of fifty. At each stage of the long journey of her body from Lincoln to Westminster, Edward built lovely and well-known crosses to commemorate his beloved. Few English kings have loved more deeply. His loss of Eleanor may well be taken to mark the real turning-point of his reign.

Other old companions also were passing, and Edward entered suddenly on a bleak and profitless time. His bitterness against Robert Winchelsey was one of his few remaining passions, apart from his consuming devotion to his office and his dedication to the Scottish war. He sent his treasurer Walter Langton, bishop of Coventry and Lichfield, to complain against his archbishop at the coronation of Clement V in 1305, accusing him of being spiteful and perverse. In February 1306 Pope Clement suspended the Archbishop and summoned him to answer the charges. On 19 May 1306 Winchelsey left England for Avignon, never to see Edward again. This was the last, and perhaps the most dubious, triumph of Edward's life. He died shortly after, directing that his bones be carried at the head of his soldiers who would go forth under his son to conquer the Scots; though he may have felt a foreboding that it was the Scots, not his mediocre son, who would prevail. He willed that his heart should be carried on the final Crusade he had never been able to make.

There were many things he had left undone; but the greatest things had been well and truly achieved. Under Edward, England had nobly met the greatest challenge of the age. Old habits and traditions had been expanded to provide the beginnings of a new polity in which order and liberty would flourish; the territorial state had taken on shape and substance without destroying feudal ideals. Unity had been preserved in spite of deep political differences, and England had kept and enhanced her position in a fiercely contending world. All these things owed something to the temper of the age, but much also to the character of the first Edward. He left an imprint on his country which lasted for many generations, and gave it a tradition of service and compromise which time has not even yet entirely destroyed.

4

EDWARD II AND EDWARD III

1. DEGENERATION OF POLITICS

CONTRARY to what might be expected at first sight, the reigns of the next two Edwards were complementary, and both were in sharp contrast to that of Edward I. The period covered by their two reigns began in discord and by the end of Edward II's rule was clouded by disaster; the government and policy of Edward III were to a significant extent a reaction against the failures of his father. They were an attempt to recapture the loyalty of Englishmen to their king and to retrieve the fortunes of the monarchy. The third Edward's reign, unlike his father's, was brilliantly successful for many years; but in spite of all the successes its end was marked by gathering clouds, even if these were not as dark and stormy as those of 1326 and 1327.

Edward II has baffled posterity by his character and actions, as he may have baffled some contemporaries. Like his father he had good looks and bodily strength, but unlike Edward I he had little intelligence. He excelled in outdoor sports which his contemporaries regarded as unfitting; and he depended so completely on 'favourites' that his morals, as well as his strength of will, came into question. His father had banished the first and best loved of these, Peter Gaveston, a Gascon knight who had been his foster-brother and playmate in the royal household, and to whom he was deeply attached. Peter's banishment ended with Edward I's death, and the young Gascon proceeded to ride the heady crest of royal favour. He received £50,000 of the money forfeited by Walter Langton, bishop of Coventry and treasurer, whom Edward had disgraced immediately after his accession to the throne; and he was made earl of Cornwall on 6 August 1307. With his earldom he received all the lands which had belonged to Edmund the previous earl who had been one of the wealthy magnates of England. He may also have received a present of £100,000 taken from Edward I's treasury. Many other favours were heaped upon him. He even became keeper of the realm whilst the new king went to France to fetch his twelve-year-old bride Isabella, daughter of the French king Philip IV and destined to be a cause of tears to both England and France.

The barons hated Peter as a Gascon upstart who sharpened his wit on their foibles and flaunted his powers over the king; but it is doubtful if the clash of personalities accounts for the nature and extent of the movement against him. These are, indeed, the subject of much debate; but it seems probable that they are to be explained by many causes. The growth of government, problems of foreign policy, and the aftermath of the quarrels of Edward I's reign all combined with distrust of Edward II. In any case, whatever their mixed motives, the barons threatened to impede Edward's coronation in February 1308, and they compelled their new ruler to accept an addition to his coronation oath in which he swore to enforce whatever just laws his subjects would choose. They 'treated' together on the morning of the coronation, discussing the king's 'election', and they 'recognized' him as their ruler during the ceremony, thus emphasizing the importance of their free acceptance of his person as their king. Shortly afterwards, in the same year, they issued a Declaration distinguishing between the person and the office of their ruler; and they justified violent opposition to the one if it was in the best interests of the other. How far they intended these actions to be merely a means of extracting the ordinances of reform which they believed that Edward had promised at his coronation, or how far they intended to express novel ideas of the ruler's subjection to his own subjects, it is impossible to say. But at least it is certain that nothing quite as damaging to the theoretical basis of the royal power had been set forth in any previous baronial declaration; though the *addiciones* to Bracton and the *Song of Lewes* had probably pointed the way.[1]

That important issues were at stake is shown by the tenacity of the barons in developing their opposition, and by the uncompromising attitude of the monarch acting in defence not only of his 'favourite' but also of his royal rights. The magnates were young and head-

---

[1] These difficult questions are discussed in my *Constitutional History 1216–1399*, vol. II, pp. 85–107. The Ordinances of 1311 are discussed *ibid.*, 112–21.

strong: the eldest of them, once chief of the king's council, was the earl of Lincoln, aged fifty-six. Most of the others were in their thirties or even younger: Thomas of Lancaster, another of their natural leaders, may have been born in 1277. He was the king's cousin and first lord of the royal blood. There were no men of great stature, except perhaps the earl of Lincoln. Two groups stood out who had regional solidarity and special interests. One was composed of lords of the Welsh March, and the other of northerners pre-occupied with the problem of the Scots. In the political conflicts which now arose they tended to stand together. The opposition to the king could also count on considerable support elsewhere, including the common people. On the whole, public opinion tended to hold that Lancaster stood 'for the justice of the Church and of the realm'.

Following up their initial actions, the opposition magnates in the same year obtained the exile of Peter Gaveston. Using the medium of parliament they got an 'award' against Peter decreeing his exile despite the bitter opposition of the king. Edward, for his part, gave Peter a consolation prize in the shape of additional income and the position of king's lieutenant in Ireland. Even so the exile did not last long. By 1309 the favourite was back in England and in power; though five earls refused to attend a council 'because of Peter', or to be present at the opening of the parliament of February 1310. When they did arrive, they defied a royal prohibition and appeared in full armour; and they loudly complained against evil counsellors. It was apparent that there would be no peace in England until the personal rivalries had been resolved one way or another; but the deep issues which had been raised were probably even harder to settle. The situation was, indeed, a typical fourteenth-century clash of extremes in which the monarch and his subjects became hope-lessly entangled in conflicting interests of every kind, but in which one question gradually seemed to emerge as paramount: whether, in the final analysis, the king or his magnates should be supreme in the state.

In 1310 and 1311 the pendulum swung far over in favour of the magnates. In the former year Edward was compelled to appoint twenty-one lords to reform both his household and his realm. The bulk of their reforms concerning the realm were issued in a parlia-ment. These were The Ordinances of 1311. The key decision, as was to be expected, was to repeat the exile of Peter, who was condemned to sail from Dover before 1 November; he was to be treated as a public enemy if he returned. This was not only a personal matter; it was the focal point on which the headlong attack of the lords met the unyielding opposition of the king. Even apart from this, however, the magnates now took the opportunity of imposing humiliating restrictions on Edward. He could not, they decreed, quit the realm or make war on anybody at all without their assent in parliament. They claimed the right to share in the appointment and dismissal of councillors and ministers, which were to take place in parliament. Thus, both the growing bureaucracy and the intimate advisers of the king were subjected to the influence if not outright control of the subjects, imposed through the assembly which Edward I had dominated and treated as an instrument of his rule. It was an assembly, moreover, in which knights and burgesses were attaining some small importance and dignity. They even swore, alongside the magnates, to uphold the Ordinances of 1311.

The barons might exile Peter Gaveston; but Edward could not bear to have him away from his side. Gaveston had sailed from the Thames on 3 November, but after some uncertain wanderings he soon rejoined the king. The two defied the Ordinances and the Ordainers and spent the Christmas of 1311 together at Windsor. Edward sought a revision of the baronial enactments and on 18 January 1312 proclaimed that Peter had been exiled against the laws and customs of the kingdom, which the king by his coronation oath was bound to maintain. Meanwhile Edward sent Peter away from the court, to hold the custody of Scarborough castle where it was hoped that he would be out of harm's way. Against such defiance the lords could give but one answer unless they wished to accept the defeat of all their pretensions and aims. Archbishop Winchelsey excommunicated Peter, and the Ordainers besieged and captured him by 19 May 1312. His personal safety was solemnly assured, but he was nevertheless executed with indignity and abuse. His real executioner was the earl of Warwick, his most implacable personal foe; but he was beheaded at Blacklow Hill, on land belonging to Lancaster, and by two Welshmen of Lancaster's retinue. All the opposition earls except Pembroke agreed. They argued that they had acted within the law in destroying a public enemy, even though they had broken a solemn promise and brought special dishonour to the earl of Pembroke, from whose custody Peter had been taken to his death whilst the earl was briefly absent on a visit to his wife.

The murder or execution of Gaveston was a landmark in this troubled reign. It deepened hatreds and destroyed the unity of baronial opposition; and it raised again the ultimate question of the nature of the royal power, brought into question by the king's inability to defend his closest friend. Nor could the harm it inflicted be eradicated by a public apology at Westminster by Peter's destroyers. They had thrown away the support of public opinion and presented Edward with important allies. He could hope to establish his leadership and ascendancy by reviving his father's aggression against Scotland. Despite the protest of the distrustful earls who claimed that the campaign needed their consent, Edward was able to make an impressive effort against Scotland in May 1314.

During the quarrels between Edward II and his barons, Robert Bruce had consolidated his position in Scotland and carried his war against the English far into the northern counties. His ravages of Northumberland, Westmorland, and Cumberland served a double purpose: they weakened his enemy and they brought him wealth, not only from plunder but even more from the enormous sums he levied on the various communities if they wished to buy off his attack. In 1311, when Edward was deeply embarrassed by the Ordainers, the men of Northumberland offered £2,000 for a truce. At the same time the towns of Hexham and Durham were pillaged and largely destroyed.

English reaction to these attacks was hesitant and ineffective. The king and magnates were so deeply divided that they could not accompany each other to war. Finally, a crisis occurred when Robert Bruce besieged Stirling castle, whose strategic importance had been clearly shown in the wars of Edward I. The garrison agreed that if an English army of relief had not approached to within three leagues of the town by midsummer 1314 they would surrender. Compelled by this challenge, Edward in May 1314 gathered together a force whose size, to contemporaries, was extremely impressive. Its numbers may well have reached the figure of 20,000, including the earls of Gloucester, Pembroke and Hereford. To oppose them, Bruce may have had between 6,000 and 10,000 men, but the Scots were well placed between Stirling castle and the little river Bannock to the south. The English army was supplied with archers, and Edward himself is said to have been told that 'a great part of the exploit will come to footmen'. But contrary to all the lessons of the past and egged on by the younger leaders, the king and his advisers ordered a preliminary attack with two unsupported bodies of cavalry. When these preliminary thrusts were repulsed, the English spent the night of 23–24 June preparing for a major crossing of the Bannock, and many of them had probably got across by the morning of the 24th.

On that day battle was joined. The Scots fought in schiltrons, the English once again put their trust in cavalry. Gloucester, who advised caution, was accused by Edward of treachery. Sir Henry de Bohun, nephew of the earl of Hereford, sought to achieve immortality by vanquishing Bruce in single combat, but the Scot split his head with a battleaxe in a famous though reckless act of *prouesse*. The cavalry made no impression on the schiltrons, whilst the English archers were largely immobilized in the rear. The young earl of Gloucester, who had not waited to don the surcoat which might have saved his life (by frugal Scots who had an eye for rich ransoms), died early in the fight. When their lances proved useless against the resilient and disciplined schiltrons, the English knights were reduced to hurling their swords and maces, which littered the empty space behind the serried ranks of Scottish spears.

Altogether, the fighting at Bannockburn lasted, on and off, for two days, and was often close and bitter, the issue hanging in the balance. It was finally decided when some Scottish camp-followers and guerrillas came to join the fray and the southerners thought this was a reserve force. Now at length they fled in disorder. Many were slaughtered, or suffocated in the river and marsh. Hotly pursued, Edward first tried to take refuge in Stirling and then headed towards Dunbar, whence he and the few who were with him fled by sea to Berwick. There was equal bravery on both sides, but victory went to the army with the greater spirit and confidence, aided by better leadership.[1]

For England and for Edward, Bannockburn was a major disaster. Domestic politics were deeply affected for the worse, whilst in foreign affairs the alliance between the Scots and the French was made secure to last for a hundred years. Nevertheless, the results were not all bad; indeed the battle may be compared in its significance with that of Bouvines almost exactly a century before. Both were fought

[1] May McKisack gives a good account in *The Fourteenth Century 1307–1399* (Oxford 1959), with a reference to controversial writings on the subject on p. 35, n. 6. Additional references are given by G. W. S. Barrow in *Feudal Britain* (London 1956), p. 407, n. 1. The best treatment of the whole period is by the same author in *Robert Bruce and the Community of the Realm of Scotland* (London 1965), pp. 300–29.

on foreign soil. Both were military disasters, even though at Bouvines the English forces played only a minor part. Both consolidated a kingdom which tended to be hostile to England. And both, indirectly, contributed to English liberty.

For Scotland, Bannockburn set the seal on what has been described as the collaboration between Robert Bruce on the one hand and the community of the realm of Scotland on the other, difficult though the latter is to define. The idea of the community of the realm had sustained all the Scottish opposition to Edward I and it had been appealed to by Wallace, who described himself as 'William Wallace, knight, Guardian of the kingdom of Scotland . . . by consent of the community of the realm'. Bruce appealed to it to sustain him as king. By the battle of Bannockburn he triumphantly vindicated his claim to the Scottish throne and his revolutionary bid for leadership of the community of the Scottish realm.

For the Scots, Bannockburn was the unique triumph of the spirit which was later expressed in the famous Declaration of Arbroath in 1320. This bore the seals of eight earls and almost every leading magnate, and may perhaps be regarded as the first appeal for national independence in modern history. Its pith and marrow lay in the well-known words which, however much they failed to be reflected in actions of many Scots between 1296 and 1314, remain a monument to Scotland in this period:

> For as long as a hundred remain alive we are minded never to bow to the dominion of England. It is not for glory, riches or honour that we fight; it is for liberty alone which no good man surrenders but with his life.

Edward did, it is true, make a great effort to undo the consequences of Bannockburn when in June 1319 he led 'all the Erllis' against the Scots in Berwick; but this only provoked Bruce into a terrible ravaging of the north; and it led to the rout of local levies at the Chapter of Myton, so-called because of the number of priests who were slain, having rallied to Archbishop Melton in defence of hearths and homes. As a result of this reverse Edward ended his siege of Berwick, together with his attempt to restore his tarnished reputation and the fortunes of war. By 1322 the Scots were ravaging the north as far as Preston and into the heart of Yorkshire. Edward II himself was nearly captured at Byland in the North Riding of Yorkshire and the country was stricken with panic. Andrew Harclay, earl of Carlisle, was executed shortly afterwards for treasonable negotiations with the Scots by which he tried to put a halt to their pillaging and slaughter.

After the disaster of 1314, it is said, Edward II 'denied nothing to the earls'. Lancaster soon overshadowed the land; in 1316 he was sworn of the council under conditions which, as one chronicler said, enabled him to add to and subtract from the Ordinances of 1311 as seemed best for the king and the realm. England was torn by strife and calamity. The year 1315 was a time of bad harvests, followed by famine 'such as our age has never seen'. Even the purveyors for the royal household could scarce discover bread. Meanwhile, Edward and Thomas showed in their relations the evil consequences which flowed inevitably from the combination of over-weak ruler and over-mighty subject: 'Whatever pleases the lord king', it was said, 'the earl's servants try to upset, and whatever pleases the earl is called treachery by the servants of the king.'

Protracted negotiations brought a kiss of peace between the two main opponents at Leake on 9 August 1318; but the conditions of stalemate which it reflected satisfied neither. Thomas resented political frustration and insecurity; Edward chafed under limitations on his powers. The drift towards extremism which had begun in 1308 could not be stemmed by a papering of the cracks; political turmoil seemed destined to continue until it resulted in a triumph of extremes. There was an exchange of angry letters in which Edward complained of Lancaster's gatherings of magnates and the earl accused the king of ignoring the Ordinances. Some efforts at mediation were, indeed, made by a so-called 'middle party', whose leader was Aymer de Valence, earl of Pembroke, and which was supported by many prelates. A secret indenture has survived, dated 24 November 1317, between Pembroke and Lord Badlesmere on the one hand and Roger Damory on the other, whereby Roger undertook to act with the utmost diligence in inducing the king to be ruled by their advice. The 'middle party' achieved a temporary ascendancy and obtained some worthwhile results. These included a continuation of the peace and the reissue of Magna Carta. Also, the Ordinances were extended to provide a reform of the king's household in the Household Ordinance of York. Temporary reconciliation with France was cemented by Edward's homage to Philip of France at Amiens in 1320, and in return he recovered control over Ponthieu. Harvests improved and wheat fell from 3s 4d to 6d a bushel.

Nevertheless, as was almost inevitable, the extremists finally triumphed and the counsels of moderation were disregarded.[1] Edward restored his trust in favourites; whilst the barons revived extreme purposes of reform. The new favourites were men of ability and of good standing. Hugh Despenser, the father, was the son of Hugh Despenser, justiciar of the barons in the days of Simon de Montfort, who had fallen at the battle of Evesham. Hugh Despenser, the son, had been knighted with Edward, when he was prince, at Easter 1306, and in 1309 had married Eleanor, daughter of Gilbert de Clare, Earl of Gloucester. Together they monopolized the king's ear. Fortified by the royal favour, they added to their estates the rich lordship of Glamorgan in the Welsh March, thus alienating the Welsh Marcher lords on a double count. Lancaster was not loath to fish in such troubled waters, and he revived his ambition to place a curb upon his ruler. He sought to create a coalition of Marcher and northern magnates, and to unite with both so as to create an irresistible movement. His purpose was to revive both the baronial aims and the unanimity of 1308. His revival of the Declaration of 1308, as well as his persistence in ideas associated with the Coronation promise, show how extremist political thinking underlay his practice of revolt; and this fact goes far to explain, if it does not justify, the bitterness of the royalist reaction in 1321 and 1322.

Lancaster's ambitious schemes achieved only partial success. At the village of Sherburn-in-Elmet in Yorkshire, the northern prelates advised 'a friendly agreement and unity' between king and magnates, explaining that they could not join Thomas because they feared an invasion by the Scots. Nevertheless, the Marchers and Thomas continued their purpose alone. War began in the Marches. Thomas and his allies set out with a brave show for Westminster, to demand the exile of the Despensers and to face 'the inexorable anger of the king'. For long, Edward refused to listen to their demands, despite the intercession of many of his subjects, including Pembroke, the archbishop of Canterbury, Queen Isabella, and the citizens of London. The conflict of wills even gave rise to talk of deposition[2]; but in the end there was a compromise, expressed in an agreement in writing

---

[1] My 'Negotiations Preceding the "Treaty" of Leake, August 1318', in *Studies in Medieval History Presented to F. M. Powicke*, pp. 333–53.

[2] *Vita Edwardi Secundi Auctore Malmesberiensi*, in *Chronicles of Edward I and Edward II*, (R. S. edited by W. Stubbs, 1882–3), vol. II, p. 258. For details see my 'Sherburn Indenture and the Attack on the Despensers, 1321', in *E.H.R.* vol. LXIII (January 1948), pp. 1–28.

which was read aloud. The king conceded to the barons the exile of the Despensers, with accompanying reforms; the earls conceded to the king an indirect condemnation of the dangerous baronial Declaration of 1308. This, at least, seems to be the only explanation of the fact that the first article of indictment which they now made against the younger Despenser was that he had supported the Declaration of 1308. This looks like a tortuous but nevertheless effective way of renouncing the extreme views they had propounded in the Declaration.

To this extent, it may be argued, the movement of 1321 was less extreme than that in the year of the coronation; but the moderation was based on expediency, not on principle. That extreme views were still in favour may be seen from two treatises which were probably written at this time. They were pro-baronial, and were intended among other things to gain the sympathy of knights and burgesses. Such a courting of 'popular' support was in itself radical, recalling the great innovator Simon de Montfort. The treatises were the *Modus Tenendi Parliamentum*, probably written in 1321,[1] and a closely related *Tract on the Office of Steward*. Both incorporated ideas of action in parliament against unworthy ministers, of the dependence of the ruler on the support of his people, and of the importance in parliament of the burgesses and knights. The tracts were a landmark in the growth of the parliamentary assembly, and in the broadening of the idea of sovereignty (to use a modern phrase), so that it resided, not in the king in his court and councils, but in the 'whole realm in parliament'. In their own way, they were almost as extreme and alarming to good royalists as the Declaration of 1308. Hence, the crisis of 1321 was not really dispelled by the exile of the Despensers. As in 1318, neither side was satisfied. The king, in particular, neither forgot nor forgave, and very soon he was able to bring about a royalist reaction based on an extremism on his part as pronounced as any that the barons themselves had shown between 1308 and 1321.

Edward opened his attack on the opposition as early as the autumn of 1321 by capturing the castle of Leeds in Kent, whose custodian, Lady Badlesmere, had refused hospitality to the queen. Having thus

---

[1] See my *Constitutional History 1216–1399*, vol. III, pp. 324–9, where the problem of the *Modus* is discussed with reference to recent literature. V. H. Galbraith's arguments are generally convincing, though it is hard to believe that the *Modus* represented only moderate liberal opinion. There is an excellent recent discussion by John Taylor, 'The manuscripts of the "Modus Tenendi Parliamentum" ', *E.H.R.*, vol. LXXXIII (October 1968), pp. 673–88.

assembled a large army, he turned against his real enemies, the Marcher lords and his cousin Lancaster. He shrewdly chilled any possible northern sympathy for Thomas by accusing him of intrigue with the Scots (Lancaster failed in his efforts to call an assembly at Doncaster where he might make a reply); and when the lords and commons of England were now confronted with a hard choice between two extreme solutions to the political impasse, they general-ly, but perhaps reluctantly, supported the claims of the king. Out-numbered, and retreating northward, Thomas was stopped short at the crossing of the Ure in the plain of York. One of his chief allies, the Earl of Hereford, was ignominiously slain by a Welsh pikeman who thrust his spear upwards through the planks of the bridge which Thomas was attempting to cross. Surrendering to superior force, and taken prisoner to Pontefract, Lancaster stood before the king and seven earls and heard himself sentenced to death for notorious misdeeds. There was no judgment in parliament, and the voice of the 'people' was not heard. On 22 March he was taken out, dressed in mean clothes and on a sorry mount, and beheaded before a jeering crowd.[1]

Thomas's vision, such as it was, of an England ruled by the king and his *comites* the earls lay in ruins, and royalist extremists replaced the extremists of baronial opposition. Nevertheless, the Lancastrians had stood for a cause and their appeal had transcended their personal shortcomings. Some men believed that Thomas was a martyr for church and state.[2] The king had to place armed guards around his burial place to keep back the weeping mourners. A chapel was erected on the site of his execution; pilgrims from all parts of England donated most of the funds. People flocked to kneel before the tablet Thomas had set up in St. Paul's to commemorate the Ordinances. When he died, royalism was riding high; but what he stood for could not be destroyed; and the circumstances of his death played their part in ensuring that the pendulum of politics would soon swing again.

2. Failure and Deposition of King Edward II

Meanwhile, the royalists carried out a thorough and meticulous restoration of the monarchy. The process against the Despensers was annulled, and the well-known statute of York in 1322 prohibited

---

[1] *Annales Paulini*, in *Chronicles of Edward I and Edward II*, vol. I, p. 303.
[2] M. McKisack, *op. cit.*, p. 69.

for ever the imposition by the king's subjects of reforms which were against the royal power. The claim of the barons to decide what was good for the king and kingdom was denied, and by implication the conduct of public affairs was once more restored to the ruler in the manner of Edward I.[1] The king's advisers would no doubt have liked to counter more specifically the Ordainer's appeal to public opinion; but they could not afford to alienate the Commons. Hence, they recognized the participation of the commonalty in parliamentary affairs, but they did not concede them any specific powers; and they excluded the possibility of any recurrence of parliamentary 'awards' against the servants of the king. Altogether, the Statute of York rejected, as far as this was possible, all the main aims and methods of baronial opposition since 1307. One innovation which could not be explicitly condemned was the new coronation oath of 1308, part of the solemn act of accession to the throne; but the significance of its innovations was at least partly destroyed.

The boldness and thoroughness of this restoration must command our admiration. Nevertheless, it was still an extreme solution to the problems of government, cast in an antique mould. It denied to the barons the right not only to extreme measures of reform, but even the right to make limited and moderate demands and, indeed, to initiate reforming movements at all. If it had remained intact, it is safe to prophesy, it would have become an important landmark in the creation in England of absolute monarchical power.

It was, however, unlikely that Edward II, who had failed so signally to prevent the undermining of royal power in 1308 and 1311, would now be able to achieve such a royalist revolution. The Despensers were restored; but their lavish acquisition of estates in south Wales did nothing to make them more beloved by the Marcher lords after 1322 than they had been before. The earl of Pembroke pledged his support to Edward in peace and war; but the Lancastrians were unreconciled. The halting of the Scottish war by a thirteen-years' truce in 1323 was sensible and beneficial; but it left Bruce all his gains; and medieval Englishmen were never grateful for such concessions to the realities of foreign affairs. There were sound reforms in chancery and exchequer administration; but perhaps

---

[1] The exact meaning of this statute has been much debated. Some conflicting views are discussed in my *Constitutional History 1216–1399*, Vol. II, pp. 134–56. See also Gaines Post, 'The Two Laws and the Statute of York' in *Speculum*, vol. XXIX (1954), 417–32; J. H. Trueman, 'The Statute of York and the Ordinances of 1311', in *Medievalia et Humanistica*, vol. X (1956), pp. 64–81.

these weighed less in the scales of baronial opinion than the huge
deposits which Hugh Despenser the younger made with Florentine
merchants in England, money that can hardly all have been honestly
gained.

The remarkable feature of these years is the speed with which all
England fell away from the king after the complete triumph of his
cause in 1322. Miracles soon began to be talked of, associated with
the 'martyrs' of the opposition. In Bristol, disturbances arose in
which a knight with the ominous name of Sir Reginald de Montfort
was involved. In 1323 Roger Mortimer, a prominent Marcher
enemy of the king, escaped from the Tower, hardly without connivance in high places, and offered his services to the French king
Charles IV. Most important, Lancastrian opposition showed dangerous signs of reviving vitality, so much so that in 1324 Edward had
Thomas's condemnation formally read and enrolled in the records of
parliament.

Finally, by devious processes and for reasons not fully apparent,
Edward's own wife turned against him. The estrangement must
have gone far when her estates were sequestrated in September 1324.
Sent to France in March 1325 to mediate between England and
France in a dispute over Gascony, she gradually revealed her complete hostility to Edward. She was successful in negotiating terms
of accord with France; but these included the performance of
homage by her husband for his French lands. Whether or not she
foresaw and even planned the consequences of her settlement we
cannot say; but it would have taken no great genius to anticipate
that Edward would not perform homage in his own person, and
that the obvious substitute would be his son Edward, thirteen years
old in November. At any rate, this is what transpired; and when the
young Edward had arrived in France to do homage for his father,
Isabella herself, together with the prince, refused to return. Soon
afterwards she made her position crystal clear by entering into a
liaison with Roger Mortimer. This shocked even the ladies of Paris,
but does not seem to have alienated her supporters at home. The
bishop of Hereford declared in the parliament of 1326 that if
Isabella rejoined her husband she would suffer death at his hands;
but whether this would have been for treachery or infidelity he did
not specify.[1]

The defection of his own queen made Edward's failure certain;

[1] *Historia Roffensis*, in H. Wharton, *Anglia Sacra* (London 1691), vol. I, p. 367.

but added to this was the fact, which became increasingly apparent, that the movement against him was universal; this is what gives it its deep significance. Isabella was known to be planning an invasion, helped by soldiers of Count William II of Hainault, to whose court she and Mortimer had retired when Paris became uncongenial. She betrothed her son to William's daughter Philippa, and obviously plotted to replace Edward II on the throne. Against this threat, the very sailors of England refused to defend her shores 'because of the great wrath which they had towards Sir Hugh Despenser'; and when the little force of invaders landed in East Anglia in September 1326 they 'found favour with all'. The common people of London gave vent to their feelings by dragging the bishop of Exeter, Walter Stapledon, a former pillar of the king's administration, from his horse; they led him through the streets to Cheapside to be beheaded with a butcher's knife. The gates of the city were flung open for Isabella and her allies.

The movement thus given a hero's welcome had its tawdry aspects, but it was no mere baronial revolt. It was a rising of all politically articulate Englishmen. It swept Edward and his ministers away like chaff before a storm. Bristol refused support to Hugh Despenser the elder, and he was condemned to death for misdeeds which were notorious to all. His son was similarly condemned 'by all the good people of the realm, great and small, rich and poor, by common assent'. Edward himself was captured at Neath Abbey on 16 November, deserted and forlorn, seeking escape to Ireland or protection in the hills of Wales. The drama of the collapse of his power is heightened by the personal elements involved; but it needed far more than these to create the unanimity with which Edward was overwhelmed. Clearly, Englishmen of all walks of life objected to his advisers and condemned his royalist solution to the problem of politics. Thus, both extremes of political action, baronial and monarchical, had now been attempted and had failed. It remained to be seen whether a compromise could be achieved in the difficult circumstances of rebellion, regicide, and usurpation, under a minority dominated by a former paramour and an erstwhile unfaithful queen.

Edward was formally deposed, not by parliament, of which he himself was the head, and which could not formally exist without him, but by the Estates of parliament which had been summoned in his name, reinforced by Londoners representing the *populus*. The whole realm of England was conceived as assembled at Westminster to join in deposing the ruler just as they had joined in his 'election' in 1308. It was this assembly which was asked by the bishop of Hereford if it preferred the son to the father as its king. A 'parliamentary' delegation had threatened Edward II in prison at Kenilworth. Through the mouths of two bishops they had warned the king that if he should refuse to resign his throne the people would reject both him and his son. Clad in a black gown, in tears and half-fainting, he had agreed. It grieved him, he said, that his people should be so alienated from him as to want to cast off his rule; but that if his son were accepted in his place he would bow to their will. The son was then produced before the assembly at Westminster with the words *Ecce Rex vester*; and there were few or none to join the courageous William Dene, bishop of Rochester, who went in peril of his life by refusing to join in the singing of *Gloria, laus et honor* to the newly designated king.[1]

We need not disentangle here the nice mixture of abdication and deposition by which Edward was dethroned. The essential fact was, as the archbishop of Canterbury declared, all the clergy and people of England considered him deposed. He was rejected by all the community, probably including the lowest as well as the highest in the land. After his deposition, his enemies had no real alternative but to put him to death. When petty brutalities failed to destroy him, this was probably achieved at Berkely Castle in September 1327 by searing his bowels with a hot iron so that his body could be exposed to the public with no sign of a violent death. There followed the hypocrisy of an elaborate funeral, where Isabella no doubt tried to look like a widow bereaved.

For many reasons the deposition of Edward II and his replacement by Edward III proved to be a landmark in English history. It perhaps did more than any other crisis to lessen the aura of divine approval and essential inviolability which surrounded the office of the king. It is true that there had been depositions outside England and talk of deposition within; but up to this point the English rulers since 1066 had shared with their cousins in France the protection and majesty that came from centuries of uninterrupted possession of the throne. Subjects might oppose and rebel, but they had not, even in 1216, actually put a monarch off his throne for the abuse of his royal

[1] The depositions of Edward II and Richard II are discussed in my *Constitutional History 1216–1399*, vol. II, pp. 284–327, with reference to recent debates.

power. Now, all this long tradition was shattered; and after this politics in England could never again be the same.

It may be that at the end of his reign Edward II was as much sinned against as sinning, but judged by the long view of history it was better perhaps that he died. He himself had created the conditions for his own destruction; nor was the rejection of high royalism too dearly purchased even by the cruel destruction of an anointed king. Apart from the brutality of 1327 it was perhaps necessary to establish once for all that not even a ruler blessed by the Church and fortified by immemorial tradition was unlimited in his power. There was, in effect, a distinction between the office and the person, as had been asserted in 1308. The essence of the kingship was preserved even if the person of the ruler was destroyed.

But after Edward's death it was the manner of his dying rather than of his ruling which tended to be remembered. It was his cruel death and not his foolish life which made his tomb at Gloucester the centre of a cult. His features, carved over his tomb, looked down poignant and unforgettable; and his death, like Lancaster's, helped to destroy those by whom he had been destroyed. Like Thomas, Edward found more love and honour in death than life: the extremes for which both had stood were in time forgotten; and in death the king and the earl paved the way for a reconciliation of political discords which they had never been able to achieve while they were alive.

3. Accession and Minority of King Edward III

If the deposition and death of Edward II made a profound impression on English history, so did the manner of his son's acquisition of personal rule. The one dealt a great blow to the monarchy; the other gave it a new lease of life. The one marked the nadir of English politics since 1216, the other issued in the age of Crécy and Poitiers. The one ended the life of an unfortunate ruler, the other began the active reign of one of the most successful kings who ever sat upon the English throne. Finally, the one reign had witnessed a recourse to political extremes; the other saw the triumph of compromise and harmony through which the ancient political heritage was revived and preserved.

In 1327 Mortimer and Isabella together seized the reins of government, Edward III being as yet only fourteen; but they were dependent on support from the Lancastrians who had helped to overthrow

Edward II. Henry earl of Lancaster was made keeper of the king, with the counsel of twelve magnates; the young king took substantially the same coronation oath as his father; and there was even a movement to canonize Thomas of Lancaster. But all this was merely a façade. Mortimer became earl of March, extended his lands in south Wales, and 'seized for himself the royal power and the government of the realm'. There was much to be said in favour of the peace he made with Scotland and France in 1327 and 1328; but the treaties were negotiated from a position of weakness, not of strength; and the concessions made to Robert Bruce at Northampton gained for the agreement the title of the 'shameful peace'. It recognized Robert Bruce as independent king of Scotland. It restored to his country its boundaries under Alexander III who had died in 1286. It provided for a marriage between David Bruce who was four years old and Edward II's young sister Joan of the Tower. It is said that there was some agreement to return the Stone of Scone to the Scots, but that the abbot of Westminster and the Londoners refused to allow this to be done.

There was inevitably a rising opposition to the course of events both at home and abroad; to destroy this Isabella and Mortimer engineered a devious and treacherous plot against Edmund of Kent, half-brother of Edward II, and friend of Lancaster. They persuaded Edmund that Edward II was still alive and encouraged him to write and talk of an insurrection. His misguided efforts obtained wide support. When all was ready Isabella and Mortimer charged him with treason. Despite an abject submission he was condemned to death. From morning until evening he stood outside the walls of Winchester whilst a search was made for an executioner. In the end a condemned criminal was found who was willing to cut off Kent's head in return for his own life.

The plot which had destroyed Kent was revolting, not even justified by results. His death only paved the way for a still more dangerous opposition by the young king himself, impatient for power, and perhaps at odds with the whole régime. There seems to be no evidence that Edward had to be stimulated to action by Lancaster: he was quite capable of acting alone.[1] He found natural allies in young magnates like William Montagu. He hatched a plot, complete with all the stratagems of fiction, including a password to be used in correspondence with the pope (*Pater Sancte*, written in his

[1] But cf. M. McKisack, *op. cit.*, p. 101.

own hand, the earliest known surviving handwriting of an English king). Through a secret passage he made his way in October 1330 into the castle where Isabella and Mortimer resided during a meeting of the Great Council at Nottingham. He and his young conspirators overpowered the guards outside Isabella's chamber and seized her lover, despite her plea that he should 'have pity on the gentle Mortimer'. On 29 November Roger was condemned by his peers to be hanged and drawn as a traitor. Isabella was sent to honourable exile in the country. She had an ample allowance of £3,000 a year and a library consisting of Arthurian romances, epics of Charlemagne, and devotional books. She died in 1358, wearing the habit of the Poor Clares. With her removal in 1330 a new epoch in the history of the monarchy began.

4. THE WARS OF EDWARD III

The monarchy established by Edward III was based on co-operation, instead of rivalry, between the king and his magnates. Its definition is to be found in the proclamation of 1330, that 'we wish all men to know that in future we will govern our people according to right and reason, as is fitting our royal dignity; and that all matters which touch us and the estate of our realm are to be disposed of by the common council of all the magnates of our realm, and in no other manner'.[1] To this purpose Edward brought the physique, temperament and intelligence of his grandfather, and a charisma that was uniquely his own, unless perhaps he shared it with Richard I. To the same purpose he also brought a truly feudal attitude to warfare, as an activity in which both a good knight and a good king could find honour and profit as well as a sense of duty performed. It was entirely fitting that one of the basic considerations of his restored monarchy should be expressed later by Froissart, chronicler of chivalry, who believed that 'the English will never love or honour their ruler unless he be victorious in war, and especially against those who are richer and more powerful than they'.[2] There was only one great flaw, by contemporary standards, in such a view elevated to be a principle of policy; but this was fatal. Victory in war could never be certain, whilst failure might bring the whole political edifice to the ground.

[1] The extract is translated in my *Constitutional History of Medieval England 1216–1399*, vol. II, p. 174; its importance is discussed *ibid.*, p. 164.
[2] Quoted *ibid.*, II, 32.

Meanwhile, young Edward set about the conciliation of erstwhile baronial, and especially Lancastrian, opposition. He made a Lancastrian prelate, John Stratford, his chancellor in 1330, and supported Stratford's promotion to be archbishop of Canterbury in 1333. He consolidated ardent support among the younger nobles by a famous creation of earls in 1337, including the young Henry of Lancaster, who became one of his most renowned generals and built the famous Savoy palace out of ransom and spoils wrung from the castle and town of Bergerac. Thus, ancient feuds were appeased and Lancastrians welded to the support of the throne.

In his policy of war, Edward III has been considered to be little more than a rash and irresponsible adventurer, but this seems to leave out some important considerations, particularly the consequences which had flowed from Edward II's failures in warfare. At any rate, rightly or wrongly, the young Edward began an era of formidable military aggression by the English almost as soon as he had obtained the reality of power. He turned a blind eye on the expedition into Scotland of disinherited Scots under the leadership of Edward Baliol, pretender to the Scottish throne, which resulted in a victory at Dupplin Moor near Perth in 1332. When Baliol was driven out of Scotland shortly after, Edward himself intervened and decisively defeated the Scots at Halidon Hill near Berwick, in 1333. In this first battle of his long reign, Edward already showed his military genius. He dismounted his knights and sent their horses to the rear. He placed his archers on the wings of his 'battles' of infantry, so that they could decimate the Scots who fought in their traditional array. His victory was complete, and the relations of England and Scotland which had been established in 1328 were dramatically reversed.

Finally, when Philip VI of France held by his alliance with Scotland, England and France drifted towards war. Philip's encouragement helped to keep Scottish resistance alive, just as Scottish assistance was later to help France after 1415. By 1337 Edward openly accused Philip of fomenting the Scottish war. Meanwhile, Robert of Artois, condemned as a traitor in France, sought refuge and revenge in the English court; and Edward in 1336 laid an embargo on the export of English wool to the Netherlands, seeking to detach the Count of Flanders, Louis de Nevers, from Philip, and to gain his lands as a springboard for hostilities against France. The embargo, intended to starve the looms of Flemish weavers and so influence their ruler, was followed by the gentler persuasion of a well-endowed embassy to Hainault, to purchase allies. Philip for his part, on 24 May 1337 declared Gascony confiscate to France 'on account of the many excesses, rebellions and acts of disobedience committed against us . . . by the king of England, duke of Aquitaine'. In October 1337 Edward laid claim to the throne of France.

The cause of the outbreak of the Hundred Years War which is most often quoted was this claim of Edward to the French throne through his mother Isabella. But though this was an important diplomatic asset to the English king, it contributed little to the outbreak of the struggle. Curiously enough, one cause that was probably more important was the project of a joint Crusade by Edward and Philip which was at one time strongly urged by popes John XXII and Benedict XII. Philip collected a fleet at Marseilles and was ready to despatch it in August 1336; but at the last moment Benedict postponed the expedition indefinitely. The French king saw no reason why the ships should be wasted, and moved them to the Channel ports for possible service against the Christian English instead of the infidel Turk. This gesture was enough to destroy any glimmering hope of peace. The war was, at bottom, a conflict between two emerging territorial states, each consolidating itself within its own borders and thrusting aggressively beyond.

The first engagement of the war was a raid on the harbour of Cadzand by Sir Walter Manny in November 1337, more than repaid in kind by French and Genoese raids on Hastings, Rye, Portsmouth, and Plymouth. In the summer of 1338, 'well accompanied with earls and barons', Edward crossed to Antwerp and prepared to round up as many allies as he could for an attack on France. His most glittering achievement was at Coblenz, where the emperor, in return for English gold, provided him with 2000 men and made him his vicar-general of the imperial lands west of the Rhine; but it was not until the following summer that he could get an army together adequate for his needs. In 1339 Edward made his long delayed invasion and 'rode against the tyrant of the French with banners displayed', only to find that King Philip remained a discreet distance away at Buironfosse and refused to accept his challenge to fight. All his costly allies had availed him nothing and he was £300,000 in

---

[1] Edouard Perroy, *La Guerre de Cent ans* (Paris 1945), translated as *The Hundred Years War* (London 1951) by W. B. Wells, p. 111. Cf. G. Templeman, 'Edward III and the Beginnings of the Hundred Years War' in *Trans. Royal Hist. Soc.*, 5th series, vol. II (1952), pp. 69–88; and A. H. Burne, *The Crecy War* (London 1955).

debt. His strategy in these early campaigns of the war has been condemned as visionary and over-ambitious,[1] but it was in conformity with an English tradition which was already old. It seemed logical at the time in view of the disparity in size and apparent strength between England and France. It was defeated not perhaps so much by its inherent defects as by the unexpected plan adopted by the French, against all the dictates of chivalry as presented by the poets.

Despite this initial failure, and despite his mounting debts, Edward persisted in his effort. He detached the Flemish wool towns from the policy of Louis de Nevers, their pro-French count, though the effort cost him another £140,000 and led him to declare formally that he was the rightful king of England and of France (or of France and England when he was corresponding with European states). He also quartered the arms of France, and engraved for himself a new seal; and he had a new surcoat made, emblazoned with leopards and lilies. But though all this no doubt impressed his allies it did nothing to the French or for his war-chest; and when he returned to England for more supplies he had to leave the queen and her children as hostages for the payment of his debts.

One great achievement Edward had to his credit in the midst of his mounting difficulties. He was able to secure his communications with Flanders by a great naval victory at Sluys in 1340. The French had a much larger fleet, but it was anchored in harbour, stationary and unmanageable, whilst the English had the advantage of sun, wind, and tide. Even at sea, they adopted their formidable military formation of archers and men-at-arms interspersed, and it proved irresistible. King Philip's clown was later heard to ask his master:'Do you know, sire, why the English are cowards? Because, unlike the French, they dare not jump into the sea.' The English were so sure that they would not have to jump that they had with them a large contingent of noble ladies who were on their way to join the queen, and who had to have a special guard allotted to them during the fight. Sluys was a notable victory, harbinger of others to come; but it did not solve the problems posed for Edward by Philip's conduct of the war.

The campaign of 1340 followed the same pattern as that of 1339, with the same results. The scenes around Buironfosse were re-enacted around Tournai. Edward had to accept the truce of Espléchin on 25 September and face the insoluble problems of supplies. He had saved Gascony and England from invasion, but had failed to develop a suitable strategy or to apply his modern tactics. Hence he clearly faced the prospect of ultimately losing the war.

In his protracted dilemma he had given a free hand to John Stratford and his ministers at home, and they had adopted a liberal policy towards his subjects in order to keep up the support of the war. But in spite of this his finances had become a shambles and he felt that he had been betrayed. Even his crown was in pawn. He eluded his creditors at Ghent: 'pretending that he wanted to take a walk, he secretly rode away'. Back at the Tower of London, on 30 November, he prepared for a reckoning with his ministers and his subjects from both of whom he had become badly estranged.

The war, through the stubborn French refusal to solve it in one spectacular explosion, threatened to have an effect just the opposite of what had been desired. It brought about a clamour for reform and even threatened a revival of the opposition which had faced Edward II. For his supplies in the parliament of April 1340, Edward had to promise the abolition of all aids or charges except those imposed in parliament. In the same assembly the Commons made remarkable demands.[1] All taxes, they asked, should be 'reserved to the people', and certain peers were to be appointed in parliament to ensure this. In the king's absence these peers were to transact the great business of the land; and for this also they were to be accountable before the Lords and Commons. Such demands were a direct challenge to the royal authority; in making them, the subjects seemed to take an unwarranted advantage of the royal needs. Even so, Stratford had satisfied the Commons in one way or another; but he had failed to evoke any great enthusiasm in Edward's support, even though the king was labouring, as he firmly believed, for the common good.

Bitterly disappointed, Edward suspected the home government of indifference or worse. Political extremism raised its head once more when in November 1340 the king, after his secret return, dismissed all his chief ministers. He began a war of pamphlets and propaganda against Archbishop Stratford, thrust a number of Stratford's adherents into prison, and eventually declared that he would no longer be served by clerics but only by such servants as could be hanged if they failed in their duty. Stratford in reply

[1] My *Constitutional History 1216–1399*, vol. II, pp. 194–5. The most recent comments are by G. L. Harris, 'The Commons' Petition of 1340', in *E.H.R.*, vol. LXXVIII (October 1963), pp. 625–54.

waged the war of words as fiercely as Edward, and somewhat more expertly. He sought a hearing 'in full parliament', and plainly courted general support against his ruler or, failing that, even the crown of martyrdom ('No such thing,' Sir John Darcy told him, 'you are not so worthy and we are not so foolish.'). Even the great lords became involved in the struggle and were in danger of becoming estranged. The earl of Surrey, whose loyalty to the monarchy was beyond question, asked publicly 'Lord king, how goes this parliament? Things were not wont to be like this. They are now all upside-down. Those who should be chief men here are shut out and others who are unworthy are here in parliament, who ought not to be at such a council, but only the peers of the realm who can aid and maintain you in your great need.'[1]

In the end, Stratford was admitted to parliament, not in order to defend himself, but to humble himself before the king. On the other hand Edward's accusations were in effect shelved. Furthermore, Edward granted that in future his magnates should share in the appointment of his ministers, who should answer in parliament any charges against them. Such a concession may seem mild in comparison with those made by Edward II, but it was nevertheless an ominous portent of what might arise from the failures of the war. Edward's statutory grants to his subjects in this parliament were so far-reaching that the king's officers publicly declared them impracticable: 'they made their protestation that they had not assented to the making or forms of the said statutes, and that they could not keep them in case the said statutes were contrary to the laws and usages of the kingdom which they were bound by oath to preserve'.[2] On 1 October 1341 Edward himself repealed the 'pretended' statutes as being contrary to the law and the royal prerogative, and they were again repealed in 1343.

It is clear that a serious conflict was threatened, but it did not materialize. This does not mean that the area of disagreement was small,[3] but that the war still absorbed men's attention and that England needed Edward's leadership and authority. With these, victory still seemed possible. Edward even got the chance of a new ally, when John III of Brittany died in April 1341 and the English supported the claim of John de Montfort to succeed him, while the

---

[1] Quoted in my *Constitutional History 1216–1399*, vol. II, p. 193.
[2] *Ibid.*, vol. II, p. 200.
[3] As argued by M. McKisack, *op. cit.*, p. 179.

French supported Charles of Blois. Although John was taken captive by the French, his claim was resolutely upheld by his wife the Duchess Joan. Edward himself invaded Brittany in 1342 and gained some success; whilst Henry, earl of Derby (son of Lancaster), and Sir Walter Manny won brilliant victories in Gascony.

On the other hand the 'grand alliance' against France in the north showed clear signs of crumbling. Lewis of Bavaria began to withdraw his support as early as 1341. Louis de Nevers, the francophile count of Flanders, moved towards the repression of his rebellious subjects and greater support for Philip VI. The pro-English James van Arteveld, leader of the cloth-weavers in Flemish towns, lost popularity. He was assassinated in 1345; and despite Edward's claim afterwards that Flanders 'was never firmer in our *fidelitas*' the event went far towards wrecking all plans for another invasion of France from the north, even though he made a kinsman, Hugh Hastings, his captain and lieutenant to organize troops and allies. Meanwhile the French made a great effort in the south, where in May 1346 a large and well equipped army under the duke of Normandy aided by the duke of Bourbon, Philip VI's lieutenant in Languedoc, besieged Aiguillon, a key fortress at the junction of the rivers Lot and Garonne.

It was imperative that Edward should make a supreme attempt to restore the military and diplomatic situation; and since the attack from the north seemed now to have little chance of success, the only likely alternative was a thrust directly across the Channel or southward to Gascony. For this Edward began assembling forces towards the end of 1345. By the summer of 1346 he had about 15,000 men at Portsmouth ready to embark. His plan of campaign is quite uncertain. In the event, he landed at St. Vaast-de-la-Hogue in Normandy on 12 July 1346. His preference for Normandy over Gascony may have been forced upon him by unfavourable winds, but on the whole this seems improbable: his timetable was hardly likely to have been so rigorous that he could not wait a little longer; he had already waited throughout the month of June. On the other hand it was much shorter to sail to Normandy than to Gascony, and from the Cotentin Edward could strike either north or south, or possibly in the direction of Paris. Finally, he had a strong local ally in the person of Geoffrey Harcourt—head of a powerful Norman family which controlled land and forces in the Cotentin—who was at odds with Philip VI. Geoffrey had been at the English court since 1344 and, according to Froissart's well-known story, had strongly urged a landing in Normandy:

> Sir [he said to Edward], the country of Normandy is one of the most plenteous countries of the world. . . . If you will land there, there is none that shall resist you. The people of Normandy have not been used to war. You will find there great towns that have not been walled, whereby your men shall have such gain that they shall be the better for it after twenty years.

Thus, it seems probable that Edward had planned a landing in Normandy; but his further intentions still remain quite uncertain. We do not know for instance whether, considering the small size of his army, he planned only a *chevauchée* or hoped for a set battle, though he had consistently refused to accept the latter unless the conditions were clearly in his favour, the latest occasion being in the neighbourhood of Vannes in 1342. A *chevauchée*, a systematic raid of destruction, would reward his generals and soldiers with booty and ransom. It would deplete French resources, damage French morale, and encourage Edward's allies. It might even relieve French pressure in Gascony.

But all these advantages were uncertain. On the other hand, there were urgent considerations in favour of a set battle, though the risks of defeat in a hostile country and by a superior army were enormous.[1] An indecisive raid might win a measure of empty glory, but it might well leave Edward bankrupt of both finances and allies. Nor was it by any means certain that Edward could avoid a set battle once he had left his port of embarkation far behind. This is what he eventually got, and despite medieval lack of strategy in war, which is often exaggerated, we have probably no right to assume that he was very much surprised. As Miss McKisack has observed,[2] Edward was a superb soldier; he had had time to lay his plans; and it must be presumed that he knew what he was about.

After disembarkation, Edward besieged and sacked Caen, ravaged the countryside and turned north, presumably making towards Flanders. He found the bridges over the Seine broken, and it was only after following the south bank almost as far as Paris that he was able to repair the bridge at Poissy and cross the river.

---

[1] Even a limited failure would have exposed England to a retaliatory invasion, which was not at all impossible. Edward referred to the possibility in letters of 20 January and 15 March 1346; J. Viard, 'La Campagne de Juillet-Août 1346 et la Bataille de Crécy', in *Le Moyen Age*, 2e série (1926), p. 4.

[2] *The Fourteenth Century 1307–1399*, p. 133.

His luck still held when he also found a ford across the Somme at Blanche Tache. At this point the French with much larger forces were hot on his heels, and a major engagement became inevitable. Whether Edward now saw a chance of victory, or whether he was brought to bay by his enemies with further flight denied him, we shall probably never know. All we can be sure of is that the French were the attackers, confident of success; but this in itself does not prove that Edward had lost all control over the military situation, and that all his plans had gone hopelessly astray.[1]

In any case, the battle of Crécy which followed was a triumph of English tactics, discipline, and leadership. Edward applied all the lessons he had learned. He chose a fine defensive position, his rear protected by the wood of Crécy-en-Ponthieu, his open front sloping down to the little river Maie. He divided his army into three main 'battles', or corps, with a reserve under his personal command. Interspersed between the 'battles' were wedges of archers, armed with the formidable six-foot long-bow made of oak or ash. It was not as powerful as the cross-bow but had a more rapid fire. Nor was its power to be taken lightly: it has been claimed that its arrows could penetrate chain mail and reach upwards of 400 yards.[2] Unlike the cross-bowmen on the French side, the English bowmen were scientifically employed. This could only be done by dismounting the knights to stand side by side with the humbler bowmen, tactics which had long ago been worked out in the Welsh and Scottish wars. Neither the dismounting of knights nor the prominent use of bowmen had been a complete novelty, even in Edward I's reign, though the fire-power of the long bow was; but it was novel to mix the humble bowman and the knight in near-equality, and make the fate of any army depend on the co-operation and interdependence of both.

The French idea of a battle was still the wild and undisciplined charge of nobility on horseback which had been made immortal by the French-English Richard Coeur de Lion at Arsulf and by Philip Augustus at Bouvines. At Crécy the French knights ran down their own Genoese cross-bowmen who, shooting into the setting sun,

---

[1] General Burns's comments on Edward's thinking are given in his *Crecy War*, pp. 149, 162; Cf. Viard, *op. cit.*, pp. 45–53; H. J. Hewitt, *The Organization of War under Edward III 1338–62* (Manchester 1966).

[2] Edward even had primitive cannon with him, but they were not effective except to frighten horses, and were not used in the early battles of the war, though they soon became important in siege warfare.

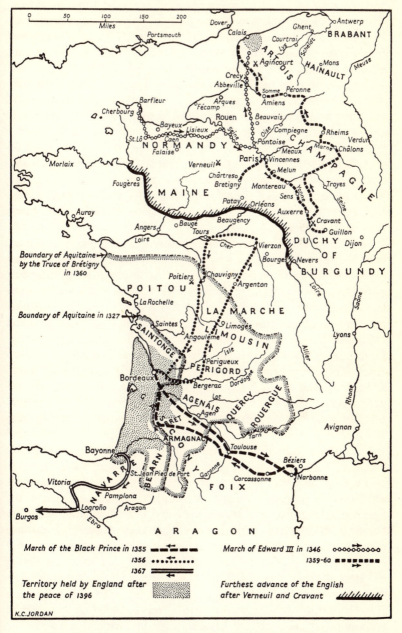

Boundary of Aquitaine by the Truce of Brétigny in 1360

Boundary of Aquitaine in 1327

Furthest advance of the English after Verneuil and Cravant

March of the Black Prince in 1355
1356
1367

March of Edward III in 1346
1359-60

Territory held by England after the peace of 1396

K.C.JORDAN

2. *The campaigns of Edward III and the Black Prince in France*

had failed to prevail against the English bowmen and had run out of arrows. Repeated and courageous assaults on the disciplined English formation were driven back. When the late summer sun finally disappeared and darkness descended, the flower of French nobility lay dead on the battlefield; only King Philip and a small section of his army retreated together to Amiens. Edward's victory was won against long odds and under desperate conditions by the kind of courage which so deeply moved Froissart. Like Courtrai in 1302 the battle was a sign of the changing world of the fourteenth century, in which the armed knight was beginning to lose undisputed command of the battlefield, and in consequence his social and political predominance began to be undermined. But we should not exaggerate the rapidity of the change. As has been observed, it was many years before the implications of the battle of Crécy were fully understood.

After his victory, which Edward refused to endanger by a pursuit of the fleeing French, he was able to lay siege to Calais, which commanded the shortest approach from England to France, and gave control over the Narrow Seas. The town was too strong to be taken by assault, so Edward built wooden huts for his army and, in the fashion of the times, was soon joined by the queen and her ladies. In this wooden town, christened Villeneuve-le-hardi, the Flemings set up a market on Wednesdays and Saturdays. After a year's siege, the brave defenders surrendered, and Calais became largely English, to be held through all the vicissitudes of war and peace until the reign of Queen Mary. Its loss, written, as she claimed, on her heart, broke one of the last links directly connecting late Tudor England with the great Edwardian age.

Meanwhile, victories accumulated in other areas. To help his allies in their time of need, David II of Scotland invaded the north of England in October 1346. But the northern barons and levies were there to receive him, and at Neville's Cross near Durham the Scottish schiltrons were surrounded and cut to pieces, mainly by the English archers. David himself was taken prisoner. It is clear that despite the great drain of the French war the preponderance of English power on the border had been wisely maintained, and that the lessons of Bannockburn had been applied against Scotland as well as in France. The year of victories in 1346 was not again rivalled in English history until 1759. It was rounded off by a belated triumph, in June 1347, for English arms in Brittany, when, at the battle of La Roche-Derrien, Sir Thomas Dagworth defeated an army several times as strong as his own. As a result, King David of Scotland was joined in the Tower of London by Charles of Blois, the French candidate for the duchy of Brittany. The effect of these striking events was that England became a major European power and Edward became a major English hero. But the Hundred Years War was not ended; indeed, as events turned out, it had only just begun.

In spite of, or maybe because of, French losses, French patriotism began to stir and French resistance to English attack became more stubborn if less spectacular. Despite his victories, Edward did not gain the support of Flanders, now ruled by Louis de Mâle who at first leaned towards France. The English could not sustain efforts like that of 1346 without intermission, and they had to accept a series of truces which gave respite to the French as well as to themselves. Edward III led an army to Calais in 1355, but there was no further great engagement until the victory of Edward the Black Prince at Poitiers in 1356.

The battle of Poitiers renewed the glories of Crécy. It resulted from one of the English *chevauchées*, carried into the heart of France. The raid of 1356 was from Gascony; and it was not led by Edward but by his son, who had gained his spurs at Crécy in nominal command of the right 'battle', and who now emerged as a great captain in his own right, equal to his father in daring and resource. He may have intended to link up with Henry Earl of Lancaster, in Brittany; but after he had got as far north as the Loire he decided to return to Bordeaux. His decision presented King John of France with a great opportunity; but John, like King Philip before him, had too many of the instincts of an irresponsible knight to make a competent general. Whether or not he was able to prevent the further retreat of the English by a flanking manoeuvre, he found them halted near the village of Maupertuis on the little river Moisson which lay on the road from Paris to Bordeaux, and there he showed the French once again how pitched battles against the English ought not to be fought.

A good many choices of action were open to John; but like Philip VI in 1346 he chose to give full play to the defensive tactics of the English by a frontal attack. It is probable that he had the greater army, though this is disputed; but the English had a formidable defensive position, shielded by hedges. A preliminary cavalry charge against them was repulsed with great loss. The French had learned enough to dismount the bulk of their army, but successive attacks by three 'battles' of knights on foot were no more successful. After all, dismounted knights without support were no great improvement on impetuous cavalry, against English tactics and discipline.

The battle was finally decided by a flank attack on the French by cavalry under the Gascon Captal de Buch, a stratagem frowned on by a modern French writer for a lack of chivalry. King John himself led the last French attack, unmistakably gallant and full of *prouesse*. It failed like the rest. As a later Frenchman would have said, 'c'est magnifique mais ce n'est pas la guerre'. The king was taken prisoner, his captors almost tearing him apart in their eagerness to lay hands on a king's ransom. The Black Prince made up for such conduct by treating John with elaborate courtesy; but this did not prevent the English from keeping him in London as a pampered and honoured guest through whom great wealth and heavy concessions could be extracted from his subjects, temporarily disunited and demoralized.

There seems to be no real doubt that at Poitiers the English were most anxious to avoid a battle. The prospects that the French would repeat the mistakes of Crécy may not have seemed good, and Prince Edward was so pessimistic about his chance of victory that he may have offered weighty concessions in return for an unmolested retreat. As it turned out, the victory brought much glory but did not decide the issue of the war. One of its consequences, indeed, was that the French finally adopted the English view of 'unchivalric' war. Because of this, their knights who died so courageously at Poitiers helped to ensure France's ultimate triumph even in their utter defeat.

5. Edward III, Monarch of Chivalry

For France, one immediate consequence of the disaster of 1356 was the tragedy of the Jacquerie, a revolt of peasants reduced to despair by the ravages of the English and the Free Companies. The latter were mercenaries recruited from all parts of Europe who served both sides (but especially the English) and pillaged mercilessly and indiscriminately. For England, the victory set the seal on the monarchy of Edward III and its policy, and concealed the weaknesses beneath. It is hard to strike a balance of losses and gains for this, as for any, military struggle. The English people lost blood and treasure the value of which cannot be computed; but they gained in a sense of national identity and in an increase in the importance of the ranks below the great nobility, without whom the war could not have been successfully waged. Though the magnates gained most in affluence and individual importance, the Commons increased their voice in national policy and in parliament, even though they showed signs of political immaturity and were dominated by the Lords. They applauded victories and glory but were reluctant to pay the inevitable price. Their attitude was negative; they refused responsibility but reserved the right to criticize; and their criticism was increasingly formidable since they had developed a control over the purse which could paralyze the conduct of the war. It is unlikely that historians will ever agree entirely as to these and other items in the balance of gains and losses; but most would agree that the war affected nearly every important aspect of English life.

The impact of the war on the French and English monarchies is perhaps a little more obvious. Both rulers claimed unprecedented obedience and loyalty, but also had to face unprecedented demands which grew out of a greater dependence on their subjects for support. In the long run the French king gained more power from the bitterness of defeat than the English king from the splendour of success; but at first it was Edward who profited more. He fought and ruled in the company of his great lords, and he trained distinguished professional soldiers who were not of the high nobility and were fanatically devoted to his service. Sir John Chandos, one of the greatest of Edward's professional captains, told the earl of Oxford, for all who cared to hear, that he himself served the king with sixty lances while the earl only served with four and had, moreover, waited to be ordered by the king to go abroad. Wherefore, Chandos concluded, 'I may of right be served and walk before you, since my dread lord the king of England and my lord the Prince [Edward] will have it so.'[1]

Edward not only fought in the company of his magnates, he also married his children to them. The eldest, the Black Prince, achieved what was a rarity in the Middle Ages, a marriage based on mutual attraction. He married Joan of Kent, who was a noted beauty but had little dowry to bring with her, and was still married to her second

---

[1] Quoted in my *Constitutional History 1216–1399*, vol. III, p. 40.

husband, the earl of Salisbury, when Prince Edward and she fell in love. The king's second son died in infancy. The marriage of the third son, Lionel later duke of Clarence, was more in keeping with the custom of the times. He had been born at Antwerp in 1338 and was married before he was four years old to Elizabeth, daughter of the earl of Ulster. This was a marriage for land, but after the death of Elizabeth Lionel married for money, gaining the hand of the niece of Bernabo Vísconti of Milan and a wedding-portion of two million gold florins. Lionel's daughter by his first marriage, who was wedded to Edmund Mortimer, bequeathed to the Mortimers of the next generations an important and dangerous claim to the throne.

The king's fourth son, John of Gaunt, cemented the alliance of Plantagenet and Lancaster by marrying Blanche, daughter of Duke Henry; and John ended by inheriting the vast Lancaster estates. He contributed much to a growing tradition of the privileges and responsibilities of the lords of the royal blood. His second marriage was to Constance, daughter of Peter the Cruel, ruler of Castile and Leon. It was his son Henry, by his first marriage, who usurped the throne in 1399.

Edward's fifth son, Edmund, who was made earl of Cambridge in 1362 and in 1385 became the first duke of York, married as his first wife Isabel of Castile, his elder brother's wife's sister. He hardly played the part in the politics of Richard II's reign which befitted a great prince of the blood, and his lack of vigour as regent during Richard's absence in 1399 contributed greatly to the triumph of his nephew Henry. His two sons by his first wife were both conspicuous in the reign of Henry IV.

Edward III's sixth and last son, Thomas, who was born at Woodstock, followed the pattern of taking a bride from the English nobility and was married to a co-heiress of Humphrey Bohun, earl of Hereford. He was made duke of Gloucester in 1385, and was destined to act the part of a great prince in the politics of Richard II.

Thus, like any other English landowner, Edward III looked after his sons' interests; but by so doing he created strong ties between leading members of the aristocracy and his successors on the throne. His sons were all loyal, and his settlements created no problems in his lifetime. It was only in the conflicts of Richard II's reign, and after the usurpation of 1399, that the princes of the blood created an additional danger for any ruler who could not maintain Edward's friendships with the greater lords.

The unity between Edward and his barons engendered by the war was strengthened in 1352 by the Statute of Treasons, an extremely moderate and limited definition of the offences for which a subject, if condemned, could be hanged and drawn as a traitor and thus forfeit all his estates. But it did include one new offence, the act of levying war against the monarch, an inclusion which was an important step away from feudal notions of a vassal's right of violent opposition to an unjust lord. The addition reflected the increasing majesty of the king; though perhaps, as Maitland argued, earlier kings of England had not been able to forbid vassals the dubious luxury of 'legal' revolt because they had themselves been vassals of the king of France. Edward III was the first king since the Conquest who owed homage to nobody, because he claimed that he was king of both England and France, and so did not owe homage to the French ruler for any lands.

Thus Edward, by his personality and wars, did much to create an English nation. His popularity extended far beyond his magnates. All his subjects were drawn together by common dangers, common endeavours, and common victories. They had a deep admiration for his personal exploits. They loved the glamour and gallantry of his court. They were touched by the English mottoes embroidered on his coat and by remarks which showed a spontaneous love of his native land. In return, Edward showed that, like his grandfather, he trusted and depended on the community of his people. He consulted them freely about his wars, and he accepted an important increase in the work of Lords and Commons in parliament. Nationalism is a word which has many definitions; but there are some grounds for believing that Edward, despite his pursuit of the will-o'-the-wisp of a French crown, was the first truly national ruler to sit on the English throne.

After the battle of Crécy, the Lords and Commons in parliament 'all thanked God for the victory that He had granted to their liege lord . . . and said that all the money they had given him had been well spent'.[1] In 1363 the Commons thanked God 'who has given them such a lord and governor, who has delivered them from servitude to other lands'.[2] In this period, Englishmen for good or ill first began to glory in their identity as opposed to Frenchmen or Scots. Of course there were much deeper causes of the beginnings of English patriotism. There was the growth of the territorial state,

[1] *Rot. Parl.*, vol. II, p. 159. [2] *Ibid.*, vol. II, p. 276.

of institutional centralization, and of English language and literature. Nevertheless, a not inconsiderable cause is to be found in
Edward's personality and wars.[1]

But there was inevitably a reverse side to the coin. Wars are
always expensive and can seldom be made to pay for themselves.
Edward had a normal income of only about £30,000 a year, not
enough for the most limited military campaign. For the rest, he
could borrow from the Bardi or Peruzzi or later from native merchants like William de la Pole of Hull; and he could strike bargains
with the wool merchants of England. In 1337, for example, in return
for a monopoly, a group of merchants agreed to buy and export
30,000 sacks of wool for his use. But the foreign merchants wanted
security; the English merchants and the king failed to agree; and
later efforts to exploit wool, notably in 1338, did not succeed.
Edward was driven into an increasing dependence on parliamentary
subsidies, for which the consent of the Commons was just as important as that of the Lords.

At a council in Northampton, only a fortnight after the king's
departure for Flanders in 1338, several of the Lords protested that
some of Edward's recent changes ought not to have been made
without the consent of the magnates in parliament. By September
1339 the king found it expedient to declare his needs to a full
parliament, through John Stratford, chief of his council at home.
In October he spoke in person to the Lords and Commons, but he
had no immediate success. The Commons wanted time to consult
their constituencies; and both they and the Lords united to ask for
the abolition of the *maltolt* on wool. The custom which Edward
could levy without asking for parliamentary consent went back in
origin to 1275, but Edward had far exceeded the amount to which
he was thus entitled. In January 1340 the Commons did, indeed,
make an extra grant of 30,000 sacks of wool to meet the king's needs,
but they imposed conditions which were so important that they
were sent by the council to Antwerp for the personal consideration
of the king.

Even after the contribution which the battle of Crécy made to
the king's prestige, his subjects showed that they were not willing
to tolerate any encroachment on their constitutional rights. The
attempt of the king and the greater merchants to control the custom

[1] For an illustration of the effect of these, see *The Poems of Laurence Minot* (Oxford,
2nd edition, 1897), edited by Joseph Hall, especially p. xiii.

on wool to their mutual advantage ended by 1347 with the disintegration of the 'estate' of merchants. The right of the Commons in
parliament to assent to the customs was finally established between
1340 and 1373. In 1348 the Commons not only made the grant of a
subsidy on conditions, they also asked that when a petition of theirs
had been answered by the king, the answer should not subsequently
be changed.

The same gradual establishment of enlarged constitutional claims
by the Commons is apparent in relation to military service. The
longer the French war lasted, the more clearly it became apparent
that whatever it meant to the king and the great lords, to the Commons in parliament it was an opportunity for constitutional demands.
Nor did even the victory at Poitiers and the truce of Brétigny
give Edward any long respite from the need to increase their burdens
and face their increasing demands.

The truces and negotiations which followed the victory at
Poitiers showed how illusory was the hope that England could
swallow her greater and richer neighbour, despite French disunity
and military inadequacy. At Brétigny in 1360 a draft treaty was
agreed upon by which King John's ransom was fixed, as were the
lands which Edward was to hold in full lordship. On the other
hand, Edward promised to renounce his claim to the crown of
France and to all lands not specifically ceded to him. But the renunciation and the cession were not carried out, nor was this ever very
likely. Both sides probably thought that they had conceded too
much. In any case, permanent occupation by the English of great
areas of land in Gascony, Poitou, and Calais, and its adjacent counties
was an insurmountable obstacle to a final peace. King John, after
being released by Edward, returned to England to die in captivity
in 1364; his sons who had been left as hostages with the English
king failed to honour his pledges, and he felt that his knightly
honour demanded that he return.

When the war was later resumed, the French under leaders like
Bertrand du Guesclin showed that they had learned wisdom from
misfortune and lost none of their courage in defeat. Both they and
the Scots showed the resilience and strength which the territorial
state bestowed on them as well as on the English. Until exceptional
circumstances arose the English were never able to repeat the glories
of 1346 and 1356 in spite of the great victory won by the Black
Prince at Nájera in 1367, fighting to put Pedro the Cruel on the

throne of Castile. The war with the French themselves was renewed in 1369. Instead of being an asset and a source of internal harmony in England, it became a burden and source of domestic disunity and strife. It only needed a naval disaster in 1372 brought about by the Black Prince's intervention in Spanish affairs, and the utter failure of the great *chevauchée* of 1374 by John of Gaunt his younger brother, to revive and expand the extremism in English politics which had been quiescent since 1341.

Signs of a new age of unrest had, indeed, begun as early as 1371, when Lords and Commons in parliament petitioned the king to dismiss his clerical ministers and to replace them by laymen. This was the re-assertion of an old claim of the community to influence the selection of the king's servants, a claim which, unlike that of 1311, was now fully shared by the Commons as well as by the Lords. Edward so far yielded that he dismissed Thomas Brantingham, his treasurer, and William Wykeham, bishop of Winchester, his chancellor and replaced them by laymen; and the gathering storm might have passed by if military successes could have been achieved. As it was, it broke with some violence in the famous Good Parliament of 1376.

6. THE GOOD PARLIAMENT AND EDWARD III'S OLD AGE

The Good Parliament witnessed the breakdown of Edward III's long effort at reconciliation with his subjects, and finally revealed in its fullness the weakness of his policy. The Commons led the attack on his government, as they had in 1340–1. Their attack was not made against the king, who was failing in health and engrossed with his mistress, Alice Perrers, though still universally admired; it was made against Edward's advisers and servants, William Latimer, his chamberlain, Richard Lyons, one of his financial advisers, and Alice Perrers herself.[1]

The chief innovation of the Good Parliament was Impeachment, whereby the Commons accused in a body and those who were thus indicted were given judgment by the Lords. Procedures were borrowed from Common Law, but what really mattered were the new methods of accusation and judgment. Judgment by the Lords

---

[1] This much debated question is discussed in my *Constitutional History 1216–1399*, vol. II, pp. 205–26. Recent writings on the subject are J. G. Bellamy, 'Appeal and Impeachment in The Good Parliament', *B.I.H.R.*, vol. XXXIX (1966), pp. 35–46; and G. Lambrick, 'The Impeachment of The Abbot of Abingdon in 1368' in *E.H.R.*, vol. LXXXII (April 1967), pp. 250–76.

was itself no novelty; but it had previously been a privilege which could be claimed only by the peers, not a means of punishment to be inflicted upon both commoners and lords. Indictment by the Commons in a body was an innovation which was only made possible by a growing sense of the unity of knights and burgesses, expressed by the first recorded election of a Speaker of the Commons, Sir Peter de la Mare. The new procedures paved the way for the formal enunciation of the notion of High Court of Parliament, which was to be important and conspicuous for a century, and for the notion of ministerial responsibility to the nation as well as to the monarch which marked the beginning of a new age in the history of bureaucracy.

The Commons indicted the king's servants of peculation, and voiced the suspicion that Latimer had been personally responsible for the loss of fortresses in France (actually, these had been surrendered in negotiations for peace). The trials were carried out in an atmosphere of high excitement and religious devotion which anticipated that of the Long Parliament even if it led to no comparable results. The initiative lay with the Commons, but nothing could have been achieved without the support of the Lords. From this point of view, the turning point of the whole movement of attack on the court, for this is what in effect it almost certainly was, is to be seen in the appointment on 24 May of ten or twelve lords to reinforce the existing council of the king. Without their common assent and advice, no great business was to be done. These lords of the council, thus created, were not intended to act as a brake on the king, who was at Eltham nursing his health, though chroniclers told darker tales of his activities there. It is much more probable that they were intended to override the opposition which John of Gaunt had shown from the start to the proceedings of 1376. Such an opposition was formidable indeed, for Gaunt was the most active and important of the king's sons, and was acting as his lieutenant during Edward's absence from parliament.

John of Gaunt's attitude was a tragic disappointment to the Commons, for he was head of the Lancastrian interests as well as a Plantagenet; but it is probable that his essential purpose was simply that of defending the interests of the Crown, threatened by the unprecedented procedures and claims of the Estates. He was, in fact, not able to defy the movement of the Commons, even though their accusations against the king's advisers were essentially political and were never actually proved. The knights and burgesses were probably supported by the earl of March, who allowed his Steward to be Speaker of the Commons, and by bishop William Wykeham who had the political defeat of 1371 to avenge. They may even have been encouraged by the Black Prince, whose motives are uncertain, and who in any case died in the midst of the Good Parliament's exciting events. With this support, and perhaps also widespread sympathy, the Commons and Lords were able to condemn Latimer and Lyons to imprisonment, and Alice to banishment from the royal court. Alice had been accused of receiving £2,000 or £3,000 a year from the royal treasure, of having used maintenance and bribery in the law courts, and of having brought dishonour and ill-fortune to the king and to the realm.

Though the Commons made extreme claims, they preserved a semblance of moderation by asserting that they protected the interests of a ruler who could not protect them for himself: they thus avoided a direct attack on the king's authority. John of Gaunt had wisdom enough to bow before the storm which his early arrogance provoked; but he also had power enough to undo the achievements of the Lords and Commons once they lost their collective strength through the dismissal of parliament. He undid all the acts of the parliament in a great council which was summoned in the autumn of 1376. All its leaders were punished one way or another: Peter de la Mare, for example, was thrust into Nottingham gaol. Ugly rumours were stilled by creating the Black Prince's nine-year-old son Richard prince of Wales, duke of Cornwall, and earl of Chester, and by recognizing him as his grandfather's heir. When Edward III's last parliament met in January 1377, Richard was introduced as the formal president of the assembly, and the chancellor in his opening address declared that 'No Christian king nor any lord in the land had so noble and gracious a wife or such sons . . . as the king has had. For all Christians had the king in dread, and by him and his sons the realm of England had been reformed, honoured and enriched as never before.' The royalist reaction was surprisingly easy and complete, which says much for the underlying strength of the monarchy Edward III had created. Edward himself died at Shene on 21 June 1377 after one of the longest and most glorious reigns in English history, and with his death new characters and problems entered the political scene. There began a deterioration of politics, and a slow triumph of the extremes which was not to end until the deposition of his successor in 1399.

This did not become immediately apparent. A closing of the ranks and a strengthening of unity resulted from the prospect of a dangerous minority. The Commons mentioned the boy Richard in the same breath as the Son of God. The lords seemed to be united in his support. It is true that John of Gaunt was involved in angry words with William Courtenay, bishop of London, when the latter attacked John Wyclif, Gaunt's 'ally' of 1376. In consequence, anger flared up in the streets of London; and Gaunt's arms, which were publicly displayed in Cheapside and elsewhere, were reversed as an accusation of treason. But peace, and the proper heraldic arms, were both restored, and the enemies of 1376 were all reconciled. Throughout, John proved himself conspicuously faithful to the government of Richard's minority. Many dark things have been surmised against him in relation to the government, but no concrete evidence has ever been adduced. His character remains an enigma, blackened unmercifully by his foes.

Among the many deeds which have been rightly or wrongly held against him, is his liaison with Catherine Swineford, whose sister was married to Geoffrey Chaucer; but such alliances were a commonplace in high quarters. They were one of the consequences of the *marriage de convenance*, and part of a social pattern in which high and low alike lived lives which were conspicuously lacking in restraint. Compared with his father's relations with Alice Perrers, Gaunt's liaison was decorous, almost respectable. It was exceptional in that he was faithful in his infidelity and took the trouble to legitimize and cherish his offspring, the famous Beauforts of a later age. He was probably neutral in English politics after 1377, and in 1385 turned his back on them completely whilst he pursued his claim to the throne of Castile.

Thus Edward's reign ended as it had begun in an atmosphere of crisis and failure. It is unfair to judge him, as Bishop Stubbs did, by modern standards; but the fact remains that the problems of his own age were unsolved, and in the final analysis were insoluble, by his policies. They were too complicated and too intractable for methods which were inspired rather by ideals of chivalry congenial to Froissart than by the insights and patience of a great statesman at any age. Edward gained brilliant successes by his personal virtues and his military skill. He won the love and admiration of his subjects, and a fame that carried far down into the future until obscured by the somewhat narrow idealism of the nineteenth century. But he had not quite got the breadth and depth of an Alfred or perhaps even of Elizabeth. He gained an invaluable breathing space in a troubled age, giving his country internal peace and stability and a new sense of harmony; and perhaps that was essentially what his country required. If he did not solve problems he provided material and opportunity for solutions. It is doubtful if he would himself have rated his achievement much higher. It seems certain that it should not be rated any less.

5

RICHARD II

1. ACCESSION AND MINORITY

THE reign of King Richard II began in crisis, continued in conflict, and ended in utter failure. This was not because Richard was deficient in intelligence, courage, or even in character, but because he inherited the same difficult problems as his grandfather, and because he himself was lacking in precisely the qualities he most needed and which his grandfather fortunately had. Above all, he proved to be no warrior king and man of well-considered action such as his subjects admired and as was demanded by the needs of the time. His intellectual gifts did not include the realism which his father and grandfather both possessed. He would have liked to be, like them, a true *preux chevalier*; but instead of the instincts of the warrior he possessed only the more exotic and less popular qualities of the aesthete, loving art, literature, and music, and the pleasures of the mind. His true emblem was the handkerchief he adopted, not the sword which he never successfully employed.

Richard was the son of a great general, Edward the Black Prince, and a great beauty, Joan the 'Fair Maid of Kent'. He had been born at Bordeaux on 6 January 1367, and his education had been supervised by two knights of the Garter, Sir Guichard d'Angle and Sir Simon Burley. His reign, which began on 21 June 1377, the day his grandfather died, thus opened with a minority, the third since the death of King John. Like its predecessors, it was a time of danger and crisis, not lessened by the fact that the French marked the occasion by plundering the south coast of the kingdom from Plymouth to Rye. Thomas Walsingham had no doubt his reasons for proclaiming the day of Richard's coronation as one 'of joy and gladness . . . the long-awaited day of the renewal of peace and of the laws of the land, long exiled by the weakness of an aged king and the greed of his courtiers and servants'[1]; but he must have been aware of the weight of the burden that would fall on the shoulders of the precocious boy who had inherited his grandfather's mantle, and must have questioned Richard's ability to succeed where even the great Edward at the finish had failed.

Richard's coronation was celebrated with great pomp and dignity, and was the first recorded occasion to include the appearance of the king's champion, in the person of Sir John Dimoke; but though Richard's claim to succeed by hereditary right was emphasized in the ceremony, his royal powers were obviously in some danger of being undermined. Yet the reign began with signs of harmony. Gaunt behaved, as indeed might have been expected, with loyalty and with some restraint. He was reconciled to the Londoners and the bishop of Winchester. Peter de la Mare was pardoned and released. The duke presided assiduously over his nephew's coronation, and walked beside Richard to Westminster carrying the sword *Curtana*. The occasion was one to mark the ending of old quarrels and suspicions; and harmony was strengthened shortly afterwards when Gaunt made a spectacular declaration of his loyalty to the king.

But such harmony did not and perhaps could not continue. There was a vacuum of power which too many were anxious to fill. Nor were tempers cooled by the continuing failures of the French war, notably John of Gaunt's repulse by the French from St. Malo, or by the necessary arrangement of a council of regency dominated by lords, which ensured a secure succession to the throne but could not fail to increase the ambitions of the magnates, already inflated by the needs of the French war and the conciliatory policies of Edward III.

The Peasants' Revolt which occurred in June 1381 produced a crisis which temporarily united most of the aristocracy in support of the established order; but it probably helped in the end to broaden the gap between Richard and his magnates. Its causes were both political and economic: on the one hand, disappointment and frustration at the failures of the French war and the inability of the Commons to achieve ambitious reforms in the Good Parliament; on the other, peasant discontent shown in demands for the abolition of villeinage, and resentment at taxation especially the poll taxes, so that one rebel demand was for no further impositions 'save the

[1] *Chronicon Angliae* (R.S. 1874), p. 155.

fifteenths which their fathers knew and accepted'. An important area of discontent was in Essex and Kent; but the rising would have been much less serious but for the support it received from the mass of the Londoners.[1] Nor was the discontent confined to London and the south-east. Other, minor, insurrections occurred as far away as Norfolk, Winchester, and York. Wherever they occurred, the risings of 1381 were not caused simply by oppression and despair. On the contrary, an important cause in many areas is to be found in expanding ambitions and hopes.

By 5 June the men of Kent and Essex were on the move. The beginnings of the revolt were unorganized and were apparently provoked by the misdeeds of royal commissioners in Essex and by the actions of John Legge, a royal serjeant at arms, in Kent. But it had been fomented by agitators like the famous John Ball, with his deeply significant rhetoric:

> When Adam dalf and Eve span
> Who was thanne the gentilman?

The aristocratic Froissart was keenly interested in the movement and put eloquent words into John Ball's mouth:

> Good people, things cannot go well in England, nor will they until all goods shall be in common and there shall be neither villeins nor gentles, but we shall all be one. Why should he, whom we call lord, be a greater master than us? . . . They have ease and beautiful manors, and we have hardship and work, and the rain and the wind in the fields; and it is through us and our labour that they have the wherewithal to maintain their estate.

Cryptic messages had been in circulation warning of the approaching hour, and there may have been liaison between the discontented in London and those of the countryside.

As the revolt progressed, the rebels from Essex and from Kent banded together, though they preserved their own identities and organization. They were mainly peasants, but there was a smattering of others, including one or two knights. The numbers of those who revolted are impossible to tell. They were large enough to deter those in authority from an attempt, after the early stages of the revolt, simply to crush it by force. The magnates who were in or near London would not advise a direct military attack on the rebels, especially after the entry into the city, and other ways of dealing with the movement had accordingly to be found.

[1] See my 'Peasants' Revolt in 1381', in *Speculum*, vol. XV (January 1940), 5pp. 12–3.

The Kentishmen moved to Rochester, Maidstone and Canterbury. In the cathedral, they interrupted Mass to cry out to the monks, bidding them elect one of themselves as archbishop, for the present head of the Church, Simon Sudbury the Chancellor of England, was a traitor who would soon be beheaded. On 11 June the Kentishmen and men of Essex began their march on London. By this time they had elected an obscure but capable individual named Wat Tyler as their leader. On their way they sent word to Richard, who had taken refuge in the Tower, that they were coming to destroy the traitors around him and to save him, and that they wished to speak with him at Blackheath.

Richard was too young to make decisions for himself in such a crisis; his general policy was probably dictated by an inner council, including the chancellor, Archbishop Sudbury and the treasurer, Sir Robert Hales. It seems probable that it was as a result of their advice that the government adopted a policy towards the rebels which was compounded of conciliation and deceit, and that this policy was accepted by the magnates, even though it involved some frightening experiences for the king.

On Thursday 13 June Richard was rowed down the river, presumably in order to land and parley with the rebels; but his advisers at the last moment forbade him to leave the royal barge. In consequence, the peasants forced their way into the city, helped by sympathizers within, and without having to fight. According to Froissart they found the gates of the city closed; but the commons of London, many of whom were in agreement with them, gathered together and asked: 'Why are these good people not allowed to enter the city? They are our people, and all that they do is for us.' With this view of the part played by the common people of London almost every contemporary chronicle agrees.

The commoners were urged on by so-called 'traitorous' aldermen, notably Sibley and Horne; but these were never punished for their deeds, and perhaps for a very good reason. They were responsible for much that followed after the rebels got access into the city; but they were not therefore traitors to the king. The rebels themselves were profoundly loyal to Richard. Their watchword was 'wyth whom holdes yow?', with the reply 'wyth kynge Richard and the trew communes'. Their discipline contrasted sharply with that of the Jacquerie in France. To punish the aldermen who sympathized with and encouraged them would have involved a condemnation of very many of their fellow-citizens, something the London jurors of 1381 greatly wished to avoid.

Once they had gained entry the rebels burned houses belonging to those whom they regarded as harmful to the king, including Chester's Inn which was the bishop of Lichfield's palace where John Fordham, keeper of the privy seal was living, and where they helped themselves to the episcopal liquor. They also sacked John of Gaunt's splendid new palace, the Savoy, and burned it to the ground, forbidding plunder in the destruction of the property of one whom they disliked above all on public and political grounds.

John of Gaunt himself was absent in the north during the insurrection. Alarmed by the news that reached him from the south, he asked Henry Percy, earl of Northumberland, if he might seek safety in Bamburgh Castle, but was refused. As a result, he retreated to Edinburgh to the protection of the Scots. Richard's advisers in London strongly condemned Percy's act, but it reveals clearly the extent of the hostility which Gaunt had aroused.

Nevertheless, the rising of 1381 was caused by much more than hatred of John of Gaunt or even local discontent in Essex, Kent, and London. There were many other local grievances. The prior of Dunstable was forced to concede a charter to his villeins. In Winchester the craftsmen rose against the authorities. At York, Scarborough and Beverley the unrest was that of townsmen not of peasants. At St. Albans William Grindcob organized a contingent of rebels to go to London. He also ran riot over the estates of the abbey, and forced the abbot Thomas de la Mare to seal a deed of manumission. At Bury St. Edmunds, John Wrawe and his followers pillaged houses and the church of Cavendish, and carried the head of the king's chief justice, Sir John Cavendish, into the city on a pike. They executed the prior of the abbey, whom they found hiding in a wood, and they extorted a deed of manumission from the subprior.

There were similar risings in Cambridgeshire, where the peasants beheaded Sir Edmund Walsingham, a justice of the peace, and made an attack on Cambridge University. Corpus Christi College was sacked and burned. Records of the university were destroyed in the public square, and its privileges were surrendered to the town. One of the best known leaders of revolt was Geoffrey Litster, who led his followers into the town and castle of Norwich, where he banqueted in state waited on by captive knights, two of whom he sent to London to get him a pardon from the king. He was eventually suppressed by Henry Despenser, bishop of Norwich, who had defended Peterborough abbey against the rebels and now captured Litster at North Walsham, shrived him, and executed him on the spot.

Meanwhile, in London, after a series of crises, the rebellion eventually died away. Wat Tyler and his followers opened the prison and beheaded a number of lawyers and Flemings, but they had, and could have, no constructive ideas. From the Tower, Richard could see the flames spreading. The time for a meeting with the rebels had clearly arrived. Accordingly, Richard designated the time and place as Mile End at seven o'clock on the following day.

The decision involved some dangers for Richard but more for the ministers whose heads had been demanded. The chances that they might flee from the Tower whilst attention was distracted were small. Once at Mile End, Richard would be a hostage in the hands of the rebels. The Tower could not be defended without putting his life in danger. Nor was it likely that the peasants would leave an avenue of escape unguarded. Sudbury and Hales must have known all these things, yet they may well have concurred in Richard's decision; the king was not later accused of having thrown his chief ministers to the wolves. On the whole, it seems probable that he knew better than the author of the *Anonimalle Chronicle* the debt he and England owed them, although it was one which posterity never recognized.

The interview at Mile End did, in fact, cost the two prelates their lives. As was to be expected, a contingent of rebels gained access to the Tower. There, the ministers awaited their fate; an effort by the archbishop to escape had been thwarted by an over-observant and over-curious woman. Sudbury and a few others were dragged out of the Tower and executed. Their heads were paraded through the city and afterwards set up on Tower Hill. Meanwhile at Mile End Wat Tyler and his followers knelt before the young ruler crying 'Welcome King Richard: we wish for no other king but you'; but they also demanded the heads of traitors, the abolition of villeinage, and land at fourpence an acre. The king granted all their requests, except that he only conceded the punishment of traitors by law. He endured some private fears and subscribed to some public duplicity, but he had the satisfaction of witnessing the first successes of the policy which Sudbury and Hales had prescribed.

After Mile End, some rebels did indeed disperse; but many

persisted in their assembly, and it was found necessary to concede still another meeting between them and the king, this time at Smithfield. Here, their demands were extreme, bordering on the fantastic. They included requests for the abolition of lordship in England, and for the confiscation of the estates of the Church. It is doubtful if Wat Tyler expected such demands to be taken seriously. He behaved with insolence, especially by toying with a dagger in the presence of his king. He used insulting words to members of Richard's entourage. Finally, the interview was terminated by William Walworth who, helped by a squire named Standish, mortally wounded Tyler, apparently goaded beyond endurance by what he saw and heard.

This act nearly brought disaster to the king, and it is almost impossible to believe that the murder was actually plotted by Walworth and the courtiers, as has been supposed. It is much easier to think that Wat did not want a royal policy of conciliation to succeed. In any case the rebels drew their bows and got ready to attack. Nor is there anything to show that any plans had been made to deal with such a crisis. Richard himself saved the situation. He spurred his horse forward and demanded of the rebels 'Sirs, will you shoot your king? I am your captain, follow me.' At this juncture William Walworth, who was later knighted for his actions, made his somewhat ill-timed ride *ventre à terre* back to London. Against all reasonable calculations, the help he obtained there was sufficient and in time. The rebels finally dispersed, and their great revolt was ended save for the dreary business of enquiry and punishment which, it must be said, was performed without conspicuous cruelty.

The formidable and surprisingly orderly revolt accomplished virtually none of its immediate aims, but left a deep mark on the memory of contemporaries. It was, indeed, a landmark in the political, if not the economic, evolution of the common people. It marked the beginning of the 'rising' as an important factor in English public life. It was far more than a movement of agrarian discontents. The actions of the Londoners show how significant were the broader causes of the unrest and how closely they were related to events in Westminster and London between 1370 and 1380. The whole movement shows a new ambition and an enlarged political consciousness in classes hitherto largely outside the periphery of political life, combined with an ancient tradition of common action by the community of the shire.

For Richard, despite his great moment at Smithfield, the rising proved on the whole to be something of a disaster. It cannot have failed to imprint on his mind an exalted notion of his importance in the eyes of his subjects, especially those in humbler stations whom he rarely encountered. It has been observed that their astonishing readiness to accept him as their captain after Wat Tyler was heady flattery for his self-esteem. On the other hand, the course of events may have given him an exaggerated notion of the value of duplicity. His reply to the Essex men who asked after the revolt for a ratification of the promises made at Mile End is well known: 'Villeins ye are', he said, 'and villeins ye shall remain.' His betrayal of trust, however necessary, was an unfortunate beginning to a reign which was always to be overshadowed by duplicity and mistrust.

Many other circumstances of these early years combined to deny to the young Richard any real chance of recreating the harmony which had been achieved by Edward III. One scandal which reveals the underlying tension of his first years involved two obscure squires, Robert Hawley and John Shakell, who were in dispute with Lancaster over the ransom of an important Spanish prisoner, and who had been imprisoned. In the summer of 1378 they escaped to sanctuary at Westminster but were pursued by the Constable of the Tower. In dragging them from the abbey, a sacristan was slain and Hawley was murdered on the steps of the altar. The crisis which arose involved John of Gaunt who had claimed the prisoners, William Courtenay bishop of London who had denounced the act of the Constable, and John Wyclif who by inference defended it; and it led to dire threats by Gaunt against the bishop who had declared excommunication against violators of sanctuary. Altogether, the scandal greatly discredited the whole government. The episode was of no lasting importance; but it shows how tempers were on edge and how uneasy were the times.

During all the years of minority, a council of regency dominated for the most part by lords ruled the king and the kingdom. It was not popular; in January 1380 the Commons showed their distrust of the régime by asking that the lords of the council be discharged and that Richard be permitted to rule with only the advice of his chief ministers; but such a request was quite unrealistic. Both tradition and precedent supported the claim of the great lords to have the responsibility of government in the minority or incapacity of the king, and the Peasants' Revolt made no difference in this situation.

In the following November the lords appointed Richard, earl of Arundel, and Sir Michael de la Pole to counsel the king and govern his person; and though Richard was already beginning to evade such restrictions on his freedom, they could not be openly defied.

Another element of discord was provided by the fiasco of a crusade led in 1383 by the fighting bishop of Norwich who had distinguished himself against Geoffrey Litster and his peasants. The purpose of the crusade was to strike a blow for the 'English' pope Urban VI and against his opponent in the Great Schism (which had begun in 1378), the 'French' Pope Clement VII. The project was essentially aimed against France; its main purpose was to regain English predominance in Flanders. It was passionately advocated by Bishop Despenser, not only as a notable service to God and the true succession to the throne of St. Peter, but also as an alternative to John of Gaunt's proposal to attack France through Spain in pursuance of his claims to the throne of Castile. For both projects Pope Urban had promised a plenary remission of sins. Gaunt had the support of the king and the lords, but Despenser caught the ear of the common people. In the end the debate was largely decided when the French defeated the Flemings at Roosebeke on 27 November 1382. As a result of this battle Charles VI and the duke of Burgundy were able to enter Bruges, seize the goods of English merchants, and order the cessation of commercial relations with England, dealing a heavy blow at the whole English wool trade as well as intimidating all potential allies.

Against this disaster the crusade proposed by Despenser seemed to offer a cheap remedy. It could be financed by the offerings of the people. It would drain French troops from the south where they threatened Gascony and Spain. It might restore the Anglo-Flemish alliance fatally damaged by the battle of Roosebeke. Yet, in spite of these arguments, the idea of such a crusade was both cynical and dangerous. Religious fanaticism could not be channelled and harnessed to political needs as easily as Despenser seemed to believe. The more experienced magnates were lukewarm and sceptical. The strongest support of the idea came in the end from the Commons, who were blinded by specious argument and the appeal of parsimony. Lay magnates were excluded from the leadership of the proposed expedition. Altogether, it is clear, the Crusade was launched in a mood of near-hysteria. Despenser himself took command, and though he was a man of enterprise and force and had fought in Italy, he was no strategist or even tactician. The failure of his emotionally inspired and half-trained army was almost certain from the start.

The army left England on 16 May, despite a last-minute attempt by the king to prevent it from sailing, and bogged down ignominiously in an ill-advised siege of Ypres. When Philip of Burgundy came to the support of the city, Despenser beat a hasty retreat. He returned with his disordered followers to face the bitter anger of his disillusioned countrymen. In the autumn parliament of 1383 he was actually 'impeached' in the presence of the king himself, now sixteen years old. Whether or not, as has been suggested, the government wished to 'capture' the new procedure of impeachment which had been used against it in 1376,[1] the king and his advisers clearly wished to dissociate themselves from the recent fiasco; though Despenser suffered no more than the deprival of his temporalities for two years, and most of his captains were imprisoned for only a very short time. The whole episode provides a sorry contrast to the well organized and successful expeditions against France which had marked the reign of Edward III.

The failure of Despenser opened the way for Gaunt's proposal to attack France *via* Spain; but before this attack could be organized there were further signs of deteriorating domestic politics. In a stormy parliament of April 1384, when Arundel complained of misgovernment, Richard told him to go to the devil. Shortly afterwards a Carmelite friar named John Latimer told the king, after a celebration of Mass, that Gaunt was plotting his murder, and Richard showed some inclination to believe the story, incredible though it would seem. But on the friar's way to custody, pending further investigation, he was seized by a band of knights, who were mainly Lancastrian, and cruelly tortured to death. Thomas of Woodstock was so incensed by the whole episode that he broke into the king's room and swore there that he would slay anyone, including Richard himself, who accused his brother of Lancaster of treason. Finally, it may be recorded that when the archbishop of Canterbury remonstrated with the king about his choice of advisers the latter drew his sword and made as if to strike Courtenay through the heart.

It is probable, though this is debatable,[2] that Richard and his

---

[1] See T. F. T. Plucknett, 'State Trials under Richard II' in *Trans. Royal Hist. Soc.*, 5th series, vol. II (1952), pp. 159–71; Margaret Aston, 'The Impeachment of Bishop Despenser', in *B.I.H.R.*, vol. XXXVIII (1965), pp. 127–48.

[2] The problems are discussed by A. Steel, *Richard II* (Cambridge 1941), e.g. pp. 106, 117.

advisers made a fateful decision in these years by showing themselves lukewarm to the counsels and assistance of the duke of Lancaster who had upheld the royal cause in 1376 and 1377. They now lost his services for an indefinite period by endorsing his expedition to Spain, a decision nearly as shortsighted as their support of Despenser's crusade. Gaunt's claim to the throne of Castile was through his marriage to Constance, elder daughter and co-heiress of Pedro the Cruel. It had become urgent when Henry of Trastamara died in 1379, and when the king of Portugal refused to recognize his successor and appealed to the English for aid. In August 1385 John of Avis made this appeal almost irresistible when he won the battle of Albujarotta, finally gained the crown of Portugal, and repeated the invitation for Lancaster to give Portugal his support. The duke now had the prospect of a valuable ally in his effort to establish his claim to Castile. In these circumstances it really seemed possible that he might establish English power in the Iberian peninsula as a formidable threat to France in the south. He might even compel the French to seek a reasonable peace and free England from the burden of a war which had plainly turned against her. This was all the more necessary since Richard showed in 1385, the fateful year of decision, that he was quite incapable of following in the footsteps of Edward III. He led a great army against Scotland, France's ally in the north; but he achieved nothing, seeming to justify Walsingham's gibe that his courtiers were far less expert on the battlefield than in bed. Nor was there much hope of a better understanding between Gaunt and his nephew. On the contrary, discord reached such a pitch that Gaunt felt compelled at one point to take refuge in his castle at Pontefract, provisioned and garrisoned for war.

Hence it is not surprising that on 8 March 1386 Richard II in full council recognized John as King of Castile. On 9 July the duke sailed from Plymouth harbour, leaving Richard to his own ambitions, his extravagances, and the counsel and friendship of his confidants, especially Robert de Vere. From the point of view of England, Gaunt's foray was quite unsuccessful. But it was not entirely unrealistic, and Gaunt himself did very well out of it. In the end he married one daughter, Philippa, to the king of Portugal and another, Catherine, to the heir to Castile. He got for himself the payment of £100,000 and an annual pension of £6,000. In return, he renounced

---

[1] But Gaunt has been strongly criticized by P. E. Russell in *The English Intervention in Spain and Portugal in the Time of Edward III and Richard II* (Oxford 1955), pp. 523–5.

his claim to Castile. It was not a bad bargain.[1] Unfortunately it kept him from England until November 1389, and meanwhile irreparable damage was done to the relations between Richard and the baronage at home.

By 1385 the bitter conflicts and antagonisms of Edward II's reign had been fully revived. It became crystal clear that the long reign of Edward III had only shelved, not solved, the clash of political ideas which had contributed so much to Edward II's 'martyrdom'; and that Richard's minority was promoting discords similar to those which had long ago resulted from the aggressive policy of the young Henry III. The chroniclers turned against him. They thought that he was 'greedy of glory'. Thomas of Walsingham had asked, as early as the end of 1381, what profit was there in writing down statutes in parliament when the king in his secret council kept changing all that had been determined not only by the Commons but also by the Lords.

Alienated from his 'natural' advisers, Richard was committed to rule through such men as Sir Simon Burley and Sir Michael de la Pole, together with Robert de Vere, earl of Oxford. He turned in upon himself and exploited his 'regality'. He stressed pomp and majesty, making his courtiers kneel before him, and turning away from the intimacy and familiarity which had in the main served his ancestors well. In this he did but follow a trend of his times. Kings everywhere used their courts to enhance their dignity and power, just as courts reflected the growth of their majesty. Richard's essential misjudgment lay in his inability to refrain from excess. And if the course he followed was ultimately fatal to himself it was also disastrous to his intimates whom contemporaries, followed by some modern writers, made the scapegoats of his indiscretion. When the king confiscated the property of some Londoners, Walsingham records, justly or unjustly, that the courtiers fell on it like harpies. They were, he recorded bitterly elsewhere, more devoted to Venus than Bellona. All the court became suspect. When in 1385 Richard planned his great expedition against the Scots, he was credited by the lords with ulterior designs, and it was partly because his campaign was lukewarmly supported that it so miserably failed.

2. The Struggle for Power

The storm broke immediately after Gaunt's departure, in the parliament of October 1386. The immediate cause was the threat of invasion from France and lack of faith in Richard's ability to organize a defence, but deeper causes are also apparent. The king proposed to go in person against France, requested a heavy subsidy, and announced the title of duke of Ireland for Robert de Vere. The Lords and Commons, for their part, demanded the dismissal of both the chancellor, Michael de la Pole, and the treasurer, John Fordham, bishop of Durham. The issue was squarely joined when the king replied that he would not, on their account, 'move the least boy of his kitchen'. His sharp tongue may have again betrayed him; but the exact form of words was not important. What mattered was that Richard's subjects had revived the old notion of expanded participation in government by the subjects, and that this had been contemptuously refused. The issue had been presented before, in November 1383, when the lords accused Richard of depending on foolish advice and suggested that they themselves bore the weight of government On that occasion Richard had warily and discreetly rejected their advice.[1] Now, he was not prepared to be conciliatory, and each side was committed to a position from which there was no obvious line of retreat.

Thomas Woodstock, the king's uncle, and Thomas Arundel, bishop of Ely (brother of Richard, earl of Arundel and Surrey), bore the request of the subjects to Eltham, speaking in the name of all the community of parliament; they quoted an 'ancient statute' to justify the threat that, if Richard did not attend the assembly in person, it might dissolve itself without voting any supplies.[2] The king's angry reply once more revealed the depth of the quarrel; he accused Lords and Commons of plotting against him, and threatened to seek aid from the king of France. The envoys, thoroughly provoked, threw caution to the winds and revealed that the Estates did not shrink from thought of deposition if the king refused to be governed by the laws of the realm and the advice of his lords. This was only another form of the old threat of violence set forth in the Declaration of 1308, and now brought up to date. It was enough to break Richard's resistance. He returned to parliament; and the process of Impeachment which had been used in 1376, though not formally proclaimed, could now be directed against the king's advisers without further open opposition. It proved to be a weapon

---

[1] My *Constitutional History 1216–1339*, vol. II, p. 230.
[2] It is not easy to see bishop Arundel as the great mediator as he seems to be presented in Margaret Aston's *Thomas Arundel* (Oxford 1967), pp. 164, 343.

not only against royal ministers but also against the whole fabric of royal authority. Thus by 1386 the old extremism of 1308–1326 had been fully and tragically revived.

Seven charges were laid against Michael de la Pole, accusing him of 'many frauds and certain betrayals of the king'. Three of them were maintained, all political rather than criminal; and Michael was condemned to fine and imprisonment. Since his gaoler was his friend Sir Simon Burley, and he was able to provide entertainment in his captivity for no less a person than the king, his punishment though spectacular was hardly severe. But this did not lessen its significance. Not only had the king's resistance been broken, but also the responsibility of the king's ministers to the Estates, calling themselves the community of parliament, had been successfully asserted. 'The parliament of 1386 dramatically showed what the passage of time had done to the greatest institution of the State, which in 1322 had been claimed by the monarch as subject to his influence. However these achievements appeared to the reformers, they must have seemed to the king's supporters like a direct and inescapable challenge to the royal power.'[1]

Richard's humiliation was completed by the appointment of a council to hold office for a year, dominated by lords and described by Henry Knighton as having the government of all the realm. The king was now nearly twenty: Henry III's minority had ended when he was nineteen; Edward III's when he was seventeen. As a ruler entitled to his full authority, Richard made no secret of his resentment and fears; he protested *in pleno parliamento* that 'on account of anything done in the said parliament, he was unwilling that prejudice be incurred by himself or his crown'. Moreover, it was plain that though he had lost a battle he did not believe he had lost a war. Defeated in parliament, he appealed to the whole community of his people. In 1387 he went off on an unprecedented 'gyration' through the midlands and the north, seeking to raise popular support. He recruited archers in Chester and north Wales, retaining them in his service with badges of golden crowns. He asked many sheriffs if they could raise forces for him in the shires and influence parliamentary elections there, only to be told that all the commons favoured the lords. He obtained a promise from the Londoners to stand by him as his royal majesty demanded.[2] Finally, by propounding a famous

[1] My *Constitutional History 1216–1399*, vol. II, p. 63.
[2] Ranulph Higden's *Polychronicon*, edited by J. R. Lumby (R.S.. 1886), vol. IX, p. 104.

set of questions, he received a condemnation from his leading judges, at Shrewsbury and Nottingham, of the ideas and actions of the opposition in 1386.

The judges agreed that the commission set up in the last parliament derogated from the king's prerogative, and that those who had procured it, or even advised the king to accept it, deserved to be punished by death. Those who had compelled Richard to make it should be punished as traitors; and so also should those who in other ways prevented the exercise of the king's regality and prerogative. The king, the judges agreed, ought to determine the business of a parliament, not the Lords and Commons; and it lay in his power to dissolve parliament at his will. Similarly, the king had the control of his servants, who were not to be impeached by his subjects. Nor did the judges fail to condemn similarly the revival of old 'statutes' against the king and the judgment on Michael de la Pole.

Richard thus, in his turn, went to extremes; but it must be admitted that he had received extreme provocation. He could claim that nearly all the offences listed in 1387 were those of 'accroaching the royal power' which had always been an unforgivable crime. Accroaching, which means drawing to oneself the royal power, had been held to be treason in 21 Edward III, in the case of a knight of Hertfordshire who assaulted and detained one of the king's subjects till he paid him £90. The king's action could be defended on the ground that the statute of 1352 ought to be widened to meet changing conditions, though it is fairly obvious that this should have been done by agreement in parliament, not by the king and his judges alone. The action of 1387 is perhaps the first unmistakable proof of the harshness with which Richard would have pursued this struggle if he had obtained a clear advantage. It was one of the things which put the opposition, in spite of their mistakes and excesses, on the side of liberty.[1]

The king was irresistible in public debate; but though his subjects might applaud him they would not give him reliable support. It was tragically misleading that on his return to London in November he was greeted like a victor home from the wars. When the earl of Arundel, the duke of Gloucester, and Thomas Beauchamp, earl of Warwick, issued circular letters of propaganda, the Londoners told Richard they would fight against his enemies but not against his

---

[1] My *Constitutional History 1216–1399*, vol. II, p. 238.

friends. Sir Ralph Basset protested his loyalty; but he declined to risk his neck for the sake of the duke of Ireland (Robert de Vere had been given the unprecedented title of marquis of Dublin in 1385 and that of duke of Ireland in 1386). Despite Richard's efforts, public opinion had not really been won over. The three lords could, with impunity, 'appeal' (formally accuse) the king's friends and servants on 14 November at Waltham Cross, and demand their trial in parliament; and Richard had no option but to agree.

The fact that Richard and the three Appellants retired to drink in apparent amity in the king's chamber should not obscure the more important fact that another great crisis had arisen. Nor could this be averted by the escape, with Richard's obvious connivance, of most of those who had been accused; indeed, this so enraged some of the lords that they wished to depose their devious king on the spot. Nor did an attempt at armed resistance by Robert de Vere achieve anything, except to prove that at least one of Richard's friends had spirit enough to dare, if not to die, in his cause. In point of fact, Robert did not even come near to dying. He gathered Cheshire levies and advanced towards London, but his forces were trapped at Radcote Bridge and dispersed, just before Christmas 1387, escaping in a thick December fog,[1] though a good many were lost in the marshes and some were despoiled by the forces of the Appellants. De Vere swam across the river to safety, discarding most of his armour. The only result of importance from this episode was that the three Appellants were now joined by Henry of Derby (Bolingbroke), son of Gaunt, and Thomas Mowbray, earl of Nottingham.

There was no doubt about the extremism of the opposition which now faced Richard: it was ready and eager to trample his royal pretensions in the dust. Before parliament met, the Appellants beat Richard into submission by a threat of deposition. They actually withdrew their homage for a time, and might have deposed their king altogether if they could have agreed on a successor. The assembly which Richard was forced to call met on 3 February 1388, and soon became known as the Merciless Parliament. The formalities of its opening presented an entirely misleading picture of royal majesty, with the king sitting in state on his throne flanked by his loyal peers. The real sovereigns of England appeared in the shape

---

[1] This is according to one modern writer. Another has it that Robert escaped 'in the falling dusk'. The chroniclers are not clear on the point (*Polychronicon Ranulphi Higden*, edited by J. R. Lumby, R.S. 1886, IX, 112; *Chronicon Henrici Knighton*, edited by J. R. Lumby, R.S. 1895, p. 254).

of the five Lords Appellant, arm-in-arm before the crowded assembly dressed in cloth of gold, kneeling before their ruler and protesting that they had never thought or imagined the death of their king. It took two hours after this for Geoffrey Martin, clerk of the crown, to read out on their behalf thirty-nine articles of accusation against Suffolk and de Vere and three others, 'reading rapidly, in the midst of parliament'. It is recorded that the hearts of some who heard were struck with sorrow and the faces of others were swollen with tears; but few can have been as desolate or distraught as the young king who sat lonely upon his throne, and wore his hollow crown, and witnessed the destruction of his dearest friends.

Legal obstruction of the proceedings was tried and found unavailing. Judges were consulted, who declared that the procedure adopted was not upheld by the Common Law of England or the Civil Law of Rome; but the Lords declared that the Court of Parliament was supreme and could make its own procedures and laws. Armed with this new definition of the parliamentary assembly the lords condemned Michael and his associates as traitors, exposing them to the extreme penalties of a barbarous execution and forfeiture of their estates. As in 1376 and 1386 the offences were essentially political; they included that of accroaching the king's power and taking advantage of his youth. Richard's advisers, it was claimed, had made him follow evil counsel, and give *signa* or emblems to his followers such as had been given by no previous king. The Appeal was merciless and the conclusion foregone, but there was more behind them than private vengeance and lynch law.[1] If the accused did not get justice, they nevertheless got the forms of justice, administered by the highest court in the land.

Nicholas Brembre was the only one of those appealed who was immediately available; the others were in hiding or had escaped. He was produced in parliament and offered to defend himself by battle 'as a knight should do'. The king tried to protect him, but there was a furious clamour. The Appellants threw down their gages of battle and others followed suit till the descending gloves looked 'like a fall of snow'. A committee of twelve peers did not find anything to make Brembre deserving of death; but strong pressure by the Appellants eventually got this opinion reversed. Meanwhile, the former chief justice Tresilian was discovered in

---

[1] Conflicting opinions are discussed in my *Constitutional History of England 1216–1399*, vol. II, pp. 252–69.

hiding. As he had already been condemned in his absence, he was dragged on a hurdle to Tyburn and there put to death. On the following day Brembre, too, suffered a similar fate.

Robert de Vere had been smuggled overseas, having reached London after Radcote Bridge, it is said, disguised as a groom; but Sir Simon Burley had been captured and put in Nottingham castle. He was now tried, together with three other familiars of the king. Burley was widely respected and almost certainly innocent of any wrongdoing. He had powerful friends. Henry Derby wished to save him, as did the duke of York and the earl of Nottingham. Queen Anne pleaded in vain on her knees before Arundel. In the end, Simon and the others were condemned to be hanged, drawn, and quartered, though Richard did his old adviser a last small service by commuting this to simple beheading. Finally, at the prayer of the Commons, the Appellants were granted the sum of £20,000 to requite them for their expenses in destroying the traitors and saving the realm.

It is easy to describe their conduct in the harshest terms, but perhaps this does not do them full justice. Hatreds there were in plenty. Men were literally playing the game of politics for their lives. But they were playing it on the stage of parliament. All England in a sense was looking on, and despite appearances to the contrary Englishmen were not entirely indifferent to deeper questions of right and wrong. Beneath the formal procedures was not only a clash of personalities and the vendetta of puzzled and vindictive men, but also the question of sovereign power in England and how it should be exercised. Richard believed that he was defending the essence of his regality; a supporter warned him that if he did not fight back he would be in danger of becoming the shadow of a king. The lords believed that what was at issue was their ancient right to share in the government of the realm.

When it was all over, the king renewed his coronation promise[1] and the subjects their homage; but there could be no return to the harmony of 1377. The king had been humiliated, but his inherent powers had not in fact been destroyed. A small group headed by the bishops of London and Winchester was appointed during the parliament, with no terminal date, to be continually attendant on him, and it was decreed that nothing was to be done without their

[1] Perhaps, though not very likely, simply because as suggested by Thomas of Favent, Richard had been a minor when he took the oath in 1377; *Historia Mirabilis Parliamenti*, edited by M. McKisack (Camb. Misc., vol. XIV, 1926), p. 24.

consent[1]; but this could not prevent him from sooner or later continuing the struggle. Whatever outward forms were preserved, the harmony of politics which Edward I had at one time achieved, and Edward III had restored, had now been completely destroyed.

3. THE ROYALIST REACTION

On 3 May 1389 Richard suddenly entered the council house and asked the magnates his age. On being assured that he was in his twenty-second year, he claimed the rule of his household and his kingdom, including the free appointment of his councillors.

> You know well [he said] that for twelve years of my reign I and my realm have been ruled by others, and my people oppressed year by year with grievous taxes. Henceforth, with God's help, I shall labour assiduously to bring my realm to greater peace and prosperity. Up to now I have been allowed to do nothing without my protectors. Now, I will remove all of these men from my council, summon to advise me whomsoever I will, and transact my own business myself. I therefore order as first step that the chancellor shall surrender to me the seal.[2]

He made token changes, and for the time seemed to be content.[3] In January 1390 he modified the designation of the members of his council, in what T. F. Tout considered as a curious comedy, but by which he seems to have deprived the lords of the council, except Lancaster and Gloucester, of any exceptional powers. All this was significant, but it was, and had to be, only the beginning of a royal restoration. There was no halfway house in the journey which Richard had begun. Peace was maintained, not because either side was satisfied, but because Richard was content to bide his time and was careful not to give the magnates an obvious occasion for a revival of the coalition of 1388.

Indeed, there were signs of willingness to compromise, perhaps helped by the return to England of John of Gaunt in 1389. In February 1392 the king promised not to recall his exiled ministers, whilst the lords promised to stand by him and allow him full power to reign. But this still made Richard a king by sufferance, saddled with the memory of a deep wrong and humiliation; and there is little doubt that he was far from satisfied. Shortly before this, in November 1391, he had welcomed, if he did not initiate, a parliamentary

---

[1] Higden, *Polychronicon*, vol. IX, p. 178.
[2] Quoted by T. F. Tout, *Chapters in the Administrative History of Medieval England*, vol. III, p. 454.
[3] *Rot. Parl.*, vol. III, p. 258. The problem is discussed in my 'Fact and Fancy in Fifteenth-Century English History' in *Speculum*, vol. XLII (October 1967), pp. 673–92.

petition which asked that he be held as free in his regality as his predecessors. He was so warm in protestation of friendship to his lords, 'by whose *nobilitas* the diadem of our nobility is chiefly honoured and sustained',[1] that Sir Thomas Talbot rebelled in Cheshire to save him from such friends as Lancaster and Gloucester; but his true feelings were more probably revealed when he struck the earl of Arundel to the ground in Westminster Abbey for being late at the funeral of his queen, Anne of Bohemia, polluting the Abbey with blood.

He soon seems to have set a deliberate and uncompromising course towards absolutism as the sure and final answer to his political problems. To achieve this end, he consolidated his powers by many and varied means. He sought glory and military experience by an expedition in 1394 to Ireland, where English authority was sadly decayed. In 1396 he made a treaty of peace with his arch-enemy of France, Charles VI. His marriage to Charles's daughter Isabella gave him the same connection with France that Edward II had possessed through his wife of the same name; and he used this in a way Edward had never ventured to do, in order to bolster his royal power. He had never liked the French war and never pursued it vigorously. Indeed, in 1386 he had told the envoys who visited him at Eltham that he might even appeal for help against the Lords and Commons to the king of France whom his subjects thought to be his mortal enemy. Now, he bound Charles VI by a clause in the marriage treaty to give him support, if need be, against his own people. Thus Richard threw aside the cloak of moderation and appeared openly for what he was, a king who would aspire to the rank of Emperor, with visions of power and glory which bordered on megalomania. It has recently been claimed that, all appearances notwithstanding, he did not aim at despotism[2] though he did aim at absolutism; but such a distinction seems to be over-subtle. It is doubtful if it really helps us towards an understanding of Richard's actions in the last fateful years of his reign.

The great year of decision came in 1397, when Richard humiliated the Commons for supporting a bill by Thomas Haxey aimed at waste in the king's household. The Lords supported the king in his anger, and possibly only the fact that Haxey was a clerk saved him from death. More significantly, Richard proceeded to restore the

[1] *Foedera*, vol. vii p. 746.
[2] R. H. Jones, *The Royal Policy of Richard II: Absolutism in the Later Middle Ages* (Oxford, 1968), p. 182.

judges condemned in 1388 for their pronouncements of the previous year. Finally, he struck at the heart of opposition, the Lords Appellant themselves. He invited them to a great banquet, which Walsingham compared to that at which Salome danced before Herod; and when the earl of Warwick attended he was thrust into the Tower. To Arundel, Richard offered a solemn oath of personal safety if he would surrender. On the advice of his brother Thomas, the earl was foolish enough to accept. Gloucester, who would not be enticed, was fetched by Richard himself, riding down to Pleshey by night; and when the duke begged for mercy he was told that he would get as much as he had shown to Burley in 1388, for whom Queen Anne had pleaded in vain. Gloucester was shipped off to Calais and secretly despatched. Richard, by leaving two of the Appellants unharmed, had effectively employed the method of *divide et impera*. He was to employ similar tactics against the remaining two Appellants in 1398.

The immediate obstacles in Richard's path lay in these two Appellants and also in the great institution of parliament, through which the Lords and Commons had humiliated their king in 1388. These obstacles were now attacked simultaneously. The assembly of September 1397 was told ominously that Richard had summoned it in order to be informed if the rights of the Crown had been diminished. It proved to be entirely amenable to the king's designs, which included its own virtual immolation. To prepare for what was to follow, Sir Thomas Percy was appointed proctor of the clergy, so that through him the clerics might assent to the shedding of blood. Sir John Bussy, Speaker of the Commons, turned the instrument of Impeachment against those who had developed it, by impeaching Archbishop Arundel; and the leading prelate of the realm was condemned to forfeiture of temporalities and banishment. Then Richard proceeded to take over also the process of Appeal which had been used against his friends in 1388, and to turn it against his enemies. By this process, the earl of Arundel was accused in parliament by eight lords, prominent amongst whom were the kinsmen of the king, and sentenced to death, the penalty being announced by John of Gaunt, on command of the king, the temporal lords and the proctor of the clergy. The trial was presided over, with no show of leniency, by Gaunt in his capacity of Steward of England. Richard Arundel's execution on Tower Hill was watched, among others, by his own son-in-law, Thomas Mowbray, one-time Appellant of 1388, now turned royalist Appellant of 1397, who must have witnessed the result of his handiwork with very mixed feelings. He had no doubt also similarly watched Warwick in parliament when, 'like a wretched old woman' the earl 'confessed all, wailing and weeping and whining that he was guilty of everything, traitor that he was'.[1] His confessions gained for the penitent perpetual banishment to the Isle of Man. During all these proceedings, Richard freely used armed men to overawe the parliament. Before it was prorogued prelates, lords and knights of the shire swore before the shrine of Edward the Confessor and elsewhere to uphold all that had been done.

The last stage in the royalist restoration and the triumph of Richard's extremism, occurred in the reassembled parliament at Shrewsbury, far away from the influence of London, in January 1398. The questions put to the judges in 1387 were read, and the serjeants-at-law advised that the king had been counselled properly and loyally. The earldom of Suffolk was restored to the heirs of Michael de la Pole. The king received the customs on wool and leather for life. Oaths were sworn to maintain the acts of the assembly; attempts to undo them were to be treasonable. Finally, Richard turned against the last two Appellants. Mowbray, now duke of Norfolk, had confided to Derby, now duke of Hereford, his fears that both were about to be destroyed. Richard ordered the latter to report the warnings in parliament, though how Richard had heard of the conversation is uncertain. In any case, he had the matter brought before a committee of eighteen magnates and others; and he gave this body, slightly changed in personnel, power to examine all outstanding petitions presented in parliament. The committee ruled that there should be a duel between the two dukes; but at the last moment Richard intervened and banished them both, Hereford for ten years and Norfolk for life.

The committee itself was later subjected to even more devious manoeuvres; and Richard seems to have intended to use it in his attack on parliament itself. The record of its appointment was so falsified as to enable it to deal not only with petitions but also with all other matters and business moved in the presence of the king.[2] With its functions thus expanded, it could act in most matters instead of parliament itself; and since Richard was now financially solvent, he was under no compulsion to summon another assembly.

[1] Adam of Usk *Chronicon*, edited by E. M. Thompson (London 1876), p. 16.
[2] The modern debate on this question is discussed in my *Constitutional History 1216–1399*, vol. II, pp. 290, 308–9. Other interpretations are given by M. McKisack in *The Fourteenth Century 1307–1399*, p. 486 and by R. H. Jones as above, pp. 90–1.

As a contemporary writer said, 'the king got the whole power of government given over to him'. He could, as the chronicler saw, continue the sessions of parliament where and when he wished, using only the truncated form of the committee of 1398.

No such extreme scheme of royal ascendancy had ever been propounded before, not even in 1322. In order to sustain it, even if Richard's intentions were not so far-reaching as suggested above, he would have to undertake a severe and consistent repression of the disaffection which was bound to arise. He would have to go still further along the road to open tyranny. Nor was he reluctant to do so. He surrounded himself with a 'fellowship' of retainers as his bodyguard, wearing the badge of the white hart. He compelled individuals who had offended him to purchase pardons at his discretion, a clear violation of the Common Law; and he extracted 'blank charters' from the representatives of whole counties which had given support, real or fancied, to his enemies. The purpose of such charters is obscure. They were sealed by the representatives and were presumably to be filled in by Richard in whatever way he chose; though just what he had in mind was never made clear. In addition, he extracted loans from friend and foe alike; and, as a precaution against possible discontent, he made many individuals renew their oath of loyalty. In a characteristic style of extravagance and bravado, and as a sign of his great majesty, he caused a lofty throne to be built for certain occasions, where he sat from dinner-time to vespers, and when his eyes fell on anyone in the hall, that person had to kneel. In all this, he leaned heavily on the counsel of such men as Bussy, Bagot, and Green, who were more than mere sycophants, but who were not from among the circle of the magnates of the realm.

4. FAILURE AND DEPOSITION

Two important events brought an end to Richard's unpopular régime. One was the death of John of Gaunt in January 1399, and the other was a second Irish expedition in the following May. The former tempted Richard to disinherit Hereford, giving the opposition a focus and a leader who had everything to gain and little to lose. The latter gave an opportunity to the discontented which must have surpassed their greatest hopes. Together, these two events evoked an explosion that was in any case inevitable, but which proved to be unexpectedly violent. The universal reaction against him showed that Richard had profoundly miscalculated the temper of his people, and had alienated every section of them, the commonalty equally with the lords. The really surprising thing is not that his subjects now fell away from him completely, but that they had not done so before. Of course the extent of his tyranny had not become apparent before 1398. Moreover, Richard had earlier possessed a genuine case for a movement to strengthen the royal power, and could point to grievances which he had long endured. His charge in 1389 that he had been subject to constant control during the last twelve years was substantially true, and a tutelage so prolonged must have shocked the sensibilities of all true royalists. His enemies had been unrestrained and vindictive in their hour of success, and were timid or naive during the royalist restoration. They were opposed by old loyalties and ancient traditions. Nevertheless they stood, however imperfectly, for the preservation of political liberty, and events now showed that they had the support of all Englishmen who had a political voice to be heard.

In July 1399 Henry Bolingbroke landed at Ravenspur in Yorkshire, near the centre of his support. He had only a small following, but he was joined by 'all the people of the north country', led by their natural leaders, Henry Percy, earl of Northumberland and Ralph Neville, earl of Westmorland. His success was made doubly certain by the incapacity of Richard's regent, Edmund Langley, duke of York, and by the action of the duke, not easy to understand, in throwing in his lot with Bolingbroke when the latter reached Berkeley on 27 July.

It was at this point that a rising for redress of grievances and in defence of liberty began to turn into a dynastic revolution, though Henry probably had sworn soon after his arrival that he sought only his rightful inheritance and that he would never claim possession of Richard's throne.[1] In spite of his enlarged claims he still found no opposition. Richard returned from Ireland, landing at Milford Haven, and wandered through Wales, in vain seeking supporters. He probably planned to join the earl of Salisbury, whom he had sent to raise forces in north Wales and Cheshire, but Bolingbroke himself was in Chester by 9 August. Richard finally surrendered to

---

[1] The latest discussion of this vexed question is in my 'Fact and Fancy in Fifteenth Century English History', in *Speculum*, vol. XLII (October 1967), pp. 673–92. There is a valuable discussion of Richard's policy in the last years of his reign by Caroline M. Barron, 'The Tyranny of Richard II', *B.I.H.R.*, vol. XLI (May 1968), pp. 1–18. His deposition was examined in my 'Deposition of Richard II and the Accession of Henry IV', in *E.H.R.*, vol. LIV (April 1939), pp. 215–39.

Archbishop Arundel and Henry Percy at Conway castle. Even here, under these conditions, he was probably promised the retention of his crown. Percy is said to have sworn this on the Host, though we do not know whether he deceived Richard or himself. The final change in Henry's attitude towards Richard seems to have occurred on the road between Conway and London. Henry decided to seize the throne since all the portents were favourable. The charge of perjury which this decision gave rise to was to haunt the royal House of Lancaster for many years.

Bolingbroke himself took charge of Richard at Chester on the London Road, in what must have been a poignant interview; and together they journeyed south, Richard to imprisonment and death, Henry to climb the steps of the throne. His usurpation presented a difficult constitutional problem, though a negligible political one. There was one clear precedent in 1326–27; but now, as then, there was no constitutional authority competent to dethrone a reigning monarch. The nearest thing was the 'whole realm of England' gathered together, who might be regarded as having power to undo what they had done symbolically at the time of Richard's coronation, when they had acclaimed his elevation to the throne. Henry was able to issue writs in Richard's name, calling a meeting of parliament; and though parliament itself could not act officially without the actual presence of the monarch, Richard could be officially recorded in the Rolls of Parliament as deposed by the *Estates* and *populus*, the latter including many Londoners.

By this body, representing the community of all the realm, the usurpation was sanctioned and applauded. It was justified by a nice blending of Divine providence, election, and hereditary right. All were reflected in the formula which Henry adopted in making his solemn claim to succeed Richard:

> In the name of Fadir, Son, and Holy Gost, I Henry of Lancastre chalenge yis Rewme of Yngland, and the Corone with all ye membres and ye appurtenances, als I yt am disendit be right lyne of the Blode comyng fro the gude lorde Kyng Henry therde, and thorghe yat right yat God of his grace hath sent me, with helpe of my Kyn and my Frendes to recover it: the whiche Rewme was in poynt to be undone for defaut of Governance and undoyng of the gode Lawes.[1]

Henry did not ask for the realm of England, he 'challenged' it. He did not plead for recognition as king, he came to 'recover' a

[1] *Rot. Parl.,* vol. III, pp. 422–3.

right already recognized by God. Nevertheless, words and formalities could not destroy the underlying realities in 1399 any more than they were later able to in the Yorkist usurpations. The realities were those of magnate co-operation in Henry's seizure of the throne, and of popular support. Modern historians rightly insist that Henry IV was not, as Stubbs claimed, a ruler by grace of parliament, with all the consequences which flowed from the parliamentary creation of a king; but we must not go to the other extreme and ignore the importance of the role played in the usurpation of 1399 by the Commons and the Lords. Stubbs correctly grasped the spirit of Henry's succession, even if he was wrong in his description of the form. It not only negatively swept away the whole pretentious structure of Richard II's tyranny; it also, more positively, introduced a new era of government by consent.

Richard himself was probably murdered at Pontefract, some time in February 1400. He was just thirty-three. Adam of Usk saw him in the Tower of London not long before his death, and reported the words he heard there, so often quoted: 'My God! a wonderful land is this and a fickle; which hath exiled, slain, destroyed, or ruined so many kings, rulers, and great men, and is ever filled and toileth with strife and variance and envy.' Thus, 'musing on his ancient and wonted glory and on the fickle fortune of the world [a favourite theme of the age], Adam 'departed thence, much moved at heart'.[1]

It has been thought that in his later years Richard suffered from a loss of control, the onset of a mental malaise: thus, if he is to be regarded as sane from 1397 onwards, it was with the sanity of a man who pulls his own house about his ears. But we must not exaggerate his extravagances, conspicuous though they were.[2] They can be matched, for instance, by those of John, who is seldom regarded as lacking in sanity, or by Elizabeth Woodville, after her marriage to Edward IV, who caused her own mother to curtsy to her even in the privacy of her own royal chamber. Richard played for high stakes, in the grand manner, and he lost; but this does not make his conduct either entirely foolish or inexplicable.

He was defeated not so much by forces he could see and measure as by the complex and baffling changes which were occurring in political life. The growth of the territorial state, with its own

[1] My *Constitutional History 1216–1399*, vol. II, p. 324.
[2] See L. C. Hector, 'An Alleged Hysterical Outburst of Richard II', in *E.H.R.*, vol LXVIII (January 1953), pp. 62–5.

loyalties and sanctions, gave a new incentive to old struggles for power and created new suspicions and hostilities. Both the king and the lords used its institutions to expand their political power and serve their particular interests. Both feared to see the new conditions it created turn to their disadvantage, so as to destroy effective monarchy on the one hand or the liberty of the subject on the other. They do a great disservice to history who make the issues of Richard II's reign only those of power and personality; the measure of Richard's tragedy is only to be seen, it seems likely, against the background of his times and the light of problems which neither he nor his opponents really understood. Richard had profound defects of temperament; but his assets were considerable and should not be discounted because he failed where few, very few, rulers would have managed to succeed. Nor, we may see with the hindsight of history, was his cause wholly harmful for England. Its weaknesses were manifest, even to his own generation, whilst those of his opponents were largely obscured by propaganda and overshadowed by success. He died for a mistaken notion of the monarchy as well as for his failure in a remorseless struggle for power; but his rival and successor, Henry Bolingbroke, had to defend many of the royal 'liberties' for which he had stood. Nor could even his enemies strip him altogether of the dignity and courage with which he unwillingly renounced his crown at the end. The most they could do was to starve him to death and show his corpse to the people to prove to the unbelievers that their ruler had died a natural death.[1]

---

[1] There are different stories about his death, discussed by A. Steel in *Richard II*, pp. 286–8.

6

ENGLAND IN THE AGE OF WYCLIF

1. SOCIETY AND THE PLAGUE

THE social progress which had taken place in the thirteenth century did not continue uninterruptedly in the fourteenth. The gap between technological and scientific advance on the one hand, and the growing needs of an increasing population on the other, became dangerously great. Alongside this, the disintegration of the manor and social conflicts within the town caused far-reaching dislocations of the established order. Hence, the fourteenth century was a period of conspicuous stresses and strains which might have proved crippling in a society which was not fundamentally progressive and strong.

The reign of Edward II was a period of transition from the age of boom and expansion to one that has been described as a period of regression, though this description must be taken with a good deal of reserve. The reign was marked by a well-known famine, which was part of the great European famine of 1315–17. A few years later, there were disasters from rain and floods; in Kent, over 4,000 sheep were lost from such causes in 1324–26. The ravages of war added to natural catastrophes in the north; they reduced the income of the priory at Durham from £4,526 in 1308 to £1,931 in 1340–41. There began a period of falling prices for agrarian produce and of rising wages, which affected adversely the 'high farming' of the previous century, by which lords organized their demesne lands so as to produce on a large scale for the market. They now found it more profitable to lease their demesnes, commuting labour services for rents. An example of this process is to be seen in the increase of the income from leasings by the Bishop of Ely of his demesne lands at Wisbech Barton from £2 13s 4d in 1320 to £48 10s 6d in 1345.

Conversely, the agricultural income from his manor of Shelford dropped by more than half between 1325 and 1333.

The changes thus initiated were powerfully reinforced in Edward III's reign by the famous Black Death, the bubonic plague which began in 1348–49 and recurred at intervals, notably in 1361–62 (the *mortalité des enfants*) and 1369.[1] It reached England by way of trade routes from the East, and was carried by rats and fleas. Its deeper causes were not only lack of sanitation and medical knowledge, but also greater concentrations of population, the consequence of prosperity and demographic growth. Its symptoms were fever and swellings in the armpits and groins, and the dark spots on the skin which earned it its title. Medical skill was not great enough to diagnose its cause or provide a cure. It carried off up to 40 per cent of the population, and by the end of the century may have reduced the population by half. Its incidence was even greater in the towns than in the country: Boccaccio made his storytellers in the *Decameron* go out into the countryside to escape its peril. To their credit, the clergy suffered more than the laity, partly on account of their ministrations to the dying. Nearly 50 per cent of the beneficed clergy succumbed in Exeter, Winchester, Norwich, and Ely. The Archbishop of Canterbury himself, the learned Thomas Bradwardine, died along with some of the highest nobles in the land.

The mortality of the plague may have been greater in the more crowded cities, but the consequences of decline in population were probably more striking in the countryside. This was because the plague reinforced tendencies already existing to bring about a sharp increase in the disintegration of the manor, and in the discontent which was engendered by the old labour services, even though these were already in decline. That these consequences were not even more disruptive of the pattern of land-holding was partly because of the recuperative power of the peasantry, but even more because of the reservoir of landless men in all villages, in the shape of younger sons, landless labourers and *famuli*, who normally owned no more than cottage and garden but were now often willing to enter into holdings on the traditional terms, including villein service. Wealthier peasants also took advantage of the situation to increase their already sizable lands, moving into the yeoman's estate. There are

---

[1] Details about the various kinds of plague are given by J. M. W. Bean, 'Plague, Population, and Economic Decline in England in the Later Middle Ages', in *Econ. Hist. Rev.*, 2nd series, vol. XV (1962), pp. 423–37.

even extreme cases of freemen who were willing to contract away their freedom in order to get possession of villein land. Many land-lords reaped a substantial profit from the dues they received from the unprecedented changes in the holding of lands.

The efforts made by individual landowners to meet the crisis are now very well known. At Ramsey the labour dues on some manors were reduced in order to encourage the villein to cultivate his own land, and additional holdings were allocated. Wage-labourers and other landless men were encouraged to assume the new responsi-bilities and opportunities thus created. The result was a rapid process whereby most of the holdings made vacant by the plague were provided with tenants. Nevertheless this caused serious dis-ruption of demesne cultivation, which was harder to remedy. As has recently been said, the rising cost of labour and the difficulty of getting it, together with a low demand for agricultural produce, caused lords to cease cultivating marginal lands and to lease their demesne lands to men who would take them at a fixed rent and thus share the risks as well as the profits.

At Ramsey, the plague greatly reduced the amount of labour available for boon work at harvest and similar times. There was a tendency to develop pastoral instead of arable farming, with a consequent saving of man-hours. Some economic recovery occurred in the 1370s and 1380s, but this was followed by a further depression; and in the early years of the fifteenth century there were far more drastic adjustments than even those immediately after the Black Death. As time wore on it became clear that the old demesne economy of most of the Ramsey estates had, in fact, disappeared, not again to return.[1]

The more general effects of the plague in the countryside were falling prices and (despite the reservoir of landless men) labour shortage, coupled with a sharp rise in wages (60 per cent in the ten years after 1348). There was a sense of uncertainty together with other signs of a traumatic experience, intensified by the belief that the plague was God's punishment for sin, a belief that contributed to the spread of the Flagellants from the Low Countries to England. Their processions, with flogging of backs and prostrations in the form of a cross, reflected the near-hysteria of the times. The general need for readjustment encouraged peasants to react against labour

[1] J. A. Raftis, *op. cit.*, pp. 251–66; F. R. H. Du Boulay, *The Lordship of Canterbury* (London 1966), p. 219.

services; but the shortage of labour, on the other hand, encouraged the lords to hold on to their legal claims. The result was growing friction, exemplified by the Ordinance and Statute of Labourers in 1349 and 1351.

These were the repressive measures of the landlords; but they also reflected ideas of social justice which seemed to most people to be applicable to the crisis of the age. Through them, the Commons in parliament pegged wages at the rates existing before the plague. All landless men up to the age of sixty had to accept these rates and give their own lords just claim on their work. No master was to offer more than the generally accepted rate of wages. Prices were to be 'reasonable'. Infractions of these rules by the peasant might be punished by whipping or branding. The lord escaped with a fine.

As we might expect, these repressive measures were highly unpopular with the peasants, both wage-labourers and villeins. Fugutive villeins became more numerous, especially from estates near London. The register of the Black Prince contains many instances. There were refusals to work and instances of peasants banding together to resist the Acts and to seek redress in the courts. Lords, too, resisted or evaded the decrees of the government, and there were even cases where they actually abducted serfs from each other, causing bitterness all round. Nothing, in the end, could resist a movement towards greater emancipation of the peasant which was helped by many converging factors: the demographic decline; the influence of the wool trade, now supplemented by the manufacture of cloth; the transition from 'high farming'; the changes in wages and prices; and finally the slow increase in the importance of the peasant in the activities of the community, notably in war.

One general by-product of the accentuated change in the structure of the agrarian society was the hastening disintegration of the manor, the growth of individual enterprise, and the emergence of the yeoman farmer: 'Wherever we look, we find standing out from the ordinary run of tenants with 15 or 20 acre holdings small groups holding 100 acres or more.'[1] Transactions in land reached an unprecedented volume. They betoken a new stratification of the peasantry. The old hierarchic order did not dissolve; indeed, in some ways it became more pronounced. But it was much more

---

[1] R. H. Hilton, 'Peasant Movements in England before 1381', in *Econ. Hist. Rev.*, 2nd ser., vol. II (1949), p. 130. The leasing of demesne land and the stratification of the peasantry which it encouraged are illustrated by the same writer in *The Economic Development of Some Leicestershire Estates* (Oxford 1947), especially pp. 94–105.

elastic and, in the new conditions of life, on the whole more efficient. Rented lands were not always as well cultivated as in the days of large-scale exploitation by the lords; the enterprise of the new tenant was not by any means always an improvement. But it did confer more dignity on the more favoured individual and induce more enterprise and initiative. England paid a high price for the emergence of the yeoman farmer, but probably the price, in the long run, was not too high.

The enactments of 1349 and 1351, and the constant friction between landlord and peasant, were an important cause of the Peasants' Revolt of 1381 described briefly above; though they were complemented by political causes such as the Poll Taxes of 1377, 1379, and 1380, and the political struggles of 1376 and 1377. The Revolt itself was a landmark in English economic as well as political development. It did not have any very evident immediate effect on the process of commutation or on the disintegration of the manor, though it was said to have persuaded Thomas, Lord Berkeley to abandon direct cultivation of his demesne, and though between 1391 and 1411 Thomas Chillenden established leaseholds everywhere on the Christ Church estates, providing food for the monks elsewhere. In any case, the movement of 1381 left a permanent impression on the inherent dignity and worth of the individual peasant. The widespread 'rising' in time became a recurrent and important feature of English history, though later movements were more political and less agrarian. At the very least, its first great manifestation caused a widespread feeling of panic which lasted for very many years.

There was no real recovery in this century from the decline in population and productivity which followed the Black Death. The time was one of abandoned villages, falling population, contracting cultivation, and of conversion of arable land into pasture.[1] But for the individual peasant, at least, it was one of increasing rather than diminishing well-being. Rents tended to be reduced. Entry fines were diminished or remitted. Labour services were going, even though they were far from completely gone. It did not harm the small farmer if some demesne lands were not rented out but went out of cultivation altogether. He was at least relieved of the kind of pressure that had arisen in the thirteenth century from demographic

[1] W. G. Hoskins, in *Medieval England*, edited by A. L. Poole (Oxford 1958), vol. I, p. 31; A. C. Chibnall, *Sherington, Fiefs and Fields of a Buckinghamshire Village* (Cambridge 1965), p. 121.

increase and inordinate competition for land. Though less was produced, there were fewer mouths to feed. There are even signs of an increased consumption of meat, vegetables, and beer hard to reconcile with the picture of a general decline.[1]

It is true that there was much economic stress and strain all over Europe which had repercussions in England. The frontiers of the East were closed to trade by Mongols and Turks. Northern Italy and Flanders were afflicted by class strife, by unemployment, and by the bankruptcy of great financial agencies. Declining trade encouraged restrictive legislation and trade practices. There was increasing friction between the urban aristocracy and the unprivileged citizens. But modern scholars have departed far from the theory that there was a general economic recession in the fourteenth century after the famine of 1315–16, and the Black Death of 1348–49.

2. TRADE AND MANUFACTURE

There were, indeed, encouraging signs of vitality as well as of recession. One was the rise of cloth weaving, destined to be a very great industry and already a source of wealth at the end of the fourteenth century, even though it was accompanied by a steep decline in the export of wool. Export of wool to Flanders reached its peak in the late thirteenth and early fourteenth centuries when in some years 30,000 sacks were exported. There were particular reasons for the contrast between 40,000 sacks in 1353 and an average of only 9,000 in the decade 1390–99; but there is no doubt that a serious decline had occurred, quite apart from variations in the staple system. By Tudor times, ships were to carry abroad little but cloth.

The cloth industry was still very humble at the beginning of the fourteenth century, exports being small and imports perhaps averaging 10,000 cloths a year. In 1326 it was felt necessary to discourage the wearing of foreign cloth by forbidding it to commoners with income of less than £40 from land; though this may have been sumptuary legislation aimed against ostentation by the poor; and we know that much of the cloth used by the rich had been woven at home. Exports may have averaged 6,000 cloths

[1] Recent writings on this controversial question are referred to in my *Constitutional History of England 1216–1399*, vol. III, pp. 201–2, and *Constitutional History of the Fifteenth Century*, pp. 321 and 332–3, where I accept much of the argument of A. R. Bridbury in *Economic Growth, England in the Later Middle Ages*. But cf. the writings of M. M. Postan referred to in these volumes.

before the Black Death, reduced to a trickle in the years just after, and rising to 16,000 by 1366–68. The large number of 43,000 a year was reached in 1392–95.

The reasons were varied. England had abundant water and water-power for fulling. In contrast to her comparative stability, conditions in Flanders became very unsettled. Exports were encouraged by the fact that English merchants were beginning to penetrate profitable new markets in the Baltic and the North Sea, whilst Italian merchants began to carry cloth to the Mediterranean. The government of Richard II's minority even tried to establish reciprocity between Hanse privileges in London and the privileges of English merchants in the Hanse towns. Again, the custom which English kings imposed on exported wool placed the foreign manufacturer at a disadvantage, apart from the fact that Edward III once suspended the export of English wool altogether. Finally, there was positive encouragement to the English weaver by the fourteenth-century rulers. Edward II in 1326 promised 'suitable franchises' to cloth-workers. Edward III encouraged Flemish weavers to immigrate into his realm, and by 1360 a colony of them was established in York, though some had been there for at least a century. According to a tale by the antiquary Thomas Fuller, Edward actually sent secret agents to tell the Flemings 'how happy they should be if they would but come over into England, bringing their mystery with them, which would provide their welcome in all places'. In 1344 the king caused proclamation to be made in London against attacks on foreign cloth-workers. Evidently, their mystery had not guaranteed them a welcome everywhere.

English cloth virtually captured the home market by the end of the fourteenth century, and was firmly established in many markets abroad. It was very much a cottage industry, developing most in the valleys of the Pennines and Cotswolds, where sheep and water-power were plentiful, but also continuing in some of the larger towns. Small villages like Leeds or Bradford in Yorkshire or Tiverton in Devonshire became large, whilst old centres like Lincoln, Stamford, and Beverley declined. The expansion in weaving took place in spite of a demographic recession. How this recession affected the domestic consumption we cannot say. In any case, a great industry had now been established which for centuries profoundly influenced English politics and economics.

Another sign of vitality in the fourteenth century was the appearance of the English capitalist. The merchants were so important that Edward III summoned an assembly of them at Nottingham in 1336 to help him finance his projected French war. In 1337 William de la Pole of Hull and Reginald Conduit of London set a pattern by lending heavily to the king on the security of wool. William himself in the end raised the enormous sum of £100,000 for the king before he refused further loans. In 1337 Edward III took over the monopoly of the wool trade, and arranged with a syndicate of English merchants to purchase the wool compulsorily and sell it abroad; out of the proceeds they were to advance him £200,000 free of interest and were to recoup themselves out of the customs which they were permitted to farm. The scheme failed, and by 1339 Edward owed £300,000.[1] Many merchants went bankrupt. This happened, for example, in the case of Walter Chiriton, Thomas Swanland and their associates, who advanced Edward £4,000 on the eve of his Crécy campaign. They also guaranteed the king £50,000 a year, and in return got the farm of the customs on wool estimated at £60,000 a year. But financing on this scale was too much for them and ended in disaster by April 1349. Such experiences brought large schemes to an end after 1353, though loans from London merchants to the king on a lesser scale were an important feature of governmental finance, especially under Richard II and Henry IV.

Though the efforts of the early capitalists met with some conspicuous failures, they nevertheless provide clear evidence of the rising vigour of English finance. Another sign is provided by the Merchants of the Staple, organized for the marketing of wool and first established at St. Omer in the spring of 1314. By an ordinance of the previous year all English merchants had been compelled to send their wool to this depot for taxation and control. They set up a government for themselves, consisting of a limited group of Merchants of the Staple and a mayor. The scheme ran into much opposition, and there was conflict not only as to the use of their powers by the governing merchants but also as to the location of the Staple. After a number of experiments the Staple was located at Calais in 1363 under the control of twenty-six of the greatest merchants in the land. After this there was for some years a measure of agreement and peace.

The Company of the Merchants of the Staple was, in theory at

[1] See E. B. Fryde, 'Edward III's Wool Monopoly of 1337', in *History*, vol. XXVII (1952), pp. 8–25, and p. 150 above.

least, a national organization. It was a Fellowship embracing all England in its membership and its interests. It owed its existence to the organized merchants in wool and to the king, both of whom sought to profit by it. In particular, Edward III wished to use his control over all wool exported abroad in order to strengthen his credit and to supply him with resources and bargaining powers in his conflict with France and in his search for allies. The Fellowship of the Merchants wished to use their collective strength to protect their interests and enhance their profits. To this end they co-operated closely with the ruler, though this sometimes led to their great loss. They were one more sign of the rise of the English merchant and the broadening economic horizons of the emerging English state.[1] One reason for the failure of the Staplers to expand was their limitation to the traffic in wool. But other merchants were not so restricted. The charters which some of them obtained from the duke of Brabant in 1296 and 1305 showed that they had an organization in his lands which was not limited to trade in any one commodity, and by which they had their own mayor, assembly, and court. By Henry IV's reign the society of Merchant Venturers was trading vigorously in many commodities with all the Scandinavian countries and around the Baltic and North Sea in competition with the great German Hanse League.

Meanwhile there are also signs of vigour on the much lower level of local manufacture and exchange. It has been said that the tendency of workers to organize themselves in fraternities, mysteries and gilds is among the most remarkable social phenomena of the later four-teenth century.[2] Some gilds, like the parish gilds, were for a purely religious purpose. Others united together those in particular trades or crafts. Others again were associations of merchants, successors to the earlier merchant gilds, though with somewhat different aims. Merchant and craft gilds normally contained three types of members: masters, journeymen (who worked for wages), and apprentices. Their organization and outlook pre-supposed the existence of small-town conditions of manufacture and trade. A master-craftsman usually bought his own raw materials or, more often, worked on materials supplied by his customer; and he sold his products in his shop or stall. There was no intermediary in such a case, and only a

---

[1] For brief comments and a reference to recent writing, see my *Constitutional History 1216–1399*, vol. III, p. 197.
[2] M. McKisack, *The Fourteenth Century*, p. 373.

small establishment. The purpose of the gild was to serve both the members and their clients. Thus, bad work was not only unprofitable in the long run, it was also disgraceful. That is why working at night was frequently banned. The craft embodied in its regulations a whole social system into which the individual was completely absorbed.

The origins of the gilds go back to the thirteenth century, but it was in the fourteenth that they developed their full stature, especially in relation to the town government. They were recognized as having control over their members in the day to day practices of their trade, and their courts were empowered to deal with petty disputes and infractions of their rules. As in the case of other medieval groups, considerations of private or corporate profit and of public welfare were intermingled. As the *Bristol Book of Ordinances* said, 'Diverse ordinances have been made on the working of woollen cloths to the intent that good and true cloth shall be made in the town, as well for the preservation of the good fame of the same as for the profit which they shall take on the sale of their cloth.' It has been stated that it is difficult to rise from a study of these and similar ordinances without a feeling that, in the best days of the gild, the professions of good faith and regard for the 'common profit' were not devoid of real meaning.[1] The gild's scrutiny of the work of its members was constant and minute, and punishment for bad workmanship which brought discredit on the whole fraternity was severe. From the same regard for profit and for the dignity and fairness of its relations with the public, the gild often fixed wages and prices. In arrangements made by the Shearmen of London in 1452 it was laid down that if a master employed 'any foreign man', that is a stranger who was not a member of the gild, the wardens of the gild and their assistants were to see the stranger at work, 'and conscientiously set his salary' between the master and him.

It was out of this mixture of shrewd business calculation, collective pride, and the personal relationships in small and intimate communities, that there developed also the system of the apprentice. This was well established by the end of the thirteenth century, and during the fourteenth it spread throughout England. It was not everywhere obligatory, but it had a very general appeal. It gave prospective members of the craft a generous training, often in the home of a master to whom he was bound, a training which at its

[1] E. Lipson, *The Economic History of England*, vol. I, 5th ed. (London 1929), p. 297.

best included far more than the simple attainment of skills. When a youth in Ipswich was apprenticed to a barber for seven years it was stipulated that he be given suitable clothing, shoes, bedding, board, and chastisement.[1]

The system enabled the gilds to keep up the quality of their members and their work. For a variety of reasons, pressure to enter the gilds increased during the course of the fourteenth century, and apprenticeship was one means by which undesirable elements could be excluded. In 1388 the government itself tried to stem the drift from agriculture into the cities and crafts by decreeing that all who served in husbandry till the age of twelve should continue to do so. It was similarly decreed in 1406 that no one in cities and boroughs might place his child to be an apprentice unless he had land or rent to the value of twenty shillings a year. It is true that there was some opposition to this enactment, particularly where the demand for apprentices was greater than the supply. But it reflected a genuine need to keep up standards and the quality of the gild. The same purpose was shown by attempts to restrict the number of apprentices which any one master might employ. By 1406 the happy times of small beginnings, when an apprentice might become a member of the master's family, and might hope to inherit his business and even with luck to marry his daughter, were beginning to pass away.

Another threat to the old structure of the gilds was an increase in the number of journeymen. From one point of view the journeyman was the natural complement to the master and the apprentice but from another he was redundant. A craftsman who had served his apprenticeship (usually for seven years) or had otherwise become skilled in the trade, and did not become a master, became a workman for daily wages. He was not a member of the gild, and his interests were not, like the apprentices, roughly identical with those of the master. He was not recognized as a member of the city community and his master might have to answer for his misdeeds. He was probably necessary for the functioning of the gild, but he was not necessary to its essential purpose. In the early days there was no gulf between master and journeyman and, as far as we know, no great friction. All three classes of gild brethren could work together in reasonable harmony, with common backgrounds and some share in a common social life.

[1] Mrs. J. R. Green, *Town Life in the Fifteenth Century*, vol. II (London 1894), p. 120, n. 1.

But as gilds became more powerful, entry more difficult and expensive, and master craftsmen wealthier and more ambitious, the number of journeymen who had no expectation of becoming masters gradually increased. Lines of division became more apparent. 'If any serving-man', said one London gild, 'shall conduct himself in any other manner than properly towards his master, no one of the trade shall set him to work until he shall have made amends before the mayor and aldermen.' This, Mrs Green assures us, was true of a great number of trades.[1] One ominous sign of diverging interests was the appearance of the gild of journeymen, caused ultimately by the threat that they would sink to the level of permanent wage-earners. In 1303 servant workmen were forbidden to make provisions to the detriment of their trade or of the people. Complaints about their demands for higher wages multiplied after the Black Death. In 1396 the Saddlers of London complained that the serving-men (journeymen), called yeomen, wore a livery and held meetings once a year to the great prejudice of their craft; they formed groups (*covins*) in order to raise their wages excessively. The Bakers were to denounce a similar brotherhood in 1441. Thus, by the increase in the number of journeymen, the old harmonies of the early gilds were steadily impaired.

Alongside the economic purposes of the gilds were their religious and social aims, almost equally important. Most craft gilds had a patron saint and maintained lights on his altar. They organized plays and pageants for the sake of religion and for a contribution to social life. Benevolent work for sick or indigent members was partly religious. Free grammar schools were founded and maintained. Mutual aid was enjoyed and freely given. Members were bound together by a lively loyalty. Despite the increasing frequency of signs of change, the craft gilds were to last far into the modern period. In the fourteenth century they added colour, warmth, and vitality to the life of the towns and cities, and showed once again the strength of the medieval group.

Gilds contributed much to city life, but they did not eliminate discord between rich and poor, privileged and unprivileged, gild and gild. This increased rather than diminished. In 1364 the mayoral election at York was disturbed for a day and a half by riots; in 1380 the mayor was chased out of the city, and the *communes* organized to

[1] Mrs. J. R. Green, *Town Life in the Fifteenth Century*, vol. II (London 1894), p. 122, n. 2.

defend themselves. In Bristol, a 'popular' party, led by John Le Taverner (Mayor 1312–13) was involved in the famous rebellion of 1312–16. In London Queen Isabella invited the *commune* to rebel in 1326; and the 'people' helped to depose Edward II in 1326–7 and made John of Gaunt flee for his life in 1377. In 1376 John of Northampton tried to harness popular unrest to his side in his conflict with rivals in the city. In particular, he opposed the fishmongers, by agitating in favour of cheap fish. He achieved some success and shook the oligarchic government of the city. But his innovations were abandoned in 1394. The commonalty of the city aided the rebels in 1381, and contributed to the violent politics of the city under Richard II.

In Exeter, new regulations were drawn up in 1345 because mayors and stewards had been acting to the 'intolerable impoverishment' of the city. The closing years of the century were marked at Lincoln by bitter quarrels between the 'more worthy citizens' and the commonalty. A petition of the citizens of Norwich in 1378 explained that many of the *commune* had of late been 'very greatly contrarious'.[1] But despite such signs of friction there was no appreciable diminution in the vitality of the towns. The townsman played a steadily increasing part in national affairs, and began to direct his interest outwards to Westminster; but his first and best love continued to be the crowded, lively city at his door.

3. The Aristocracy

Group life on a much higher level and organized in a very different way was also a feature of the society of the aristocracy. This life, despite evident stresses and strains, was equally abounding in social well-being. The great lords lost income as a result of falling prices and rents; in the 1390s John of Gaunt's council caused an inquiry to be made into his declining income from land. But they gained by the centralization of their estate management, by the profits of war and the indirect rewards of Bastard Feudalism, and by the union of estates through marriage which was usually a cold-blooded business transaction. It is hard to say whether or not the ransoms and booty of the Hundred Years War outweighed the steady cost of great expeditions and the occasional ransom which had to be paid out by an unfortunate individual; but there is little doubt

---

[1] W. Hudson and J. C. Tingey, *The Records of Norwich*, vol. I (Norwich 1906), p. 64; J. W. F. Hill, *Medieval Lincoln*, p. 359.

that conditions favoured the enterprising magnate, however strong the threat of a general economic decline.[1] This was especially the case where any particular lord had access to the apparently limitless royal bounty, which had always been the most important avenue to the enhancement of baronial estates. Splendid living and lavish hospitality in the great households of the time do not suggest any significant reduction in aristocratic incomes, and few magnates seem to have got heavily in debt.

Henry of Lancaster may serve as an illustrious example: he was a pattern of chivalry in his age as well as a most successful general. He began as a hero of Edward III's Scottish war. He was present at the naval victory of Sluys in 1340 and gained brilliant victories in Gascony and Poitou between 1345 and 1350. In 1350 he also took part in the sea fight off Winchelsea; and in 1351, for a change, he crusaded in Prussia and Poland. In 1356–57 he fought in Brittany and Normandy, and accompanied Edward on his last campaign to France in 1359. Out of the profits of the castle and town of Bergerac which he himself captured he built his great palace, the Savoy. He was made Sheriff of Staffordshire for life; in 1345 he became earl of Lancaster; in 1351 he was made duke, and his county of Lancaster was made a palatinate. He was earl of Lincoln from 1337–61 and Earl of Moray from 1359–61. We do not know the balance of his profits and expenditures, but he probably gained a great deal from his loyal and valuable service to the Crown.

The aristocracy continued conspicuously its highest function of war, but also reflected in its way of life the influences of a changing environment. It partook effectively in the conduct of the French and Scottish wars, but also contributed lavishly to social and political groupings engendered by court life and Bastard Feudalism. The royal court was renowned throughout Europe for its chivalry, as was Edward, its charismatic central figure. His famous Round Table was founded in 1348; after a great tournament at Windsor in 1344, Edward had sworn to follow Arthur's footsteps. His Order of the Garter was the most select and famous in Europe. Its motto, *honi soit qui mal y pense*, was said to have been derived from an episode when the Countess of Salisbury, a celebrated beauty

---

[1] These interesting questions are discussed by K. B. McFarlane in 'War, the Economy and Social Change, England and The Hundred Years War' in *Past and Present*, vol. XXII (1962), pp. 3–13, and by M. M. Postan in 'The Costs of The Hundred Years' War', in *ibid.*, XXVII (1964), pp. 34–53. Cf. G. A. Holmes, *The Estates of the Higher Nobility in XIV Century England* (Cambridge 1957).

honoured by the king's love, lost her garter at a ball given to celebrate the fall of Calais.

The initiation of the Order was celebrated by a state banquet in the great tower of Windsor Castle, then being rebuilt, together with the chapel of St. Edward, which was enlarged into the chapel of St. Edward and St. George. The Order consisted of only twenty-six knights, including the king, bound by a lasting bond of friendship and honour. It included Edward the Black Prince and all the leading magnates of the land. Edward sent his heralds to publish the news of it in the leading countries of Europe. The memory of Crécy and later the fame of Poitiers covered it with glory. It had later imitators in various courts, but it never had a peer.

Feasting and dancing were a conspicuous feature of Edward's magnificence. The king himself was the embodiment of *prouesse* and also of courtly romance, revelling at Windsor clad in white and silver, with his tunic embroidered with the words

> Hay, Hay, the whitë swan!
> By Goddes soul I am thy man.

Chroniclers described the courtiers kissing and embracing as they danced. Of Edward's court in its early days, Froissart wrote feelingly: 'I could not tell or recount in a day the noble dinners, the festivals, the entertainments, the gifts, the presents.' The poet of chivalry made no secret of the love of fighting and the eagerness for booty and ransom in the aristocracy, but he also talked seriously of their chivalric ideal. How far this had reality is, of course, an open question. Richard II perhaps bore unconscious witness to its significance to contemporaries when he exclaimed when not far from his death, *Je suis loyal chevalier et oncques ne forfiz chevalerie.*

In Froissart's day the tournament was becoming more and more a spectacle, governed by strict rules and chivalric etiquette, and a great social occasion; though Edward III's near and dear friend William Montagu, earl of Salisbury, was slain in one in 1344. It had become quite transformed since the days when William Marshal had risked life and limb to win 500 tournaments and make a fortune from his booty. William Langland made Piers the Plowman enumerate the duties of a knight in words which strikingly omit the practice of war:

> In couenaunt that thou kepe · holy kirke and my-selue
> Fro wastours and wyckede men · that this worlde struen.
> And go hunte hardiliche · to hares and to foxes.

To bores and to brockes [badgers] · that breketh adown myne hegges
And go affaite [train] the faucones [falcons] · wilde foules to kille;
For suche cometh to my croft · and croppeth my whete.[1]

Complementary to this were developments in the formal education
of the nobility. A knowledge of letters gradually became a matter
not only of increasing interest but also of a growing necessity. It
showed in the king himself, and we may quote V. H. Galbraith's
summary:

> From 597 to 1100 it is exceptional for a king to be able to write at all,
> or to read Latin; in the twelfth and thirteenth centuries kings learn to
> read Latin but do not (even if they can) write it; in the fourteenth and
> fifteenth centuries they are taught in youth both to read and write
> Latin but in fact are far more occupied with French and English.[2]

Signs of noblemen skilled in letters multiply in the fourteenth
century. Hugh Despenser, the father, had a library of books. A
bible in French, containing the Old and New Testaments, was
illuminated for John de Wells and his wife before 1361. An earl of
Salisbury bought a French *Petrus Comestor*, taken from the French
king at Poitiers, for his wife. Guy Beauchamp, heir to the earl of
Warwick, bequeathed forty-two books to Bordesley Abbey. Sir
Simon Burley, confidant of Richard II, also had some taste for books.
Thomas of Woodstock possessed a considerable library. The heroes
of late fourteenth-century metrical romances of knighthood were
occasionally lettered, and the capacity for listening to fine books was
admired. It has been claimed that the marked taste for mystical literature among the more devout early in the fourteenth century pre-
supposes a thorough grounding in dogmatic and moral instruction.[3]
Henry, duke of Lancaster (*c.* 1300–61) was a celebrated diplomat
and scholar, and one of the original knights of the Order of the
Garter, but his *Livre de Seyntz Medicines* was one of the most remarkable religious works of the fourteenth century. The aristocracy was
not only more literate but it was also probably more active in its
patronage of literature. It may well have contributed much in this
way to the revival of alliterative verse, commented on elsewhere, in
the middle years of the fourteenth century.

The intense social life engendered by Bastard Feudalism and new

---

[1] *Piers the Plowman*, edited by W. W. Skeat (Oxford 1886), vol. I, pp. 195–6 (B. VI, 24–33).
[2] 'Literacy of Medieval English Kings', *British Academy Raleigh Lecture on History* (London 1935), pp. 7–8.
[3] W. A. Pantin, *The English Church in the Fourteenth Century* (Cambridge 1955), p. 191.

fashions of chivalry was reflected in the importance of the minstrel at one end of the scale and in the architectural development of dwelling-places at the other. Homes of the nobility were now obviously evolving from the fortress of the High Middle Ages to the mansion of the Tudor Age. They were built for comfort, elegance, and social life, as much as for security; though this is hardly true in the case of those accessible to the Scots or the French. Such a building was Michael de la Pole's fortified manor of Wingfield in Suffolk (1384), of which Thomas Hearne the painter said, 'upon the whole, this Fabrick seems to have been formed rather to inspire the idea of dignity, and to oppose a popular tumult, than to resist an enemy'.[1] The fourteenth-century baron himself had not yet become the Tudor courtier and politician; but by the end of the century he was clearly well on the way.

4. MIDDLE CLASSES

The classes in between the common people and the magnates may not have reflected as clearly the development of social life, but there is scattered evidence to suggest that they imitated the nobility in this as in other matters, and that they were gaining sophistication and responsibility for the welfare of their local communities. The heavy burden of administrative work and the conduct of business created a growing habit of letters and experience in administration. Sir Peter de la Mare in 1376 was Steward of the earl of March. London merchants like John Pecche a London wine-merchant, and Richard Lyons another London merchant, were important in national politics in the period 1376–80. William Walworth and John Philpot, both successful traders, were made war-treasurers for the government by the parliament of October 1377, and the former was conspicuous in 1381. Nicholas Brembre, leader of the victuallers in London, was closely associated with Richard II, and was appealed in 1388. The Commons showed both courage and an unprecedented initiative in the Good Parliament of 1376. Meetings of the shire court were dominated by the stewards of the great lords; but they were essentially composed of the smaller gentry; they were the place where the knight of the shire and others of comparable status met together for social contact as well as the business of the shire. Chaucer's franklin attended regularly:

[1] A. L. Poole, *Medieval England*, vol. I, p. 122.

> At sessiouns ther was he lord and sire;
> Full ofte tyme he was knight of the shire.

At home, his hospitality was outstanding:

> An housholdere, and that a greet, was he; . . .
> With-oute bake mete was never his hous,
> Of fish and flesh, and that so plentevous,
> It snewed in his hous of mete and drinke,
> Of alle deyntees that men coude thinke.[1]

Not only were all levels of society busy in the social life of their own groupings, and moving about the countryside, but individuals also occasionally improved their fortunes and crossed the barriers of the rigid hierarchical order. Clement Paston, living at the end of the century, is a good example of how changes could begin. He ploughed his own modest farm of five or six score acres, and he married a bond-woman; but he sent his son to Eton, though it made him go into debt; and he helped his descendants to achieve a real measure of importance in East Anglia. Like the magnates, knights could make their fortune in war. In 1347 Sir Thomas Dagworth was offered £4,900 for his prisoner, Charles of Blois, whilst Sir John Harleston's share in a French knight amounted to £1,583 6s 8d. William of Windsor, husband of Alice Perrers, was said to be 'an active and valiant knight, rich with great wealth acquired by his martial prowesse'. The duke of Gloucester complained to Richard II that his policy of peace disheartened the poor knights, squires, and archers of England whose comforts and stations in society depended on war.

The wars affected social relationships in another way. They worked strongly to emphasize the importance of individual merit rather than formal rank, even though they added to the stature and authority of successful generals who were very frequently great lords. It is difficult to exaggerate the importance of Sir John Chandos's claim, quoted above, to have precedence over the earl of Oxford. Chandos, like Sir Robert Knollys and Sir Thomas Dagworth, was not of noble birth, and for this reason did not obtain the status of banneret until later in his career; but he was a Founder Knight of the Order of the Garter nevertheless.

Trade as well as war added to the movements in society and to the social contacts of the gentry. Some new knightly families made or had made their money in trade. Adam Fraunceys, for example, was

---

[1] *The Works of Geoffrey Chaucer: The Canterbury Tales: Text,* edited by W. W. Skeat (Oxford 1894), p. 11.

a successful fourteenth-century mercer who bought the manor of Edmonton. A son obtained the manor of Cobhams in Essex and was knighted, whilst his sister married into the nobility. Other such families were founded by the sons of successful lawyers, like the Cobhams and Scropes. An inquisition held in Middlesex in 1353 lists seven London names among thirty holders or groups of holders of knights' fees or fractions of knights' fees. As is well-known, Langland complained that 'soapsellers and their sons for silver have been made knights'.

5. THE PEASANTRY

The one group that lost rather than gained in the vitality of its group life was that of the peasants. The disintegration of the manor brought new sources of energy and initiative into their lives, but took away old sources of strength. One result characteristic of the century was agrarian discontent. Geoffrey Chaucer could effectively conceal this in his picture of the poor ploughman who lived in perfect peace and charity, loved God, paid his tithes and helped his neighbours; but his contemporaries were less restrained. Langland implied that the peasant of his day was less content than formerly with a diet which lacked hot fish and flesh; and Gower left no doubt that the villager, in his view, was full of arrogance and discontent. Formerly, he says, cheese and milk had been a feast for the peasants; they had dressed in hodden grey; and 'then was the world of such folk well ordered in its estate'. Now, they worked little, and dressed and fed like their betters, so that ruin stared everybody in the face. He believed that the common folk suffered from madness; though he also stressed the commonplace that a serf could be as comely and intelligent as a baron, and had the same human blood in his veins.

Thus, in the course of the century, the peasant lost some of his environmental support and contentment; but he gained in emancipation and dignity, and in a more general appreciation of Gower's aphorism about the fundamental equality of men. It is unlikely that any writer in England at the end of the fourteenth century would have used the words of a distinguished Franciscan, Alvarus Pelagius, near its beginning, describing European villagers in general:

> For, even as they plough and dig the earth all day long, so they become altogether earthy; they lick the earth, they eat the earth, they speak of earth; in the earth they have reposed all their hopes, nor do they care a jot for the heavenly substance that shall remain.

A century later, the Dominican St. Antonino, archbishop of Florence, would declare of peasants in general that 'living like beasts, they sometimes die the death of a beast'; but his description of their sins lacks the fine flavour of their inferiority which appears in the twenty-two items of his predecessor; and if either had been in England he would have had to reckon with a peasantry which was exceptionally favoured by circumstances and, accordingly, had achieved a rather higher status than those in many parts of the West.[1]

In England, despite the accentuation of some class distinctions and in particular the increasing wealth, luxury, and ostentation of the great lords, it seems likely that the gulf between the top and bottom of society had begun to shrink by the end of the fourteenth century. Some peasants became poorer whilst others became richer, but wealth is not the only criterion. Individualism was growing in society, and the common man was beginning to find a place in literature. It was no longer possible even for a disdainful courtier to adopt the contemptuous attitude reflected in Walter Map's *odit anima mea servos*, reflecting fashionable prejudice at the court of King Henry II.

6. MILITARY SERVICE

Military service affected all ranks of society. At the highest level it gave rise to Bastard Feudalism, one of whose characteristic features, that of service by indenture and for pay, is illustrated by an agreement of 1341 between the king and Edward Montagu, who agreed to serve in Brittany for forty days with six knights, twenty men-at-arms, twelve men more lightly armed, and twelve archers. For this he got wages of £76. More important, though less common, were indentures for life.[2] Among the well-known abuses arising from the new feudal relations were those of livery (a great noble-man's livery might protect a wrongdoer from just punishment), maintenance (by which a lord might abuse his general obligation to vouch for his followers in the courts), and intimidation. Such abuses became endemic. Already, in the Statute of Westminster I, Edward I forbade maintenance by his own officials, and Edward II condemned it in 1327. The first parliamentary complaint against peacetime retinues was in 1331. The first specific legislation against indentured

[1] Cf. the interesting 'half-proverbial rhymes and epigrams' quoted by Eileen Power in *C.M.H.*, vol. VII, p. 749.
[2] G. A. Holmes, *The Estates of the Higher Nobility in Fourteenth Century England*, p. 83.

retainers came in 1390. Bastard Feudalism has been blamed for growing disorders in the country, which culminated in the fifteenth century and, it is claimed, contributed almost as much as failure in government to the catastrophe of civil war. On the other hand, it has been argued, the real trouble was not the impossibility of handling the problems created by the new pattern of feudalism but the personal inadequacies of some English kings. The lords with their retinues never got out of hand under Edward III, nor was Bastard Feudalism the cause of their rebellions and political claims under Richard II.

Any increase in their military power was probably more than balanced by the rise of the bowman in the age of Crécy and Poitiers, the beginnings of artillery, and the sporadic but probably increasing use of the popular levies. The importance of the bowman is very well known, but that of the popular levies is not.[1] Yet, as G. G. Coulton has said, behind the magnates and their retainers Edward III had in his wars 'a whole nation in arms'. The use of these levies, at least in England and Scotland, was greatly extended by Edward II. After Bannockburn, for example, Edward called out all the footmen of Yorkshire to serve at the cost of the vills. In 1315 levies were ordered to serve the king for forty days, at the cost of themselves and their neighbourhood; in 1316 one man per vill was to serve sixty days at the cost of the vill. In 1318 certain towns were to provide footmen to serve for forty days at local expense (London supplied 200 armed foot). Similar requests were made throughout 1319–26. For the Boroughbridge campaign of 1322 there were heavy demands. London was asked to grant 500 foot for forty days at the cost of the city, then forty days paid for by the king. Coventry sent 100 men for forty days at the cost of the city. After Boroughbridge the demands became heavier still. Lincolnshire, for example, was at one time asked to supply 4,000 foot, well-armed and furnished with expense money. There were 12,000 on one Scottish campaign, of whom 7,000 spent four weeks at local expense.

The lords were used extensively to array the levies. An instance picked at random is that when Richmond and Lancaster and forty-two other lay lords acted in this capacity in 1318. Lords of vills were ordered to arm and prepare their tenants. In 1322 the king commanded lords all over England to raise both horse and foot: the northern lords were to arm and array all tenants between sixteen

[1] The best account is by M. R. Powicke, in *Military Obligation in Medieval England* (Oxford, 1962).

and sixty. In the end, however, Edward II's attempts to develop the militia were prevented by a general opposition, and his innovations were condemned after his downfall, in the Statute of 1327.

Edward III depended more on his lords than did his father, but even he tried to extend his claims on the service of the militia. It has been calculated that Edward's armies on occasions contained levies whose numbers in comparison with that of others was in a ratio of five to two. Hobelars (infantrymen mounted for mobility on small horses) made up almost one-quarter of the army which faced the Scots in 1327, and half the army were archers.[1] In 1345 Edward ordered all men to serve who had at least £5 worth of land, bringing followers in strict proportion to their wealth; though in 1346 individuals were only asked to provide the archers. However, the forces so provided were for service overseas, and the measure, according to the chronicler Adam Murimuth, caused fierce opposition. All these innovations were strongly resisted in parliament. Finally, in 1352, the king agreed that no man should be obliged to find men-at-arms, hobelars, or archers, except those who held land by such service.

This statute did much to bring to a close a century of great experiment. The attempt of the government to extend its use of the levies had failed; but the long effort clearly shows the importance of the levies, and the political consequences must have been considerable. There was probably a connection between the rise of the bowman and the increasing appeal to the levies on the one hand, and the epoch-making rebellion of the peasants in 1381 on the other.

The skill and discipline of the peasants had been taught them in part by the government itself. Nor could they have failed to derive from their experiences an increased sense of their importance in the state.

7. RELIGION

In religion the century showed similar divergent tendencies. New forces arose to threaten the old pattern of religious life but conservatism triumphed in the end. The laity began to achieve a greater role in religious worship. The Lords and even the Commons claimed increasing authority in religious affairs. There was an unprecedented rise of mysticism; and the mystics, as well as reformers like John Wyclif, emphasized the importance of the individual, high and low,

[1] Ranald Nicholson, *Edward III and the Scots* (Oxford 1965), p. 27.

and his ability to effect direct contact with God. Finally, the religious
life of England became slightly more English; there were unprecedented attacks on the Papacy, owing much to the Avignon
Captivity and the Schism; and reformers looked more than ever to
the English king and, more significantly, to parliament. But there was
no religious revolution, and both the ecclesiastical hierarchy and the
orthodoxy of belief alike in the end weathered the storm.

The twin pillars on which the Church depended were the two
'monarchies', spiritual and secular; and the king and the pope for
the most part found it possible to continue the pragmatic co-
operation which had followed the struggles of Edward I's reign.
But the co-operation developed steadily in favour of the secular
rather than the spiritual power. The papal tenths that were levied
on the Church in England between 1301 and 1324 amounted to
about £230,000; but this sum was quite illusory. Most of the
receipts from such taxes went into the hands of the king, like the
three-quarters of the triennial tenth raised by Clement in 1309. It
has been calculated that Edward II got £255,000 in taxes from the
clergy, three-quarters of which was obtained by his share of papal
taxation.[1] The pope got the unpopularity of such taxation; the king
got most of the cash. Edward III permitted Innocent VI to raise
money from the English clergy to contribute towards the ransom
of King John of France, because this went straight into his own
pocket; but he only allowed Gregory XI to collect three-fifths of the
amount he proposed in 1375 in return for concessions on provisors
and other matters. When Urban VI tried in 1388, and Boniface IX
in 1391, the English clergy were sternly reminded that such taxes
were illegal.

Failing to develop any system of regular taxation, the popes had
to develop other levies on the clergy. Their expenses were heavy,
as were those of the cardinals. The latter lived in great style as
befitted princes of the Church, and had to find money for themselves
and their households. They are not altogether to blame if, failing
a regular income from the pope, which they would not have liked
in any case because of the dependence it would have brought, they
used all kinds of devious means to gain wealth.

The pope himself used his *plenitudo potestatis* to expand very greatly
the provision of papal nominees to vacant benefices in the Church

[1] Details are given by W. E. Lunt, *Financial Relations of The Papacy with England to 1327*
(Cambridge, Mass. 1939).

at the expense of all other parties involved. Innocent III had asserted that in principle at least all ecclesiastical offices were at the disposal of the Vicar of Christ. In 1265 Clement IV decreed that all benefices falling vacant by the death of an incumbent while he was visiting the Curia should be reserved for the pope's disposal. The Avignon pontiffs extended the categories of reserved benefices until these included a majority of the major offices of the Church, including those of archbishops, bishops, and abbots. They strongly condemned pluralism in their public decrees but encouraged it by their acts. Both John XXII and Benedict XII insisted on their right to provide to lesser benefices in ecclesiastical patronage. Clement VI (1342–52) began his pontificate by offering benefices to all poor clerks who would claim them at Avignon within two months of his coronation.

Papal provision to benefices, it has been said, was simply part of the growing centralization of the Church; it was centralization applied to patronage, just as appeals to Rome and the use of judges-delegate represented centralization applied to the judicial system. It was not, it has been argued, in itself an abuse; indeed, it was capable of being used as an instrument of reform. But it is very doubtful if the advantages were nearly as great as the disadvantages. These were made even worse by the growth of a practice of granting expectations to benefices not yet vacant. More than one such exptecation could easily be granted, defrauding the first recipient, bringing in revenue from competing suppliants, and leading to litigation in the Curia, with still more profits for the judges who heard the case.

The Curia did not, in other ways, give its services for nothing. All archbishops, bishops and abbots thus 'provided' had to pay heavy fees besides a formidable 'service' tax, generally fixed by the fourteenth century at a third of the estimated annual income of the benefice. Lesser benefices were paid for by 'annates', fixed at a year's income as assessed (at a low level) for papal taxation. In addition, the popes claimed the income from a reserved benefice during its vacancy. Disputes over benefices were very numerous. Not infrequently there were rival claimants by papal provision. On the other hand, a papal provision might be challenged by deans and chapters or by laymen. Any one of these disputes might conceivably be taken to the Curia, where expenses were heavy, both in fees and in bribes. All kinds of privileges were for sale in the Curia, such as legitimization, permission to hold benefices *in absentia* or in plurality.

Many were sought by petitioners who were under age or without the necessary qualifications of literacy or experience.

> Voiz of a clerk [it was said] is sielde i-herd
> Ne were he never swich a clerk, silverles if he come.[1]

Notwithstanding such resolute attacks on abuses as the papal bull *Execrabilis* of 1317, the venality of the papal Curia, which sixty years later was to be condemned by St. Catherine of Siena in the strongest terms, continued throughout to be the greatest single source of weakness in the Church. An English monk could write in this period:

> Why does the pope presume to make greater exactions from the clergy than the emperor himself from the laity? . . . Lord Jesu, either take the pope away, or diminish the power that he presumes over the people; because he who abuses his power deserves to lose his privilege.[2]

The king and the magnates might condemn the practices of the Curia; but they themselves co-operated in them.[3] Pope and king, and even pope and lords, found it advantageous to join hands against lay patrons and cathedral chapters, even though both the magnates and the high clergy were dissatisfied. In the end the most resolute opponents of the practices proved to be the Commons in parliament, who were excluded from the profits of the system.

Influenced by such weaknesses, the clergy of the fourteenth century failed to meet the challenges of their age, even though in most respects they were as good as their predecessors, and in some may have been better. It is true that the scholar-bishop of the previous century now became less prominent. Leadership in the Church tended to be taken by ministerial and aristocratic prelates. Such bishops were not always bad, though the former had to be absent from their spiritual duties, whilst the aristocratic Thomas Arundel, made bishop at the age of twenty, had little to commend him. On the other hand, William Courtenay, son of the Earl of Devon, who was made archbishop after the murder of the lowly born archbishop Sudbury, was one of the best prelates of his age. The ministerialist John Thoresby, who became archbishop of York after long service

---

[1] *Political songs . . . from the Accession of Edward III*, edited by T. Wright, 2 vols. (R.S., 1859–61), vol. I, p. 324.

[2] The so-called Monk of Malmesbury in *Chronicles of Edward I and Edward II*, vol. II, p. 198.

[3] In 1329, Edward III wrote on behalf of Robert Wyville (for the see of Bath and Wells) to 24 cardinals, papal relatives and officials; W. A. Pantin, *The English Church in the Fourteenth Century*, p. 67.

in the king's chancery, had great integrity and zeal; but others were far less attractive. Some of these were neither aristocratic nor ministerial. Walter Reynolds, archbishop of Canterbury (1313–27), owed his promotion, it was said, to his skill in dramatics. Bishop Robert Stretton of Lichfield (1360–85) may have been of limited learning; and Adam Orleton, who held three bishoprics in succession between 1317 and 1345, was an unscrupulous politician. The chronicler Adam Murimuth said that the pope could never have appointed Robert Wyville to Salisbury (1330–75) if he had seen him first.[1] But it is just as easy to find good bishops who had obtained promotion essentially by their merits, men like Thomas Brinton of Rochester, the most famous preacher of his day.

Lower officials in the Church showed more clearly its failings. There was much absenteeism in cathedral chapters, where rich canonries and archdeaconries were to be had; and the same is true of the parish clergy. Non-residence was general and accepted. John Wyclif himself practised it. It has been said that in some districts the unbeneficed clergy who served in appropriated livings outnumbered the beneficed clergy by two to one. John Mirk, writing a handbook for parish priests at the end of the century, assumed that his reader would be a 'hired man' working as assistant to a priest, or as chaplain to a lord, not as rector of a parish.

The standard of education among the parish priests was very low: some had no knowledge at all of the Latin which was the language of their Church. The ordinary priest did not go to a university: all the education he got was attendance at a cathedral school or local grammar school, if there was one in his neighbourhood, perhaps run by friars; or he may have learned by helping a senior priest. On top of this, the standards of the ordinary clergy were depressed after 1348 by the effects of the Black Death; at least there was a difficulty in finding suitable candidates for clerical office. There was not only illiteracy but also downright ignorance among the parish clergy, and little evidence that they greatly inspired their flocks, despite Chaucer's poor parson who

> . . . Cristes love, and his apostles twelve,
> He taughte, and first he folwed it himselve.

They were often so poor that there was nothing, not even an absence of farming on their part, to distinguish them from their neighbours.

[1] *Continuatio Chronicarum* by Adam Murimuth, edited by E. M. Thompson (R.S., 1889), pp. 60–1. Robert had written 'special letters' for the queen.

In consequence of what G. G. Coulton called a great religious revival at the end of the thirteenth century, the Archbishop of Canterbury proclaimed that every parish priest must preach at least four times a year, approximately as set forth (as we shall see) by William of Pagula; but the proclamation was little obeyed. Nor could this deficiency be supplied by pictures on the church walls: it is remarkable that the idea of these as the poor man's Bible can have been taken seriously.

Despite the frequent poverty and occasional illiteracy of the parish priest, the Church protected his rights and dignities zealously because he was part of the hierarchy of clergy, set aside by its intermediary position between man and God and with a divine mission symbolized by the episcopal laying on of hands. He had the power of the confession and the right to judge and even to punish in important moral questions, including usury, witchcraft, and the marriage laws. Parishioners who had not made a will had to do so orally on their death-bed. The priest's person was sacred: no ordinary confessor might absolve a man who had wilfully assaulted him. His goods and chattels were also under special protection. His church was a sanctuary for at least forty days. He had a right, enforceable by excommunication, to tithes of wheat and similar crops, which would have made many parish priests comparatively well-to-do if the livings had not been appropriated. His other perquisites included the *heriot* or *mortuary* of the next best beast on the death of a tenant. There is no wonder that discontent was strong among the poorer sections of the population who suffered most, and gained least, by the system which had grown up in the Church.

There were, indeed, more writers than ever who were ready to teach the parish priest, if necessary in verse, what he should preach and how he should live. An early example is a work entitled *Oculus Sacerdotis* by William of Pagula. It began by instructing the priest how to hear confessions:

> And the priest ought to enquire of the penitent, if he was drunk, how he got drunk, whether perchance because he did not know the power of the wine, or because of guests, or because of an exceeding thirst coming upon him . . . .[1]

William even included advice to expectant mothers and the bringing up of the very young child. He touched on behaviour in church, and enjoined every priest to expound in English, four times a year, the

[1] W. Pantin, *op. cit.,* p. 197.

fourteen articles of faith, a proper knowledge of the seven sacraments, seven works of mercy, seven virtues, the ten commandments (plus two of the Gospel), and seven sins. He also prescribed remedies against such sins. Finally, he gave special instructions for the priest himself, especially on the sacraments. His treatise was imitated and in some ways improved upon by his successors. All this devotional literature reveals an earnest regard for the effectiveness of the fourteenth-century parish clergy. Its limited success was due to the accumulation of adverse circumstances rather than to a lack of understanding of the problem or of zeal.

The friars, who had contributed so much in the thirteenth century, now offered no real help to the parish clergy. The quarrels which their activities engendered increased rather than diminished. Their low reputation is reflected in bitter lines by the poets Chaucer and Langland. Gower claimed that they seriously menaced the purity of family life. Their internal dispute on the subject of absolute poverty was a traumatic experience for the whole Church, not ended even by Pope John XXII's condemnation of the dogma of Christ's own absolute poverty, which had been authoritatively declared by an earlier pope and had been accepted as a cardinal belief by the Franciscans themselves. Pope John was openly defied by Michael of Cesena, the General of the Order. The quarrel, together with the holding of property, continued; and the greed of the individual friars did not cease to be notorious. Langland noted

> . . . how that freris folwed · folke that was riche,
> And folke that was pore · at litel prys thei sette,
> And no corps in her kirkeȝerde · ne in her kyrke was buryed
> But quikke he biquethe hem auȝte · or shulde helpe quyte her dettes.[1]

The monkish orders were not notoriously corrupt, but were becoming restricted clubs for members, mainly from the upper classes, who wished to live in semi-retirement from the world. Entry could be quite expensive, but once admitted the monk found that life was not hard. There was a constant tendency to obtain relaxation of austerity in food and even in the daily routine. So strong was the desire to eat flesh that in 1337 Benedict XII permitted the use of the misericorde: this was a chamber midway between refectory and infirmary in which the monks might eat the flesh forbidden in the refectory. The only restriction left was that

[1] *Piers Plowman*, B. XIII. 7–10; edited by W. W. Skeat, vol. I, p. 386.

only half the community could use the room at any given time.[1]
Chaucer's prioress committed a serious but very general offence in
setting aside the basic rule of seclusion.

A 'wage-system' was established, whereby payments were
received by individual monks for work done or dignities and degrees
attained. With these they could buy clothes, books and jewelry.
The taste for private apartments spread downwards from the prior;
and in one way or another many of the aged or important monks
had their own private rooms. The monastic orders no longer
provided inspiration or leaders to the laity, even though it became
the custom to send monks to graduate at the universities. The
economic changes of the fourteenth century, which affected the
monks in the same way as other owners of estates, meant that the
monks more and more became *rentiers*, and substantial smaller
gentry like Chaucer's reeve and franklin took over their former influence in the countryside. They ceased to be a necessity or even an
integral factor in the country's economic stability.[2]

It does not justify the whole system to point out that many deserving
people benefited by it, as well as many undeserving, and that it was
in any case beyond reform by any individual, or by any one generation. It became harder to defend in the fourteenth century because of
the increasing education and sophistication of the laity. The development of a more educated laity helped to vitalize religion; but, on
the other hand the more literate and sophisticated laymen became,
the more they must have been conscious of the shortcomings of
the clergy. Their increasing place in the Church can be seen in the
size of the new structures, and the growing role of the congregation.
This was also reflected in the development of both the sermon and
the confession. The new religious activity of the layman can be seen
in the devotional book of Henry, earl of Lancaster. Lady Cobham
who died in 1344 had a degree of religious piety, described in a
sermon given by bishop John Sheppey at her funeral, which puts
her in the same category as the earl, though we do not know whether
she could read or write.

In spite of such devotion, anticlericalism rose to an unprecedented
height. It found expression in 1341 in the hostility to clerics of the
king himself. In 1376 the Commons presented a petition described

---

[1] The English Benedictine Chapter complained that this, which still amounted to a
prohibition on alternate days, was too strict for 'modern' monks who were no longer
capable of the self-denial of their forerunners.

[2] M. D. Knowles, *The Religious Orders in England* (Cambridge 1955), vol. II, pp. 357–9.

as 'a bill against the pope and the cardinals'. Clergy and chivalry, they said, had given place to simony and greed. Traffickers in holy things plied their trade in the sinful city of Avignon. The pope did not feed his flock but sheared it. His cardinals were England's enemies, who despoiled the country when they visited it. In this time of jubilee[1], it was said, a great gladness would be deliverance from evils fatal to the wellbeing of Church and State.

The famous Acts of Provisors in 1351 and Praemunire in 1353 were a direct challenge to the *plenitudo potestatis* of the pope. By the former, King Edward in parliament decreed that there should be free election to all elective benefices in England and free presentation by those who had the right to do so. By Praemunire, the statute Henry VIII was to use in 1534, Edward forbade cases to be taken to the papal Curia which were cognizable in English courts; and thus at a stroke he formally prohibited the bulk of appeals to Avignon, even though his prohibition turned out to be as yet largely a matter of form.

These enactments in fact made little immediate difference. On the one hand, even before they were decreed the king had possessed ample power to protect his subjects if he had wanted; on the other, because the existing system met his needs so well, he made no serious and consistent effort to put the new laws into effect. Nevertheless, the enactments were important for the way in which they were made, if not for the way they were applied. They were the creation, not of the monarch alone, but of King, Lords and Commons; and thus matters of the highest religious import were formally recognized as being in the cognizance of all the laity of the realm, even though Richard II seemed to believe that they were essentially his own concern when he came to reissue the Act of 1353 in the 'great' Statute of Praemunire of 1393.

Lords and Commons also worked together to oppose two minor papal exactions: the ancient hearth tax of Peter's Pence, owed since Anglo-Saxon times and commuted for a payment of nearly £200 a year; and John's tribute of 1,000 marks a year, now hopelessly in arrears. When Pope Urban V (1362–70) tried in 1365 to enforce full payment, Edward III brought the matter before parliament; and the Lords utterly denied King John's right to concede such a tribute, and declared that they and the Commons would resist it to the end. The

[1] This was a reference to the coming celebration of the fiftieth anniversary of Edward III's accession to the throne.

opposition to papal demands almost inevitably expanded to join hands with radical notions of reform which were gaining ground in many parts of Europe, and which in England found particular expression in John Wyclif and his far-reaching attack on the whole existing structure of the Church.

John Wyclif was a Yorkshireman of obscure origin, possibly born about 1330 in the Lancastrian Honour of Richmond. During the period between 1350 and 1370 he became one of the most notable scholars at Oxford; but about 1371 he was attracted into politics and into the royal service. His activities as a politician and religious reformer detracted from, but were also complementary to, his achievements as a scholar. Here, Wyclif was at his best. In philosophy, it was said of him, he was reputed to be second to none and, in the disciplines of the Schools, incomparable. He was 'holden of full many men the greatest clerk they knew then living'.

Like all reformers Wyclif was essentially a child of his generation, expressing in his life and works the inner conflicts of his age, but also its burning idealism, its courage, and its faith. 'Confusion and discord in metaphysics and theology,' it has been said, 'this was the climate in which Wyclif's opinions were moulded'[1]; but Wyclif also reflected a passionate belief that, with the help of God, the ills of Christendom could be cured. In this belief, both his theology and his philosophy led him in the end to advocate changes which his contemporaries believed to be heretical and which in many respects anticipated Martin Luther, but which he himself regarded as supported by Holy Scripture and the traditions of the early Church.

Prominent among his conclusions was an attack on the whole intermediary role of the priest between the individual and God; and this involved even the pope himself despite his claim to be the vicar of Christ. Closely connected with this attack was the concept of predestination and the invisible Church of the elect. Also connected was Wyclif's reverence for the Bible, which resulted in its translation into English. All these views tended to enhance the contribution of the individual layman to religion; and it was in line with this that Wyclif argued for reform of the Church by kings and laity if the clergy themselves were unable or unwilling to carry out a reformation.

In propounding his views on reform, Wyclif came to run a risk of martyrdom, but he had not in his veins the pure blood of the

[1] J. A. Robson, *Wyclif and the Oxford Schools* (Cambridge 1961), p. 31.

martyrs. He had a burning zeal to bring men face to face with Christ; but he held a prebend at Aust as an absentee; and he was probably human enough to resent the fact that he lost the warden-ship of Canterbury Hall, Oxford, through a dispute with his monks. He also lost a prebend at Lincoln which had been promised, but which was given to the immature son of one of the pope's mercenary captains. Finally, for reasons unknown, he failed to obtain the bishop-ric of Worcester to which he had some expectation. Whether or not a little less ardour for reform would have gained him more promotion is a question which can never be answered; but it seems uncharitable to argue that the lack of promotion provided any signi-ficant part of his motives as a champion of reform.

His dedication to reform, in face of the urgent needs of his age, led him more and more bitterly to assail those whom he regarded as the stubborn defenders of abuses: the 'regulars' whom he had long denounced; the friars whom he had at one time regarded with some favour; the 'Caesarean' clergy; and even the pope himself, who finally emerged as a potential and even actual Anti-Christ. Meanwhile, in line with his belief that reform might be looked for at the hands of the laity (if the clergy themselves failed to provide it) he became active in politics. He was a *clericus peculiaris* of the king as early as 1371, and by the time of the great crisis of 1376 he was an open 'ally' of John of Gaunt. He influenced political opinion against the payment of tribute to the pope and justified the violation of sanctuary. He thus made himself doubly obnoxious to the bishops, but gained only a dubious and limited support from the politicians. The limitations on their support became clearly evident after the publication of his *Confessio* in 1381, in which at length and after much searching of heart he brought himself to pronounce on the difficult and potentially explosive problem of the miracle of the Eucharist.

In the sacrament of the Eucharist, according to the teaching of the Church, men saw no visible change, but the bread and wine were nevertheless annihilated. There was a twofold miracle, of creation on the one hand and of annihilation on the other. But this, for Wyclif, was impossible. All that he saw around him, with the eyes of an extreme realist, was a reflection of the mind of God, which was eternal and unchanging. No part of it could be simply annihilated. God had made this impossible, even for himself, because of his eternal knowledge which could not be diminished or changed.

It is important to remember that Wyclif did not deny the miracle by which the priest created the body and blood of Christ in the sacrament of the Eucharist. He did not reject the significance of the vital and central act which renewed Christ's promise of salvation through His grace. He merely sought a formula which could be reconciled with his philosophical realism: 'that as Christ is at once God and man, so the sacrament is at once the body of Christ and bread—bread and wine naturally, the body and blood sacramentally'. But in fact he rejected what had been proclaimed as a dogma at the Fourth Lateran Council, and he publicly challenged the Church's claim to be the infallible repository of the truth by virtue of the promise of Christ.

For this action in particular, which alienated all his orthodox supporters, he has been regarded as little more than a child in politics; though he should perhaps be regarded rather as a scholar who could not surrender his highest dedication, which was the pursuit of truth through the reason given him by God.[1] In any case, Wyclif's attitude towards transubstantiation, added to his other heretical views, has been used to support the contention that his extremism not only prevented the success of his own efforts, but also harmed the cause of religious reform for many years to come. It is argued that he actually helped to perpetuate the abuses against which he fought so hard: leaders of the Church after his time tended to identify reform with heresy and to oppose even a reasonable change.

But perhaps such views exaggerate the possibility, in Wyclif's day, of effective reformation without a radical challenge to existing practices and ideas. Perhaps also they fail to take into sufficient account the nature of the universal crisis which had arisen in the *Respublica Christiana*: when the Church as a whole was torn by bitter conflicts about poverty; when cardinals and pope were deeply divided; when the Avignon Captivity and the Great Schism caused widespread scepticism and distress; and when the laity, especially kings and princes, were claiming dangerous powers and privileges in their relations with the Church. Wyclif was not the only man to be stirred into new ideas of reform in the years preceding the Conciliar Movement. It is easy to exaggerate the gulf that separated him from Martin Luther and his age.

[1] Two small volumes which give different interpretations of Wyclif's character and aims, which have been debated ever since his days in Oxford, are K. B. McFarlane's *John Wycliffe and the Beginnings of English Non-conformity* (London 1952), and John Stacey's *John Wyclif and Reform* (London 1964).

Wyclif and John of Gaunt have both been condemned for this failure of reform; the one for provoking it, the other for allowing it to happen. But perhaps both have been harshly dealt with. In the last years of crisis, indeed, each was on the horns of a dilemma, compelled to sacrifice immediate profit for what was considered to be the greater good. Gaunt's difficulties need not detain us. They were those of a politician, perhaps even a statesman, for whom it was folly to endanger a precarious political stability by supporting an uncompromising reformer. Wyclif's difficulties were more complex and baffling, arising from the conflict between a reformer's dedication and a scholar's inescapable obligation to the pursuit of truth regardless of the consequences. He was always, perhaps, a philosopher first and a reformer only second, despite all his passion for Christ. This is well illustrated by the scholastic logic which lay behind his pronouncement on transubstantiation which sacrificed on the altar of truth the hope of powerful support in the cause of reform.

The truth seems to be that Wyclif's ideas, though fine and inspiring to many, were too far in advance of the times to have more than a limited and transient success. Opposition mounted fast after 1376. In that year, Adam Easton, English clerical envoy at the papal Curia, wrote to the Abbot of Westminster asking for copies of Wyclif's writings; and he may have been one of those who moved the pope to attack the reformer in 1377. Wyclif still revered the pope and later expected much from the election of Urban VI in 1378. But in February 1377 he was summoned before the bishops in London to answer charges against him. Later in the same year, Gregory XI issued five Bulls against his teaching, urging the university of Oxford and the king to arrest this 'master of errors'; and in 1378 John appeared before the bishops at Lambeth and was prohibited from maintaining certain condemned theses in the Schools. In 1382, in an assembly of clergy at Blackfriars, many of his conclusions were condemned as heretical or erroneous; and though an earthquake which accompanied the council was claimed as a divine sign in his favour, the same claim was made for themselves by his foes. Later, in spite of eloquent support by colleagues at Oxford, his views were formally condemned by a committee of twelve doctors, voting seven to five. Greater excommunication was threatened against all who taught or heard them. When Wyclif's adherents appealed to Gaunt for support, he too bade them submit. Wyclif himself was commanded to be silent. His books were sent to the archbishop to be judged. This ended open support of the reformer in his own university, where he had so long been an honoured and influential teacher, and a heavy blow was struck at the freedom of academic thought and debate.

That Wyclif failed to retain active political support in high quarters is not surprising. What is surprising is the extent to which, for a time, he received the very highest protection. In the council of February 1377, Wyclif was defended by John of Gaunt himself. In that held at Lambeth in 1378, he was supported by the queen-mother, Joan of Kent, who commanded that no public judgment be given, as well as by the London mob which broke into the session. John of Gaunt even went in person to Oxford to urge Wyclif's silence on the matter of transubstantiation. Indeed, Wyclif's influence lived on strongly, even after Archbishop Courtenay's thorough condemnation of his teaching in 1382, not only in the Lollard movement he inspired but also in the Schools. Here, indeed, his views almost escaped condemnation, except for those on the annihilation of substance; and the learned Thomas Netter admitted later his profound admiration of them whilst he was a student at Oxford. Their influence persisted into the fifteenth century. In 1407, Archbishop Arundel was still prohibiting them from being taught in public places of Oxford or Cambridge, and in 1410 Wyclif's works were still being publicly burned in the university where he had taught. Not until after this did attempts to teach his philosophy officially cease.

But neither Wyclif nor his scholarly disciples in Oxford sought to promote their faith by martyrdom. Wyclif himself died peacefully in bed at Lutterworth in 1384; but in 1415 it was ordered that his bones be cast out of consecrated ground; and in 1428 his ashes were scattered into the river Swift, a gesture by Bishop Fleming on orders from the Council of Constance backed by an urgent demand of Pope Martin V. 'Thus', as Thomas Fuller wrote, 'this brook hath conveyed his ashes into Avon; Avon into Severn; Severn into the narrow seas; they, into the main ocean. And thus the ashes of Wickliff are the emblem of his doctrine, which now is dispersed all the world over.' Those of his disciples who were put under pressure recanted, and some ended up in very high office. Philip Repingdon, for example, became chancellor of Oxford, confessor to Henry IV and, ultimately, bishop of Lincoln. Bishop Fleming had himself 'played with heresy in his youth': he was the pert young scholar at Oxford whom Thomas Arundel had wished he could 'swap with a rod'.

Under Richard II, Wyclif's teachings, or at least some of them, were supported by a number of prominent laymen, among them Sir Thomas Latimer and Sir John Montagu, future earl of Salisbury. Contemporary chroniclers claimed that Lollard preachers could depend on the favour and even the outright adherence of a group of knights, some of whom were actually in the king's household. When Latimer was summoned before the council in 1388, he possessed heretical pamphlets and books. His dwelling at Braybrooke had become a centre of Lollardy. Montagu is said to have removed the images from his chapel at Shenley in Hertfordshire. Also strongly suspected were Sir Lewis Clifford and Sir John Cheyne, both with access to the royal court. In 1395 a group of knights felt so strong that they may have subscribed to a manifesto setting forth Lollard views. It was said to be from 'poor men, treasurers of Christ and his Apostles'; and it was attached to the doors of Westminster Hall and St. Paul's.[1]

But the glory of sacrifice and martyrdom for Wyclif's dream of reform belongs in the final analysis to the humble and poor, preached at and exhorted by men like William Smith, the first obscure layman we know of who supported the movement. Alongside him was William Swinderby, the most eloquent Lollard of them all. Gossip had it that Smith was deformed and ugly. When he failed to persuade a young woman to become his wife, he renounced the eating of flesh and wearing of shoes, and he became a teetotaller. He taught himself to read and write and became a Lollard preacher. When threatened by persecution, Smith showed a characteristic reluctance to suffer martyrdom and disappeared from history into the wilds of Wales, but not before he had made many converts to his cause.[2] In 1389 eight inhabitants of Leicester who were denounced before Archbishop Courtenay as heretics included a scrivener, a parchmenter, a tailor and a goldsmith. John Fox was elected mayor of Northampton in 1392; but he aided and abetted Lollards in his city, and in April 1393 he was dismissed and imprisoned.

After 1395 Convocation took a stronger stand against Lollardy. The prelates asked the pope to urge Richard II to stamp it out. In 1397 they demanded the death penalty for heretics who refused to repent. The movement which was to lead to the statute *De Haeretico*

---

[1] See the names given by M. McKisack, *The Fourteenth Century*, p. 521, n. 1. Cf. *Rogeri Dymmok Liber*, edited by H. S. Cronin (London 1921), Introduction, pp. xxvi-xlii.
[2] K. B. McFarlane, *John Wycliffe and the Beginnings of English Nonconformity*, p. 103; J. A. F. Thomson, *The Later Lollards 1414-1520* (Oxford 1965).

Comburendo of 1401 had begun. When this massive reaction set in the fate of Lollardy was sealed. Though the movement had support in high places, even extending to the king's court, the time had not yet arrived for a revolution in Christian practice. The repression of freedom which followed was an enormous price to pay for the continuance of the unity of the Church and the old comforting ways of Christian worship; but it preserved many things that were good as well as many that were bad. To some, such repression can never be justified; to others, the value of what was preserved was, on the whole, worth even the very heavy price that was paid.

One other conspicuous result of the defects of institutionalized religion and of the increasing devotion of the laity was the great and attractive movement of English mysticism. This was most significant, not only because it had affinities with a more general rise of individualism, but also because it revealed the strength of the deep and persistent Christian piety. The essence of mysticism, as at all times, was an insistence on the transcendental virtue of direct communion between the individual soul and God.

The English mystics were not rebels and emphatically not heretics; on the contrary, like William Langland who may claim to be in their company, they offered zealous obedience to Holy Church. On the other hand they lived apart and claimed a unique and direct inspiration by God, to be achieved outside the ordinary channels provided by the sacraments and services of the Church. They wrote at least part of their work in English and won the respect of the devout layman as well as the clerk. Like St. Francis before them, and Meister Eckhart in Europe, they were in danger, at times, of drifting into heresy. Despite their humility and devotion, their whole movement was in some sense a protest against the failures of institutionalized religion; but their continued fidelity to the Church shows also the inner strength of the established order, despite its obvious defects. The leading English mystics were Richard Rolle (1300–49) of Hampole, of Thornton-le-Dale in Yorkshire, together with the unknown author of *The Cloud of Unknowing* and Walter Hilton, an Augustinian canon who died in 1396. Hilton had lived near Newark and wrote the *Scale of Perfection*. The peace and serenity of Hilton and the author of *The Cloud* have been contrasted with the controversies and scandals of the age of Wyclif and the Great Schism; but, despite that, they represent in part a reaction to the same deep problems of the age.

It has been observed[1] that the fourteenth century saw neither monk nor friar nor bishop canonized. The one canonized saint was an obscure prior of a house of Austin canons at Bridlington. But if the century produced no saints, it nevertheless produced its fair share of good prelates, great issues, and courageous ideas of reform. In religion, as much as in any other aspect of life, it was the age of stress and strain. The career of its complex and still enigmatical greatest reformer reveals the conflicting forces which were at work. The ferment of the age did not destroy the old beliefs and the old forms of worship, but it did leave a legacy for all Christians to whom it offered the logic for a pattern of reform. For Englishmen there was the memory of an English movement, born and nurtured in Oxford, offering to the commoner a gift of the English Bible, and making its own contribution to the markedly English Act of Supremacy of 1534.

8. Intellectual Life

In the intellectual life of medieval England, a new period began with the fourteenth century, marked by a bitter clash of extremes in spite of the *via media* which had been opened up by Robert Grosseteste. The stimulation of scholars to new violence in controversy was mainly offered by William of Ockham, a one-time Oxford scholar and teacher who made his contribution to English learning chiefly from abroad. He developed his system of thought by 1320, when he was probably not more than thirty years old, and died in 1350. His writings not only led a violent reaction against the intellectual system of Aquinas, but also posed a serious threat to many accepted assumptions and traditions of Christian philosophical thought.

Instead of the dominant conception of knowledge as arising from the apprehension of universals through their reflection in particular objects, Ockham taught that only individual things had true existence. Universals were only names, signs standing for a group of particulars which the human intellect had observed to have something in common. Thinking in terms of universals was both possible and useful, but these should not be confused with realities. Whereas Aquinas had taught that what is known is the universal, Ockham taught that what can possibly be known is only the particular. Aquinas's philosophy led the thinker back to the mind of God; Ockham's kept the

[1] A. L. Poole, *Medieval England*, vol. II, p. 435.

philosopher preoccupied with the world around, and left God to
theology. For Ockham it was impossible to ascend from the particular to the mind of God by any process of human reason, for there
was no possible connection.[1] There was, indeed, a universal order;
but this was not based on God's knowledge but on his inscrutable
will. God Himself, except for His revelation, must remain unknowable
and unknown.

Ockham did not dream of denying the efficacy of revelation or of
questioning Christian dogmas. He merely argued that the essence
of religion was not reason but faith. Its truth lay in the Bible, the
teachings of the Church, and the communion of the individual with
God. This attitude could be, and was, compatible with deep religious
faith. It has sustained scientists through the centuries. Nevertheless,
the Ockhamist, like the radical Aristotelian, lived in a mental climate
which was alien and hostile to traditional Christian ideas. A
clash between Ockhamists and traditionalists was probably inevitable.
Indeed, it has been argued that it was the only way towards the rise
of modern science, a development which was not possible, despite
Grosseteste and Bacon, as long as speculation was rigidly controlled
by the postulates of religion; though this argument may underestimate the capacity for development inherent in Christian
thought.

The reaction aroused by Ockhamism can be seen in Thomas
Bradwardine, who was a Fellow of Merton from 1323 to 1335.[2] He
was a noted scholar and became archbishop of Canterbury shortly
before he died of the plague in 1349. His opposition to the prevailing
nominalism made him cling all the more firmly to St. Augustine
and his neo-Plathnism. His work probably did something to cause
scholars at Oxford, after two decades of upheaval, to return to more
conservative ways. Another famous scholar to join the fray was
Richard Fitzralph, archbishop of Armagh, who died in 1360. His
antipathy to Ockhamism was so strong that he experienced a 'conversion' against the methods and aims of the Schools, turning his
back on them, as he claimed, in favour of the absolute and divinely
revealed truth of Holy Writ. Through Scripture, he averred, God
had now dispersed the cloud of error which had enveloped him

---

[1] J. A. Robson, *op. cit.,* p. 24. Ockham, it is argued, placed the faithful before the
absolute and incomprehensible liberty of God.

[2] See Gordon Leff, *Bradwardine and the Pelagians: a Study of his 'De Causa Dei' and its
Opponents* (Cambridge 1957), and the comments of E. F. Jacob in *The Journal of Ecclesiastical History,* vol. IX (April 1958), pp. 94–96.

when he was croaking in the swamps with frogs and toads. His conversion almost led him into sheer anti-intellectualism. It was a revulsion against the whole process of learning which had led to such extremes of destructive speculation, and it has had its parallels in the twentieth century.

A more extreme reaction, as well as greater ability, is to be seen in his younger contemporary John Wyclif. The reformer was the foremost opponent of the *via moderna* of Ockhamism, and the most extreme defender of the old Augustinian traditions according to which Christian speculation was still directed towards an absolute knowledge of God. He believed that knowledge of the truth was to be obtained by a logical and metaphysical process. Its pursuit was by way of a ladder of wisdom which led to a knowledge of universals; here the ultimate reality was to be found, imperfectly reflected in the particulars which the Ockhamist so highly esteemed. The universals were the eternal exemplars existing in the mind of God. Knowledge of them was, in some sense, knowledge of God. This, Wyclif believed, was 'the reason why God does not permit the School of universals utterly to fail'. Wyclif felt this so deeply that he almost made his realism a test of orthodoxy.

To combat his opponents no effort was too great. Hence, Wyclif became a man of extremes, driven both by his nature and by his convictions. His extremism helped to preserve something that was precious in the great Augustinian heritage, but it aroused unnecessary bitterness and helped to make scholasticism in England after his day timid and sterile though there is no evidence that even without Wyclif it would ever have recaptured the vision of Grosseteste. Wyclif himself was a devout disciple of Grosseteste the philosopher and theologian, but not of Grosseteste the man of science. It is certain that he helped to prolong an emphasis on metaphysics and logic which had ceased to bear important fruit. Thus, after his day, the pursuit of truth began to assume a different form and the outlook of a whole age gradually slipped away. The scholastic effort to unite the findings of human reason and the data of revealed truth lost its force and appeal; the overwhelming power of a great system of thought was broken; and men were free to move forward on different lines towards a world dominated, eventually, not by the Christian tradition but by the findings of modern science.[1]

[1] M. D. Knowles, *The Evolution of Modern Thought* (London 1963), p. 335; J. A. Robson. *op. cit.*, p. 154.

9. LITERATURE

In the field of English writing and the visual arts the fourteenth century was perhaps the most remarkable period of the whole Middle Ages. It witnessed a spectacular triumph of the English spirit in both poetry and architecture, and produced the first great work of literature with a primary interest in the common man. It was a momentous period in the development of what, for want of a better term, we may call nationalism in both politics and art.

The transition from the thirteenth to the fourteenth century is marked in literature by the *Cursor Mundi* of about 1300, written in English and relating the story of the world from the creation to the day of doom. The reason for the use of the English language, it was explained, was that French rhymes were everywhere, but there was nothing for those who only English knew. The writer himself was learned, literary, sympathetic and, judging by surviving manuscripts, very successful. Not far removed in time was Robert Mannyng, author of *Handlyng Synne*, an English translation of a French aid to the confession. He improved on the original version (William of Waddington's *Manuel des Pechiez*) and made notable use of anecdotes and illustrations from the homely life of his day; he has, indeed, been called the most skilful storyteller of his time. He was essentially didactic and a severe moralist. Tournaments, he believed, were the occasion of all the seven deadly sins. If every knight loved his brother, they would not be held, for they encouraged pride, envy, anger, idleness, covetousness, gluttony, and lust. Mystery plays also earned his censure as occasions for sin (miracle plays were just passing out of the hands of the clergy into those of the laymen).

The *Cursor Mundi* and *Handlyng Synne* show the vitality of written English at the turn of the century. After 1300, it has been said,[1] there can be no doubt that English is the language of the country. Its triumph as the literary tongue was delayed by traditions derived from the Conquest, and by the prestige of French culture and language, but hastened by the rise of English patriotism and the political and administrative needs of the court. As an example of such needs, it may be noted that as early as 1258 the Provisions of Oxford were drawn up in Latin and French, but sent to the shire courts accompanied by letters in English. In the same period, when Richard of Cornwall was elected Emperor in 1257, one of his assets

---

[1] R. M. Wilson, 'English and French in England 1100–1300', in *History*, vol. XXVIII (March 1943), pp. 37–60.

was his knowledge of English; which tongue, Matthew Paris explained, 'is similar in sound to German'. Edward I assured his
subjects in 1295 that there was a danger the French king would
invade the land and extirpate the English tongue from the earth.
In 1362 a statute required all pleadings and judgments in all courts
to be in English, since French was 'much unknown in the realm'.
Parliaments began regularly to be opened by a speech in the
English tongue. In 1385 Trevisa agreed with Higden, whose
Polychronicon he was translating, that since the Normans came to
England Englishmen had been forced to leave their own language
and do everything in French. But, he added, since the Plague
everything had changed. Now, in all the grammar schools English
had again been accepted as the primary language. Children learned
French from English, and not English from French. Accepted as
the universal mother tongue, it could hardly be long before English
triumphed as the language of the court as well as of the countryside.

The individual writer who contributed most to this was Geoffrey
Chaucer. Chaucer was a protégé of the court, and he began his
writing under strong French influence.[1] He derived much from the
Roman de la Rose and from the French poets Machault and Deschamps,
not to mention the Italians Petrarch and Boccaccio. But he ended by
being as English as the pilgrims to Canterbury whom he portrayed.
His father was a London wine merchant and collector of customs;
and he lived most of his life in London. As an esquire, probably of
Lionel, duke of Clarence, he helped to invade France in 1359 and
was captured and ransomed. In June 1367 he received an annual
salary as valet in the king's household. At about the same time his
wife Philippa was lady-in-waiting to the queen.[2] A third attachment
to the royal circle came in 1371 or 1372, when Philippa's sister
Katharine Swineford became the acknowledged mistress of John of
Gaunt. On 8 June 1374 Geoffrey was appointed comptroller of the
Customs and Subsidy on wools, skins and hides in London, a post
he held until December 1386. He was no ardent politician or
reformer. His advice was 'Tempest thee noght all croked to re-
dresse'.[3] He survived the political crises of both 1386 and 1388
though he lost his comptrollership in the former. Nor was his

---

[1] D. S. Brewer, *Chaucer* (London 1961), p. 16.

[2] After Queen Philippa's death in 1369, Geoffrey's wife transferred to the service of
Gaunt's second wife Constance.

[3] From the *Balade de Bon Conseil*, quoted by Loomis, 'Was Chaucer a Laodicean?' in
Essays and Studies in Honour of Carleton Brown (New York 1940), p. 148.

position at court shaken by the deposition of Richard II. Indeed, his income was increased rather than diminished as a result of the usurpation of the throne by the son of his old patron in 1399.

Chaucer's work was all the more significant since it came from one who wrote under court patronage, betraying some of the preferences we should expect. He dwelt on the virtues of knighthood as well as the perfection of God, even when translating Boethius. His *Troilus and Creseyd*, probably written between 1374 and 1386, was a great and original masterpiece, and is claimed as the fore-runner of the English novel; but its hero was the 'verray parfit, gentil knight'. The same is true of Chaucer's greatest masterpiece, *The Canterbury Tales*, which he may have first pondered over when he had to surrender his comptrollership in 1386 and retired to his Kentish home.[1] This remarkable work displayed superb talent and shows how close Geoffrey could come to the common man; but he still reflected the outlook of a poet of the court. He did not, like Langland, give a new significance to the poor. He talked of villagers, but usually of the village aristocracy. Similarly, the lower citizenry of London had a scant place in his great panorama, though he saw them daily in the streets. He showed warm affection for the poor parson and the scholar, but each of these was an aristocrat in his chosen sphere. His most constant affection remained for the knight of chivalric romance:

> A Knight ther was, and that a worthy man,
> That fro the tyme that he first began
> To ryden out, he loved chivalrye,
> Trouthe and honour, freedom and curteisye.

Nevertheless, one of the very significant things about Geoffrey Chaucer is that he shows English literature rising above the limitations of the aristocratic courtly tradition. Another is that he achieved a new status for the English language, although it has been claimed that more than half the words he used were French or were derived from French words. His writings may also show the royal court itself broadening its interests and sharing some of his attitude. Hence, Geoffrey not only created a new versification but also contributed towards a new outlook. The 'miracle' of his *Canterbury Tales* should perhaps be placed alongside that of the

[1] Father Gervase Mathew, who generously allowed me to read the proofs of his *King Richard II* (London), believes that the tales belong to quite different periods and that often Chaucer used old material in a new framework. Sections may have been read at court.

earlier building at Gloucester[1] as one of the outstanding achievements of a remarkably creative age.

Compared with Chaucer, his younger contemporary Gower, though a very distinguished poet, has been called a man of talent rather than of genius,[2] though more recent writers find this judgment harsh. He wrote in Latin, French, and English, but did not possess the freshness, humour, or versatility of Chaucer. He early followed in Chaucer's footsteps and can be regarded as a poet of the court; but he was financially independent, and he showed his independence by turning against his patron Richard II. In his early writing he followed the usual courtly style by dedicating his efforts to the king and made the usual courtly references to Richard II:

> Richard by name the Secounde,
> In whom hath evere yit be founde
> Justice medled with pite [an echo of the coronation promise],
> Largesce forth with Charite.[3]

But he changed the dedication of the *Confessio Amantis*, whose first version was completed in 1390, when Richard began to 'play the tyrant'; and he presented the work not to the king but to England. This must have taken considerable courage. In a later work, the *Vox Clamantis* (between 1385 and 1402) he not only called Richard an undisciplined youth but also in a revision of the text lectured the king on his royal duties, declaring that the God-given beauty of his person should be matched by the virtue of his soul. For the last eight years of his life he was associated with the court of Henry IV and was described on one occasion as 'the king's esquire'. On another occasion he called himself Henry's 'oratour' and he dedicated English and Latin poems to the Lancastrian king.

Gower's anger extended from crowned fools who did not live up to their high office to uncrowned fools who laboured in the fields, but who worked little and aped their betters. It included the lords who ignored the danger which arose from the pride of the common folk. In him, the Chaucerian tradition lost some of its urbanity, but it did not cease to include an interest in all manner of English folk.

A new portent, of a different kind, was the development of archaic, alliterative verse, written in a north-western dialect, about

---

[1] See section 10 below.
[2] *Cambridge History of English Literature*, vol. II, p. 134.
[3] *The Works of John Gower*, edited by G. C. Macaulay (Oxford 1901), *lib*. VIII, lines 2987–90; vol. III, p. 469.

the middle of the century, probably coming not from the royal court but from the baronial hall. The verse was more than a mere survival of what seemed destined to disappear before the forces of change. It was also, probably, a literary revival of much significance. It sang of the chivalric virtues (its hero was often a knightly super-man), and its audience was expected to be aristocratic and informed. It seems to have been patronized by nobles who were in opposition to royal policy.[1] The outstanding example is *Sir Gawain and the Green Knight*, a polished and accomplished poem. Whatever its origin and purpose, the alliterative verse is part of the emergence to ascendancy of the English language in English literature. It forms part of the great Chaucerian era of change.

A fourth and superb contribution was by William Langland, 'gaunt poet of the poor', as John Richard Green called him. Langland was sustained neither by magnates nor by the court. He was never more than a poor chantry priest with no rich patron and no wealthy friends. He rubbed shoulders with the wealthy in the streets of London, men who wore furs, rich garments and gold collars; but he would not greet them fittingly. He probably originated in the west country near the Malvern Hills, but he lived and worked in London. He wrote alliterative verse, clearly not intended for the halls of the great, and less polished and finished than *Sir Gawain*. It would not be very far from the truth to call his verse a poor man's *Sir Gawain*, remembering, however, that even Langland's writing was probably too scholarly and sophisticated to be read to most of the poor.

Langland was born about 1332 and it is generally agreed that he was the sole author of *Piers Plowman*, the three redactions of which were probably made in 1362, 1377, and 1393.[2] It is a truly epic poem, justifying the ways of God to man and setting forth the ideals which had to be reactivated in society if the Christian world was ever again to go on the greatest of all crusades, the pilgrimage to the heavenly Jerusalem.[3] The well-worn copies of it show convincingly that Langland wrote for a different audience than did Chaucer. He tended to ridicule the courtier, vain and boastful, who laughed aloud at his own jokes.

---

[1] Dorothy Everett, *Essays on English Literature* (Oxford 1955), p. 48.

[2] These dates are provisional. For the most recent discussion of the texts see the volume by Gervase Mathew, *King Richard II*, mentioned above.

[3] D. W. Robertson and B. F. Huppé, *Piers Plowman and Scriptural Tradition* (Princeton 1951), p. 235.

William's poem is full of moral indignation about the failings of all classes of society; but also it shows a unique interest in and compassion for the sufferings of the poor. Its hero Piers is Peter, and is ultimately identified with Christ himself; but he is also a plowman, representative of honest toil, who all his life has 'Dyked and delved · and done what he hight/Within and without . . .'. Unlettered but upright, 'None are sooner saved · more settled in conscience/Than poor people as plowmen · and pastors of beasts'. There is still truth in Jusserand's concept:

> Piers Plowman shall feed everyone; he is the mainspring of the State; he realizes that ideal of disinterestedness, conscience, reason, which fills the soul of our poet; he is the real hero of the work. Bent over the soil, patient as the oxen that he goads, he performs each day his sacred task; the years pass over his whitening head, and, from the dawn of life to its twilight, he follows ceaselessly the same endless furrow, pursuing behind his plough his eternal pilgrimage.

> I wil worschip ther-with · Treuth, bi my lyve
> And ben his pilgryme atte plowe · for pore mennes sake.[1]

With such compassion Langland struck a new note in English literature. Typical of his outlook is his interest in the *comune* and *communes*:

> þanne come þere a kyng·knyȝthod hym ladde,
> Miȝt of þe comunes made hym to regne.[2]

It is hard not to believe that there were political implications in such lines, challenging and dangerous in the years around 1381. If there were, *Piers Plowman* marks the coming of age of the literature of England in a way that was all its own. Indeed, its author has some claim to be regarded as the most original of all the writers of this extraordinarily original age.

10. ARCHITECTURE

In architecture, the Decorated style, despite its extravagances, seemed destined to endure for a long period; but this was not to be the case. Though it had adherents far into the fourteenth century, the predominant fashion, in England at least, abruptly changed very

---

[1] B-text, VI, 103; J. J. Jusserand *Piers Plowman* (London 1894), p. 119.
[2] The meaning of *comunes* has been discussed by Donaldson in *Piers Plowman, the C-text and its Poet* (Yale, 1949); cf. P. M. Kean in 'Love, Law, and *Lewte* in *Piers Plowman*', in *The Review of English Studies*, N.S., vol. XV (Oxford, 1964), p. 241, n. 3; and my 'Fact and Fancy in Fifteenth Century English History' in *Speculum*, vol. XLII (October 1967), pp. 685–86. Gervase Mathew believes that for Langland the *commune* meant primarily the community of the kingdom conceived as a single organism, living and diseased (*Richard II*, as above).

soon after the decade 1327–37. After that a new style, usually called
the Perpendicular was followed in ninety per cent of English building. It was widely adapted to domestic architecture during the
fifteenth century and employed in the universities as late as 1637.
It remained uniquely English; at least, it never took root on the
continent of Europe, however much individual traits were reflected
abroad. Thus, historians are confronted with a sudden and surely
very significant change in architectural fashion which did not, like
previous changes, essentially express the pervasive culture of
Christendom whose main centre was in France. In its most characteristic features it was an English phenomenon, not to be fully
explained except in terms of the English scene.

The distinguishing feature of the new style was the use of the
straight line, both vertical and horizontal, and the emphasis on the
ogee curve. It expressed a fondness for geometrical design, and for
net-and-fan-vaulting by which the divisions into bays was almost
completely obscured. The combination of Gothic curve and a
rectilinear pattern looks at times like an attempt to reconcile ir-
reconcilables; but the attempt achieved a remarkable success.
Perhaps it is not altogether fanciful to see in the astonishing triumph
of a style which might well be called paradoxical, a reflection of new
forces at work in England in the mid-fourteenth century, and of a
new national mood. The confidence and high endeavour of the
period of the Decorated style continued, but not so exuberantly.
They had brought great triumphs but also some disasters. In the
period roughly coinciding with Edward III's reign, there was a new
spirit of reaction against venturesome innovations (in scholars like
Richard Fitzralph and John Wyclif, for example) and a new search
for discipline, unity, and harmony. Nor was the new mood immune
from movements like growing secularism and the increasing importance of what we may call the common man. The churches built
in the new style, it has been said, were more secular, with flattened
roofs and a tendency to obscure the idea of a city of God on earth,
soaring up towards the heavenly city. They began to cater more for
the individual, especially in chantry chapels and effigies, than for the
community of the Church; for the laity rather more and for the
clergy rather less. They were built more for the congregation and
the sermon, whose significance in Christian devotion steadily
increased.

The earliest significant surviving example of the new architectural style is that which was provided by the rebuilding of the choir at Gloucester cathedral. The south transept was probably rebuilt between 1331 and 1336.[1] A landmark in its adoption throughout England was its use in the church at Edington in Wiltshire. Other famous building occurred in the presbytery at Winchester, built between 1345 and 1366, and in the new choir at York, begun in 1361. There was no repetition at that time of the massive reconstruction of churches which had been witnessed in the thirteenth century, and which occurred in the parish churches of the fifteenth. Nevertheless a new style of great beauty and discipline took possession of England in the second half of the fourteenth century. The antiquarian, William Stukeley, said in the eighteenth century that 'The cloysters in this cathedral [of Gloucester] are beautiful beyond anything I ever saw.'[2]

Modern writers tend to reject the view by which the new style was attributed to a 'miracle' at Gloucester, largely independent of borrowings from abroad.[3] It is argued that, on the contrary, the style was essentially introduced into England by master-masons connected with the royal court. The origin of many of the ideas it incorporated was France, particularly the Sainte-Chapelle which had been built by Louis IX. The modern view emphasizes the importance of the royal court; the older view stressed the contribution of Gloucester. The one dwells on eclecticism by experts; the other was concerned with the mood of a community. Both have important truths; and they are not entirely opposed.

The emphasis on the part played by the royal court is of the utmost importance; but so is the recognition of a mood and tension at Gloucester which makes it not altogether inappropriate to talk of a 'miracle'. The Perpendicular style is inseparably connected with the

---

[1] There has been much controversy on the beginnings of the Perpendicular. In the main I follow J. H. Harvey in 'The Origin of the Perpendicular Style' in *Studies in Building History*, edited by E. M. Jope (London 1961), pp. 134–65. Mr. Harvey cites various modern contributions to the problem and discusses in particular the significance of building at St. Stephen's Chapel, London. His conclusion is worth giving at length (p. 149): 'From what has gone before it will be seen that the architecture of St. Stephen's Chapel, though it formed part of the movement which led to the establishment of Perpendicular as a ruling style, did not have a specifically Perpendicular character, even in the western porch completed only after 1344.' This should be contrasted with the strong assertion of Paul Frankl in *Gothic Architecture* (Harmondsworth 1962), p. 152, and with Geoffrey Webb, in *Architecture in Britain in the Middle Ages* (Harmondsworth, 2nd edition, 1965), pp. 133–6.

[2] Geoffrey Webb, *Medieval England*, vol. II, pp. 474–5. There is a plate of Edward II's tomb at Gloucester (Plate 85).

[3] The term 'miracle' is taken from G. G. Coulton's *Art and the Reformation* (Oxford 1928), p. 20.

'martyrdom' of King Edward II at Berkeley (not very far from Gloucester) and the great political tragedy of his reign. It was the mood which this created, and the concourse of pilgrims who flocked to his tomb at Gloucester, bringing piety and homage and rich offerings, which perhaps did most of all to inaugurate a new period in the history of English ecclesiastical architecture. In the words of the local chronicler:

> After the king's death, his venerable body was refused by certain monasteries hard by [Berkeley castle where he had been murdered] . . . for fear of Roger Mortimer and Queen Isabella and their accomplices. Yet Abbot Thoky fetched him from Berkeley Castle in his own chariot, sumptuously adorned and painted with the arms of the monastery, and brought him to Gloucester, where the abbot and all the convent received him honourably in their solemn robes, with a procession of the whole city, and buried him in our church in the north aisle, hard by the high altar.[1]

This was in 1327. By 1331 the transformation at Gloucester had already begun. The new building was started in that year with the refashioning of the south transept. By 1377, the year of Edward III's death, the new style had obtained a complete mastery over the English mind.

Thus two influences were happily united to produce a 'miracle', but both were intimately connected with the monarch and his court. And after 1331 the royal influence and entourage continued to promote the new style. Edward III himself donated rich gifts to Gloucester in 1337. Of the great building enterprises which contributed to the spread of Perpendicular—at Canterbury, Winchester, and York—the first two can reasonably be called works of the court school, and the third had affinities with it. Individuals who were connected with the royal entourage were prominent in building enterprises. Among them was Henry Yevele, a master-mason of the court. William of Wykeham, the great builder at Winchester after about 1360, had been surveyor of the king's works at Windsor, including works for the Order of the Garter. Edington, active at Canterbury after 1379, had been the king's treasurer from 1344 to 1350. John Thoresby who built at York had been chancellor. His work on the eastern front of the cathedral was one of the architectural triumphs of the century.

Thus, the new Perpendicular style flourished because of its own intrinsic beauty, because it suited the mood of the court and the

[1] *Chronicle of Gloucester Abbey*, edited by W. H. Hart (R.S., 1863), pp. 44, 48.

nation, and because it was linked in the public mind with a great traumatic experience caused by the life and death of an unfortunate king. Because it was so intimately connected with the English scene it bore a unique imprint of English genius and taste and reflected the national mood. It is perhaps not without a broader significance that it kept its hold unchallenged over the affection of most Englishmen for the remainder of the Middle Ages. Some minor notes of extravagance were introduced by Richard II and the Lancastrians. A great panel which Richard commissioned at Westminster, probably dated between 1394 and 1400, showing an aloof and majestic portrait of himself, may have been intended to promote his views on regality[1]; and the beautiful Wilton Diptych, about the same time represented Richard, heir to the two heroes Edward III and the Black Prince, kneeling before the Virgin. The subject was probably the king's coronation, always present in his mind; and the Diptych like the panel was intended to reflect Richard's majesty. Majesty of another kind was expressed when Richard II's builders made themselves famous by their use of the hammer-beam, a structure of wooden vaulting invented by the great fourteenth-century carpenters, which was used to erect a roof at Westminster Hall with a span of 67 feet. Henry IV set up a screen at Canterbury with six portraits of his predecessors, each about seven feet high. It has been claimed that the Lancastrians wanted to bring their monarchy within the received iconography of the Universal Church. But the grace and disciplined beauty of the new style were not seriously affected by these extravagances. Architecture continued to reflect the mood of a remarkable age in English history, when order and harmony struggled, in the end successfully, against strong and conflicting forces, and when amid all the powerful influences of the *Respublica Christiana* the English nation unmistakably began to take shape.

[1] Joan Evans, *English Art, 1307–1461* (Oxford 1949), p. 83. Some interesting comments on the Wilton Diptych, with reference to recent writing, are given by Gervase Mathew in *Richard II.*

7

HENRY IV AND HENRY V

1. The Lancastrian Usurpation of the Throne

THE reigns of Henry IV and Henry V were linked together like those of Edward II and Edward III. The latter is hardly to be understood except in the light of the former. Both Henry V and Edward III were under heavy pressure to indulge in foreign wars of aggression in order to escape from the difficulties which had faced their predecessors. Together, Henry IV and V were responsible for the revival of the Hundred Years War, a struggle which had already brought much harm to England and France, and was to bring even more before it was ended in 1453.

By his usurpation of 1399 Henry Bolingbroke established a new dynasty but he did not really begin a new period of history. He owed his throne to the support of both the aristocracy and the *plebs*, and he paid his obligation to both, but he also defended to the best of his ability the royal powers which he had usurped. He was heir to traditions of baronial opposition to kings, strong in the Lancastrian house and in his own youth, but he was also heir to an illustrious line of Plantagenet kings. Hence, his reign was a compromise between what his supporters expected and what his predecessors had claimed. He performed a brilliant tight-rope act, beset by multiple dangers both foreign and domestic: in the circumstances it was an achievement merely to survive. But he did not and could not change the course of history or dramatically banish the tensions of the age by a new kind of constitutional rule.

Before his accession to the throne Henry Bolingbroke was already by far the richest man in England, and he brought all his wealth as a dowry to the throne. Its content had been increased in 1380 by his marriage to Mary de Bohun, a co-heiress of the earldom of Hereford.

In addition to his wealth and power, he had more than the average share of ability combined, in his youth, with a chivalric and adventurous disposition. He had been born in 1367, too late to share in the glories of the early Hundred Years War; but he had made up for this by adventures in Lithuania and Prussia in 1390 and 1391, and by a 'grand tour' to Jerusalem. Wherever he went he travelled with a great retinue, accompanied by his household musicians, sending heralds before him to announce his coming, and distributing alms. His valour and skill in arms were unquestioned, unlike his cousin's. By way of contrast, he was also a student of moral philosophy. He had learned politics when opposing Richard II in 1386 and 1388, young though he was, and had helped to rout Robert de Vere at Radcot Bridge; but he had earned himself no great honour by acquiescing in Richard's destruction of three of the Lords Appellant in 1397, and this action did not prevent his own exile in 1398. His revolt in 1399 was mainly caused by Richard's confiscation of the Lancastrian lands on the death of his father, John of Gaunt; it was, he proclaimed at Ravenspur, to recover these that he had returned. But we need not conclude that his condemnation of Richard's 'tyranny' was no more than political expediency, and that he had learned nothing during the mismanagement of Richard's later years.

Henry Bolingbroke may have landed with the initial purpose of claiming his estates; but he was quick to profit by the fact that all England fell away from Richard; and, indeed, he must have known from the start that he could never be secure in England until Richard had been destroyed. In such circumstances the oath he took not to seek the throne was made to be broken. Somewhat ironically his perjury may not have been necessary. Public opinion would probably in any case have been in his favour, and the sentiment of the community was becoming a cardinal factor in politics. The long-term consequences of this were bound to be profound.

Whatever the exact truth of what transpired, obscured beneath a cloud of Lancastrian propaganda, it is clear that when Richard surrendered to Northumberland at Conway Castle he must have known that, except for a miracle, his death was assured. He was compelled to resign his throne during the morning and afternoon of 29 September, signing the document with his own hand and, it was claimed, saying that as far as he was concerned he would wish

Lancaster to succeed him. He was not allowed simply to resign; he was also indicted for his misrule, and it was universally agreed that he was unworthy to be king. His deposition was a consequence of action or inaction by the whole nation. Whatever the precise terms of Henry's claim to succeed, he did in fact owe his throne not only to his own efforts and to his immediate supporters, but also to the judgment of all the community on an unworthy king.

Hence, he was always in some sense a ruler on sufferance: like his own judges he held office *dum se bene gesserit*. His Lancastrian dynasty had to establish itself, like that of the Yorkists sixty years later, by favouring a movement of reform; and it succeeded because of popular support, even though its founder had led an aristocratic revolt. In the end the 'usurpations' of both 1399 and 1461 bound the king and the 'people' more closely together, and helped to create a new structure of politics in which the feudal hierarchy which had dominated England for so many centuries began to give way, even though slowly and almost imperceptibly, before the 'national' order of the early modern state.

2. THE TROUBLES OF HENRY IV

These changes began to show themselves even under Henry IV though their full consequences were long delayed. The weakness of the king's position encouraged demands for concessions on the part of his supporters and conspiracies against him by his enemies. They compelled Henry to fight a continuous battle 'against pressures from all sides that tended to diminish the royal 'liberties', and prevented the constructive effort, of which he was almost certainly capable, to restore political harmony. The disharmony which persisted throughout his reign ruined his health before the reign was halfway over and encouraged his son, Prince Henry, to look for an easy solution to domestic problems in the glories of a foreign war.

The Welsh were, somewhat surprisingly, Henry's first and strongest enemies; they had been incorporated into the English kingdom ever since Edward I's Statute of Wales. The king was actually leading an attack on Scotland when the formidable Welsh revolt of Owain Glyn Dŵr began. The revolt expressed in part the deep discontents of a society which was in unwilling transition from tribalism under ceaseless pressure from England. It also expressed the fears which beset Welsh nationalism, strong in a growing consciousness but threatened with decline. It favoured Richard's cause as against Henry IV, though the reason for this is not clear. What is certain is that Owain developed his revolt after an obscure quarrel with Reginald Grey of Ruthin, a member of Henry's council. He quickly had himself declared Prince of Wales, on 16 September 1400, and burned Ruthin on the 18th. By the end of 1401, despite successful actions by Henry Percy against him, he had obtained control over most of north Wales. Negotiations for peace having failed, Owain tried to get help from both Scotland and Ireland. Meanwhile, in 1402, he captured Reginald Grey near Ruthin, and shortly afterwards also made prisoner Edmund Mortimer, younger brother of the earl who had died in 1398. An English campaign of 1403 failed, partly from bad weather, despite some successes by Prince Henry; and English hopes suffered a further reverse when Mortimer married Owain's daughter and became his father-in-law's candidate for the English throne (he was the grandson of Lionel of Clarence).

By the end of 1403 the rebellion which had begun as an isolated revolt engulfed much of Wales, recalling the successful movement of Robert Bruce which had freed Scotland in the days of Edward II. 'All the Welsh nation', a contemporary wrote, 'are concerned in this rebellion.' An approach towards unity in Wales was accompanied by growing division in England. Mortimer was soon linked with the disaffected Percies whose revolt began in 1403. Moreover, a final ingredient was added to the Welsh movement when, in this same year of gloom for England, French help was effectively given to Owain. His movement had plainly moved far from the personal quarrel with which it had begun, and had acquired strength enough to provide a challenge to the whole structure of Anglo-Welsh relations which had been created, apparently to endure indefinitely, by Edward I.

In 1404 the story of Welsh success continued. The key fortresses of Harlech and Aberystwyth were lost. Owain negotiated a formal alliance with France and dreamed of a Welsh Church independent of Canterbury. In 1405, though with the hindsight of history we can see the turn of the tide, he and his allies, now including Northumberland, could plan to divide all England between them. Owain's share, if we may believe a somewhat dubious record, was to reach eastward as far as the Severn, the Trent and the Mersey. Northumberland was to have the northern counties including Northampton and Leicester. Mortimer was to receive all the rest. Well might Welsh hopes run high, for a French expedition landed at Milford Haven in August and Carmarthen was taken by storm. Welsh forces even moved eastward to within sight of the city of Worcester.

But, despite failure abroad and dissension at home, Henry weathered the storm; and in the end the superiority of English resources began to turn the scales. The French were not in a position to redress the balance in favour of their allies, and the strength of the Edwardian system in Wales proved itself in the time of need. Prince Henry took over the English counterattack and pursued it with vigour. He perfected in Wales the military skill which he was later to use on a larger scale in France. By 1407 he had so impressed the Commons by his achievement that they formally thanked him in parliament. By 1408–9 the major fortresses in central Wales were once more in English hands. Mortimer died during the siege of Harlech in 1409, and his three daughters fell into English custody. In 1413 Owain himself, his cause lost, went into hiding, never to reappear. His rising had been a costly episode. It had grievously beset Henry IV, but had not changed the fundamentals of Anglo-Welsh relationship, governed by the wealth and power of England and the gallantry but comparative poverty of Wales.

Scotland, which was larger and stronger than Wales, by a lucky series of accidents gave Henry less trouble. War was indeed threatened, and raids were encouraged by English weakness in 1399 as a result of the usurpation; but the Scots were divided by one of their characteristic feuds. George Dunbar, earl of the Scottish March, quarrelled with the earl of Douglas, both wishing to ally a daughter with the heir to the Scottish throne. Hence, Dunbar joined the English whilst Douglas followed the tradition of Bruce. Henry was not indisposed, despite his own problems, to take advantage of this quarrel. He was compelled by his very weakness not to repeat the concessions made by Isabella and Mortimer under like circumstances in the 'shameful' peace of 1328. He also wanted to forestall common action by the Scots and the French. Hence, he found time amidst all his distractions to lead an army into Scotland in 1400, though he failed to achieve any result. He took his claim to overlordship very seriously, searching old precedents, but the Scots were quite unimpressed: they had heard such claims before. They relied on the less sophisticated argument of war.

Unfortunately for them, and as it turned out almost as unfortunately for the English, a raiding force, including a large part of their aristocracy, was defeated in 1402 by the Percies at Homildon Hill. Seven Scottish magnates were killed and twenty-eight were made prisoner. The Percies gained great glory, Henry himself lost countenance, and the border was temporarily secured. But Northumberland refused to follow custom and surrender his most important prisoner Douglas to the king, though he yielded up other important captives in the parliament of autumn 1402. The crisis to which this formed a prelude was more dangerous and harmful to England than Homildon Hill itself was to the Scots.

The English victory of 1402 was thus not the piece of good fortune for Henry that it appeared at first sight, but better was to come. When James (later James I), heir to the Scottish throne, was being sent to the court of France in 1406 to protect him from his own future subjects, he was captured at sea by Norfolk pirates. The regent, Albany, who cherished his office, was in no hurry to obtain James's release; indeed, he intrigued strongly and successfully against it. The result was that James, a gifted poet destined for a tragic end, remained in England until 1424, returning to Scotland with an English bride, Joan Beaufort, and a policy of peace with England which had become his second home.

Thus, both countries were fortunate for a time in the preservation of a precarious peace, Scotland more so perhaps than England. Even though she was stronger than Wales, she was a poor country. Aeneas Sylvius Piccolomini, a visitor in James's reign, found her a poverty-stricken land. The roofs of the houses were of turf and the doors of ox-hide. Bread was a luxury. The common people lacked refinement and the women were attractive but not conspicuously chaste. In short, he could describe the country as a 'barren wilderness'. But it developed apace in the fifteenth century. Its first *studium generale* was sanctioned at St. Andrews in 1413; in 1451 a second was established at Glasgow; and a third was created at Aberdeen in 1495. Economic conditions also improved, something which would have been very unlikely if the cruel wars of King Edward I had been revived.

France proved to be tenacious in enmity, though failing by reason of internal divisions to make use of her great opportunity. Charles VI had plenty of reason for opposing the usurpation of Henry; Richard II had not only married his daughter Isabella but had also gone far towards allaying the deep quarrel between England and France. Consequently, Charles demanded Isabella's return to France, with her dower. The first part of his request, at least, was promptly met; but the second was not so easily conceded, and French threats of an invasion of England multiplied. Nor was it possible to build up an effective coalition against France on the continent by the marriage of Henry's children and the payment of English gold, the latter a policy familiar to English rulers since John.

The signing of preliminaries of a lasting truce with France herself, at Leulinghen in August 1401, was the best that could be accomplished but the Channel was vexed by a fierce war of privateers which inflamed the relations between Henry and many of his neighbours, and led between 1403 and 1405 to the burning of English ports. Meanwhile, the French attempted to encircle Gascony, and the city of Bordeaux itself had to fight for its life, or at least for its English régime. Nor did France fail to embarrass England by supporting rebellion in Wales.

Providence saved Henry in France just as in Scotland; in this case it was the madness of King Charles VI and the degeneration of French politics into civil war. One landmark in this process was the murder of the duke of Orléans at the instigation of the duke of Burgundy in 1407; a second landmark was to be the murder of duke John of Burgundy by the Armagnacs at Montereau on 10 September 1419. These acts of stark tragedy reveal the bitterness of the aristocratic struggle for power, intensified rather than allayed by theories of the rights and duties of lords of the blood, upon whom devolved the government in the incapacity of the king. The only problem for Henry, after 1407, was which side to support in the struggle of Burgundians and Armagnacs. Outside France also his prospects improved. He signed a commercial truce with Flanders and Brittany in this year, and in 1408 he patched up a peace with the Hanseatic League. In view of these successes, his dynasty might be regarded as accepted by its chief neighbours, or at least it could be argued that its full acceptance was only a matter of time.

3. Henry IV and his Subjects

In fact Henry's greatest danger proved to be not abroad but at home. His supporters claimed to share the fruits of a common victory; but the attempt to meet their various demands revealed the underlying divergence of their views. There was, indeed, a common reaction against the spirit of Richard's recent policy. It was agreed that all good laws should remain[1]; that the king should be counselled and governed by the honourable, wise and discreet persons of the realm; and that he could not change the laws at his will. Such generalities were profoundly important, but they could not cover all the practice of the constitution. Beyond this, Henry was prepared to make concessions but he was not prepared at any time to make a revolutionary change. He had not usurped a throne in order to liquidate its powers; indeed, he got a 'grant' from the Commons in 1401 that he 'should be in as good liberty as his ancestors before him',[2] presumably including among these all kings up to Richard II. He did not really trust the 'people'; and his lords trusted them still less. It is wrong, indeed, to imagine that, because the Estates and 'people' had helped him to the throne, he embraced any notion of 'parliamentary' rule. No such thing was possible, in any case, in the conditions of the early fifteenth century; and, if it had been possible, the experiment would have been entirely dominated not by the Commons but by the Lords.

The net result of the political balance of the reign was that the Commons did, indeed, strengthen their position; but they did not do this nearly as much as they would have liked. They preserved their basic and essential control over the purse; but they did not establish any revolutionary claims upon the king. In spite of Henry's dire financial needs they made fewer grants to him than they had to Richard (Henry's income was probably only £90,000 a year compared with Richard's £116,000), for they were very mindful that Henry enjoyed the income of the vast Lancastrian estates and they deplored the heavy expenses of his court. They had not supported a revolution in order to pay higher taxes, and Henry in consequence was poorer as a monarch than he had been as a pampered Lancastrian prince. The favourite project of the Commons was the resumption of royal grants and leases; they urged this in the first parliament of the reign, and it was their ambition for the next half-century. They were particularly suspicious of the household of the king and queen, and of the aliens who were housed there and enriched.

---

[1] My *Constitutional History of the Fifteenth Century*. p. 6.
[2] My *Constitutional History of the Fifteenth Century*, p. 43. A more recent discussion is by A. L. Brown, 'The Commons and the Council in the Reign of Henry IV', in *E.H.R.*, LXXIX (January 1964), pp. 1-30.

As a consequence of all this, Lancastrian finances were never adequate, and the situation became steadily worse as Lancastrian popularity diminished. As early as 1401 the treasurer wrote to the king to say that there was not enough money in the Treasury to pay the messengers who were to carry letters to the council. So hostile were the Commons to taxation, that when in 1404 they offered an extra grant to meet the king's grave necessities (an income tax on land and chattels), they ordered all records of the tax to be destroyed.

The result was a pattern of heavy borrowing, extending for many years. Borrowing had greatly expanded the powers of government as early as Edward I's reign; now it became necessary in order to avoid a complete failure of administration. The interest on loans was ruinous, and the cumulative burden of debt fantastic; Sir John Fortescue later recognized that chronic debt was one of the fatal evils besetting the whole Lancastrian régime. The refusal of the Commons was not yet, as it later became, an expression of distrust in Lancastrian methods of government; it was merely a part of the effort made by the Commons to exploit the political gains they had made in 1399. They were extremely ambitious and perhaps a little unrealistic. It was probably as well for England that their power after 1399 was not greater than it was.

They favoured strong methods of promoting efficiency in the governmental handling of the taxes. In 1406, despite Henry's assertion that kings were not wont to render account, they got a parliamentary audit. They may even have proposed that councillors should be made personally responsible for refunding moneys which had been misspent; but if they did, this proposal was very properly refused. Their favourite means for curbing governmental extravagance, however, came to be a very dangerous reliance on the council. This reached its height in 1406 when they proposed that grants warranted by officers, and even those by the ruler under his signet, should be authorized by the conciliar body which thus obtained a power of veto over the disposal of his own wealth by the king.

It was not so much the king's normal council to which the Commons turned for reforms, but rather certain specially appointed lords of the council with exceptional powers. The delegation of such powers to these lords was potentially more dangerous to good government than the immediate evils which the Commons sought to correct. Nor was it really practicable to place a limitation on the powers of the lords of the council by making them answerable to parliament. The inability of parliament to curb their aristocratic ambitions and quarrels was to become very evident during the minority of Henry VI. Thus, in 1406, it may have seemed a step towards good government to obtain from Henry a pronouncement that he wished to be counselled by the wisest lords of the realm, and that these should have the survey of all that would be done for the good government of the kingdom;[1] such a step may in any case have seemed justified by the illness of the king. But the extent to which Henry was really incapacitated is not certain, and the proposed restraints were probably unwelcome. In any case they advanced one stage further the growing threat of aristocratic control.

The expedient of a council dominated by the lords was not new, and it had generally failed to produce anything but strife. It achieved little more success under Henry IV than it had under Richard II. In the parliament of 1407 the chancellor and lords of the council declared that they had received neither gratitude nor thanks for their labours, and wished to be excused. In 1410 King Henry accepted another council dominated by lords and led by Prince Henry and Henry Beaufort; but in 1411 he rejected 'any manner of novelty in his liberty and franchise as entirely and comprehensively as any of his ancestors and predecessors in the past.[2]

The policy adopted by the Commons was premature and likely to be unfortunate; but the more general claims for an enhanced status of the Commons in parliament were both beneficial and difficult to deny. They were not only a consequence of usurpation, but also of the long, slow rise of the Commons in importance ever since the reign of Henry III. Henry's attitude towards such claims was, as we have seen, ambivalent. His hostility to some of them led him not only to insist on his traditional rights, but also to go as far as to encourage a movement in 1407 designed to limit the Commons' all-important control over the purse. He similarly showed himself to be hostile, or at best lukewarm, towards the 'communing' between Lords and Commons which had, in the past, favoured the lower rather than the upper House. But in practice the Commons enjoyed a freedom and importance under Henry which they had not

[1] Translated in my *Constitutional History of the Fifteenth Century*, p. 239.
[2] *Ibid.*, p. 244.

experienced since the Good Parliament. The latitude they claimed is well illustrated by their attack of 1404 and 1406 (probably) on the temporalities of the clergy, an attack so violent and outspoken that it drove Archbishop Arundel to seek support against it from the secular lords. The Commons' growth in status may also be seen in the promises by which Henry assured them adequate time for debates and protection against the practice whereby the king listened to un-authorized reports of transactions in the lower House. Henry further promised to have the business of parliament engrossed, if possible, before the Commons' departure, so that nothing should be included gratuitously; and he conceded that the knights and burgesses should be consulted if any existing statute should be changed.

All this was important; but it involved no revolution. What the Commons might have hoped for after 1399, and what they did not get, was some clear improvement in their status, some movement towards greater equality with the Lords, such as they had seemed on the point of gaining in 1376, but which had been withheld, in spite of the great precedents of 1341 and 1376, throughout the whole reign of Richard II. This is what gives a particular significance to the claims of the Speaker, Sir Arnold Savage, in 1401, when he spoke of parliament as a Trinity and of its procedures as parallel to those of the Mass; and to the Commons' assertion of an enhanced status in the parliament of 1414, which is referred to briefly below. Nothing came of these claims; but despite some modern scepticism they reveal new aspirations. They point the way towards a time, not too far distant, when all members of parliament, like all participants in the Mass, would share the indivisible unity and equality of the Trinity. As Sir Arnold assured Henry, 'to have the hearts of his people is the greatest treasure and riches of the world to every king'.[1]

These hopes were not fulfilled, despite favouring circumstances, because (to use a much criticized term of Bishop Stubbs) they were premature. Henry would not be a king on sufferance, least of all to the Commons; and for good or ill he forfeited the chance of purchasing unshakeable support from the *plebs* by really significant concessions to their representatives in parliament. The result was that, in the end, the Lancastrian dynasty built its hopes upon, and virtually surrendered to, the growing power of the magnates of the land.

Contrary to a tradition which owed much to Bishop Stubbs, the magnates were the greatest gainers from the Lancastrian usurpation.

[1] Translated in my *Constitutional History of the Fifteenth Century*, pp. 300, 301.

As a result they consistently offered by far the most serious threat to the reality of kingly power. Henry's policy towards them was much more devious than that which he followed towards the Commons, and it was far less successful. He began by showing extreme leniency to Richard's former magnate supporters, revealing not only the aristocratic sympathies which informed his movement, but perhaps also a desire to use them as a balance to the Percies in the north. Richard had made them marquises, dukes and earls, when he openly moved towards absolutism in 1397. They included Edward, son of Edmund duke of York, whom Richard had made duke of Albemarle, Thomas Holland, grandson of Joan of Kent and formerly duke of Surrey, John Holland similarly duke of Exeter, John Beaufort who had been created marquis of Dorset, and Thomas Lord Despenser whom Richard had elevated to the earldom of Gloucester. They were unpromising material for Henry's purpose if indeed he looked to them for support, since many had Plantagenet blood in their veins, and since he had reduced them from their high rank, to become merely earls of Rutland, Kent, Huntingdon, and Somerset and Lord Despenser. In January 1400 they plotted a rising in which a priest named Richard Maudelyn was to impersonate King Richard. It was reported by Rutland to Edmund, duke of York, his father, and thus brought to the notice of the king. The rebels had neither timing nor ability. Intimidated by Henry's prompt reaction, and lacking any real support, they fled to the west country, to be caught and executed by the 'people' in Cirencester and Bristol, where memory of the tyranny of Richard was strong. Back in London, the archbishop of Canterbury gave thanks to the Blessed Virgin for 'rescuing the most Christian king from the fangs of the wolves and the jaws of wild beasts'. The main significance of the rising is that it shows a nation more bitterly divided than Henry's easy success in 1399 seemed to show. There was no easy road to the achievement of political unity, and Henry had to lean heavily on his own supporters, with no gratuitous assistance from his erstwhile political foes.

In fact he had no effective counterweight to the Percies. They had done much to put Henry on the throne, and were deeply dissatisfied with their rewards, even though they were high in the king's councils after 1399, and were almost unchallenged in their control over the Scottish March. Henry Percy had been appointed Warden of Carlisle and the West March as early as 2 August 1399, by a commission under the seal of the duchy of Lancaster. Percy was also active in national affairs and in those of Owain of Wales. He spent heavily in the course of his many duties, and was only slowly repaid; but this was hardly an adequate reason for revolt and, indeed, he was not really unfairly treated. His quarrel with Henry over the prisoners captured at Homildon Hill was a symptom of growing strain rather than a significant cause of rebellion. We are driven to the conclusion that, inflated by his victory of 1402, Henry Percy and his son Henry (Hotspur) felt themselves strong enough to challenge the whole tenor of Henry IV's settlement of 1399, and the measure of continuity of royal policy which it expressed.

By July 1403 the Percies were in revolt. Hotspur, at Chester, issued a proclamation referring to Henry IV as Henry of Lancaster, and declaring Richard to be still alive. He prepared to join forces with Owain of Wales and Edmund Mortimer. He and his father appealed by propaganda to both magnates and *plebs*, proclaiming their loyalty to Henry but their desire to cleanse his council. They acted, they said, in the public interest; but they allied with the public enemies, Glendŵr and Mortimer, and probably aspired to be king-makers, to nobody's profit but their own. Grievances such as that arising from taxation by Henry without the advice of the Estates in parliament, against his promises of 1399, recalled the aims of earlier baronial opposition; but Henry's cautious policies since 1399 had ensured that there would be no general response.

Englishmen were in no mood for civil war, and saw no reason for a change of masters. The crisis of rebellion was sharp, but it was also short; and it did not really shake Henry on his throne. He beat Hotspur in a race to reach Prince Henry's headquarters at Shrewsbury. He disposed of Hotspur's army outside the city, offering negotiations to the last, but fighting resolutely when these were refused. The confused battle was fought until nightfall; but in the end Douglas and Thomas Percy, earl of Worcester (brother of Northumberland) were captured and Hotspur slain. The body of the impetuous Hotspur was exposed at Shrewsbury and later distributed to various towns, the head going to Micklegate Bar in the city of York.

The fate of Northumberland himself is surprising and significant. He was retreating, outnumbered and without hope of success, when Henry offered, in return for his formal submission, to restore him to favour. Being restored to favour meant, as it turned out, being stripped of castles, estates, and offices, and kept under close guard; but it was generous nevertheless. Henry, as nearly always, was percipient: he knew the value of moderation and the Percy strength in the north; he was doubtless aware that the deeply respected Richard Scrope, archbishop of York, had been spoken of as a supporter of the opposition; and he hoped by conciliation to avoid further trouble. As usual, his head ruled his heart. But trouble could not be avoided; and it had an alarming feature when it came. A rising, led by Archbishop Scrope in 1405, made an appeal to all classes; its propaganda stressed the subjection and annihilation which threatened the secular lords, as well as the unbearable taxes on merchants and commons. It was a northern revolt; but its propaganda made a strong appeal also to the south. However, it was easily crushed at Shipton Moor, where the leaders were tricked into submission and the army melted away.

Perhaps because of the dangerous appeal of the movement, by reason of its leader and its propaganda, Henry put aside moderation in his punishment of Scrope. He had the archbishop tried by a secular court (though Sir William Gascoigne resigned from the tribunal on the ground that the Archbishop could not be tried by a secular court), and he executed him despite his immunity as a priest and leader of the Church. Henry may have argued that Scrope had too many admirers, both lay and clerical, to be left alive. The archbishop had, indeed, been followed to Shipton Moor by members of all four mendicant orders; the Franciscans among them had been stripped of their clothes by the royalists and left to run away. Even dead, the archbishop could be dangerous. Miracles were worked at his tomb.

Northumberland was, of course, behind Scrope's revolt, and Henry moved north from York to punish him. The time for moderation was plainly past. For a while, the old earl avoided capture by taking refuge in Scotland. From there, in 1406, he made his way into Wales, later to France, and back to Scotland again in 1407. He finally tried a desperate invasion of the north of England in 1408, and was defeated by the Sheriff of Yorkshire at Bramham Moor, losing his life.

The Percy revolt did much to throw Henry heavily on the support of the countryside, with consequent demands by the Commons. But what had done even more to save the Lancastrian dynasty was the failure of the magnates to give the rebels support. Hence, in the long run, the rebellions of 1403 and 1408 brought the Lancastrians and the aristocracy more closely together, rather than driving them apart. The north became a stronghold of Lancastrianism, in spite of loyalty to the Percies and to Scrope. Scrope's martyrdom was not all waste. Some of his ideas would be revived by the Yorkists, whether by accident or design. On the other hand, apart from their own 'affinities', the Yorkists would find support not so much in the north as in the more radical south and east.

Thus, by methods and intelligence one cannot but admire, Henry IV survived the consequences of his usurpation and the attacks on his position which had resulted both at home and abroad. The remainder of his reign is mainly a story of declining health, perhaps aggravated by remorse for Scrope's death. Soon after the revolt Henry became very ill at Archbishop Arundel's manor at Mortlake, and lost consciousness from a stroke. He was thought to be dying, as also was to happen again in December 1408. After this, there are frequent references to his medical advisers. Whatever he suffered from, apart from the stroke, it was not leprosy as contemporaries believed; but there is no doubt that his trials and difficulties made him neurotic, and his later years have provided fine material for moralizing about the emptiness of worldly ambition and the inevitable price that is paid for transgressing the moral laws.

The decline of the king was accompanied by the rise of Prince Henry, who, in August 1408, was probably just twenty-one years old. His rise to power and responsibility began so early in his life that he must have found some difficulty in finding time for the youthful excesses Shakespeare later talked of; though these were no doubt real enough, so real at least, that there may have been some kind of a 'conversion' when he became king in 1413. In any case, he was formally given charge of north Wales and the Marches when he was thirteen. In 1406 he attended meetings of the king's council at the age of nineteen, and in 1407 he was publicly thanked for his victories over Owain of Wales.

From this time on he was allied in politics with Henry Beaufort, who had been made bishop of Winchester in 1404; and he became increasingly at variance with his father. He and Beaufort seem both to have leaned heavily on the support of the aristocracy, and they served on the aristocratic council of 1410. In 1411 they had become so estranged from Henry that Beaufort suggested that the king should resign his crown in favour of his son. Prince Henry and his supporters were obviously a powerful force in politics, and it was their influence which resulted in English aid being given to the Burgundian side in the French civil war. An English expeditionary force helped the Burgundians to defeat the Armagnacs at St. Cloud on 9 November 1411. The English forces were soon persuaded to leave France, by gold from the coffers of the duke of Orléans, but their intervention in 1411 was a clear portent of more massive intervention to come.

In the midst of these critical events, King Henry died on 20 March 1413. His reign had brought him more trouble than glory; he must often have sighed, in spite of the glittering prize of 1399, for his affluent easy days as son and heir to John of Gaunt. Nevertheless, in some matters his achievement was great. Most of all it lay in the fact that he had reversed the trend of Richard's last years, and set England's face once more towards her destiny of reconciling liberty and order in the modern state. In other matters, however, his success had been strictly limited. He made an irreversible choice, though this was perhaps inevitable, when he allowed his dynasty to become dangerously dependent on the aristocracy. From this, despite all the play of contingencies, flowed much of the tragedy of fifteenth-century politics; and this was already presaged when he died, lonely and worn out. The fruits his appetite had demanded in 1399 had proved unexpectedly bitter, and death must have seemed more and more like a happy release.

4. The Rule of Henry V and the Resumption of the French War

Henry V succeeded to the throne at the age of twenty-six and died at the age of thirty-five. His character has been as variously interpreted as that of Edward III, and for essentially the same reason. His admirers and detractors alike have judged him by the outlook of their age, changing their point of view from generation to generation, especially in relation to the fundamental problem of war. But later generations have reached a surprising degree of agreement in recognizing Henry's essential greatness. They have come near to Stubbs's view; though it is interesting to contrast Stubbs's appreciation of Henry's qualities, as those of one of the greatest and purest characters in English history, with his condemnation of Edward III.

In point of fact Henry V and Edward III had a good deal in common. Each had a great responsibility for the Hundred Years War. In Henry's case the temptation to revive the claim to the French throne, with its consequence of a major struggle, was reinforced by the need to strengthen the Lancastrian dynasty. Once the war was begun, Henry's conduct of it entitles him to be regarded as one of England's great rulers. He had high intelligence and some genuine piety, combined with a love of justice and a capacity for heroic labour. It can be said that his personality was in harmony with his destiny. We may forgive him a measure of hypocrisy, not unknown to some political leaders in any age. His negotiations preliminary to the resumption of war were probably quite insincere, but they served a political aim. We may discount his declared purpose of ending the long effusion of blood between England and France. On his death-bed he was said to have professed that his dream had been to unite Christendom against the Turks and 'to build again the walls of Jerusalem'; but he must nevertheless be given a large share of the responsibility for the war; and his calculated decisions to this end led, in fact, to the shedding of a great deal of French and English blood.

It has been argued that the tragedy of his reign was that he gave a wrong direction to national aspirations and led his people into a chimera of foreign conquest by which they were exhausted, and which postponed their commercial expansion for nearly a hundred years. But perhaps this is to abuse the hindsight of history. France, like Scotland, was an unresolved problem for Englishmen at the beginning of the fifteenth century. No king could ignore it, and few or none could have turned their back on the opportunity for solving it in England's favour which was presented by the French situation under Charles VI. The war did, indeed, bring terrible consequences and would have been better avoided; but the course of English history might still have followed a very similar path. Commercial expansion did in fact occur, and was restricted not so much by the struggle in France as by the bitter hostility of commercial rivals who guarded the Baltic and the Mediterranean, just as, a century and a half later, broader oceans were claimed as a monopoly by the Spaniards and the Dutch.

At any rate, the resumption of this French war served one immediate purpose: it cemented English domestic unity. Henry had strong support for his venture; three dukes, eight earls, two bishops, and about eighteen barons, accompanied him to France in 1415. But, before the effects of the common action became fully apparent, the disunion it was intended to overcome which had survived all his father's efforts, was clearly shown by a plot against him on the eve of his departure, headed by Richard, earl of Cambridge. Cambridge was not the prime mover, nor the most active conspirator, but he was the titular leader. He was a son of Edmund of Langley, younger brother of John of Gaunt; his elder brother was Edward, former duke of Albemarle and afterwards duke of York. Finally, by his first marriage he had been brother-in-law of Edmund, earl of March, and thus allied to the Mortimers. His first wife Anne was descended from Lionel of Clarence, Edward III's second son. His second wife Maud Clifford linked him with the Percies. These marriage affiliations are now somewhat tedious, but they were immensely important at the time. England was coming to be dominated by the princes of the royal blood; and both Richard's royal blood and his other connections were calculated to have a strong appeal.

The projected rising amounted to no more than an abortive intrigue. The conspirators felt obliged to inform Edmund, earl of March; Edmund as great-grandson of Lionel of Clarence had a legitimate claim to the throne, and was to be proclaimed king, but he promptly informed Henry V of the plot. March saved himself by this act, but the conspirators were executed as traitors. It was an inauspicious though in itself unimportant beginning to what was to be a brief but glorious reign.

Henry's invasion of France was even more systematically prepared for, and more backed by all the national resources, than Edward III's great expedition of 1346, even though the army which landed near Harfleur on 14 August 1415 was comparatively small. The groundwork had been laid by diplomatic negotiations with Burgundy and Flanders which assured at least their friendly neutrality. Since Henry took with him only about 2,000 men at arms and 6,000 archers, he has been regarded as contemplating only a large-scale raid; but this is unlikely. He must have remembered what little effect had resulted from such raids under Edward III unless they served to bring about a major engagement. He began more ambitiously than Edward by besieging Harfleur before he made his *chivauchée*; and since the siege was unexpectedly long, and his losses heavy, his march was to that extent curtailed. But it was made, nevertheless, and the result was closely parallel to that which had attended the campaign of 1346.

After the siege of Harfleur, Henry's force was no more than about 900 men at arms and 5,000 archers, but it was a disciplined and formidable force. Henry proposed to traverse a hostile territory from Harfleur to Calais. If he could repeat the story of Crécy, so much the better. Defeat he refused to contemplate, though his generals pointed out its possibility. After a long march along the bank of the Somme, looking for a crossing, he made his way over on 19 October, between Béthancourt and Voyennes, his men tired and weakened by the weather and the scarcity of food. On 24 October, when a very superior French army finally barred his path to Calais, he prepared for a supreme effort near the village of Agincourt. Whether or not he proposed to the French to renounce his conquests and pay compensation for his destructions, in return for a free passage to Calais, remains doubtful. The chroniclers are not agreed. Henry faced very heavy odds, amounting to perhaps eight to one, and cold reason may have overcome hot valour; but, considering the price of surrender, this is hard to believe. In any case, the outnumbered English waited, through the darkness of 24–25 October, for a desperate encounter. It rained all through the night.

At nine o'clock in the morning the English moved towards the narrow gap between two woods through which their road lay. Henry commanded the centre, the duke of York and Lord Camoys each commanded a wing. The French plan was to ride over their enemy by sheer numbers. The English, on the other hand, still put their faith in the archer, braced by the men at arms, each bowman equipped with a sharpened stake prepared long ago at the crossing of the Somme. It was to be planted before him at the opportune moment, in face of the cavalry charge. He would be the first to receive such a charge, standing as he did in front of the knights and organized in open order, in clusters of two hundred. His exposed position was one to try the nerve of any man. If the archers broke or failed, ultimate disaster for everybody was assured.

The French attacked down the narrow lane in three great masses, the first or vanguard alone consisting of 5,000 to 10,000 men; whilst on the wings there were special forces of knights to dispose of the English archers. The result was stark disaster. The whole majestic body of French nobility failed to do more than dent the English line. They were jammed helplessly in the narrow gap. They were butchered 'like sheep' where they stood. Many were taken captive, for ransom; but these threatened to outnumber their captors, and a mistaken cry that reinforcements had arrived caused Henry to order them all to be slain. The French losses were enormous. The English lost no more than 300 men, including the duke of York and the young earl of Suffolk. English discipline had once more triumphed over French valour uncontrolled. A 'great victory, glory to God in the highest', the victors proclaimed.

What the victory brought is debatable. Very little, some historians argue: only Harfleur, hard-pressed and far from impregnable. But the harvest was nevertheless rich in such intangibles as English unity and English prestige. It enabled Henry to contemplate a long war, and to undertake a systematic conquest of Normandy, something Edward III had never been able to do. How was Henry to know that, just as much as Edward, he was building on sand? He enjoyed much glory, and was flattered by a visit to England in 1416 of no less a personage than Sigismund, Holy Roman Emperor, anxious to mediate between England and France. Sigismund made a deep impression, distributing Henry's gold, which he had received in presents, to English courtiers and nobles, who thus enjoyed their king's generosity at second hand, and were dutifully grateful to both benefactors. It was not Sigismund's fault if his intervention was unavailing and that the war continued. In the end Henry got out of the visit a treaty of mutual help and alliance with the emperor, for what it was worth, which was sealed on 15 August. On paper, the English position among the powers of Europe was now extremely strong and that of France extremely weak.

For the next stage of the war, Henry obtained by various taxes on both clergy and laity the huge sum of £136,000. On 23 July 1417 he embarked with a new army of some 12,000 men (10,000 effective). He had made plans for systematic conquest and he proposed to winter in France, itself a novel move. Caen was captured (an objective repeated long afterwards in the allied landing of 1944), and Falaise fell in February 1418. Meanwhile, Henry's ally, John the Fearless of Burgundy, who had been worked on by long and tortuous negotiations, enveloped Paris from the east, Chartres being captured in October. By February 1418 there were Burgundian garrisons at Mantes and Rouen. The English advanced into the Cotentin and also began the reduction of Maine.

The seizure of Paris itself by the Burgundians, who formally entered the city in June 1418, gave them the responsibilities of government and changed their attitude towards the English. There were moves towards creating a united front with the Armagnacs against Henry, and towards getting help from Scotland and Lorraine. But in spite of this defection Henry captured Rouen in January 1419, not before the garrison had put out many of the old and weak to die in the ditch around the town.

Nevertheless, his position, between the Burgundians in Paris and Normandy to the north, and the Armagnacs to the south, looked strong but was in fact weak. The French he conquered did not show any desire to support him. The Scots responded freely to the recruiting activities of the Count of Vendôme; there was talk of volunteers up to 10,000 men. The Castilians promised Henry's enemies a fleet. The Armagnacs emerged as the real defenders of France. The English might still have obtained favourable terms from the Dauphin and the Armagnacs, but they hankered after those set forth in the treaty of Brétigny. They believed they could still play off the Burgundians against the Armagnacs and hold out for their far-reaching claims; but time was not as it seemed to be really on their side. Forces were soon to begin stirring in France which would change the whole complexion of the war.

This is true even though negotiations now included a firm project of marriage between Henry and Catherine, daughter of Charles VI, whom Henry glimpsed for the first time on 2 May 1419, being much impressed by her beauty and charm. As against this, an alliance was concluded in the following July between the duke of Burgundy and the Dauphin, intended to end forever the feud of Burgundian and Armagnac. The bright prospects this raised for France were, it is true, shattered by the Armagnac axe wielded by Tanneguy du Chastel, which felled the duke as he entered the fenced enclosure at the bridge of Montereau on 10 September to concert measures with the Dauphin against Henry. The sequel to this was the famous treaty of Troyes sealed on 21 April 1420, binding English and Burgundians together. Henry was to marry Catherine and inherit the French crown on the death of her father. Meanwhile, he was to exercise the regency made necessary by Charles VI's ill health.

The treaty of Troyes provided the cornerstone of English policy after 1420 and, indeed, sustained all their conduct of the war. It was agreed to by all the subjects of both Henry and Philip, and was not to be abrogated without their consent. But it was not supported by a sentiment of friendship between two peoples or by mutual self-interest. Indeed, in matters of trade and commerce, England and Burgundy were hostile rather than friendly; and in matters of sentiment Burgundy was drawn to France rather than to England. The murder at Montereau had temporarily obscured both sentiment and self-interest, but this would not endure; and if ever Burgundy and Armagnacs came together again, the foundations of English conduct of the Hundred Years War as renewed by Henry V would be effectively destroyed.

Though the English won victories and gained ground after 1420, and though Henry was married to Catherine on 2 June in this year, and was received into Paris in state in December, the foundations of the English position in France were never secure. The vision of England and France perpetually united under one ruler was magnificent and had some basis in history; but the current was flowing strongly against it. To keep the 'state' of Normandy loyal required roughly 4,700 men on permanent guard, mostly English. Nor could military superiority be taken for granted. Despite all her disunion and the disasters which befell her, France was wealthy, her knighthood was gallant, and her size and strength made it impossible to subdue her with the limited resources of England even with the best organization the age could produced.

At Baugé, in 1421, the Duke of Clarence was defeated and slain because he outrode his archers and fought with his men-at-arms alone. It is true that Bedford more than made up for this minor disaster, at Cravant in 1423 and at Verneuil in 1424, by maintaining the traditional English formation. It is true also that the hard-fought engagement at Verneuil was disastrous for the Scottish allies of the French; out of 6,000 of them few survived, and the dead included the earl of Douglas and his son and the earl of Buchan. This was a great victory for England, and showed that the English had discovered a fine general. But nothing could make up for the death of Henry V from dysentery in 1422. Though opinions have varied about Henry and his war, he should almost certainly be regarded as a great general, inspiring his troops, conscious of his limitations as well as his strength, filled with a burning conviction of the justice of his cause. Nor did he lack stature as a statesman. He gained and held the loyalty of his subjects at home as well as in the field. During his short life-time England became one, finely tempered for the work he had taken in hand. Unlike Edward III, he did not live to see the flower of victory wither in his hand; and it was left to his successors to reap a bitter harvest of defeat and disillusionment from the war he had quite deliberately begun.

8

HENRY VI

1. The Years of Minority

KING HENRY VI was the first and most eminent victim of his father's policies. This is true even though his reign was unique in the history of post-Conquest England by reason of the weakness and ineffectiveness of the ruler. John had been untrustworthy and unprincipled, and Stephen had been easygoing and too magnaminous for his times, but no earlier monarch after Ethelred the Unready had been so lacking in the attributes necessary in a medieval king. The nearest was perhaps Edward II, who paid a terrible price for his shortcomings; but even Edward might possibly have been a respectable ruler in more propitious times. Henry VI had only scholarly learning, piety, and good intentions to commend him at a moment in history that demanded heroic virtues, the capacity for great decisions, and inflexibility of purpose. His reign was bound to be disastrous for England, as disastrous almost as that of Charles VI had been for France.[1]

England suffered by the death of Henry V, not only in the French war but also in the domestic problem which that war aggravated rather than solved. Both problems were, indeed, inseparable. The war demanded unity and sacrifice at home; but unity and harmony at home depended largely on the success of the war. The nominal rule of a baby, less than twelve months old in 1422, invited discord and frustrated the war effort. After 1422, indeed, the Hundred Years War slowly brought, for England, exactly the opposite consequences from those which Henry V had anticipated, despite his claim that he had on his side the justice of God. From 1422 to 1455 England saw

[1] Comments on his character are in my *Constitutional History of England in the Fifteenth Century*, p. 16, and in R. L. Storey's *The End of the House of Lancaster* (London 1966), pp. 34-8.

an almost uninterrupted decline towards civil war. This was not so much the product of aristocratic selfishness and violence as of a web of circumstances that no individual or group of individuals could control.

Henry had done what he could before his death to arrange for his son's rule. By his will Henry's brother John, duke of Bedford was to control Normandy and fight the war, whilst England was to be ruled by a council of regency, dominated by lords, and under the direction of Humphrey, duke of Gloucester, Bedford's younger brother. Humphrey had been designated by Henry, and this designation was approved by parliament, to hold the office of lord protector as long as Bedford was abroad; but he was not given the powers he thought should be rightfully his. Humphrey wished to be *rector regis et regni*, like the earl marshal had been in 1216, with all the councillors subordinate to him and advising him as he temporarily exercised the authority of the king. The lords of the council believed, on the contrary, that it was they who should exercise the royal authority, whilst the protector defended the king's person and, if necessary, his realm. At the most, Humphrey should be chief councillor. Thus, the lords, acting in parliament during its session, and at other times acting in the council, proposed to rule the land in the long minority of the king.[1]

In the bitter political struggles which followed, Duke Humphrey generally received the support of the Commons, inside and outside parliament, and regarded himself as the spokesman of the poor who could not or dare not speak for themselves. He laid great stress on the special responsibilities of the lords of the royal blood. The lords of the council were generally supported by Bedford, anxious to have aristocratic co-operation in his war, and by the lords in parliament, who in 1428 endorsed the solemn claims which the lords of the council had made in the previous year:

> And the just God would never have my lords of the council stand in such great doubt and peril as they think they do, unless they be free to govern by the said authority [of the king], and acquit themselves in all things in a manner they think expedient for the king's advantage, the public good of his realms and lordships, and the free execution of his laws.

[1] The problems of this settlement are the subject of vigorous debate by modern historians. Reference to recent literature is given in my 'Facts and Fancy in the Fifteenth Century' cited above. Some comments are made also in R. L. Storey, *The End of the House of Lancaster*, pp. 38–9.

Thus,

> the execution of his [the king's] authority stands at the present moment in his lords assembled, either by authority of his parliament or in his council, and especially in the lords of his council.[1]

There emerged, in the prolonged conflicts which arose between Humphrey and his opponents, a genuine clash of political ideas. Both sides in the struggle were, in fact, loyal to the duty of preserving the royal authority intact; but Humphrey may well have pointed to the danger of oligarchical control breeding aristocratic faction and struggles for power; whilst the lords of the council could proclaim the danger that a great lord of the blood might forget the ties of kinship, seduced by the temptations of power, as indeed happened later in the case of Richard III. The divisions which Humphrey both feared and fostered led directly to those which, broadened and deepened by events, contributed much to the Wars of the Roses and the change of dynasty which were to take place between 1455 and 1461.

Humphrey was tenacious and aggressive in attempting to wrest control over the government from the lords of the council, though he never ceased to proclaim his unswerving loyalty to the king. He took time off from the domestic struggle in 1424 in order to lead an army into Hainault, seeking the lands of his wife Jacqueline of Hainault and endangering the friendship of Burgundy; but on his return in 1425 he called on the authorities of London and the Inns of Court to help him against the lords of the council, and in particular against Henry Beaufort, now once more chancellor. Beaufort in turn summoned Bedford home to end what threatened to become a civil war: 'as you desire the welfare of the king our sovereign lord, and that of his realms of England and France, and also your own well-being and ours, hasten hither', Beaufort wrote. Humphrey's ambitions were checked; but the quarrel continued, even though Henry VI was crowned king on 6 November 1429, and the duke resigned his title of Protector, keeping only the title of chief councillor. He was still, after Bedford, the leading prince of the blood, and in April 1430 was made the king's lieutenant and warden of the kingdom whilst Henry went to be crowned king of France. There were still many vicissitudes until 1437, when new arrangements were made for the exercise of the royal authority, finally superseding those of 1422. In May 1432, for example, Gloucester described himself as willing to

---

[1] My *Constitutional History of England in the Fifteenth Century*, pp. 248–9.

act as chief councillor with the advice and assistance of the other lords; he still did not concede them an authority equal to his own.

The arrangements of 1437 followed closely the pattern of 1406. They gave the day-to-day government of England largely into the hands of a council still dominated in fact, if not in form, by the great lords. It was headed by Duke Humphrey and Henry Beaufort, and included the archbishops of Canterbury and York, bishops, earls, and officers. In fact, as Humphrey found to his cost, it tended to be entirely controlled by the archbishops of Canterbury and York. Some matters of grace were reserved to the king. Others 'of great weight' were not to be concluded without his advice. But the government of England remained largely in the hands of the council and the court.

Humphrey, because of his ambitions and his pride, stood largely alone; but he had the intermittent support of the *plebs*, notably the Londoners and the Commons in parliament. It has been said by a weighty authority on the period that he made himself the idol of the middle class. He gave to the *plebs* an idea of their importance in politics which they had not enjoyed since the early part of Henry IV's reign; he certainly destroyed the unanimity of aristocratic support to Henry VI; and he prepared the way for a later effective opposition. He emphasized notions of the rights and duties of a great prince of the blood which were becoming anachronistic and which were in any case to be destroyed by their abuse by Richard of York and Richard III; but he was nevertheless the forerunner of the Yorkist opposition and of Yorkist royal policy under Edward IV. Hence, the Minority of Henry VI, in spite of its complicated personal quarrels, is to be compared in its political and constitutional importance with that of Henry III from 1216 to 1227 and with that of Edward III.

2. The Ending of the Hundred Years War

Meanwhile, as violence began to take possession of the domestic scene, defeat began to emerge over the horizon in France, each the counterpart of the other. Abroad, Bedford strove valiantly to preserve and even extend Henry's conquests; but he met with increasing pressure from the former Dauphin who, since 1422, was King of France. One ominous feature of the war was the poignant career of Joan of Arc, magnified in its contemporary significance by modern writers, but nevertheless dramatically illuminating the change which was occurring in the war. As has been said, there is no more astounding or more moving story in history than that of the peasant girl who became the commander of an army, saved her country from mortal danger, and herself died a martyr for her religious and patriotic faith. Joan symbolized not only the enduring strength of France but also the growth of French patriotism; and it was this, above all, which spelled the doom of English hopes of conquering any substantial part of the country.

Joan was born at Domrémy between Champagne and Lorraine, probably in 1412. She was the youngest child of well-to-do peasants, and could neither read nor write. In her work as a shepherdess she had time for quiet contemplation, and pondered the 'great sorrow' of France. She heard voices; St. Michael appeared to her as a knight surrounded by angels; and she decided that her destiny was to drive the English from the land. The first French captain she approached advised that she should have her ears boxed and should be sent back home; but she persisted and in the end obtained an interview with Duke Charles of Lorraine. Eventually, in 1429, dressed in men's clothes and escorted by six men, she obtained an audience with Charles VII himself. Every schoolboy knows how she recognized the king although he hid among his courtiers. This was at the town of Chinon. She told Charles: 'I am come with a mission from God to give aid to you and to the kingdom, and the King of Heaven orders you, through me, to be anointed and crowned at Rheims.'

Thus the justice of the cause which had been proclaimed by the great Henry V was challenged by a humble shepherdess. The French believed her because they wanted to believe. The English disbelieved, but feared. The amazing thing is that she succeeded. She got herself equipped with banner and armour and household. She obtained command of an army of 7000 or 8000 men; and she relieved the key city of Orléans, besieged by the English under Salisbury and later under Talbot, both famous generals of the age. Joan inspired the defenders and disheartened the attackers. After ninety days of siege, Talbot retreated on 8 May 1429. Joan's dreams were authenticated; her mission justified.

The inspired French showed what they could do by winning a brilliant victory over the English at Patay on 19 June of the same year. The details of the battle are confused. One of the English commanders, the famous Sir John Fastolf, was accused by a French chronicler of cowardice, but it is likely that his actions were mis-understood. What seems clear is that the French outnumbered the English and also outmanoeuvred them, another sign of the changing times. In consequence of their defeat the English beat a general retreat. On 17 July Charles was crowned at Rheims, Joan kneeling before him. She exclaimed, 'Gentle king, now is fulfilled the good pleasure of God', and expressed a wish to retire from her appointed task. Her request was refused, but her claim that God's work had been accomplished was justified. It did not really matter, after Charles's coronation, that the treason she feared undermined her influence and that on 24 May 1430 she was captured by the Burgundians in a minor engagement. Her essential purpose had been achieved.

Joan was sold to the English for 10,000 gold crowns. She was tried before a tribunal of the Inquisition, declared a heretic who had relapsed, and condemned to the stake. Political intrigue and professional jealousies accompanied her to the end. She died with courage and fortitude with the word 'Jhesu' on her lips. Well might an English bystander exclaim, 'We are lost; we have burned a saint'.

Historians will no doubt always disagree as to the importance of Joan's part in the war. Many other factors besides her influence were at work on the side of the French. Nevertheless, it was no accident that her year of victory was the turning-point: after 1429 English fortunes steadily waned and French power consistently grew. The decisive event was the ending of the Anglo-Burgundian alliance. This had always been weakened by incompatibility of purposes, reinforced by commercial friction. It was further damaged by a quarrel between Humphrey of Gloucester and Philip the Good of Burgundy, who challenged Humphrey to a duel. John, duke of Bedford, did what he could to retrieve Humphrey's blunders, but he died in September 1435. Above all, the failure of the alliance was made certain by a reconciliation between Philip the Good and Charles VII, which the latter purchased at a heavy price, but which did much to end the long bitterness left by the tragedy of Montereau. The treaty of Arras, by which Philip finally loosed himself from England, was sealed in April 1435. The young Henry VI wept when he heard of Burgundy's defection. His tears were prophetic. He was weeping, had he known it, for the whole foreign policy followed by the dominant party in his court, for the English possessions in France, and for himself and his son Edward, still unborn.

But there was more behind the changing fortunes of the war than either patriotism or diplomacy. Frenchmen had found a new ruler as well as discovering a new saint. King Charles VII, who succeeded his father in 1422, was an inglorious leader, but he was *le bien servi*. Under his direction his subjects put order before constitutional liberty, a fateful choice which coloured all their history up to 1789. A great series of *Ordonnances* provided efficient and up-to-date military service. The right of levying troops was reserved to the king alone. The reforms gave the king something like a standing army, an important element of which consisted of archers enlisted in the parishes. In the end, even the nobles were paid, and for the first time became amenable to discipline and centralized direction exercised by the king.

Artillery was greatly developed and some cannon were mounted on gun-carriages. Ships of war were acquired. The French armies became even more efficient than the English, and the gallantry and indiscipline of Crécy and Agincourt became things of the past. Regular taxation was imposed to maintain all this organization, including the famous *gabelle*, a compulsory tax on salt, first made general and permanent by Philip VI, and the *taille*, a direct tax which came to be levied annually, by the royal authority alone. It had been accepted as a permanent imposition, in fact if not in law, during the reign of Charles V. But the tax had later been discontinued, and it was Charles VII who finally endowed France with a new and co-herent system of finance, just as he endowed her with a new, efficient, and disciplined army. The sacrifices this entailed were only apparent in the long course of history. For the present, the positive virtues were enough to enable the French to begin the long piece-meal reconquest of their country, freeing her alike from the English and from the free companies who intermittently preyed mercilessly on the countryside.

As against the advantages enjoyed by the French, slowly feeling their way towards national unity, England suffered the disadvantages of a minority and of rule by Henry VI. Their king was beloved for his virtues; but he was also simple-minded and amenable to control by courtiers and priests. His long rule repeated many of the tragic features which in France had marked that of Charles VI. Even her earlier successes worked against England, for they wedded men's minds to the strategy and tactics of the past and obscured the realities of the present. England, not France, had now to endure the internal divisions which tend to accompany a losing war, and had to fear the invasion of her soil by the enemy. The result was a stubborn, courageous, but hopeless struggle to maintain the English conquests. With no victories won, no booty gained, and no rich captives taken, the new phase of the war was far more expensive than the old, and the consequences in England more disastrous. It says much for English tenacity and valour that the phase lasted from 1435 to 1453.

3. The Failure of Lancastrianism

In the years that followed 1437, a court group controlled both king and council, and in some matters imposed their will on both parliament and the community at large. Their policy was to magnify the king's authority, much of which was in their hands, whilst keeping the king himself in tutelage. The distinguishing features of their régime were their evasion of ancient traditions of consent, and their preference for the advice of great councils of lords over that of Lords and Commons in parliament. They systematically refused to allow free contact between the king and his subjects, and they rejected any special claims of the lords of the blood to defend the interests of the king or of the realm.

Such a political order was plainly dangerous to the hard-won liberties of Englishmen. But it had certain incurable weaknesses. It was inextricably bound up with Henry's personal incapacity, and with a foreign policy of peace with France even if this involved great concessions. Both by reason of its evasion of English constitutional processes and of its apparent sacrifice of English interests abroad, it had to be pursued in an atmosphere of court intrigue and secret diplomacy which engendered widespread opposition. Whether or not the ruling 'party' was animated by superior wisdom and by willingness to sacrifice popularity for the good of their country, which is very doubtful, its leaders were bound to incur the bitter opposition of Duke Humphrey, supported increasingly by the commonalty. A good many strands of evidence combine to suggest the conclusion that a political explosion was in the making in the years 1440 to 1447, and could not long be deferred.

It is not surprising, therefore, that in these same years there were bitter political struggles, marked by a systematic and ruthless attack on Duke Humphrey. This was led by William de la Pole, successively earl, marquis and duke, of Suffolk; but it was almost certainly made with the agreement of Beaufort and Kemp, and with the active support of Adam Moleyns, bishop of Chichester and clerk of the council. It was not without provocation; in 1440, for example, Humphrey made violent accusations against the king's advisers in general, and against Beaufort and Kemp in particular, which almost amounted to an impeachment.[1] But the reaction which in the end overwhelmed him was even more violent. It showed clearly a degeneration of politics after 1437 which was undermining the very basis of Lancastrian rule.

In 1441 Eleanor Cobham, who had succeeded Jacqueline of Hainault as Humphrey's wife in scandalous circumstances, was accused of being the 'chief author of . . . acts and false deeds' performed by persons who intended to destroy the king by 'their false working and craft'. She was, it was said, guilty with them of witchcraft, and she was solemnly tried for felony and treason by all 'the principal clergy of the realm'. The accusers and judges alike were her husband's political enemies. She escaped with a penance, 'the which . . . she fulfilled and dede righte mekely', and imprisonment for life. In prison on such a charge, and with the possibility of a burning such as that which her 'clerk' Roger had suffered, Eleanor was no doubt a hostage for her husband's good behaviour; though, considering Humphrey's character, his good behaviour must still have remained a matter of considerable doubt.

The attitude of the ruling 'party' towards Humphrey of Gloucester may perhaps be illustrated from a well known interview between Henry VI and French ambassadors in 1445, at which Humphrey and other lords and advisers of the king were present. This interview was part of prolonged negotiations for peace and was described in great detail by the French ambassadors.[2] It was dominated by William de la Pole, earl of Suffolk. The king appears to have been little more than a figurehead, smiling and making an occasional platitudinous remark. Humphrey of Gloucester was plainly snubbed and ignored; it was probably mostly for his benefit that Henry at one point said in English (Henry also spoke good French): 'I am very much rejoiced that some who are here should hear these words: they are not at their ease.' The whole interview was a public and unmistakable expression of the extent to which Humphrey's political fortunes had sunk since

[1] My *Constitutional History of England in the Fifteenth Century*, pp. 52–6.
[2] Part of the document is translated *ibid*, pp. 61–5.

he was Protector from 1422 to 1429, and since he was the king's lieutenant during Henry's absence for the coronation in France.

But Humphrey was still a great prince, with powers to influence public opinion and to arouse hostility against the faction which controlled Henry. This was all the more so since the negotiations with France from which Gloucester had been largely excluded in 1445 were still continuing, with an outcome which was likely to be most unpopular. It was because of this political conflict that Humphrey may have been murdered on 23 February 1447 as he attended a parliament at Bury St. Edmunds. He was silenced before he had an opportunity, if such indeed was his intention, of repeating and surpassing his earlier passionate accusations against those privy advisers who were usurping the authority of the king.

The evidence for murder is largely circumstantial, but it is persuasive.[1] Humphrey was isolated from his friends as soon as he reached Bury St. Edmunds, and was imprisoned in his own lodgings without accusation or trial. Henry's mind had already been so poisoned that he believed Humphrey threatened his safety. The king even called out the local militia to stand guard outside the town, though 'there was no doubting that it was intensely cold and biting weather', as the contemporary Richard Fox records. After this, all that Richard cared to say is that on 'the Thursday, after the arrest of the said duke of Gloucester, he died on the stroke of three on the bell'. Towards evening, it is recorded, Humphrey was disembowelled and wrapped in a waxed cloth. He was laid in a leaden chest enclosed within a wooden casket, and he was exposed to the public as Edward II had been in 1327. Such an exposure may have been advisable in any circumstances, but it cannot fail to suggest a parallel between the fate of two unfortunate men.

The reticence of contemporaries is usually discounted by modern writers. Plain accusations of murder which were made, when it was safe to do so after the Yorkist triumph in 1461, are set aside as Yorkist propaganda. But the veiled hints of those closest to the events, or their refusal to go into detail, seem on the whole to point to the conclusion that Humphrey of Gloucester was the victim of foul play. Unfortunate in his times and his character, but not

---

[1] The problem is discussed *ibid.*, pp. 23–7. A later writer, R. L. Storey, does not believe that Humphrey was murdered (*The End of the House of Lancaster*, p. 46), though he adds one interesting scrap of evidence, for what it is worth, in favour of the theory. An approver claimed that, on 17 June following, he had heard of the murder from the keeper of Gloucester Castle.

dishonourable in his intentions, he was probably murdered by his political opponents for what they considered to be the good of his country, but also and primarily for purposes of their own. His death was a political tragedy of first magnitude for all. In the words of a well-known chronicle of the period, probably written in or soon after 1460,[1] the event was 'grieved by all the people of England, taking hardly his decease'. Nor did the 'people' not know whom to blame: as a London chronicler records 'many murmurs and grievances began this year to spring up against the marquis of Suffolk for the murder of the duke of Gloucester and other things'.[2]

Thus Gloucester's death consummated the work of his life. It contributed to a genuine political movement, however unformed and intermittent, which did not cease until the Lancastrian régime, which many contemporaries thought to have committed or permitted his murder, was finally swept away. It was no accident that the tragedy of 1447 was followed by violent struggles in which his memory was invoked. This year is, indeed, as good a point as any to adopt for the real beginning of the strife which led straight to the Wars of the Roses themselves.

One crucial issue involved was the conduct of the French war. William de la Pole, who dominated foreign affairs from 1445 to 1450, is an enigmatical figure. He was a seasoned veteran of the wars, having led an army to defeat at La Gravelle as early as 1423. He was also a diplomat and statesman. Grandson of Michael de la Pole who had been impeached in 1386, he inherited high royalist traditions. A connection of the Beauforts by marriage, he shared their close ties with the old aristocracy. How he united his loyalties to the country and to the court in his service to Henry VI must remain to some extent a mystery, but this is also the case with such well-known figures as Beaufort and Kemp. At any rate, both his devotion to Henry himself and to the policy of peace are beyond question, and they probably led him into dark and questionable ways both in his negotiations with Charles VII of France and perhaps in involvement in the undeserved death of the duke.

Suffolk had given his support to the policy of peace as early as 1432 or 1433, and this was both one cause of his prominence in the years which followed and also for his ultimate undoing. After

[1] Giles *Chronicle: Chronicon Angliae (Incerti Scriptoris) de regnis Henrici IV., Henrici V. et Henrici VI.*, edited by J. A. Giles (London 1848), pp. 33-4.
[2] *The Great Chronicle of London*, edited by A. H. Thomas and J. D. Thornley (London 1938), p. 181.

3. Estates of the nobility under Edward I

4. Estates of the nobility at the time of the Wars of the Roses

the treaty of Arras, the English never had a chance of making good Henry V's ambitions in France. The tragedy was that most of them, with memories of Crécy and Agincourt to beguile them, could not bring themselves to surrender their ancient claims and ambitions in order to liquidate a war which they could no longer win. Beaufort and his allies were clear-sighted in working for peace through concessions; but they could not make concessions palatable to their countrymen. The foreign policy they pursued can, indeed, be regarded as enlightened and might have saved England great suffering; but in fact it contributed much to the destruction of the whole Lancastrian régime which it was their prime purpose to defend.

Suffolk supported the liberation of the duke of Orléans, prisoner since Agincourt, so that the duke might further the negotiations for peace, an act bitterly criticized by Gloucester in 1440. In 1444 he was sent on an embassy to France, one purpose of which was to negotiate for a French bride for the king, a matter of great importance for both foreign and domestic affairs. So grave would be its consequences that Henry assured Suffolk that no charge would be laid against him if he failed, 'by the king, his heirs, his councillors and officers, or by any of the king's people'[1]; which was an over-generous exercise of the royal power for it bound the kings's subjects as well as the king.

The bride chosen was Margaret of Anjou, daughter of Duke René and niece of the queen of France. Pawn of the court party and of Charles VII in their moves towards peace, and pledge of English desire to this end, she was the choice of the court and her betrothal to Henry was a defeat for Gloucester; though in the end it turned out to be disastrous for almost everybody who was involved. Margaret was a strong and ambitious girl only fifteen years old; before long she became a domineering and uncompromising woman. She had no understanding of English traditions and not much more of English politics, and was soon hated by the *plebs* as representing an unpopular policy in both foreign and domestic affairs. Meanwhile, however, her betrothal to Henry was regarded as a triumph for the party of peace. Suffolk himself received extravagant thanks for his work; in parliament, Gloucester and other lords rose to their feet to applaud. Nevertheless, ugly rumours soon began, to the effect that Margaret's marriage to Henry had been purchased at an

---

[1] Nicolas, *Proceedings and Ordinances of the Privy Council*, edited by H. Nicolas (London 1834–47), pp. 32–5; translated in my *Constitutional History of the Fifteenth Century*, p. 61.

extravagant price. Concessions, it was whispered, had been made to France which were so serious that the people were not told. Agnes Paston referred in a letter to news from overseas about which people were afraid even to talk.

Whatever promises Suffolk made, Henry himself wrote a letter of 22 December 1445 agreeing to the surrender of Maine; this, he told Charles he understood the French king to wish as 'one of the best and most apt means of arriving at the blessing of peace between us and you'. Just before, in the negotiations in England in which Gloucester had been publicly humiliated, there had been irresponsible talk of a summit meeting between Henry and Charles, and Suffolk had paraded his love of the French king. In 1446 the magnates disavowed all support of a personal meeting between the two kings: it was an idea, they said, which 'only our Lord has been pleased to arouse and instigate in you, as He knows. You have not been aroused or instigated, in any manner, by any of the lords or any other subjects of this your realm'. The Commons shortly afterwards attacked the cession of Maine. The English position in France was plainly becoming desperate, and the government just as clearly put its heart into the search for peace rather than in the pursuit of the war. It is true that in 1443 an ambitious effort had been made under Somerset, who received an ambiguous and roving command. But his campaign was probably ill-advised: in any case it was a failure. Richard of York was gradually pushed back to the north. Finally, in July 1449 Charles VII ended a series of truces by invading Normandy itself, and very shortly captured Rouen. This was the news which greeted the arrival of the members to a parliament summoned for 6 November 1449.

What began to destroy the Lancastrian hold on the country was not only failure abroad but also a distortion of the constitutional procedures at home. The policy of peace was not only unpopular in itself, but was dependent for its execution on secret diplomacy, on an exaggeration of the royal authority, and on the actions of a court party which turned its back more and more on the traditions of 1399. The events of 1440–49 proved that the Lancastrian monarchy in the hands of the weak and helpless Henry VI finally posed a threat to the liberties of the subject comparable to, if different from, that once posed by Richard II. Hence, in view of the vigorous political life of fifteenth-century England, a strong reaction may be said to have been inevitable. This actually occurred in 1450, both

inside and outside parliament. The government itself survived, as it
had survived the murder of Gloucester, mainly because of continued
aristocratic support; but it was never afterwards secure. Popular
movements failed to remove the deeper causes of unrest; but
partly as a result they were succeeded by a combination of aristocratic and popular opposition which finally swept the Lancastrians
off the throne. The question of how far this did, indeed, represent a
genuine political movement with serious purposes, or was merely
an escalation of local rivalries and conflicts, is touched on very
briefly below.[1]

4. THE STRUGGLE OF LANCASTER AND YORK

By 1450 the 'good duke' had been dead for three years, and such
discontent as existed among the lords, shown by their protest of
1446 against the 'summit' meeting, was leaderless. The folly of the
murder of Gloucester (if such it was) had perhaps already been
revealed by the increased political influence of Richard, duke of
York. Humphrey, in spite of his ambition, had always been loyal to
his king, but Richard in time became a contender for the throne.
His early discontent was probably similar to Gloucester's, reinforced
by personal ambition and experience of the government's inefficiency in the conduct of the French war. He had been the king's
lieutenant in France in 1436 and 1437. In 1440 he was engaged to
act for five years as lieutenant and governor-general of France and
Normandy. In 1443, in view of strong French attacks, the government decided not to reinforce Richard but to send out John Beaufort,
earl of Somerset, with a second army and a commission which
gave him in fact greater authority than Richard himself possessed.
Richard was starved of finances whilst Beaufort, who had been
made a duke when he received his commission, was paid £25,000
in advance. In spite of all this, and in spite of his pretentious secrecy,
Beaufort achieved nothing, and the English power in general
suffered a serious decline.

Richard's experience in France could hardly fail to make him an
opponent of the conduct of the war by the dominant faction in the
court. He had also pretentions which were in some ways more
dangerous than Humphrey of Gloucester's as a leading prince of the
royal blood; for he was descended, not (like Humphrey) from
Henry IV and John of Gaunt, but through Philippa and Edmund

---

[1] p. 310, below.

Mortimer from Lionel, duke of Clarence, John of Gaunt's elder brother. Indeed, in 1447 he was heir presumptive to the throne. Closely coincident with Gloucester's death he was himself under attack by the government for mismanaging his finances in Normandy and when he blamed Adam Moleyns for some of the rumours against him, the bishop who was keeper of the privy seal and a key figure in the government gave him an insulting reply. Shortly afterwards Richard was sent into virtual exile as king's lieutenant in Ireland. He was formally appointed on 29 September 1447; he actually departed from England in 1449.

Despite York's exile, a severe political struggle soon disrupted the country. In its early stages, Henry's piety and gentleness still won him personal loyalty and devotion, despite his disastrous subordination to the court. To support him, Henry had also the Lancastrian achievement since 1399, and the claims his House had established on the loyalty of Englishmen, especially of the aristocracy. He had also the power and resources of the crown, still great in spite of alienations and impoverishment. Finally, he had the loyalty of many Englishmen to the crown itself, symbol of the common weal.

As against Henry's piety, Richard of York had the achievements and bearing of a warrior and a knight. A story is told of a remark he made just before his death, when advisers urged him not to leave the castle of Sandal near Wakefield to engage the much superior forces of the Duke of Somerset and the earl of Northumberland. He refused, the story goes, saying that he had never kept inside a castle in France, even when the Dauphin came to besiege him, and that he would not be caged like a bird. His great wealth and his royal blood were obvious assets. Nor can the fact be overlooked that Richard had sworn loyalty to Henry and may have been genuinely loath to rebel against him, quite apart from the dangers involved. Finally there was an obvious need for Richard to find powerful political allies if he was to succeed in a rebellion; though he may, in any case, have been encouraged to take an open stand against the government by the signs of popular discontent which multiplied rapidly after 1447.

The first movement of opposition by the Commons was in the parliament which was summoned for 6 November 1449. By the time it was in session, Rouen had been captured by the French on 4 November, and Harfleur was taken on Christmas day. Public hostility to the government was high. Adam Moleyns was murdered on 9 January 1450 by soldiers awaiting transportation to France: his confession before he died was thought to have implicated Suffolk in the surrender of Maine. William Aiscough was torn to pieces by his own parishioners in the following June: he was dragged from the church at Edington where he was saying Mass and murdered on a nearby hill. Both, it was said by a contemporary, were covetous men, much hated by the common people, and held to have promoted Gloucester's death. It was in these circumstances that the Commons adopted the procedure of impeachment and used it against Suffolk, reviving memories of 1376 and 1386, and challenging the whole policy of the government, especially their conduct of the war. There were two sets of articles of indictment, one by the Commons alone, the other by Commons and Lords. They contained some charges which were widely improbable, such as that Suffolk had sold England to Charles VII and had fortified Wallingford Castle as headquarters for a confederacy organized against his own country. Other charges, such as that of receiving inordinate gifts from the king and mischievously granting moneys from the exchequer to himself and his friends, could be established, at least in part. In any case the main grievance seems to be clear. It was that Suffolk had misused his influence as one of those 'privez' to the king, and had been traitorously friendly to the French; in particular, he had been mainly responsible for the secret surrender of Maine. He had no difficulty in claiming that the whole council was involved in such transactions; but this was no defence in the eyes of the Commons. They clearly wished to discredit the whole régime in which he had played a leading part.

In this attack, the Commons assumed the initiative and bore the main burden. The Lords still, in the main, supported the king and the court. Henry himself openly favoured the accused, who made an emotional appeal to his king before ever he was attacked: 'And if it ever shall please God that I die otherwise than in my bed, my blood untainted, I beseech Him for my soul's good that I may die in that quarrel [i.e. against the French]'.[1] By this appeal, Suffolk apparently tried to intimidate his opponents and shelter behind the royal prerogative, as he had done in 1444 and 1447. But the Commons would not be intimidated, and they obtained at least enough support from the upper House to enable them to proceed.

[1] Recorded in the Rolls of Parliament and translated in my *Constitutional History of the Fifteenth Century*, p. 75; cf. R. L. Storey, *op. cit.*, pp. 50–8.

They indicted Suffolk on 7 February, for his alleged crimes; and when this first attack proved insufficient they departed from precedent and on 9 March drew up an indictment conjointly with the Lords. The co-operative approach was probably an attempt to strengthen their hand, in response to Henry's action on 12 February, when he had respited the proceedings 'until he would be otherwise advised'. In consequence of the new approach, the king again produced Suffolk for trial, on 13 March. Perhaps as a result of the increased danger to which Suffolk was now exposed, Henry on 17 March removed the proceedings from parliament altogether, on a transparent pretext, and imposed a minimum sentence on his own authority. With regard to the first bill against Suffolk, he pronounced his minister 'neither declared nor charged' concerning its horrible accusations. With regard to the second bill, he exiled Suffolk for five years. This lenient sentence was almost certainly far less than the Commons wanted. It was a flagrant exercise of the prerogative by which the effectiveness of impeachment was largely destroyed. Even the Lords, who had been ambivalent in their attitude, were moved to protest that the king had not acted with their counsel and advice; though their main purpose, as they stated, was merely to protect their traditional privileges as peers.

In the event, the harsh punishment which the Commons had failed to obtain was provided by the commonalty. Suffolk narrowly escaped capture by the angry Londoners and embarked for exile to Ipswich, after swearing his innocence before the assembled populace. But his ship was intercepted in the Channel by a royal vessel, the *Nicholas of the Tower*, whose captain was disloyal to his ruler. Suffolk was taken and summarily beheaded by an unknown Irishman with six strokes of a rusty sword. His body was flung out on to the sands. It has been argued that, mysterious as was his end, his character and aims are hardly more intelligible.[1] To one historian, it is said, he is a statesman, farsighted, loyal, and misunderstood; to another, he is an unscrupulous and blundering tyrant. The truth, it has been concluded, as so often, lies probably in between. For good or ill, Suffolk was no figure of heroic mould. He was ambitious yet timid, corrupt yet well-meaning. He was, in short, the inevitable scapegoat who atoned for the sins of others as much as for his own.

Perhaps this hardly does justice to Suffolk's intelligence or even

---

[1] *Cambridge Medieval History*, vol. VIII, p. 407.

to his courage. He was himself one of the chief architects of the policy he carried out. Disastrous as this was, it was not indefensible, even if Suffolk stooped to very low means to attain his ends. He could claim, as he did, that he laboured for the ultimate good of his country, however unpopular his methods. Perhaps this mixture of good and evil in him will never be unravelled, but he probably deserves our respect as well as our pity. What betrayed him in the end was not his own character but that of King Henry who fell short of giving him adequate support in the hour of crisis. The impeachment of Suffolk weakened both the government and the Commons, and paved the way for a new structure of politics. Opposition which had failed inside parliament had succeeded outside. The common people felt a taste of power. This both encouraged and was increased by the popular rising of Jack Cade, which revived some of the aims and methods of the Peasants' Revolt of 1381.

Disturbances occurred in many places during Suffolk's trial. A formidable movement of Kentishmen, the 'radicals' of the century between 1350 and 1450, was on foot by the beginning of June. It included many yeomen, husbandmen and craftsmen, and was more political and more sophisticated in its aims than that of 1381. The 2,000 pardons granted to individuals after the suppression of the rising included one to a knight, eighteen to esquires, seventy-four to gentlemen and one to the mayor of Queensborough. Some of these individuals had been, or would later be, sheriffs, attorneys, or members of parliament. It was strongly pro-Yorkist: Jack Cade called himself John Mortimer, cousin of Richard of York. Its leaders plainly expressed the discontents of a fairly broad section of the community. They attacked the deficiencies of the government, especially its protection of the 'false progeny and affinity' of Suffolk; and they claimed to stand for the common weal.[1] They echoed Gloucester's views on the duties of princes of the blood; and they went further than Humphrey had in their emphasis on the claim of the commonalty to a voice in politics and to responsibility for the welfare of the *Respublica*. The tone of their propaganda may be gathered from the opening words of their proclamation of 4 June: 'These are the points, causes, and discontents, relating to the

---

[1] Documents relative to the revolt, including the important proclamation of 4 June put out by the rebels, are given in my *Constitutional History of the Fifteenth Century*, pp. 80–6; (cf. *ibid.*, pp. 35–41). Some discussion of the revolt is given by R. L. Storey, *op. cit.*, pp. 61–8.

3rd day of June 1450 . . . . We trust to almighty God that with the help and grace of God and of our sovereign lord the king, and of the poor commons of England, we may find a remedy; if not, we shall die in the attempt.'

Putting forth reasoned and plausible statements of their aims, and acting with great moderation, the rebels gained unexpected support among the followers of the magnates who were with the king. Saved by this support, and strengthened by the friendship of some Londoners, they obtained entry into the city. The keys of London Bridge were surrendered to them on 3 July, and the city gates were opened for Cade by Thomas Godfrey, a spurrier clad in russet, who repeated the role of the traitorous aldermen of 1381.

But, as in 1381, the rebels had no political aims which they could accomplish. Entrance into London was not an end in itself. All that Cade could do was to satisfy his more violent followers by beheading some of the king's advisers. Among these were Lord Saye and William Crowmer, whose heads were put on two stakes or poles and brought together from time to time, as they were paraded around the city, as if they were kissing in death. Some Londoners were despoiled. Nothing constructive happened or could happen. It is not surprising that the Londoners soon 'withdrew their hearts and love'. On 5 July the mayor and aldermen, 'with the thrifty commoners', invited the veteran Lord Scales, keeper of the Tower, to issue from his fortress and destroy the rebels. The attempt was only partly success-ful; but after a bitter and indecisive struggle for London Bridge the rebels were constrained to accept a general pardon, negotiated by the prelates Kemp, Stafford, and Waynflete. On analogy with 1381 this was only a form of surrender. It marked the tragic end of a movement which had begun with high hopes and had been marked by intelligence and restraint. Cade himself was soon captured and died of wounds. His followers were left to the harsh justice of a frightened government.

The rising was not all loss, however. For a short while, as after 1381, the tide flowed strongly in favour of the Establishment and against the dangerous spirit of revolt. Even York suffered from the reaction, though he had carefully stood aloof from the revolt. Nevertheless, the memory of a moment of high achievement by the commonalty remained vivid; and great lords did not fail to take cognizance of the important factor which such 'risings', now twice repeated, had introduced into political life. This coloured their propaganda and affected their political calculations. Indeed, it had an important influence on the whole political life.[1]

The reaction of 1450 was short-lived. The following decade was, in fact, to be marked by the rise of an effective opposition to Henry VI, led by York. This was still not easy. Henry continued to be sustained by his own piety and sanctity, by the support of most magnates, and by the resources of the Crown. On the other hand the opposition had clearly been broadened and strengthened by the events of 1447 and 1450. It was also strengthened after 1454 by an alliance between York and the Nevilles which gave it a necessary basis of aristocratic support. In these circumstances the forces of authority and opposition were very evenly divided. Civil war was the ultimate produce of this nice division of forces, which created a deadlock that proved to be impossible to break by any other means.

Unrest continued among the Commons after 1450. The parliament in November of that year was pro-Yorkist and in no way repentant of its part in Suffolk's destruction. It took a great show of strength by the king and the magnates to overawe what the Londoner Gregory called the London 'ryffe raffe'. But York was not able to make political capital out of the discontent. When Thomas Young, a member from Bristol, nominated Richard as Henry's heir, he was committed to the Tower. When, in January 1452, York tried to rouse the Londoners and Kentishmen in an armed revolt, he got no response: the people 'came not to him'. But he did incite sympathetic risings in many towns in three well-marked areas, the Welsh Marches, Somerset and Devonshire, and a broad East-Anglican district stretching from Grantham to Chelmsford.

Richard clearly relied heavily on popular support: a letter to Shrewsbury is extant in which he explained his intentions and his hopes for the support of the burgesses, as well as for 'the help and support of Almighty God and of our Lady and of all the company of heaven'. His attempted coup was preceded by months of propaganda aimed at attracting the sympathy of the common people. As early as September 1451 he had written letters to win sympathy from the towns and the men of influence in Norfolk. Edmund Clere, a 'cousin' of the Pastons, brought copies of these letters to the mayor and citizens of Kings Lynn. But there is no recorded appeal for the help of the greater lords.

[1] Recent discussions are in my *Constitutional History of the Fifteenth Century*, pp. 35–41, 80–6, and R. L. Storey, *op. cit.*, pp. 61–8, 97–6.

Accompanied only by the earl of Devon and Lord Cobham among the magnates, Richard left the Marches and marched towards London. But when he sent a herald, asking for permission to pass through the city, he was refused. He accordingly crossed the Thames at Kingston bridge and arrived in Dartford on 1 March. He and his followers had artillery, and seven ships on the Thames filled with baggage and supplies, but they were quite helpless without a 'rising' in their support. A much superior royal army encamped at Blackheath. York was able to negotiate terms of surrender which included the promise that his opponent Somerset would be imprisoned and tried, but his terms were immediately disregarded. He himself became the prisoner, compelled to throw himself on the king's grace. This he quickly received. He was lucky that the group which now controlled Henry did not feel it wise to make another martyr by executing him for his offence. But the failure of his attempt to storm his way into the royal councils had been complete. According to one contemporary, 'the whole kingdom was governed by the duke of Somerset [Edmund Beaufort, nephew of the late Cardinal] and his adherents'. Nothing had been accomplished and nothing had really changed.

This was also largely true of the French war, which was now virtually lost, though the government made a great effort in 1452 and 1453 to retrieve the situation. It was probably the need for a united effort in face of imminent disaster which deprived York in these years of any appreciable support. Reinforcements were sent to Calais in 1451, and in 1452 John Talbot, earl of Shrewsbury, was despatched as king's lieutenant to Aquitaine. His intention was to make a supreme attempt to recover that vital area of English power, almost entirely in French hands. He regained Bordeaux and other towns, but lost the last great battle of the Hundred Years War, at Castillon on 17 July 1453. The English defeat was final; the battle, small though it was, marked the end of an era in which their earlier advantages had slowly disappeared. Talbot was forced by circumstances to attack French forces which were strongly defended by artillery. The head of his column was blown to pieces, and he himself was mortally wounded by a cannon ball which shattered both his legs. The French had become just as professional in war, and just as united, as the English. Nothing could be done to retrieve the disaster. England herself was now on the defensive, open to invasion, with no foothold in France save Calais.

The Lancastrians had finally failed in foreign policy as completely as in domestic affairs. It was ironical that, just before the final disaster of Castillon, a parliament of March 1453 had been warmly Lancastrian. It had even made the king a remarkable, though somewhat ambiguous, offer of 20,000 archers for the defence of the realm. Henry appeared before the Lords and Commons in person to thank them: 'We thank you warmly and do not doubt that we shall be to you a gracious and benevolent lord'. It was the last time that such warmth would be recorded between the subjects and the king.

In October 1453 Queen Margaret gave birth to a son, so that York was no longer Henry's heir. But defeat abroad had undermined Henry's whole position, and this was further weakened when, about the same time (probably in August) his feeble mind completely collapsed. The king's insanity was a tragedy for the nation but seemed like a benevolent act of providence for Richard of York. It saved him from the isolation into which he had fallen since 1450; even his enemies could not in the end deny him the office of Protector. His first protectorate, beginning in March 1454, brought him important political allies and a chance to recover the political stature which he had lost in 1452. But Henry's madness was short. He recovered by Christmas 1454, waking as from a long sleep. In January 1455 he received ministers; and 'he speke to hem as well as ever he did, and when thei come out thei wept for joye'.[1]

It was no accident that the first protectorate was followed by the first battle of the Wars of the Roses. This modern name for the struggle has, incidentally, no contemporary justification; but it would be pedantic to discard it after generations of use, especially since no satisfactory substitute has been produced. The Yorkists could not refuse to surrender their Protector's special powers; but after pasturing in the green meadow of political affluence they were not prepared to be reduced without a struggle to dependence on the clemency of the ambitious and unforgiving Margaret of Anjou who now completely dominated the king and the court.

A spark led to violence between them. After Henry's recovery, York went north to join his allies the Nevilles. With strong forces the earls advanced to Hertfordshire, protesting their loyalty and asking Henry not to believe their enemies. York claimed that he dared not go unarmed to a council which had been summoned to meet at Leicester. His protests were not even allowed to reach the

[1] *The Paston Letters*, edited by James Gairdner (Edinburgh 1910), vol. I, p. 315.

king. The forces of the earls came into contact with those of the king at St. Albans, near the scene of the proposed council, and once again York was foiled in an attempt to explain his position to Henry himself. On 22 May 1455 he finally had recourse to arms. The first battle of the Wars of the Roses took place, more the result of a political mismanagement and manoeuvring than of deliberate intention. It was hardly more than a skirmish. Few were slain. But the Yorkists had taken the decisive step of opposing the royal standard in arms. Henry himself was wounded in the neck as he watched as a helpless spectator. The rebels were victorious. They knelt before their ruler and offered every protestation of loyalty, but prepared to settle political accounts. They summoned a parliament in the king's name, with a Yorkist Speaker and pro-Yorkist Commons; they passed an indemnity for those who had fought at St. Albans; and they prepared to replace the political domination of Margaret of Anjou with their own. But blood feuds sprang inevitably from Lancastrian losses in the battle. Many a man, it was said, begrudged the bill of indemnity; and though the lords were well in their bodies, a contemporary observed, they were not well in their hearts. On Corpus Christi Eve, the Londoners armed themselves to protect York against assassination, and 'moche adoo there was'.

Henry VI's second madness in November 1455[1] brought a respite; but it proved to be only an interlude in the struggle. Margaret of Anjou was again denied the regency which she claimed. Richard of York once more became Protector. He acted with moderation, though one of his conspicuous acts was to suppress Thomas Courtenay, earl of Devon, who had been making violent attacks on his rival William, Lord Bonville. Richard was summarily dismissed on 25 February 1456, as soon as Henry recovered. Once more he felt at the mercy of the queen. Nor was he mistaken. As the duke of Buckingham reminded him about this time, he had nothing to lean on save the king's grace. Considering Margaret's attitude and disposition, this was a very unsubstantial support.

Thus England, deeply divided within herself, drifted towards political bankruptcy. She was, a Yorkist claimed, out of all good governance: the hearts of the people were turned away from those who had the government of the land. Nor can we assume that there was in all this partisan writing no element of truth. Margaret

[1] There is disagreement as to Henry's condition; see my *Constitutional History of the Fifteenth Century*, pp. 98–9.

prepared for the inevitable struggle by recruiting the knights and squires of Cheshire and mending fences in her relations with the aristocracy. But the lords no longer gave the king their whole loyalty. As one chronicler said, for want of free breathing many magnates determined to rebel and the land was rent in two, including nobles, chapters, colleges, convents, brothers and friends.

In this situation, the Yorkists were revealed to have won the decisive struggle—that for the hearts of the commonalty. 'The commons of this land', it was said, 'hated Somerset and loved the duke of York, because York loved the *communes* and preserved the common profit of the land.' In the confusions and tergiversations of the period the discontents of the 'commons' have rightly been regarded by K. B. McFarlane as being a constant factor of very great importance. From one point of view the Yorkist movement was just another baronial struggle for profit and power. Nevertheless, the support of the common people, especially of London and Kent, was what eventually turned the scales in its favour and ousted the time-honoured Lancastrian dynasty from the throne.

The first skirmishes of the struggle were, indeed, essentially aristocratic like those between the Nevilles and Percies in their family feuding and struggles for power, which were climaxed by a minor 'battle' at Stamford Bridge in November 1454. Henry's efforts to reconcile the factions in a great council at London in January 1458 came to nothing. The magnates could not be reconciled even though Henry made pious exhortations and it was agreed that York, Warwick, and Salisbury should establish a chantry at St. Albans where Masses should be celebrated for the souls of those slain at the battle of St. Albans in 1455, and that financial compensation should be paid to their families. But personal quarrels were by no means the only issues which divided the 'parties' after many years of political strife: 'the king', a Yorkist sympathizer said shortly afterwards, 'is simple and led by covetous counsel . . . the queen and those who were of her affinity ruled the realm as she liked'.[1] What seems to be implied is opposition to a whole system of government dominated by the court and the queen.

In 1459 the Yorkist lords gathered forces on the Welsh Marches and won a skirmish against the king's forces at Blore Heath. But Henry reacted with uncharacteristic vigour. As his admiring subjects said later, he laboured against the Yorkists for thirty days,

[1] Quoted in my *Constitutional History of the Fifteenth Century*, p. 101.

taking no rest except on Sundays and at times sleeping in the bare fields. At the Rout of Ludford the rebel forces melted away without striking a blow: 'God smote their hearts with cowardice and about midnight they fled.' The leaders were exiled, in a parliament at Coventry, summoned in November. But the king's victory was quite illusory. In notable political pamphlets the exiles deepened their appeal to the *plebs*; and they obtained strong support from the papal Legate Coppini and a group of prelates—an ominous sign. As Buckingham told the bishops when they made a last-minute appeal for peace: 'Ye come not as bysshopes for to trete for pease, but as men of armes.' Indeed, he and Henry's other advisers had much cause to fear the power of the bishops, added to that of magnates and *plebs*.

The situation invited the return of the exiles, and the next engagement of the war occurred on 10 July 1460. Conspicuous on the side of Richard of York at the battle of Northampton were the levies of Kent. As the armies were about to engage, Warwick 'lete crye thoroughe the felde that no man should laye hand vppon the kyng ne on the commune peple, but onely on the lordes, knyghtes and squyers'. The entrenched position held by the king's forces was flooded by heavy rain, and the guns on which the royalists relied proved to be useless in the water and the mud. The battle only lasted half an hour. The victory brought Richard almost, but not quite, to the throne. Before he could overcome opposition to his claim, he had to crush resistance in the north, stronghold of Lancastrianism. There, by his own recklessness, or by the treachery of his enemies, he was killed in the battle of Wakefield, though Shakespeare portrayed him as being mocked as a prisoner after the battle, crowned with a straw emblem of royalty. His head was publicly displayed upon the walls of York, and his cause seemed to have been irretrievably lost.

Richard had, indeed, contributed to his own defeat, not only by his rashness in battle but also by his haste in attempting to get himself crowned before he had disposed of his enemies. Nevertheless, his cause was greater than he and could not be disposed of so easily. In fact, his heir his son Edward was more formidable and could make better use of popular support, not yet exploited to the full. This was the more so since Margaret, in spite of her victory, still felt her forces to be so weak that she committed the fatal mistake of an alliance with those traditional enemies of England, the Scots. Thus strengthened, she was able to march south and defeat the Yorkist

Warwick at the second battle of St. Albans. She outmanœuvred his forces and caused confusion in their ranks, which was turned into rout by the inexplicable desertion of the Kentish men. But she could not take London. She was foiled, significantly, not by the mayor and aldermen, but by the *populus* led by a brewer and a cook. She had, in fact, lost far more through her Scottish contingent than she had gained. This made it easy for the Yorkists to spread a report that all England south of the Trent had been betrayed, and to claim that Northerners, Scots, and Welshmen ravaged the land 'as they had be paynems or Sarracenes, and no Crysten menne'.

Lack of any general support in the south caused Margaret to retreat from London. Popular support enabled Edward not only to follow her northward, but also to do so as the accepted king, raised to the throne on 4 March 1461. He could thus summon to his banner every Englishman between sixteen and sixty. With the aid of the *plebs* he could defeat the Lancastrians at the bitter battle of Towton, fought in a snowstorm on 29 March, and marked by the stubbornness of his foes. In fact his enemies seemed to be gaining the day until John Mowbray, duke of Norfolk, arrived with reinforcements for the Yorkists and unexpectedly attacked the Lancastrian left flank.

With the great Yorkist victory the most critical phase of the Wars of the Roses came to an end. England could enter upon a period of reconstruction even though she was still to be troubled for a decade by the upheavals of war. In Edward IV, the new dynasty was represented by an intelligent and resourceful ruler. During the course of political stuggles and civil war, the beginnings of a new structure of politics had begun to emerge; the commonalty began to be weakened in their attachment to the political leadership of the great lords and brought to a general though not entirely constant support of the monarch, Edward IV. A new dynasty had been set upon the throne which owed its success to promises made specifically to the commonalty of England, and which would stand or fall by the degree to which those promises were fulfilled.

Henry VI had not been on the battlefield of Towton. He had preferred to spend such a holy day as 29 March, which was Palm Sunday, praying at York. After the battle he fled through Newcastle to Berwick, which he surrendered to the Scots in return for a grant of asylum. In November he was attainted by Edward IV. He probably stayed in Scotland for four years, often accompanied by

Margaret and his son Edward. The Lancastrian cause was sustained by the stubborn courage of the queen. Henry joined a Lancastrian rising against Edward in the north of England in the spring of 1464, and was nearly captured after the battle of Hexham on 15 May when his supporters were crushed. For twelve months after June 1264, when he was deserted by the Scots, he was in hiding on the moors between Yorkshire and Lancashire, and in the Lake District. He was finally captured in Clitheroe wood, taken to Edward IV, and imprisoned in the Tower; he was too insignificant in Edward's eyes to merit the customary fate of monarchs whose thrones had been usurped, or perhaps he was saved by the existence of a more formidable heir.

9

THE RULE OF THE YORKIST KINGS, EDWARD IV AND RICHARD III

1. THE EARLY YEARS OF EDWARD IV

EDWARD IV gained the throne in 1461 as a medieval prince of the royal blood, with the help of a magnate 'affinity', but he was pre-eminently the king of transition from medieval to modern. He owed his usurpation to the support of the *plebs* as well as to that of the aristocracy. He proclaimed legitimism but strengthened notions of succession to the throne dependent upon consent, and so united medieval traditions of limited power with ideas that would one day lead to Stuart claims of divine hereditary right. He combined the traits of a medieval knight with those of a Renaissance prince. He excelled on the battlefield but preferred to negotiate rather than fight. He did something to revive the royal traditions of Edward III, but Renaissance intrigue was a conspicuous feature of his court. In most of these traits he was a model for his brother Richard, who added a final touch of Renaissance lack of principle to Yorkist policy. Had he lived, Richard might have gone down in history as the first modern ruler of England. By his death he paved the way for the 'new' monarchy of Henry VII and Henry VIII.

Yorkist rule was, indeed, in line with the changing conditions of the age. It gave England strong and solvent government freed from excessive dependence on the aristocracy. It pointed the way towards a new reconciliation of authority and liberty. For this alone, the Yorkists deserve a place of honour among the creators of the modern English state.

By any standards Edward IV was himself a remarkable ruler. Modern research has shown how older views of his laziness and debauchery came to be established, and how they did not altogether arise from the facts; though it has still not absolved him for one notable weakness which contemporaries noted: his inordinate pursuit of the opposite sex. He took vigorous measures to put down disorder. He went personally on extended judicial surveys, and he developed courts like the council of Wales and of the North which suppressed violence and intimidation by the great. He reduced or liquidated the massive Lancastrian debts, and by his vigilance regained royal wealth which had been alienated, as the Lancastrian parliaments had sought to do by Acts of Resumption. He reformed the royal household, inculcating frugality and method: it was in 1471–72 that there appeared the famous *Black Book* in which the order of an efficient household was set forth. He supplemented all this by inquiries into feudal tenures and the imposition on offenders of heavy fines.

It is true that Edward made himself notorious by imposing benevolences and forced loans on his subjects, by which wealthy citizens were compelled to make 'voluntary' contributions. He 'plucked the feathers of his magpies without making them cry out'. Since only a minority suffered, the majority acquiesced in what was a real weakening of parliamentary control over finance; and the harmony between the king and his subjects was not destroyed. Indeed, Edward's benevolences may almost be regarded as an income tax on the wealthy middle class which did not adequately sustain the business of government or war. They do not prove that Edward was not greatly dependent on the public opinion which had helped to put him on the throne.

As Sir Thomas More said later, the king 'was of visage louely, of body myghtie, strong and cleane made'. His affability is not in doubt: 'he used towardes every man of highe and low degree more than mete famylyarytie'; and he made himself beloved by the common people and long remembered after his death. Kissing the wives of the Londoners won him their deep gratitude, no mean political asset even in the fifteenth century. Few would deny that he was a fine soldier and man of action; though how far he really mastered military tactics is a matter of doubt. Finally, his capacity for finance is proved beyond question, as witnessed by his remarkable accumulation of wealth.

With regard to his inner qualities of mind, his ideals if he had any, and the essence of his policy, neither his contemporaries nor modern writers have agreed. Nevertheless, the safest view seems to be that of

John Richard Green, that Edward was a man of iron will and great fixity of purpose, who 'began to break the teeth of the sinners'. His ultimate purpose, we may believe, was to stand by the promises of Yorkist propaganda. He would give England a government which was both strong and efficient, and at the same time would approximate to the *dominium regale et politicum* of the Lancastrian Sir John Fortescue.[1] This central notion of Fortescue's important political writings was almost certainly accepted by Edward IV. The English king, Sir John argued, unlike the French, had to rule with the agreement of his subjects in parliament. They would not allow him to rule in any other way. It was by their failure in this vital matter, Sir John implied, that the Lancastrians had lost their hold on the throne. Edward's policy, inconsistent though it was at times, and dominated by contingency rather than principle, was an attempt to succeed where the Lancastrians, in the end, had most noticeably failed.

It has been claimed, indeed, that both Edward and his father were authoritarians; that they based their claim to the throne essentially on their legitimate rights as heirs to the Plantagenets; and that this militated strongly against any serious attempt on Edward's part to fulfil Sir John Fortescue's ideal. But it is doubtful if those who make this claim stress adequately the extent to which both Richard of York and his son depended on popular support. Richard, indeed, allowed the 'people' to thwart the gesture towards the throne which he had made in parliament. Edward sought the consent of the 'people' at St. John's Field on Sunday 1 March, as his first step towards becoming king. He 'took possession' of the realm as of right; but, as Prospero de Camulio, a contemporary, said, 'the people of London ... together with some other lords ... had created a new king'. His coronation finally took place on 28 June, fortified by an Act issued by the authority of parliament.

In this procedure Edward IV breathed the spirit of Yorkist opposition, however much he acted from expediency. The same spirit, on the whole, marked his conduct as ruler. He did not repeat Henry IV's dependence on parliament; partly, indeed, because he was not so dependent on the Lords and Commons for supplies and because he knew how his subjects regarded taxation. But he did place a new emphasis on the need for co-operation with all his

[1] For some interesting comments on Fortescue see A. B. Ferguson, *The Articulate Citizen and the English Renaissance* (Durham N.C., 1965).

subjects. He gradually destroyed the predominance of lords in his council, in a manner of which Fortescue would have strongly approved. He sought to create national unity in his support by an aggressive foreign policy, in the manner of Henry V. And he tried hard to heal the deep divisions in the country by a leniency to the defeated Lancastrians, either those who were still in England or those in exile at the court of King Louis XI.

Foreign policy took a high priority in his interests, as well it might. Louis XI who ruled France from 1461 to 1483 was astute, unscrupulous, and powerful. Louis saw France's great opportunity in English political conflicts, most of all in an English civil war. On the other hand he feared the possibility of another Anglo-Burgundian alliance, and he had no wish to support a losing cause. He had so little faith in Margaret of Anjou that he refused even to grant her an allowance. But Margaret's only real hope was in French help; and Louis ultimately gave her a minimum of aid in return for a promise of Calais. Edward, for his part, favoured Burgundy, as Henry V had done long before; but his policy had to be almost as tortuous as Louis's, because of the hostility of English merchants against their counterparts in Burgundy, aggravated by restrictions on English cloth, and because of a need to hide his intentions from both Warwick and Louis of France.

The problems thus created were made more complicated by differences between Edward and his chief supporter, Richard, earl of Warwick, the 'Kingmaker'. Warwick favoured an alliance with France rather than with Burgundy, probably influenced by his contacts with the 'City', where commercial rivalry with the Burgundian Netherlands was strong. Edward ultimately prevailed, and his alliance with Burgundy was established by a secret treaty in 1468, cemented by a marriage between the king's sister Margaret and the duke. But Edward did not prevail before there had been an open breach between him and Warwick, in which foreign policy was closely involved.

In domestic as well as foreign affairs, the two Yorkist leaders also became hopelessly estranged. The reasons are debatable. But they unquestionably arose in part from the character of the earl. He was not only the richest magnate in England, he was also one of the most ambitious, with an insatiable mind that could not be content. He contributed vital leadership to the Yorkist movement, though he had been defeated at the second battle of St. Albans. He may have been lukewarm in support of Edward's seizure of the throne. At any rate, when the new king proved unable to fulfil all the hopes he had raised, Warwick began to develop his own appeal to the *plebs*. A London chronicler records:

> This year [1468] many rumoured tales ran through the City, of conflict between the Earl of Warwick and the Queen's relatives. Which earl was always held in great favour by the commons of this land because of the exceedingly great household which he kept daily in every region wherever he stayed or passed the night. And when he came to London he held such a household that six oxen were eaten at a breakfast and every tavern was full of his meat; for anybody who had any acquaintance in his household could have as much boiled and roast meat as he could carry on a long dagger.

There is no doubt that he became the favourite of the Londoners and Kentishmen. We can see his desire to win over the *plebs* reflected later in his propaganda, and we can see the result in the way the commonalty of Kent and other shires followed him to war. It was just the lower strata of the community whose hopes Edward had been least able to satisfy; in any case, his most immediate need, in spite of his own propaganda, had been to come to terms with a strong section of the aristocracy. Thus the 'people' complained that he favoured men who had been his great enemies and oppressors of the commons, and one report said that the common people had been happier and less taxed under Henry VI. In these circumstances it was easy for many to believe that the true heir to the Yorkist opposition was not the king but the Kingmaker, and that the latter, not the former, now had their real interests at heart.

This alone was enough to put Edward and Warwick far apart. Its effects were increased by the victories won by the Nevilles in 1464 over the remnants of Lancastrianism in the north. It probably provides one important explanation of the famous secret marriage between Edward and Elizabeth Woodville in the same year.[1] Elizabeth was beautiful and Edward was young and impatient. The Londoner, Gregory, believed that the affair was a love-match: 'take heed,' he wrote romantically, 'what love may do'. But others were not so certain. Elizabeth was a Lancastrian widow, whose father, the first Earl Rivers, had been a fairly distinguished Lancastrian general and administrator but not of the highest nobility. He had been at one time steward of the duke of Bedford and had married

[1] This much debated marriage is discussed in my *Constitutional History of the Fifteenth Century*, pp. 146–8.

Bedford's widow. For presuming beyond his status, he had been soundly berated on one famous occasion by Yorkist leaders, especially by the Nevilles, father and son.

Such a marriage was bound to alienate Warwick, if for no other reason than the fact that it created a court which was likely in due course to challenge his influence with the king. Warwick knew as well as Edward what a power the court had been under Henry VI. Nor were some of his forebodings unfulfilled: the Woodville relatives soon began to receive promotions and lucrative grants from the king, including profitable marriages for a number of sisters. Elizabeth's brother John had been married at the age of twenty to the octogenarian duchess of Norfolk (who outlived this husband, her fourth). Nor was this all. Warwick had been urging a marriage between Edward and a French bride, prelude to his hoped-for alliance with France; and he now saw all his policy undermined. Finally, he suffered the humiliation of discovering that the king's marriage had been kept secret from him as well as from all others from May until September 1464. Many contemporaries no doubt firmly believed that the king had no need to offer marriage to Elizabeth, if all he required from her was affection. Edward must have had some powerful reasons for making Elizabeth his queen, with all the political consequence which this entailed, reasons which went far beyond his personal relationship with Elizabeth herself. As Lord Wenlock wrote to the Burgundian Hugh de Lannoy, Edward had caused 'great displeasure to many great lords, and especially to the larger part of all his council'. Surely this was something he could have easily forseen.

He may well have loved; but he probably acted also from cold political calculation. He was too strong to tolerate Warwick's pretensions, but not strong enough for an open challenge. He used the royal powers, which were rightfully his, as part of a grand design in which court and council were both instruments of a revitalized government, and in which a Kingmaker had only a subordinate place. It cannot have been a surprise to Edward that after the marriage, though the king and Warwick kept up a pretence of friendship, men knew that they never 'loffyd togedere'. In February 1465 Margaret wrote to Louis XI to tell him they had come to great division (Louis's comment was, 'look how proudly she writes').

2. EXILE AND RETURN OF EDWARD IV

Thus events conspired to a renewal of civil war. Warwick sought support from Edward's sulky and ambitious brother Clarence, and in 1469 Clarence married the Kingmaker's daughter Isabel. This uneasy alliance provided the basis for a movement of opposition which borrowed garments from both the erstwhile Yorkists and the Lancastrians. Its propaganda likened Edward's rule to that of Edward II and Henry VI. In 1469 local uprisings were fomented in the north, with Louis XI's tardy blessing. Finally, England was invaded and Edward was found largely unprepared. He had trusted the mass of his subjects to rally to him, and he never forgave them for their default. He told Commines later that up to the time of the battle of Barnet he had commanded that the common people be spared in battle, but that after this he omitted to do so 'for he had conceived a great hatred against the English people for the favour that he saw them to bear towards the earl of Warwick'.

The invasion started from Calais in July 1469. The supporters of Warwick and Clarence won a victory at Edgecote. Some of Edward's supporters were executed, including Earl Rivers. He himself was taken captive by George Neville, archbishop of York, who had donned the full armour of a knight. He owed his life and throne to the divisions and indecisions of his enemies. By October their inability to rule either with him or without him had become plain. He was able to turn the tables on his captors and resume the reality of power. By April 1470 the strange episode of a king half sovereign and half captive was ended, and Warwick and Clarence were forced into exile, to join the group headed by Margaret of Anjou at the court of Louis XI.

At this point the logic of the situation became irresistible and the three exiles created a united front against their common enemy. Their action was a complete sacrifice of principle for expediency, since Warwick had been the extreme foe of Lancastrianism, and Clarence, if he stood for anything, stood for the rights of a prince of the blood which later Lancastrian rule had denied. Margaret made the Earl of Warwick pay a heavy price in humiliation for her 'friendship'. He had to withdraw his slanders against her and, it is said, begged for forgiveness during a quarter of an hour, on his knees. Margaret completed her alliance with Warwick by betrothing her somewhat arrogant son Edward to Anne Neville, Warwick's daughter, though she stipulated that the marriage should not be completed until the Kingmaker had gone over and conquered the greater part of England for King Henry. The long hostility between them was formally if insincerely allayed, and a formidable coalition emerged with strong claims on the loyalty of Englishmen of many localities, even though it was weakened by an incompatibility of political ideas.

Faced with such a coalition, and failing as before to receive general support, Edward was unable to withstand a second invasion. Warwick landed at Dartmouth and Plymouth on 13 September, accompanied by Clarence, Jasper Tudor, and the earl of Oxford. By 6 October he was in London. Betrayed by the new marquis of Montagu, John Neville, who had wished to be made earl of Northumberland but had been fobbed off with a mere marquisate, Edward chose not to fight it out. Instead, he took a ship from King's Lynn in October 1470 to seek refuge and help in Burgundy. He was no coward, but probably acted on a shrewd assessment of the weaknesses of the coalition against him. It was as certain as anything in the uncertain politics of the age that the incompatible elements of the opposition which had dethroned him would very shortly fall apart.

His flight was followed by a Readeption of Henry VI, a sorry shadow of a king, almost an object of ridicule. When he had been found, Henry, it was said, was not worshipfully (honourably) arrayed as a prince and not so cleanly kept as should beseem such a personage. Nothing could put life into a government headed by a cipher and supported by a coalition of elements which had little or nothing in common except enmity to Edward IV. Its essence is revealed by the tragicomic episode of a royal parade around London, organized by George Neville in an attempt to strengthen the spirits of the royalists in the city, in face of Edward's approach in 1471.

> And so they went, with a small company of gentlemen going on foot before, and one on horseback bearing a pole or long shaft, at the end of which were fastened two foxes' tails, and with a small company of serving men following behind. They made the above progress, which more resembled a play than the display of a prince, made to win men's hearts. For by this means he [Henry] lost many, and won none or right few. And he was always displayed in a long blue gown of velvet, as though he had no other clothes to change into.[1]

Edward was able to organize a return in 1471, because he got support from Burgundy, including an invaluable force of professional soldiers; because he disarmed opposition by claiming only his

[1] *The Great Chronicle of London,* translated in my *Constitutional History of the Fifteenth Century,* p. 185.

ancestral lands; and because of support from a few powerful lords. At the decisive battle of Barnet, beginning in a fog on Easter Sunday morning, Warwick was supported by the 'people' and had the larger army. Edward relied on his faithful 'fellowship' of better trained men. Warwick's heavier artillery was wasted overshooting its mark. Edward's skill enabled him to deal with each wing of Warwick's forces in turn. In the mist, two Lancastrian contingents attacked each other by mistake and there was fear of treachery. Warwick was slain when his army had already been defeated and he was himself in flight—'somewhat fleinge', as the chronicler says. In the hard-fought battle, Edward had 'susteygned all the myght and weight', and 'with great violence bett and bare down afore hym all that stode in hys way'. It reveals the depth of aristocratic prejudice among the Lancastrians that Margaret's own supporters among the lords, who had failed to support Warwick in time, assured her that her 'party' would not be weaker but rather stronger by virtue of this defeat of a leader whose appeal to the *plebs* aroused their distrust.

However, the truth was brutally revealed to be otherwise when Edward crushed Margaret at the field of Tewkesbury on 4 May 1471. The queen was captured; her son was slain in flight, with or without Edward's silent consent; and Henry, who had been re-captured at Barnet, was obscurely murdered when his captor made a triumphal entry into London on 21 May. With Margaret confined and broken in spirit and the male Lancastrians dead, there was little left for their supporters to fight for, as Fortescue showed by his reconciliation with Edward in 1473. The queen herself, powerless and discredited, was eventually sent back to France in January 1476, in return for 50,000 crowns.

3. THE RESTORED MONARCHY OF EDWARD IV

The Yorkist king was more secure than ever on the throne; but the rule he established was not quite the old Yorkist régime. It was still based on Yorkist traditions, but it was not so dependent on popular support. Edward trusted neither the *plebs* nor the aristocracy as much as he had been compelled to in the past. He worked consistently to strengthen his own power, financially and otherwise. He enriched himself by 'gifts' and 'loans' from his wealthier subjects; he developed Benevolences and acquired profit by trade. In addition he revived projects of an attack on Louis XI, repaying him for his support of Warwick and Margaret; and he extorted from him by his threat of renewed war a 'pension' of £10,000 a year, promised by the treaty of peace at Picquigny in August 1475. After obtaining subsidies from his subjects in July 1474 and March 1475, he was able to do without parliament until 1478, and at the same time to pay off £12,923 9s 8d to the City of London, a feat not matched before by any English ruler of the fifteenth century.

He removed one minor obstacle to his restoration of the monarchy when he suddenly arrested and imprisoned George Neville, archbishop of York, whose temporalities were seized into the king's hands, whose mitre set with gems was made into a royal crown, and whose jewels and plate were given to Edward Prince of Wales. In 1478 he removed a second obstacle by the attainder and execution of his own brother, the 'false, fleeting, perjured Clarence', who had betrayed his allies on Edward's second return in 1471, and had been restored to favour as the leading prince of the blood. Clarence's ambitions were dangerous. He quarrelled with his younger brother Richard, the future Richard III, and he refused to attend court. He opposed the Treaty of Picquigny. He tampered with judicial procedures to favour his retainers. Finally, he was accused of being regarded by Lancastrians as heir to Henry VI. He was obviously still a potential centre for the kind of opposition which had almost destroyed Edward in 1470–71.

It has been claimed that in moving against his brother, Edward yielded to an atmosphere of hallucination and suspicion; but more probably, as earlier in the case of his marriage, he was moved by clear and cold political calculation. Clarence was attacked in parliament by bill of attainder. The charges included one to the effect that he had planned to destroy and disinherit the king and his children. Edward professed that he could still forgive his brother, in spite of all; but that Clarence was incorrigible and that in any case the country would not forgive. The Duke was condemned with the assent of both Lords and Commons and by authority of parliament. He was executed on 18 February in the Tower, probably by drowning in a bath; some contemporaries, along with Shakespeare later, believed that he was immersed in a butt of Malmsey wine; and one writer suggested that Clarence himself chose the manner of his death. Whether or not Edward had any justification for his act, he showed a fear of the power of a prince of the blood which was later to be posthumously justified in the fate of his own children, the Princes in the Tower. The probabilities are that they were murdered by his own trusted

younger brother, Richard, duke of Gloucester, grasping power by
reason of his nearness to the throne.[1]

After the attainder, Edward stood forth as dependent on no
aristocratic 'affinity', not even on his blood relations, but as a king
strong in his solvency and the efficiency of his government, demanding obedience and respect, if not love, from all his subjects alike.
His domestic régime was strengthened by his foreign policy.
Already in 1467 he had made a commercial alliance with Burgundy,
strengthened by the marriage of his sister Margaret and Duke
Charles. Now, he managed to keep the friendship of Burgundy in
spite of his treaty of Picquigny with France. He enjoyed both the
ransom gained by threat of war and the benefits of peace. He was so
strong that it is no wonder a contemporary feared that his rule was
becoming despotic. It is true that his prosperity was not quite complete. A war against the Scots in 1482 brought successes, but these
were achieved by his brother Richard, not by the king himself. His
balancing feat abroad collapsed when Louis of France and Maxi-
milian of Burgundy composed their differences by the treaty of
Arras in December 1482; but before this could seriously affect his
policies he died on 9 April 1483. Whether or not his death was
hastened by excesses, it came at the early age of only forty years.

Edward has been regarded as an empiricist who did not try to
create systems; but it is doubtful if this does him full justice. There
seems to be no reason to deny him a broad political vision even if he
often compromised with events. He both contributed to his age and
reflected its vices and virtues. He restored order and prosperity to
England, and re-established the monarchy in its old essential traditions, even if this meant adding much that was new. Abroad, he
combined the old and the new by continuing the ancient feud with
France, but at the same time accepting the loss of Guienne and turning Anglo-French hostility into a source of profit for England, rather
than a cause of mutual destruction and loss. He was a true medieval
ruler; yet he felt the breath of a new age marked by expanding commerce and broader horizons, in which men would open up new
worlds not in the Baltic and the Mediterranean but across the broader
ocean to the west. As part of his 'modernity' he did not think it
beneath his royal dignity to take as his mistress a city merchant's
wife. As a man of action and as a national leader he had something in

[1] This vexed question is discussed in my *Constitutional History of the Fifteenth Century*,
pp. 137, 159–63, with reference to recent writing.

common with the third Edward; as a Renaissance statesman he looked forward no less unmistakably to Henry VIII. His many-sided and significant figure may well be taken to reflect not in-adequately the spirit of his age.

4. Usurpation and Rule of King Richard III

Richard III had not the same significance in English history, but nevertheless his short reign stands out as a landmark. If Edward reflected in his life the union of old and new, Richard expressed this by both his life and his death. His usurpation of the throne was characteristic of the fifteenth century, but unlike those of 1399 and 1461 it ended in disaster. The throne of England was now based on foundations too broad to be shaken by the power of one individual, just as its contribution to the life of the community was too large for it to be occupied as a result of an aristocratic feud. Richard had precedents in more than a hundred years of history when he ex-ploited the rights and duties of a leading prince of the blood in order to destroy his nephews; but his crimes, real or suspected, ensured that he would have no successor in the path he followed to the throne. He lived and died within the circle of the old hierarchic notions of feudalism; but his actions helped still further to under-mine the traditions of the old aristocracy. He had many of the traits of a Renaissance princeling; but it is not without reason that he has been conventionally taken as the last medieval English king. His own mixed qualities were those of a transitional age. With his death at Bosworth the last great medieval struggle, equally conventionally known as the Wars of the Roses, finally came to an end and an era of comparative if still uncertain peace began.

Richard had lived through the vicissitudes of the Wars of the Roses. He had been courted by Warwick but kept faith with his brother Edward. He was steadfast during the Readeption, com-manded Edward's right wing at Barnet, and was in the vanguard at Tewkesbury. With his brother once more on the throne, he shared with Clarence the honours and rights of the leading prince of the blood. After 1478 he stood alone. Later, his victories against the Scots aided by a deliberate bid for popularity gained him warm support in the north. He was the last embodiment of Humphrey of Gloucester's idea of a royal prince but, as events were to show, without Humphrey's redeeming quality of loyalty. Richard, who was named Protector in Edward's will, used his office not to protect his nephews but to destroy them. His essential purpose was his own aggrandisment: his ruthless drive for power may perhaps be seen reflected in the words of a contemporary writer, even though the chronicler emphasizes the agreement of all the lords:

> The said Richard duke of Gloucester accepted that solemn magistracy which had once fallen on duke Humphrey of Gloucester . . .. This authority he used, with the assent and agreement of all the lords, commanding and forbidding in all matters in the manner of an alter-rex . . ..[1]

The exact time when he first directed his ambition towards the throne will probably never be known. From the very beginning there was a temptation to usurp the royal authority. His powers as Protector, like those of Humphrey before him, were strictly limited, and he was faced with the bitter hostility of the Woodvilles entrenched in the court. Elizabeth and her supporters wished to have Prince Edward crowned in all haste. The marquis of Dorset hurriedly laid hands on the royal treasure. Sir Edward Woodville tried to seize the fleet. If Richard allowed his dignity of Protector to be taken from him, or if what powers he had were to be diminished rather than increased, it was probable that his complete destruction would be only a matter of time.

Thus it can be said in his defence that his enemies did not leave him the luxury of loyalty and moderation. They drove him to usurpation as a measure of self-defence. For such a move he had strong assets. His formal powers could plausibly be extended. His personal capacity was well known. He offered England, or seemed to offer, stability and efficient rule—if his authority was confirmed. In these circumstances the Woodvilles' challenge even seemed to offer him an opportunity rather than a menace, for it was not really formidable, yet it enabled him to behead Prince Edward's custodians, receive formal custody of the prince, and take possession of his person. It all happened very quickly. Edward IV had died on 9 April. On hearing of his brother's death, Richard held a memorial service for him at York and swore allegiance to Edward V, calling on all the neighbouring gentry to do the same. On 29 April Richard was at Northampton on his way south, and young Edward was at Stony Stratford ten miles away, together with his uncle Anthony Woodville Earl Rivers, and Sir Richard Grey. Rivers rode into Northampton to greet the duke of Gloucester (Richard). Despite his apparently

[1] *Historiae Croylandensis Continuatio,* translated in my *Constitutional History of England in the Fifteenth Century,* p. 188.

amicable behaviour, Anthony Woodville was suddenly arrested by Gloucester on the following morning. The duke then rode on to Stony Stratford and took possession of his nephew, telling him that there was a plot to seize the government by force and that it had been necessary to arrest Earl Rivers. Edward was then placed under guard in the custody of his uncle. Rivers and Grey were beheaded at Pontefract on 25 June.[1]

It is often argued that only after these events did Gloucester drift into the murder of his princely charges and usurpation of the throne; but, on the whole, this view seems too charitable. All his actions seem to fall into a consistent pattern of a cold and deeply calculated design upon the throne. From the moment of Edward IV's death, the circumstances were probably too favourable and the temptation too great. Added to Richard's own assets were the widespread unpopularity of Elizabeth Woodville and the court, the deep divisions of the lords, and the ineptitude of the archbishop of Canterbury, Thomas Bourchier, who persuaded Elizabeth to hand over her second son to the tender mercies of his uncle. Thus, as a contemporary said:[2]

> The duke of Gloucester went to Westminster [where Elizabeth and her son were in sanctuary] and took with him the Archbishop of Canterbury. There, by persuasiveness, and because of the trust the Queen had in the Archbishop, who thought and planned no harm, she handed over to them the duke of York, a child about seven years old.

There are few more baffling acts of naivety or duplicity in the long and varied annals of the fifteenth century. Both Edward IV's sons were shortly imprisoned in the Tower.

The decisive act of treachery was the sudden execution of Lord Hastings, unshakeable in his fidelity to Edward IV and his heirs. On 13 June Richard appeared at a meeting of the council in the Tower and charged Hastings and others of plotting with the Woodvilles against the protectorate. Whether or not there was any truth in his accusation we have no means of knowing. James Gairdner preferred to follow a highly colourful story by Sir Thomas More, according to which Hastings was suddenly implicated in a charge which Richard levied against Elizabeth Woodville of conspiring with another sorceress, Jane Shore, to waste his body, showing his arm to the council in proof. His arm was indeed withered, but according to

---

[1] Details are given in P. M. Kendall's *Richard III* (London 1956).
[2] *Chronicles of London*, translated in my *Constitutional History of the Fifteenth Century*, p. 189.

More 'it was never other'. In any case, Gloucester had armed guards waiting in readiness and Hastings was seized and led out for immediate execution. A royal proclamation, apparently all prepared, was read out enumerating his treasonable acts.

There followed somewhat ineffective efforts by Richard's servants and allies to persuade Londoners of the bastardy of the two princes. Following this, in a packed meeting at Baynard's Castle, attended by very few of the common people, Richard accepted the throne. A final act, though evidence is scanty and inconclusive, was no doubt the murder of the unfortunate princes in the Tower. Richard could then be crowned king, on 6 July 1483, with all his potential enemies and rivals removed, save one, Henry Tudor, who had betaken himself in haste to Brittany. Richard surrounded himself at his coronation with unprecedented splendour and an unparalleled throng of magnates. He obtained the approval of all the Estates of the realm, acting both inside parliament and outside. But he leaned heavily on hereditary right, perhaps chiefly because his 'election' by the Estates deceived nobody, perhaps least of all himself.

Richard took his business of ruling very seriously. Despite his pretences he had still to gain the approval of his subjects, much more their loyalty. He had scarcely assumed the crown when he toured the west country to win adherents and show his determination to fulfil the duties of his office. He filled his royal council with 'the ablest men that England could then boast', and he finally established the council of the North. He encouraged trade, created an admiralty office with Sir Robert Brackenbury and Sir John Wode as vice-admirals, and he developed the royal Chamber.[1] He improved finances and for a time abolished Benevolences. He achieved some successes, but in one essential matter he conspicuously failed. He could not get the respect of the majority of his subjects, and without this all else was in vain.

Thus, he showed himself an able and effective king, but he was never free from opposition. Whilst he was in the west there was a popular movement of discontent in the south and east to which his chief supporter in his early intrigues, Henry Stafford, duke of Buckingham, lent his support. It is perhaps significant that one area of disaffection was in Kent where political awareness was strong. Buckingham was descended from Thomas Woodstock, Edward III's youngest son, and was married to a Woodville, but he had

[1] P. M. Kendall, *Richard III*, p. 312.

helped to arrest his wife's relatives and to bastardize Edward's sons. He was richly rewarded by Richard, but not satisfied. He may have wished to revive all the powers and claims of the earlier princes of the blood, and to play the role of Warwick the Kingmaker. In any event, he and the popular rebels both failed. Buckingham himself was surrendered to the sheriff of Shropshire by one of his own servants. His plea for mercy was ignored, and he was beheaded in the market-place at Salisbury on 2 November 1483 without ever being allowed access to the king.

Meanwhile, Henry Tudor, an even more formidable opponent to Richard, made abortive efforts to return to England from his exile in Brittany. His caution made him turn back, but he lived to fight another day. Henry was cool, clear-sighted, efficient, and brave. He had a good many supporters, but not enough to have challenged an accepted king. He was descended from John of Gaunt and Catherine Swineford; though Henry IV had excluded the descendents of John and Catherine, from the throne. His mother, Margaret Beaufort, had a better claim than he had to the throne, though this was tactfully ignored. She had married Edmund Tudor, and on 28 February 1457, three months after her husband's death and when she was only thirteen, had given birth to a son whom she named Henry. She was still alive in 1485; in fact, she was only forty-two years old.

Henry had originally planned to settle in France, the old haven for exiled Lancastrians, but had been driven to take shelter in Brittany. Prominent among his supporters were those who were still loyal to the Lancastrian cause which had owed so much to the Beauforts, and Welshmen who were moved by local attachment to the Tudors and by a patriotic desire to see a half-Welsh magnate on the English throne. To reinforce his claim, Henry at Christmas 1483 pledged himself to marry Edward IV's daughter, Elizabeth of York. By this, he promised a reconciliation of the chief opposing families in the long quarrel of the Wars of the Roses. Thus he had plenty of potential supporters in England; but his real strength lay in the incurable hostility which beset Richard III.

In 1485, when Henry made his long-promised landing, he had with him only about 2000 soldiers, who have been described as the sweepings of the gaols of Normandy, though they may have included also a few Scots. But he landed in Milford Haven and was sure of Welsh support; he knew he had allies in England and that

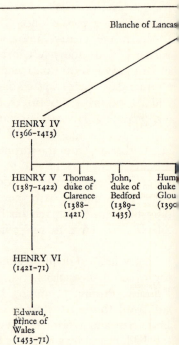

LAN

E.

Blanche of Lancas

Edward,
prince of
Wales
(1330–76)

RICHARD II
(1367–1400)

Lionel,
duke of
Clarence
(1338–68)

Phillippa, *m.*
Edmund
Mortimer,
earl of
March
(1352–81)

Roger
Mortimer,
March
(1374–98)

Edmund
Mortimer,
earl of
March
(1391–1425)

Anne, *m.*
Richard,
earl of
Cambridge
(*d.* 1415)

Richard,
duke of
York
(1411–60)

EDWARD IV
(1442–83)

Edmund,
earl of
Rutland
(1443–60)

George,
duke of
Clarence
(1449–78)

RICHARD III
(1452–85)

HENRY IV
(1366–1413)

HENRY V
(1387–1422)

Thomas,
duke of
Clarence
(1388–
1421)

John,
duke of
Bedford
(1389–
1435)

Hum
duke
Glou
(1390

HENRY VI
(1421–71)

Edward,
prince of
Wales
(1453–71)

ORK

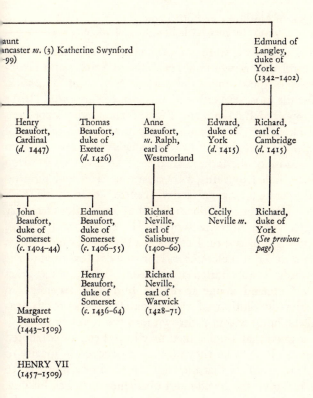

aunt
ancaster *m.* (3) Katherine Swynford
-99)

Edmund of
Langley,
duke of
York
(1342–1402)

Henry
Beaufort,
Cardinal
(*d.* 1447)

Thomas
Beaufort,
duke of
Exeter
(*d.* 1426)

Anne
Beaufort,
m. Ralph,
earl of
Westmorland

Edward,
duke of
York
(*d.* 1415)

Richard,
earl of
Cambridge
(*d.* 1415)

John
Beaufort,
duke of
Somerset
(*c.* 1404–44)

Edmund
Beaufort,
duke of
Somerset
(*c.* 1406–55)

Richard
Neville,
earl of
Salisbury
(1400–60)

Cecily
Neville *m.*

Richard,
duke of
York
(*See previous page*)

Henry
Beaufort,
duke of
Somerset
(*c.* 1436–64)

Richard
Neville,
earl of
Warwick
(1428–71)

Margaret
Beaufort
(1443–1509)

HENRY VII
(1457–1509)

treachery among Richard's followers would be the greatest of them all. The battle of Bosworth which decided the issue between Henry and Richard did, in fact, see more betrayals than any other in the fifteenth century, and they were all against Richard. A warning was pinned even on the tent of the king's chief lieutenant, the Duke of Norfolk, warning him on the eve of battle:

> Jack of Norffolke be not to bold
> For Dykon thy maister is bought and solde.

Among Richard's betrayers were two of the magnates whom he had tried most to bind with power and wealth, Lord Stanley and Henry Percy. The levies of the counties did not respond to his summons. The bishops for the most part either stood aloof or supported Henry as they had supported Buckingham. Richard tried every expedient and did not lack either determination or courage. One of his last acts was to order the execution of Lord Stanley's son, kept with him as a hostage, because of the father's treachery; an order which even his own servants failed or refused to carry out. He died fighting fiercely, in a desperate attack on Henry's centre, beset on his flank by Lord Stanley's brother Sir William, who but for Stanley treachery would have been marching to his support. His crown was found on the field of battle and placed on Henry's head by Lord Stanley. His body was carried naked to Leicester and for two days exposed to the public. Afterwards it was buried at the Grey Friars. Some years later Henry VII erected a fine tomb for him with an effigy in alabaster. At the dissolution of the monasteries, the tomb was destroyed and the body within it thrown into the River Soar.

It has been argued that Englishmen may have been so corrupted by the Wars of the Roses that they no longer believed in loyalty to their ruler. It is more likely that they felt the need of a monarch to whom they could give the loyalty and obedience that was his due. Their betrayal of Richard underlies not the bankruptcy of the monarchy but the importance of its ethical content. Henry Tudor offered a chance for the restoration of national unity and reaffirmation of the old, tested, tradition of a monarch who was not only under the law but also under God, and who would make the betrayals and rebellions of the previous century little more than an unhappy memory, to be distorted in the interests of the Tudor dynasty, and in any case to be misunderstood.

10

SOCIETY AT THE END OF THE MIDDLE AGES

1. The Age of Transition

THE opinion of scholars about society in the last century of the medieval period is sharply divided. On the one hand there are those who talk of recession and decline, on the other those who emphasize progress towards the early modern age. The truth would seem to be that the period was one of conflicting tendencies. The consequences of the Black Death, the recurrence of the Hundred Years War, and catastrophes on the frontiers of Europe, combined to produce signs of economic recession. Reaction from the extremes of the fourteenth century produced conservatism and mediocrity in scholarship and politics. Failure in high quarters led to civil war. On the other hand there was steady progress in other aspects of society, notably in the expansion of the middle class and in the changing outlook of the whole community.

The underlying changes which took place were more important than the more obvious ones. They included the continued disintegration of the agrarian group, the rise of individualism, and a more pronounced capitalism. The hierarchical order continued its outward forms, but its constituent elements became modified both in themselves and in relation to each other. English patriotism and loyalty to the *respublica* both became stronger. In religion, conservatism was the order of the day; but the age was nevertheless the prelude to Reformation. It was a time when men held fast to much that was good in the traditional way of life, but when they also moved forward to the threshold of revolutionary change.

2. Agriculture and the Countryside

In agriculture, a decline which lasted until the 1480s followed the comparative prosperity of the last decade of the century before.

There is evidence of farmhouses in decay, tenants lacking, and of more deserted villages. Though it has recently been argued convincingly that the population decline had probably been arrested by the end of the fourteenth century and that some expansion then ensued, the level in 1500 was still below that which had been reached before the Black Death.[1] In the estates of the abbey of Ramsey, there was a general worsening of conditions. Between 1460 and 1470, the abbot had to wipe all debts off his account rolls and grant out his lands in a series of long leases, hoping that good years would later make up for the bad. Similar signs, though not always as marked, can be seen also in other parts.

There were serious difficulties for the landlords, but there was no general depression of the standard of living of the peasant. The period has, indeed, been hailed, though with some exaggeration, as a golden age for the agricultural worker. Sir John Fortescue, no mean witness though an admirer of all things English, declared that the English peasant was 'the beste fedde and also the best cledde of any natyon crystyn or hethen'. He had an unprecedented opportunity to escape from his villeinage, if he wished, into the town or the cloth industry. The accessibility of the latter is strikingly illustrated by the case of Castle Combe, quoted by E. F. Jacob,[2] where in 1454 free and copyhold (villein) tenants lived in the higher vill called Overcombe and cultivated their strips around, whilst in the lower vill of Nethercombe down in the valley the weavers worked along with others engaged in the manufacture of cloth. It was even possible for a villein to amass wealth in the cloth industry whilst he kept his servile estate. In the same Castle Combe a villein named William Heyne became a wealthy clothier and left chattels at his death worth the large sum of £2,000.

Thus, the development of the cloth industry created wealth, offered opportunities to the peasant, and changed the distribution of population. That it brought prosperity to a good many communities in the fifteenth century is proved by the large and impressive 'wool' churches of East Anglia and the Cotswolds. The chronology of the changes it brought about is obscure; as has been seen, many began in the fourteenth century. In the Cotswolds,

---

[1] J. M. W. Bean, 'Plague, Population, and Economic Decline in England in the Later Middle Ages', in *Econ. Hist. Rev.*, series 2, vol. XV (1962), pp. 423–37; arguing against John Saltmarsh, 'Plague and Economic Decline in England in the Later Middle Ages', in *The Cambridge Historical Journal*, vol. VII (1941–43).

[2] *The Fifteenth Century 1399–1485* (Oxford 1961), p. 378.

places like Stroud and Chalford grew from obscure villages into thriving towns. Bradford-on-Avon owed its rise to the same cause. When the antiquary Leland visited it much later, he wrote 'all the town standeth by cloth-making'. Up in Yorkshire the West Riding outstripped York as a producer of cloth. The industry was partly organized on a primitive capitalistic basis, including small factories; but it was also a cottage industry, in which smallholders farmed their land and also had one or more looms in the house. But York itself increased its population significantly, especially after 1298 when it became a base for the conduct of the Scottish war. By the end of the century, it stood about 13,000. In view of the Black Death this must point to a massive immigration from the countryside.

The lot of the villeins who remained on the land was also improved. The law courts gave them legal rights as customary tenants or copyholders, placing them in a category very different from that which had been implied by the Abbot of Burton in 1280. Chief Justice Danby declared in 1467 that if the lord ousted his customary tenant he did him wrong, for such a tenant held his land, and his heirs after him, as securely according to the custom of the manor as any man according to Common Law. This was a heartening declaration, though its force is somewhat diminished by the modern view, different from that of Maitland, that the customary tenant had long had a title to his land by blood.

But commutations continued apace. At Crowland, the flight of villeins at the end of the fourteenth century and the beginning of the fifteenth, and the failure to find substitutes, so disrupted the cultivation of the abbey's demesnes of Cottenham and Oakington in Cambridgeshire that they were leased entirely to villeins. Such leasings were not at all uniform, but they show an unmistakable trend; and with this there was a continuation of the accumulation of holdings by the wealthier peasants. The land thus acquired was often taken for rents at the lord's will or pleasure, unprotected by the custom of the manor. That there were plenty of takers on these terms indicates an increasing exchange of lands, an increasing inequality of holdings and, with the growth of holdings of 60–80 acres, the continuing emergence of the yeoman class. Villagers might go no further than a neighbouring village, even under the same lord, where there was land or employment; but the result was nevertheless a steady weakening of the cohesion of the village group and a lessening of the old seignorial relationship between lord and cultivator, and the link between the land and the community of the vill.

Some part of the changing pattern was due to enclosure. On the duke of Norfolk's manor of Forncett in Norfolk sixteen tenants paid fines in 1404 for having enclosed their land. On the other hand, the first protests against such enclosures appear under this year, whilst the contemporary *Court Rolls* of Launton state how 'the jurats present that all the tenants, freeholders and villeins, assembled and brake an hedge of land that marked off a recent enclosure, and carried it away in contempt of the lord'. It is clear that the attitude of tenants towards enclosure might vary, but the fact of enclosure seems to be clear. At his death in 1489 a chantry priest of Warwick named John Rous left a *History of the Realm of England* in which he agitated against the destruction of villages which had occurred because certain sons of Mammon found wool and meat more profitable to produce than grain like the enclosing tenant at Forncett who in 1401 paid for a licence to have a fold for 100 sheep. Rous talked of this 'modern' phenomenon which brought dearth to the commonwealth. The early desertion of villages, which was in fact uneven and occurred most extensively in the Midlands and parts of Yorkshire, may have been caused largely by the Plague; but the later movement was probably the result of enclosure for the sake of rearing sheep or creating parks for deer.

3. COMMERCE AND GILDS

Alongside these changes, commerce increasingly affected all people's lives. The *Herald's Debate* of 1453–61 still divided Englishmen into churchmen, nobles, and others; though in the last group it distinguished between craftsmen and 'common people'. Commerce became prominent for the first time in the theories of national policy, as in the *Libelle of English Polycye*, even though the primary purpose of this piece of propaganda was to promote strength not in commerce but in war:

> Cheryshe marchandyse [the council was advised], kepe thamyralté,
> That we bee maysteres of the narowe see.

Nevertheless, commerce was the means:

> For yef marchaundes were cherysshede to here spede,[1]
> We were not lykelye to fayle in ony nede.

---

[1] The *Libelle of English Polycye*, edited by Sir George Warner (Oxford 1926), pp. 1, 25. See an important comment by E. F. Jacob, *The Fifteenth Century*, p. 346, n. 2.

Purely commercial conflicts did, indeed, assume national importance, calling for the sustained intervention of the government, as for example the long dispute between the Merchant Adventurers and the Hanse League. The former were the best known of all the associations of English merchants in the late Middle Ages. They represented a pooling of resources in an effort to penetrate markets abroad, especially Prussia, Norway, Iceland, and Spain. By the time of the *Libelle of English Polycye*, the Merchant Adventurers could boast that they bought more goods in Brabant, Flanders, and Zeeland than all other nations. They were active in all the main English ports, but especially in London, where they gathered cloth from all parts of the land for shipping to the great international marts of the Low Countries. The Adventurers of London were so powerful that they compelled all who sold cloth in these marts to contribute to their Fellowship, even the stubborn Yorkshiremen. They normally received strong support from the government, though this occasionally faltered badly, especially under Henry VI.

The fundamental cause of the conflict between the Merchant Adventurers and the Hanse was the English attempt to penetrate into the Baltic, and the strong, at times violent, opposition of the German towns. Both sides were guilty of acts of piracy and intimidation, including very damaging English attacks on Hanse shipping in 1449 and 1458. There was much governmental intervention and there were many discussions in parliament. The English made a favourable agreement in 1437, gaining reciprocity; but this was never confirmed by Prussia or recognized by Danzig, Prussia's leading port; and they were unable to keep all their gains. A second settlement, in the Treaty of Utrecht of 1473, was less favourable to them; though it owed much to Edward IV, and though there was a strong link between him and the Hanse merchants as he had returned to England in Hanse ships after his overthrow by Warwick. At any rate, through his aid the 'oold frendlyhode' between English and German merchants was patched up though not completely restored.

There were similar conflicts with Italian merchants, though these were not so extensive. In 1457 the Genoese seized ships of Robert Sturmy of Bristol as these were on their way home from the Levant. There were reprisals and lawsuits, extending to include the merchants of Southampton, whose mayor Thomas Payne was sued in the Court of Chancery by the Italians, complaining of his violence towards them. As a result he was deposed from his office by the king. In the end the Italians were more successful in their opposition to English merchant intrusions into their sphere of influence than the Germans, and the Mediterranean remained closed to English shipping for some years.

Opposition did not prevent English ports and trade from expanding. In 1414 Rye sheltered a mere handful of people but by 1493 it had five burghers assessed at £400 and its total wealth was rated at £6303. Bridport, Chester, and Plymouth also expanded. Sandwich appears to have prospered, though this was not true of all the Cinque Ports. Southampton and Bristol became large and important. In the latter, according to William of Worcester, William Canynges the younger kept 800 men for eight years employed in his ships, and 100 workmen employed on their construction. A foreign traveller later reported that London shops contained more precious metals than those of Rome, Milan, Florence, and Venice put together.[1] At the close of the fourteenth century, English trade had been still mostly by way of foreign ships, but a hundred years later English vessels carried more than half the cloth exported and about three-quarters of other goods.

4. THE ARISTOCRACY

Though commerce was obviously on the increase, the landed aristocracy remained securely dominant. The fifteenth century was, indeed, the time when their combination of social ascendancy and political power on the one hand, with Renaissance statecraft and sophistication on the other, enabled them to exploit their advantages most effectively. It has, indeed, been claimed that in the fifteenth century Bastard Feudalism threatened to destroy the constitutional and legal progress achieved since the twelfth. Through it, the argument runs, the baronage was able to make immediate dependants of the same landed gentry whom the king had used extensively to expand his government and law. The great lords more and more used the power this gave them for the purposes of aggrandizement and private war. The feuds which multiplied were ultimately transferred, as if to a supreme court, to the battlefields of the civil war. Thus, it is claimed, the breakdown of public order in England long preceded, and was not caused by, the loss of possessions and the

---

[1] Mrs. J. R. Green, *Town Life in the Fifteenth Century* (London 1894), vol. I, p. 59.

cessation of warfare in France; and the Wars of the Roses themselves were simply an escalation of private feuds.[1]

There are, indeed, signs of such an escalation. In Devonshire, the earl of Devon was at odds with William Bonville, who was a thrusting and able man, summoned to the parliament of 1449 as Lord Bonville of Chewton. In 1451 the earl led a 'campaign' against his opponents, with a force which has been estimated at between five and six thousand men. He laid regular siege to Taunton Castle, though singularly little blood was shed. It is no wonder that in the greater political conflict of the civil war Bonville supported the Lancastrians and Devon supported York.

The north was even more seriously divided. There was a bitter feud between Nevilles and Percies for influence and power. The area was remote, exposed to Scottish attack, and impossible to control, at least by the government of Henry VI. The Percies were in the main the aggressors, especially Thomas, the earl of Northumberland's second son. Born in 1422 he was endowed with excessive arrogance and showed a tendency towards violence which was outstanding even in that aristocratic and violent age. By 1453 he had become so contemptuous of royal authority that he ignored repeated summonses by the king. Royal commissions to investigate the quarrels and disturbances achieved nothing. On 13 August 1453 Thomas, now for some years Baron Egremont, gathered a force said to number 5000 men and threatened the earl of Salisbury, his son Thomas, and their wives, as they were travelling homeward after Thomas had been married at Tattersall Castle.

After this, nobody, least of all the king, could reconcile the two. Indeed, after Henry VI's illness of August 1453 Egremont and a new ally, Henry Holland, duke of Exeter, gathered together what we must call an army, including retainers from many parts of the north, together with weavers, barbers and other tradesmen from York. They seized York and tried to capture Hull. Meanwhile they engaged in much propaganda. Richard of York took the field against them and the 'rising' faded away. Exeter suffered imprisonment 'with great heaviness and right chargeable costs': the earl of Northumberland, head of the Percy clan, suffered judicial investigations. On 31 October 1454 Egremont fell into the hands of John and Thomas Neville as the result of a skirmish at Stamford Bridge. Before a commission of oyer and terminer at York he was condemned

[1] R. L. Storey, *op. cit.* (London 1966).

to pay Salisbury crushing damages of £11,200. He and Richard Percy were confined in Newgate prison, escaping by a spectacular action on the night of 13 November 1456.

There are many other instances of local disorders, some in Derbyshire, for example, which have been cited as providing a forceful answer to those apologists of Bastard Feudalism who write of its stabilizing qualities. But the problem provided by this form of aristocratic dominance is not to be solved by a simple enumeration of local disturbances. Local disturbances were one thing; an attack on the king's standard and on his anointed and crowned person was another. Men did not cross the line which divided them without serious cause or far-reaching designs; though it must be admitted that the act of crossing at the first battle of St. Albans in 1455 had in it a considerable element of chance. As K. B. McFarlane says, it is impossible to believe that York's course had been charted beforehand or that he—or indeed anyone else among the nobility—was spoiling for a fight.[1] Nevertheless it seems true to say[2] that:

> The war was fought because the nobility was unable to rescue the kingdom from the consequences of Henry VI's insanity by any other means. It does not follow that they liked the task. It is obvious, of course, that they were far from united in their attitude towards it.

It may be admitted that the methods of the new feudalism encouraged local rivalries and struggles for power, but they also helped to adapt aristocratic leadership to the conditions of the fifteenth century. And aristocratic leadership was still a necessity. The price paid for it was heavy, but the contribution it made to society was invaluable and would be for many generations to come.

Bastard feudalism not only encouraged political ambitions and turbulence but also political sophistication and governmental skill. If political sophistication may be linked to education in letters, it was certainly increasing in the fifteenth century. The spread of education was shown by the exceptional interest in learning by such outstanding characters as Duke Humphrey of Gloucester and John Tiptoft. Humphrey was a great lover of books, patron of Italian scholars, and donor of a whole library to Oxford University. Of John, Thomas Fuller later said that the axe which beheaded Tiptoft (with three blows at his request, to symbolize the Trinity) cut off

---

[1] 'The Wars of the Roses', in the *Proceedings of the British Academy*, vol. L (1964), p. 94; cf. *ibid.*, p. 95: 'only an undermighty ruler had anything to fear from overmighty subjects'.

[2] *Ibid.*, p. 97.

more learning than was left in the heads of all the surviving nobility; and this should perhaps be taken as praise of John even more than disparagement of aristocratic learning. Tiptoft's Latin oration was said to have been so polished as to move Pope Pius II to tears. Fortescue tells how the Inns of Court were patronized mainly by the aristocracy. The foundation of Winchester by William of Wykeham in 1382, because of its size and self-government, marked the beginning of a new period in English public education. Even the boys at Edward IV's court were taught, in addition to the skill and behaviour of the knight, 'sundry languages and other learnings virtuous'. Sir John Fortescue insisted that Prince Edward who was in his charge should be taught above all else the law of the land. The interest in law was commented on by William of Worcester. Finally, it may be noticed, the 'new' knight of Tiptoft's translations was expected to possess readiness of wit, pleasantness of wisdom, and knowledge of letters.[1]

Alongside this, the whole concept of chivalry on which the aristocracy was nourished continued to change, despite the insistence on old ideals by such writers as Froissart and Sir Thomas Malory. By the fifteenth century, even those who extolled the 'antique virtues' came to describe them in terms which had a direct relation to the needs and practices of contemporary life. Knighthood became, even more obviously than in the age of Langland, not only a pursuit of glory and honour, but a service to the *respublica* in matters of peace as well as of war.

Already, to Langland, true knighthood had been, if not a magistracy, at least a substitute for or supplement to magistracy. To John Gower the function of a knight was to give battle against injustices.[2] When we come to the fifteenth century, even a work like William of Worcester's *The Boke of Noblesse*, written shortly before 1461, and ostensibly reflecting the old heroic virtues, was openly concerned with the welfare of the *respublica* in such matters as foreign policy and the successful conduct of a 'national' war. John Tiptoft's *Declamacion of Noblesse*, written about the same time, gives high priority to public service alongside the cult of *prouesse*. As one of his characters says:

---

[1] A. B. Ferguson, *The Indian Summer of English Chivalry*, p. 184; William of Worcester's *The Boke of Noblesse*, edited by J. G. Nichols (1860), p. 77; R. J. Mitchell, *John Tiptoft (1427–1470)* (London 1938), p. 182.

[2] Gervase Mathew, 'Ideals of Knighthood in late Fourteenth Century England', in *Studies in Medieval History presented to F. M. Powicke* (Oxford 1948), p. 360.

DESCENDANTS OF K

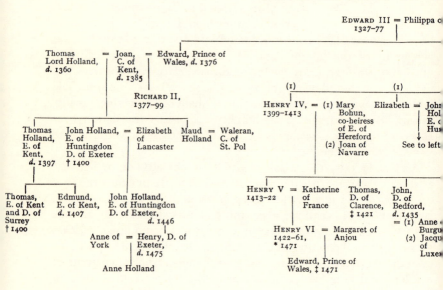

EDWARD III = Philippa o
1327-77

Thomas = Joan, = Edward, Prince of
Lord Holland, | C. of | Wales, *d.* 1376
d. 1360 | Kent,
| *d.* 1385

RICHARD II,
1377-99

(1)

HENRY IV, = (1) Mary   Elizabeth = John
1399-1413 | Bohun, | Hol
| co-heiress | E. o
| of E. of | Hu
| Hereford
| (2) Joan of   See to left
| Navarre

Thomas   John Holland, = Elizabeth   Maud = Waleran,
Holland, E. of   of   Holland C. of
E. of   Huntingdon   Lancaster   St. Pol
Kent,   D. of Exeter
d. 1397 † 1400

HENRY V = Katherine   Thomas,   John,
1413-22 | of   D. of   D. of
| France   Clarence,   Bedford,
| ‡ 1421   *d.* 1435
| = (1) Anne
| Burgu
HENRY VI = Margaret of   (2) Jacqu
1422-61, Anjou   of
* 1471   Luxe

Thomas,   Edmund,   John Holland,
E. of Kent, E. of Kent, E. of Huntingdon
and D. of *d.* 1407   D. of Exeter,
Surrey   *d.* 1446
† 1400

Edward, Prince of
Wales, ‡ 1471

Anne of = Henry, D. of
York | Exeter,
| *d.* 1475

Anne Holland

NOTE.— * = Murdered.   † = Executed.   ‡ = Killed in battle.   *d.* = Died.   D. = Duke.   M. = Marquis.   E

ARD III

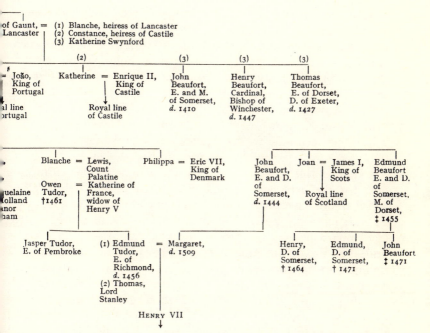

of Gaunt, =	(1) Blanche, heiress of Lancaster		
Lancaster	(2) Constance, heiress of Castile		
	(3) Katherine Swynford		

(2)   (3)   (3)   (3)

= João,   Katherine = Enrique II,   John   Henry   Thomas
King of   King of   Beaufort,   Beaufort,   Beaufort,
Portugal   Castile   E. and M.   Cardinal,   E. of Dorset,
al line   Royal line   of Somerset,   Bishop of   D. of Exeter,
ortugal   of Castile   *d.* 1410   Winchester,   *d.* 1427
                                                     d. 1447

Blanche = Lewis,   Philippa = Eric VII,   John   Joan = James I,   Edmund
          Count   King of   Beaufort,   King of   Beaufort
          Palatine   Denmark   E. and D.   Scots   E. and D.
   Owen   of   of
uelaine   Tudor,   = Katherine of   Somerset,   Royal line   Somerset,
olland   †1461   France,   *d.* 1444   of Scotland   M. of
nor   widow of   Dorset,
1am   Henry V   ‡ 1455

Jasper Tudor,   (1) Edmund = Margaret,   Henry,   Edmund,   John
E. of Pembroke   Tudor,   *d.* 1509   D. of   D. of   Beaufort
                       E. of   Somerset,   Somerset,   ‡ 1471
                       Richmond,   † 1464   † 1471
                         d. 1456
                       (2) Thomas,
                       Lord
                       Stanley

HENRY VII

t or Countess.   ↓ = Leaving surviving issue.   Many persons of no historical importance are omitted.

after that [his diligent study in philosophy and ancient languages] when I remembered me how every man which had virtue or cunning is bound to serve therewith the estate public, I gave myself wholly and fully to the public weal of the city.

Caxton's printing of *Tullius of Old Age*, a translation of Cicero's *De Senectute*, was intended for 'noble wyse and grete lordes, gentilmen and marchauntes that have ben and dayly ben occupyed in materes towchyng the publyque weal'.

Thus the fifteenth century knight was still set apart by chivalry, but his transition from the warrior to the courtier or administrator became more pronounced. In conformity with this, the tournament finally became nothing but a spectacle. Denholm Young refers to the 'futile but highly stylized and ornamental pageants of the fifteenth century'. There were heralds, ladies, tents, and crowds of spectators, feasting and dancing. Minstrels (*histriones*) recited and made music. Knights fought for the honour and love of their ladies. Tilting between only two combatants became the fashion, and the two were now separated by a barrier or 'tilt'.

As part of this general pattern the age became famous, or notorious, for the extravagance and ostentation of the nobility; but lavish entertainment was not so much an end in itself as a means to an end; indirectly if not directly it reflected the increasing aristocratic preoccupation with peace. It was an expression of aristocratic pride but also an instrument of policy. Far from being simply a sign of decadent chivalry and of a ruling class quite divorced from reality, it was also intended to win friends and adherents by advertising generosity and wealth. Indeed, magnates closer to reality than men like Richard of York or Warwick the Kingmaker it would be difficult to find. Richard Neville, earl of Salisbury, was a shrewd and capable soldier and politician, but he kept a large household as a matter of course, including eight domestic chaplains. It was not a matter of empty ostentation when Warwick and his brother George indulged in entertainment whose scale echoed throughout England when the latter was installed as archbishop of York in 1467. The duke of Buckingham dined 319 strangers on the feast of the Epiphany. The duke of Clarence had a 'riding' household of 188 servants and a 'standing' household of 299. When in 1463 the importation of wine from Gascony and Guienne was forbidden, the duchess of York got an exemption in order to import sixty tuns of wine; and Edward IV sent her another six tuns for Christmas. It has been claimed that

Warwick required six oxen daily to feed his household and distribute food, and that it was not unusual for him to cater for five hundred guests. The king himself had long ago set an example. It was said that 10,000 persons were fed in Richard II's household and that 300 worked in his palace kitchens. At Lichfield, during the Christmas of 1398, 28 cows were consumed, 26 oxen, 300 eggs and numberless fowls.

Such lavishness was not an innovation. Long before this, when Gilbert, earl of Gloucester and his wife Joan visited her brother Prince Edward in February 1293, they took with them over two hundred knights, esquires, and maids of honour. But retinues and extravagance both increased in the two hundred years that followed. According to Edward IV's *Black Book*, a duke ought to spend £4,000 a year and have 240 attendants, and a marquis ought to spend £3,000 and have 200 attendants. By 1461 the Percies may have paid out a third, or possibly even a half, of their gross revenues in retainers' fees, a sharp increase on what they had paid in 1421. 'That is the guise of your countrymen', a lawyer complained in Norfolk in 1454, 'to spend all the good they have on men and livery, gowns and horses and harness, and so bear it out for a while and at the last they are but beggars'.

The changes in manners were reflected in changes in dwellings. These showed an increasing regard for space, comfort, and elegance. Despite political unrest, defence became much less important, though the main buildings were the tower house for the lord and his family, with a rectangular courtyard for guests and retinues. The beautiful mansion of Tattershall in Lincolnshire, begun in 1434 by Henry VI's treasurer, Lord Cromwell, is an outstanding example. Its great tower had windows, some fine rooms with elegant fireplaces, a hall beside the tower, and a moat around: 'the rooms gave a remarkable impression of spaciousness, dignity and fine proportion. They were planned to be the home of a highly civilized people of noble birth.' John Norreys built an impressive house during the Wars of the Roses; but though it was built in time of civil strife it was notable for the number and size of its windows and for a design worked out on a basis of harmony and beauty with no thought for the needs of defence.[1]

[1] Joan Evans, *English Art, 1307–1461*, pp. 129, 134.

5. THE MIDDLE CLASSES

All this change meant that the aristocracy was modifying its supreme dedication to war and readiness for war, and to this extent finding a measure of identity with the great majority whose preoccupation was with the affairs of peace. In this respect they moved a step towards the middle classes; whilst the latter, for their part, moved if almost imperceptibly towards increasing affinities, in speech, politics, and even social intercourse, with the highest class, though still far removed from the great princes of the royal blood. They were without cohesion or definition; but they ranged widely and slowly expanded. Their upper ranks included gentry like the Pastons, together with rich merchants like the Celys, and successful managerial experts like William of Worcester. Their lower ranks included yeomen farmers and prosperous craftsmen. After the restriction on franchise in the shire courts in 1429, and the failure of Jack Cade's revolt in 1450, their position in the countryside was unchallenged. In 1445 it was enacted that the representatives of the shires should be knights or esquires, or at least gentlemen of similar estate.

During the century the middle classes consolidated their position in the towns. After 1381 the aristocractic and conservative element achieved greater ascendancy in London. The council of citizens existing from the earliest period lost much of its importance. The aldermen were made immovable except for good cause. Oligarchy triumphed, an example followed in most towns, though in varying degrees. In Norwich power was largely concentrated in the hands of the mayor and council, who had permanent tenure of office. Exeter fell under the control of a restricted aristocratic council. Bristol was created a county as early as 1373; its council was to be elected by mayor and sheriff, with only the assent of the commonalty. Co-option rather than election to office tended to triumph at York, though with interesting vicissitudes, as it did at Leicester and in Northampton. There may occasionally have been greater flexibility; but in general the age of the incorporation of boroughs was also the age of consolidation of the civic aristocracies after the conflicts and unrest of the fourteenth century.[1]

During the same period, even the crafts became more oligarchical in structure. Their spirit decayed, as witnessed by a weakening

[1] The interesting problem this presents is briefly discussed in my *Constitutional History of the Fifteenth Century*, pp. 330–1.

support for their pageants. They became exclusive, charging prohibitive fees for the admission of new members. In an Act of parliament in 1437 they were accused of making unlawful and unreasonable ordinances 'for their singular profit and common damage to the people'. As markets widened, trading functions were taken over by a special class of merchants, and the master craftsman was limited to the work of his hands. Small crafts amalgamated with each other. The middleman between them and the public became increasingly important and tended to reduce the craftsman to dependence.

The changes led to the development of the Livery Company. Its origin goes back to Edward III's reign, when crafts were permitted to adopt liveries as a sign of participation in a common brotherhood. In time the livery was confined to the wealthier members of the craft, who incorporated themselves and acquired a greatly privileged position. In the large towns, with the exception of London itself, they developed into general trading companies, not restricted to any one class of merchandise and quite separate from the crafts. Partly through them and their organization, the wealthy merchant became increasingly respected in the community, an aristocracy of the city parallel to the squirarchy of the shires.

Incorporation and increasing stratification may have weakened the communities of town and shire more than the earlier strife and disorders. It is a moot point. What seems to be certain is that both communities were affected by the steadily increasing predominance of the central government, so that the most important single event was tending to become the election of parliamentary representatives. In any case signs of rising status became more unmistakable. Members of the upper middle classes became not easy to distinguish from the great lords, at least in their manners and attainments. Books were more common with them. The Pastons both owned books and loved reading. Sir John Paston was an enthusiastic bibliophile; while in 1450 the great neighbour of the Pastons, Sir John Fastolf, had a good collection of books at Caistor Castle. A number of knights bequeathed books in wills proved before Archbishop Chichele. Paper had not yet come into general use to facilitate the spread of letters, but it was being rapidly adopted; and by the third quarter of the century, ordinary men and women were 'surprisingly literate'.[1] Even apprentices could write letters to

[1] H. S. Bennett, *The Pastons and their England* (Cambridge 1922), p. 112; cf. R. F. Mitchell, *John Tiptoft* (1427–70), p. 1; cf. J. W. Adamson, 'The Extent of Literacy in

their masters. Jane Shore, mistress of Edward IV, was the wife of a London goldsmith, but she could 'both read well and write'. A London baker could order that his son be brought up 'in all lernyng', and an alderman could wish his to have learning and erudition. Private tuition was available. A boy of twelve was represented as declaring that in three months at the school of a certain William Kingsmill he had learned to read and write, to make up accounts, and to speak French. William Walworth bequeathed to his brother a law library worth the appreciable sum of £100.

Some humble laymen were both literate and eloquent. Among the Lollards of the early fifteenth century, William Swinderby at Leicester is said to have taught himself to read and write. Walter Brute, another of the sect, had a considerable knowledge of Latin and a capacity for dialectic, though how he obtained these we are not sure. A carpenter's wife of Norwich was accused of Lollardy for inviting her neighbours to hear her husband 'read the law of Christ to them'. An increasing number of grammar schools and chantry schools were established. The first of many to be founded by citizens of London may have been that which was endowed in the will of a grocer in 1432 to provide 'a Bachelor of Arts, but by no means in holy orders, to keep a grammar school . . . to teach and instruct all boys whatsoever'. The Commons in 1447 spoke of 'the great number of grammar schools'.

In the early fifteenth century we meet a 'gentleman villein' in Oxfordshire. He had been brought up as a boy at New College, and was claimed by the Abbot of Abingdon as a bondman. He had difficulty in finding 50 marks, the price of manumission, for he had only a few acres of land.[1] One more general reference to literacy has been cited by Miss Abram.[2] When enquiries were made in 1466 in connection with Sir John Fastolf's will, twenty witnesses were examined. Of these, eleven were described as illiterate: they consisted of five husbandmen, one gentleman, one smith, one cook, one roper,

England in the Fifteenth and Sixteenth Centuries', *The Library*, Fourth Series, vol. X (1930), pp. 163–93; W. A. Pantin, *The English Church in the Fourteenth Century* (Cambridge 1955), p. 217; compare *Speculum*, vol. XI (1936), pp. 224–31; D. Hay, 'History and Historians in France and England during the Fifteenth Century', in *B.I.H.R.*, vol. XXXV (1963), pp. 111–27.

[1] Sylvia Thrupp, *The Merchant Class of Medieval London* (Ann Arbor 1962), p. 309.

[2] A. Abram, *English Life and Manners in the Later Middle Ages* (London 1913), p. 229. Compare J. W. Adamson's view in *The Library* as above, p. 193: 'it may be said of the English people of the fifteenth and especially of the sixteenth century that it was by no means an illiterate society and that facilities for rudimentary instruction at least were so distributed as to reach even small towns and villages'.

one tailor, and one mariner. Seven were 'literate': two husbandmen, two merchants, a tailor, a mariner, and one whose occupation was not described. One other, Stephen Scrope, could write, and the other had been a schoolmaster. A knowledge of reading and writing, Miss Abram concluded, was fairly widespread.

A good many of the nobility were descended from or had close connections with the middle classes. It has been pointed out that between 1439 and 1504 sixty-eight new peerages were created, excluding promotions from one rank of the peerage to another. Of these, twenty-one went to the husbands or sons of heiresses to old titles, but forty-seven creations were new. There was a constant influx into the peerage from rich but untitled families. The meteoric rise of a middling landowner into the ranks of the highest nobility is illustrated by the king's elevation of William Hastings in 1461. Edward IV gave William a mass of forfeited estates which enabled him to dominate the central midlands as a loyal supporter of the king, and to be a leading figure in national politics until his execution by Richard III.

Lord Cromwell, whose lineage was not conspicuously high, rose to be Treasurer, and when he died in 1455 left property worth £2,263 a year. Lower down the scale, Sir John Fastolf began as a humble squire and made his fortune out of the French war; he became an important member of the gentry out of the proceeds of one single victory at Verneuil. Thomas Chaucer, son of the poet, whose grandparents had been no more than well-to-do merchants, became accepted into the aristocracy. Beginning as a protegé of John of Gaunt, he became Chief Butler to Richard II, Henry IV, and Henry V, Constable of Wallingford Castle, and member of parliament for Oxfordshire in nine parliaments between 1402 and 1429. He was many times chosen as Speaker, served the king as ambassador, and fought at Agincourt with a retinue of twelve men-at-arms and thirty-seven archers. He became a member of the king's council and died a very rich man. The grandson of his only daughter was the earl of Lincoln whom Richard III named his heir apparent.

There was constant movement also of a less spectacular kind. Rich merchants settled in the countryside and founded families of minor gentry. Wealthy farmers like the early Pastons could become important local figures. Sir John Paston at the mid-century was called Sir John Fastolf's 'best friend and helper and supporter', was addressed as 'cousin' by the famous soldier, and received Caistor

Castle from Fastolf as a bequest. He and his successor could feud with the duke of Norfolk himself.

According to the *Boke of St. Albans*, published just after Bosworth but derived from fifteenth-century sources:'. . . in theys days opynly we se how many poore men by theyr grace favoure laborire or deservyng are made nobuls sum bi ther prudens sum bi oder virtuys . . .'. We may perhaps add to that another adage common in the century:

> Yt ys all wayes sene now a days
> That money makythe the man.

Not that there were not strong objections by the defenders of old ways and old distinctions. Lord Rivers, whose daughter later married Edward IV, could be berated heartily as an upstart in 1460 by the Yorkists themselves. As William Paston described the scene[1]:

> As for tidings, my Lord Ryvers was brought to Calais, and before the [Yorkist] lords there, with eightscore torches, and there my lord of Salisbury berated him, calling him a knave's son . . .. And my Lord of Warwick berated him, and said his father was but a squire, and brought up with king Harry the Fifth . . ..

That the old prejudices were well recognized on a lower level of society is shown by the sentiments which Froissart had put into the mouths of the peasants in 1381. They tempted the chivalric Sir Robert Salle to join them by pointing out that as the son of a mason he would never be accepted as a gentleman. William of Worcester, champion of the new chivalry, objected to the sons of lords attending shire courts to embrace and rule among the poor and simple commons of bestial countenance who desired merely to live in peace. But in spite of these defenders of lost causes, and perhaps shown by their very objections, it is clear that the fourteenth century movement from class to class continued and may even have become more pronounced.

The changes of the fourteenth and fifteenth centuries even affected the agelong classification of society into men of prayer, of war, and of work; though this threefold division was still common. Already in the late fourteenth century Thomas Walsingham referred to three classes of *proceres, mediocres,* and *pauperes*; the last two groups being subdivisions of the men of work. The *pauperes* were identified at times with the *vulgares*; in a fifteenth-century dictionary they are defined as the 'comune pepylle'. Bishop Stafford in 1433 advised

[1] *The Paston Letters*, vol. I, p. 506.

them to look for justice to the merchants and esquires.[1] This new classification did not reflect any change in the position of the aristocracy at the apex of society, but it did reflect a growing importance of the middle class. Bishop Stafford gave them a significant role to play; as *mediocres* they could fulfil what was to become a traditional function between the high and low strata of society. The strengthening of the bourgeoisie did, indeed, contribute towards a process which was leading towards the unity of all Englishmen under the Crown. More and more it was possible to claim that:

> The least liege man, with body and rent,
> He is a parcel of the crown.

Similarly, it could be argued in political debate that 'it behooves every person of the commonalty to oppose the ruin of the public good'.

6. Military Service and War

An increasing sense of this obligation may be seen in the organization of armies. For campaigns overseas this was still dominated by the traditions of Edward III's reign. The aristocracy served in person, both by tradition and preference; and from their ranks came the most famous generals, men like John, duke of Bedford. In 1415 every active baron followed Henry V to Agincourt. They and their followers were still organized by the methods of Bastard Feudalism, mainly by the use of the indenture. Aristocratic captains contracted with the king to produce the necessary 'companies'. Each knight had his own esquires and followers; and the knights, retainers of the great lords, were the *élite* of the armies. They dismounted for battle and their steeds were led to the rear by the esquires. They were formidable warriors, even in the changing conditions of the fifteenth century, with a special *ésprit de corps*.

War was profitable to the magnates, at least until the tide turned against the English after 1429. They not only received the king's pay but also took a share of the ransom won by their retainers; though the ruler demanded a third of the gains his captains made and a third of the winnings of his captains' men. In spite of all this, there was a continuing decline in the importance of the lords in comparison with other elements in the king's armies. The humble bowmen were

[1] G. R. Owst, *Preaching in Medieval England* (Cambridge 1926), p. 264; *Literature and Pulpit in Medieval England* (Cambridge 1933), pp. 352–4; Sylvia Thrupp, *The Merchant Class of Medieval London*, p. 288.

as important as ever, as for example at Verneuil in 1424 or at Patay in 1429; and they were now supplemented by the artillery, as at the siege of Harfleur in the Agincourt campaign, at Formigny in 1450, and at Castillon in 1453. The French made better use of guns and gunpowder, but the English did not ignore them. Humphrey of Gloucester, for example, was expert in their use. They were employed by Edward IV to reduce Lancastrian strongholds; and in 1464 Bamburgh Castle was breached by the king's artillery and carried by storm: 'so all the king's guns that were charged began to shoot upon the said castle'. The guns were now so important that they were 'christened' individually. Warwick also used artillery extensively; he kept his gunners busy all night at Barnet but, unfortunately for him, they consistently shot over the royalist camp. Artillerymen were specialists; but they were not of the knightly class. The development of their weapon decreased the importance of the more aristocratic cavalry and greatly reduced that of the aristocratic fortress. Finally it should be noted that in this century, despite the victories of Henry V and Bedford, the armies which the aristocracy recruited and led ceased to be strikingly successful. They lost France between 1429 and 1453, and in the Wars of the Roses the great lords on the whole were on the losing side.

Of course, these changes in warfare did not destroy Bastard Feudalism, though for various reasons it was now more talked about, legislated against, and denounced. In 1401 Henry IV enacted that with certain exceptions only the king might give livery or sign of company, but this general prohibition was not maintained: Edward IV, for example, allowed lords to bestow liveries to those who had his commission to raise men. In 1468 both liveries and retaining were forbidden; but an exception was made for members of a lord's household or council or for lawful service done. Only in the sixteenth century did indentures and liveries become largely ornamental; by that time they had ceased to serve the purposes of society and at the same time injured it with their abuse.

As the effective contribution of the magnates to warfare declined, that of the levies of the countryside became more important, especially after the advent of civil war in 1455. That civil strife would tend to increase the importance of the levies is understandable. 'Parties' could use them to tip the balance of forces; there was not the same problem of logistics which prevented their use on any scale overseas; and it could be claimed, when they were summoned during the crises of civil strife, that they were being called upon to fulfil their traditional purpose of defending hearth and home.

The usual procedure for calling out the levies was for the king to issue Commissions of Array, empowering individuals to call upon the towns and shires to supply them with recruits, and directing them to lead the recruits to the king or his lieutenant. In 1402 and 1404 the Commons insisted that such commissions should be issued only to provide troops for the defence of the realm; but as the domestic situation degenerated the Lancastrians made strong efforts to use the levies, not for defence against foreign invaders, but for use against domestic foes. They used various methods in addition to Commissions of Array. Henry VI in 1453, for example, got the Commons to grant him a body of 20,000 archers, though just how these were to be raised, and against whom, is not clear. In July 1457 he called out the *Posse Comitatus* of fifteen counties to keep order in the north. This seems to have been an attempt to call out all available levies to face a domestic crisis. That all men could be regarded as having the duty of obeying such a call was made clear by Margaret of Anjou in 1461 when she threatened death to all who did not rally to her aid.

Margaret, in fact, did not rely on the levies of the countryside as much as on the magnates and gentry, who flocked to her standard with their retinues and tenants suitably arrayed, in the same way as the cavaliers of the seventeenth century flocked to the banner of Charles I. It was the Yorkists who relied more heavily on Commissions of Array and the support of the 'commons'; though they, too, had their retainers, indentured and otherwise, and their confederacies of lords. The three Yorkist earls 'with many gentlemen and commons' met Henry at St. Albans in 1455. Richard of York and his son Edward put the same trust in the popular levies as they did in propaganda. Edward clearly laid it down that it was every subject's duty to aid the king with body and goods against either foreign or domestic foes. Nor were Warwick and Clarence behind-hand in claiming popular support. In all the violence of the civil wars the towns and shires bore a heavy and increasing burden. They were sometimes hard put to, if principles failed them, to pick the winning side; but whether individual towns came out on the right side or not, or merely trimmed their sails, the cumulative effect of their military contributions was the same. It was an increase in their status and importance in the community at large.

7. RELIGION

Changes at the other extreme, in the realm of religious affairs, also reflect the increasing importance of the common man. The century witnessed no great English churchman and no English saint[1]; though there were, indeed, some very respectable prelates. Robert Hallum, bishop of Salisbury in the early years of the century, was Chancellor of Oxford, leader of the English delegation to the council of Pisa, and later right-hand man of the Emperor Sigismund at Constance. Henry Chichele, archbishop of Canterbury from 1414 to 1443, was not unworthy of his exalted position; among other things, he promoted the appointment of graduates to high office. Adam Moleyns of Chichester and Thomas Bekington of Bath and Wells were both early humanists and able administrators. Even more conspicuous was William Grey of Ely, bibliophile and benefactor of Balliol College library.

On the other hand the Church in the mid-century had as its most conspicuous representative Cardinal Beaufort, inveterate and unscrupulous politician and worldly prelate. His loans to the Lancastrians were no doubt of immense help in time of need, but his profits were unconscionably large, quite apart from being contrary to the decrees of the Church. Adam Moleyns might be a scholar, but he had a dubious political record. He was implicated in both the notorious trial of Eleanor Cobham in 1441 and the probable murder of Gloucester in 1447. One outstanding prelate, Reginald Pecock, was broken and humiliated because of his zeal for truth and reform and his naïvety in pursuit of both.

Nor did English bishops and clergy receive help or inspiration from the papacy. The pope's problems were aggravated by both the Great Schism and the Conciliar Movement. The great Councils were called into being to restore unity to Christendom and to achieve reform in the head and members of the Church, but achieved success only in the first of these aims. The English bishops at Constance and elsewhere partook in all the efforts of the reformers, but they may be accused of being Englishmen first and faithful Conciliarists second. They were, in any case, in no position to obtain significant reforms, even if they had been more single-minded and whole hearted.

The failings of government in the Church, which had been obvious

---

[1] Dom David Knowles, *The Religious Orders in England* (Cambridge 1955), vol. II, pp. 361, 364; Denis Hay, 'The Church of England in the Later Middle Ages' in *History*, vol. LIII (Feb. 1968), pp. 35–50.

in the fourteenth century, became scandalous in the fifteenth. The Great Schism was ended by the election of Pope Martin V in 1417, but the Church fell under the control of a series of popes who showed themselves quite unable to promote the Christian ideals in the highest places of leadership and power. By the time of the pontificate of Sixtus IV (1471–84), the papal Curia had become almost indistinguishable from the court of any Italian prince. Sixtus made systematic nepotism a formidable instrument of political aggrandizement; and in the end his policy, which led to the appointment of five nephews and one grandnephew as Cardinals, was ruinous in its results. The pontificate of Innocent VIII (1484–92) brought even greater degradation, leading straight to the excesses of Alexander VI and the bitter denunciations of Martin Luther himself.

The failure of leadership in the Church was not only the failure of individuals but also of institutions. The papal monarchy, weakened by the lack of any system of co-operation and consent such as was developed in the secular states, notably in the English parliament, could not finance itself adequately or cure the abuses of bureaucracy. The weaknesses which these failures engendered proved in the end to be too strong even for the stubborn idealism and recurrent inspiration which periodically revitalized the medieval Church. Thomas Gascoigne, chancellor of Oxford in 1434 and 1443–45, summed up the influence of the papal curia in his time: 'there are three things today that make a bishop in England: the will of the king, the will of the pope or court of Rome, and the money paid in large quantities to that court; for thousands of pounds of English money were paid here in England to Lombards for exchange, to the impoverishment of the realm'.[1]

The repercussions in England as elsewhere could not fail in the long run to be disastrous. As Langland had pungently asserted cleanliness of the sheep could not be expected unless the shepherd was clean. The decadence of the papal Curia affected all ranks of the clergy, and its failures were intensified by the continued exploitation of the clergy by the secular governments and the gentry. This brought about the promotion of scholars and support of students in the universities; and it gave the king very expert clerical ministers; but it took the clergy away from their spiritual duties and made strong demands on their loyalties. It created a situation in which old inspiration languished and there was no new inspiration to take its

[1] But cf. E. F. Jacob, *The Fifteenth Century*, p. 269.

place. The monasteries became progressively more backward and stagnant, and their cost to the community harder to justify. The friars quite lost their early virtues. The secular clergy, without religious zeal themselves and with no help from their leaders, were incapable of giving inspiring leadership to others in a world which was increasingly critical of their traditions and claims.

The only Englishmen to keep alive the spirit of the martyrs or even the zeal of the first friars were the Lollards, now a humble sect with little scholarship and even less aristocratic support. As a result of their stubborn idealism and extremism, they were called upon to suffer persecution which was tempered by conciliation and patience, but which in the last extreme involved the stake and the fire. In 1401, at the petition of the clergy of Canterbury, the Statute *De Haeretico Comburendo* was enacted, which decreed that if the diocesans should find anybody breaking the rules of the Church against unlicensed preaching, he should be arrested and kept in prison until he adjured. If he proved obdurate, he was to be handed over to the king's officers to be burned. The conflict of opinion became exceedingly bitter; in 1410, for example, the Lollards or their sympathizers proposed the disendowment of the Church; whilst in 1411 archbishop Arundel made a final attack on the main source of all error, the heresy-tainted University of Oxford. He overrode the privileges of the scholars in order to carry out a visitation and impose obedience to the teachings of the Church. His action was high-handed and damaging to liberty, but it had the support of public opinion. So had his persecution of the Lollards outside the university. When the tailor Badby of Evesham was publicly burned in 1410 for refusing to recant his errors despite the persuasions of Henry, Prince of Wales, his brave determination to die for his beliefs and for his right to hold them did not win him any wide popular support.

The climax arrived in 1414, when a political conspiracy of Lollards was organized by their most powerful and influential member, Sir John Oldcastle, a soldier and a magnate who had been the friend of Henry V. He was arrested and convicted for his Lollard views in 1413, but he escaped from the Tower on 19 October 1413, perhaps with the connivance of the king, more probably by the aid of devoted friends. Finally, he plotted an armed insurrection, to be sparked by a gathering of Lollards at St. Giles-in-the-Fields near London on the night of 7–8 January 1414. The idea was to destroy Henry V and his brothers at Eltham after the Christmas festivities there. The meeting was betrayed. The Londoners did not arrive to help. The small band of rebels, mostly craftsmen or small traders, was surprised and disarmed. The conspiracy had been widespread; Bristol, for example, sent a contingent of forty craftsmen, mainly weavers, headed by six chaplains. But it was not well organized; it turned into a fiasco, and its failure marked the end of Lollardy as a political force.

Oldcastle himself escaped for a time, helped by important clerics such as the Abbot of Shrewsbury and the prior of Wenlock, as well as by devoted adherents of much lesser rank. He maintained himself for three years in the midlands and the west of England, and actually lived in his own Herefordshire manor in 1417. An attempt to capture him in a villein's house on the St. Albans estates proved a failure. Finally, he was taken in a farmhouse on the border of Wales, after a fierce fight in which he was badly wounded. He was finally drawn through the City of London and hanged at St. Giles-in-the-Fields where his hopes had earlier been destroyed.

Oldcastle was a remarkable man who deserved a better fate. The Lollardy he embraced had all the marks of a true English sect expressing a type of puritanism. It was a protest which drew inspiration from a deep if mistaken spiritualism, and from a popular mysticism: it was Wyclifism without scholastic content, adapted to the market place. It did not die out with Oldcastle. Scattered pockets persisted throughout the century. Bristol was a conspicuous centre, as it had long been for political radicalism. William Smith, one of the most active Lollards of the mid-century, was probably a leader of its dissenting community. Among his disciples was James Willis, a lettered weaver, who possessed a number of books and knew a considerable part of the New Testament in English. Another group of heretics were in the Thames valley, especially at Reading. There were gatherings at Coventry and Birmingham, with discreet members related by association or blood: the servant of a certain John Smith married John Cropwell; she brought him to her mistress for instruction. More extreme Lollards crop up in East Anglia. There was trouble in London when the veteran Lollard priest Richard Wyche was burnt in 1440: it was said that the common people considered him to have been a great man, and his associates held him as a saint. Other parts of England were affected in varying degrees, though there is little evidence of Lollardy in the north. The tenets were everywhere the same: condemnation of pilgrimages and of the worship of images, questioning the efficacy of offices performed by a priest in mortal sin, denying the authority of the pope, believing in the reading of the Scriptures as the supreme Christian authority, denying the miracle of the sacrament of the Mass. In various forms and places these teachings survived until the Reformation and made their contribution to the puritan revolt.

Outside Lollardy, the devotion of the laity was expressed in domestic piety and in the endowing of chantries for the salvation of individual souls. Provision for Masses to be sung was made by rich patrons, by gilds and by municipalities. Despite Lollardy, the sacrament of the Eucharist continued to hold its popular appeal, as did the great feasts of Christmas, Corpus Christi, Good Friday, and others such as the Feast of St. Nicholas on 6 December. Plays and pageants abounded. It is perhaps not without significance that the cult of women saints, emphasizing gentleness and pity, grew throughout the century, notably that of St. Brigit of Sweden. The worship of Mary, mother of Jesus, became a dominant feature of popular religion; it robbed Christianity of some of its spirituality, but perhaps Mary, more than all the other saints put together, brought relief from the harsh logic of the Church in matters of salvation and damnation.[1] Her cult was infinitely better than the widespread worship of relics and saints which abounded, even though, as Myrc the fifteenth century author of *Instructions to Parish Priests* wrote, 'To do God's worship to images is forbidden'.

Pilgrimages were still extremely popular. John Tiptoft, Earl of Worcester, made a famous one to Jerusalem. When William Wey, Fellow of Eton, went to the popular shrine of Compostella in 1456 there were eighty-four pilgrim ships in Corunna harbour and thirty-two of them were English. Motives for such pilgrimages were very mixed. Inevitably many had little to do with religion. A peregrination to Canterbury in Spring could be leisurely and enjoyable, though on the longer journeys hardships were great. Margery Kempe made a well-recorded pilgrimage to Rome in 1414 and one still more notable to Jerusalem, and no one can doubt the religious devotion of this one-time mother of fourteen children. She was one of the last of the medieval English mystics, who carried on the great traditions of the fourteenth century, though on a lower plane.

How deep or how spiritual all this popular devotion was, it is impossible to say. E. F. Jacob sums up his remarks on the subject

---

[1] G. G. Coulton, *Five Centuries of Religion* (Cambridge 1929), vol. I, p. 170.

in cautious but favourable terms: 'So far from running down in this period, religion, not merely in literary and artistic forms, but in the fervour of corporate devotion and in popular appeal achieves a place in the ordinary life of the country which it has seldom been accorded by historians of pre-Reformation England.'[1]

Nevertheless, despite the strength of popular devotion, Christianity was moving towards a climax, with the old ways more and more in disharmony with new forces. However much or little of consequence flowed from influences such as those of individualism, nationalism, and secularism, all contributed to a climate of opinion hostile to an indefinite continuation of privileges and abuses in the Church which had only been tolerated so long because they were bound up with noble traditions and great virtues. One development which above all others threatened destruction to the old order was the slow and inexorable accretion of power in all matters, including religion, to the central government, and in parliament to the Commons and the Lords. As part of this process, the old Statutes of Provisors and Praemunire were steadily maintained; and Pope Martin V, after the Councils, was quite unable to modify the relation of Church and State which they expressed. 'It is not the pope', he said, 'but the king of England who governs the Church in his dominions'. But it is perhaps significant that when Archbishop Chichele in 1428 shed tears in nis pleading against such secular control, he did so before the Commons of parliament, in whose hands and those of the Lords the destinies of the Church in England were coming to reside. Thus the authority of parliament was added to that of the monarch when in 1462 the privileges of the clergy were confirmed by Edward IV.

The Lords and the Commons were more hostile to the papal authority in England than was the king, since they suffered more from its abuse, and this was particularly true of the Commons. The kings themselves were often at odds with the popes; but with a growing pressure from below which threatened the whole mutual exploitation of the Church by king and pope, the royal authority came more and more to stand as a buffer between the Church and the forces of change. If this buffer should be withdrawn, the old relationships of Church and State would not continue for long.

Thus the greatest single cause of the Reformation of 1534 would not be provided by the failings of the Church or the clergy, important

[1] *The Fifteenth Century*, p. 687.

though these were, but by the changing environment of religion. Just as the classes of the lay hierarchy had moved nearer together in the secular state, so the laity moved nearer to the clergy in the *Respublica Christiana*. In the end, in England as in Germany, this destroyed the separate and privileged position of the clergy and the Church. The distinction between clergy and laity was still profound; but as Wyclif had shown, the privileged hierarchy of the Church was increasingly open to attack by the evangelist or mystic, who rejected the priests' claim to be an order apart, the only avenue to truth and salvation, and who taught the direct communion of every individual with God. What reformers were insisting on was the unity of the whole nation in religion as well as in secular affairs. Henry VIII in 1534 was not only in some sense heir to the fourteenth-century scholastic, he also garnered the fruits of an English nationhood whose emergence had been long and slowly prepared. In the final analysis all Englishmen partook in this historic movement, the humble and devout laymen even more than the aristocracy or even the monarch himself. The monarch became the embodiment of nationalism in religion, but all men tended to find themselves increasingly lukewarm to the claims and privileges of a Universal Church.

8. Intellectual Life

The century which turned its back on the more extreme teachings of John Wyclif in religion was hardly likely to develop his views in philosophy. English scholasticism did not progress at the hands of cautious and conservative thinkers like Thomas Netter, or popularizers like Reginald Pecock. Netter, who died in 1430 and had studied under William Woodford at Oxford probably in 1389 to 1390, was a great admirer of Wyclif's intellect, but not a subscriber to his philosophical ideas. He was severely orthodox and successful, confessor to Henry V (the king is said to have died in his arms), bishop of Winchester, and prosecutor of the Lollards. He forbade the discussion of controversial topics, including that of the Immaculate Conception. His orthodoxy was impeccable and his influence was great. Reginald Pecock, on the other hand, was not really in the line of the great scholastics. His intellect was not outstanding; his writings, of which the best known are the *Repressor of overmuch blaming the clergy* and the *Book of Faith*, were primarily apologetic. Fellow of Oriel from 1414 to 1424, he became bishop of Chichester in 1450, but for a variety of reasons he became unpopular. He was attacked in 1457 not only as a provocative thinker but also as an ardent Lancastrian; and perhaps his political sins were more important than his intellectual offence.

Pecock was a sincere reformer who wrote in English the better to be understood, and even created a new vocabulary where this was necessary. He was a scholastic in his confidence in reason and the syllogism. He made special appeal to the 'doom of reason' in his attempt 'by cleer witt [to] drawe men into consente of trewe feith'. He did not in any sense deny the way of understanding by faith, but he did not hesitate to apply his thoroughgoing use of reason to the Bible, to the Creed, and to the formulation of the ten command-ments themselves. Thomas Gascoigne, chancellor of Oxford, accused him of putting the law of nature above the scriptures and the sacraments.

In fact, he worshipped both reason and tradition. He accepted the judgments of Aristotle as being as valid and divinely inspired as those of the Doctors of the Church. But it is typical of his thinking that he would not accept such judgments 'azens treuth'. Similarly, he crusaded against the Lollards, but he shared one or two of their views and believed that they should be converted rather than burned. He was, in truth, more than a little conservative, and unlike Wyclif was disinclined at times to accept the logical consequences of his thought. Hence it is not surprising that when he was persecuted for his writings in 1458 he retracted his errors before he reached the point of martyrdom. We may believe that he recanted mainly because he sincerely desired to conform to the great traditions of the Church. He was confined to the abbey of Thorney where, about 1460, he died.

This remarkable appeal of a philosopher to the common people has perhaps not been given its proper significance; but the future did not lie with scholasticism, even that of Reginald Pecock. It lay with an attitude of mind developed particularly in Italy, which at some points, but by no means in all, was in sharp conflict with scholastic methods and ideas. This attitude steadily penetrated into England during the fifteenth century. While at the beginning English cultural standards were still thoroughly medieval, at the close they came within fairly close distance of those of the Renais-sance, and this change began in the first quarter of the century.[1] The humanism of Italy, based on the classics and a new attitude to

[1] R. Weiss, *Humanism in England during the Fifteenth Century* (Oxford 1941), p. 1; A. B. Ferguson, 'Reginald Pecock and the Renaissance Sense of History' in *Studies in the Renaissance*, vol. XIII (1966), pp. 147–65.

man and to learning, came to England in the person of Poggio Bracciolini, whom Henry Beaufort met at the Council of Constance and invited to accept a position in the bishop's household. His stay between 1418 and 1422 brought about no appreciable change in the intellectual interests of Englishmen, though some copies of his writings did come into English hands. But Renaissance influences soon became stronger, flowing through various channels. One was the papal Curia: Giuliano Cesarini, for example, was sent over in 1426 to procure the repeal of the Statute of Provisors. A great prince like Humphrey of Gloucester shows the mixture of old and new learning. He read or collected widely in both classical and contemporary writings, and he was a patron of Italians. He employed two well-known Italian scholars as his secretaries, and employed Tito Livio da Forli to write the biography of his brother, Henry V. But he also patronized English poets, including Hoccleve, Lydgate, and Capgrave. He even gave early patronage to Reginald Pecock.[1] The famous library he bequeathed to Oxford showed an interest in astronomy and astrology, history and rhetoric, along with medical science. The books were, in fact, wanted for broader lectures in science at the university. The new humanism was not a body of doctrine, but a return for inspiration to the classics. It was a means of intellectual emancipation because, though itself a product of scholasticism, it freed men from the weight of some scholastic postulates and assumptions. But it was not a simple rejection of the past; it represented a broadening of intellectual horizons and was thus part of a healthy movement of advance.

As in religion, so in scholarship, there was a dearth of great figures until the last decades of the century, but there was no dearth of intellectual activity. Here, as elsewhere, the most significant landmark was the printing press of Caxton in 1476. Its products appealed to a broad audience, and it provided a long list of translations into English which many could enjoy. It would be idle to deny that during this phase of transition there was a dearth in England of inspiring work in either the old or the new tradition of learning. Nevertheless we know with the hindsight of history that the way was being prepared for a new and fruitful combination of both, even if the ways of the old scholasticism were soon to be derided and its contribution to knowledge subjected to bitter scorn.

[1] H. S. Bennett believed that his title of 'The Good Duke' was derived in part from his patronage of learning: *Six Medieval Men and Women* (Cambridge 1955), p. 19.

9. LITERATURE

As is well known, the literary achievements of the great fourteenth-century writers were not continued in the fifteenth. The age of Hoccleve and Lydgate at its beginning showed a marked decline from that of Chaucer and Gower, nor did writing in the Chaucerian tradition fare much better in the long reign of Henry VI. Partly the fault lay in the Lancastrian court, preoccupied with narrow politics, with the disastrous experiment of a renewed French war, and with the court quarrels and intrigues that were conspicuous after 1422; this seems to be true even though John Lydgate was the favourite court poet of the Lancastrians until he died in 1441. It was no substitute for the old traditions of the royal court that Henry VI clothed his kingship in piety, prurience and humility, so much so that there was an attempt in his own lifetime to have him canonized. He loved clerks, learning and religion. Common people sought his intercession in their prayers, and God testified to his virtues by miracles; but the atmosphere of his court became dull and uninspiring. Towards the end, it was said of him that he held no household and maintained no wars; and a visiting knight from Constantinople marvelled 'how very few of the lords were at Court'.[1] His greatest monuments to posterity were not acts of literary patronage but the foundation of Eton College in 1440 and King's College, Cambridge, in 1441 (Margaret of Anjou similarly founded Queen's College in 1448).

In any case, authors began to look to a broader audience for their writings, an audience which was not yet either as critical or as stimulating as that of the royal court or aristocratic hall. They moved towards a time when they would no longer be forced to depend mainly on the generosity of one person or a small group of persons, and when they could begin to cater for the great body of rising middle-class men and women who, with money in their pockets and little learning in their heads, would be asking to be instructed and amused.[2] John Shirley, who died in 1456, had a large house and four shops, and almost certainly copied out numerous MSS. which would be taken by customers, read, and returned.

The old courtly poetry persisted, but its quality sadly declined. Some of the best of it actually came from Scotland; the *Kingis Quair* may be

---

[1] My *Constitutional History of England in the Fifteenth Century*, p. 102.
[2] H. S. Bennett, in *The Oxford History of English Literature*, vol. II, pt. I, pp. 115–16.

included in this, though it was probably written by James I when he was a prisoner in England. Most of its creators have been excoriated for their servile imitation and tedious verse. They showed their mediocrity by their blatant pursuit of patronage. An anonymous translator of *Palladius on Husbandry* praised Humphrey of Gloucester in 128 lines of prologue. King Edward IV later got 240 in Ridley's *Compound of Alchemy*. Loudly and needlessly the poets proclaimed their incompetence. The decadence of much of their courtly literature is beyond question, but there were some exceptions. Three writers made an important use of the old courtly themes. Of these the most significant by far was Sir Thomas Malory. His prose narrative of the old Arthurian stories, the incomparable *Morte Darthur*, was enormously popular. He has been regarded as essentially a product of chivalric decline, as a disillusioned soldier-turned-storyteller. It has been denied that he was a political thinker or even a commentator; and he has been dismissed as one who occasionally exclaimed against his times but for the most part retired into the world of long ago. But all this hardly does justice to the serious intention that seems to be apparent in his work.

Nothing is known with certainty about him. For many years he has been identified with a certain Sir John Mallory of Newbold Revel in Warwickshire. The *Morte Darthur* was written in prison: 'for this was drawyn by a knyght presoner sir Thomas Malleorre, that God sende hym good recover.' The Warwickshire knight spent much time in prison and this is a strong argument for the identification; but the imprisonment was the consequence of acts of violence and intimidation which are hard (though not impossible) to reconcile with a book which has always been regarded as the classical exposition of chivalry. It is even harder to bring the volume into the context of writings in the courtly tradition which had a serious political aim.

Quite recently, however, it has been suggested that the author was another Thomas Malory altogether; he was a son of Sir William Malory of Studely and Hutton in Yorkshire, not far from Ripon, and this identification is, on general grounds, much more attractive; though it must be admitted that there is no record in this case of imprisonment. The Yorkshire of the 1460s tended to be somewhat reactionary in politics, or at least to be faithful to Lancastrianism; but it had produced good literature, including both the alliterative *Morte Arthure* and the stanzaic *Le Morte Arthur*. The candidate from Yorkshire was of good family, and as far as we know had no disreputable background. His imprisonment, if we could assume that he went to prison, may well in those troubled days have been for purely political reasons and not a matter of disgrace. It is likely that his brother William was killed at Edgecote on 26 July 1469, fighting for the Lancastrian cause in Robin of Redesdale's rebellion; and another brother may have died fighting against the Yorkists at Towton. We may well imagine him, as we may not easily imagine his namesake, achieving sincerity and truth in the words:

> Lo, ye all Englysshemen, se ye nat what a myschyff here was? For he that was the moste kynge and nobelyst knyght of the worlde, and moste loved the felyshyp of noble knyghtes, and by hym they all were up-holdyn, and yet myght nat thes Englysshemen holde them contente with hym. Lo thus was the olde custom and usayges of thys londe, and men say that we of thys londe have nat yet loste that custom. Alas, thys ys a greate defaughte of us Englysshemen, for there may no thynge us please no terme.[1]

The King Arthur he described was more than a mere romantic figure quite dissociated from the hard realities of the fifteenth-century world. He was no abstraction at the centre of the fellowship of the Round Table; he was a leader who was responsible for the broad welfare and prestige of a kingdom. Chivalry in his hands was a practical code of conduct, suited to the needs of country gentlemen. His knighthood had a practical function in a well-established order with its headquarters in the household of a great prince.[2] Chivalry to Malory was, as it had been to Froissart and was to be to Caxton, a way of life which could still edify as well as entertain.

This was also true in the case with William of Worcester, 'gentleman-secretary' to Sir John Fastolf and thus linked with John, Duke of Bedford, in whose service Fastolf was employed in Normandy. His *Boke of Noblesse* was a manual of knighthood, and also much more.[3] It was the practical application of the chivalric values to the problems of contemporary England. It contained a strong advocacy of aggressive war against France and offered practical advice as to how the war should be won. It blamed the English gentry, not the ruler, for English failures in France, above all for neglecting the

---

[1] W. Matthews, *The Ill-Framed Knight* (University of California Press 1966), p. 48. Professor Matthews has propounded the attractive new theory referred to above.

[2] *The Works of Sir Thomas Malory*, edited by Eugene Vinaver (Oxford 1947), p. xxvii; A. B. Ferguson, *op. cit.*, p. 47.

[3] Its Prologue was recast by William's son after his father's death.

physical discipline which was part of the chivalric ideal. What William most hoped to revive by his chivalry were the qualities which made a good soldier.[1] The king should see to it that the sons of the nobility were instructed in the 'disciplines, doctrine, and usage of school of arms'.

> But now of late days, [he said] the greater pity is, many a one that be descended of noble blood . . . sets himself . . . to learn the practice of law or the customs of land, or of civil matter, and so do greatly waste their time in such needless business as holding courts, and keeping . . . a proud countenance at the meeting of sessions and shires . . ..

Besides,

> it is not well possible, nor hath been since the Conquest, that justice, peace, and prosperity hath continued any while in this land in any king's day but in such as have made war outward.

Similarly in John Tiptoft's translation of the *Controuersia de Nobilitate* by Buonaccorso da Montemagno, made about 1460, knightly character was regarded more highly than aristocratic descent, and stress was laid on service to the common weal. Tiptoft was a fine scholar as well as a great lord. All these examples suggest that the courtly tradition was still a force in English literary creation. As Caxton said later, 'read the noble volumes of Saint Grail, of Lancelot, of Galahad, of Tristram, of Perceforest, of Parseval, of Gawain and many more. There ye shall see manhood, courtesy, gentleness.'

Nevertheless, the real strength of the English literary tradition had now come to reside in lyrics and plays and in miscellaneous writing intended for a wide audience. Such writing included many works of piety, such for instance as the autobiography of Margery Kempe who probably could not write, but dictated her prose to two clerks between 1432 and 1436. It also included a very wide variety of books, covering almost every aspect of life. Sir John Fortescue broke new ground by political treatises in English. There was the start of a native antiquarian movement which owed nothing to Italian examples and a good deal to patriotic sentiment. John Russell one-time official of Humphrey of Gloucester wrote a *Book of Carving and Nurture*. The Pastons wrote vigorous and lively correspondence, now collected in their *Letters*. Political satires flourished. Chronicles such as the *Brut* were composed in the vernacular.[2]

---

[1] As Ferguson points out (*The Indian Summer of English Chivalry* (Duke University Press 1960), p. 146), nobility is defined chiefly in terms of illustrious deeds done on behalf of the commonwealth.

[2] See D. Hay in *B.I.H.R.*, vol. XXXV, as above, pp. 122–3.

Babees Books set forth good manners for children. There were popular books of travel, like the *Travels of Sir John Mandeville*, written originally in French about 1356, and in strong circulation in English during the fifteenth century. All this output of literature, good, bad, and indifferent, is of immense significance. As A. W. Pollard quoted by H. S. Bennett declared, calling attention to the great mass of 'non-courtly' poetry: 'to say that English poetry was dead when verse like this was being written is absurd. It was not dead, but banished from court.'

The creation of popular plays in the century is outstanding. Their origin went back to the thirteenth century and far beyond; but they really came into their own in the fifteenth century. In a limited sense, they may be called the nearest thing to a literature of the poor (in 1244, Robert Grosseteste had classed 'plays' with scot-ales or drinking bouts). The miracle plays of the fifteenth century were essentially a product of gilds, secular or religious. In London, for example, they were in the hands of a gild of St. Nicholas composed of parish clerks. They often fell under the control of the municipality. Their authors are unknown and were presumably obscure. As the plays became more elaborate they were paraded around the main streets of the town. The favourite time for their performance came to be the feast of Corpus Christi in May or June, and many were provided by Corpus Christi gilds.

In the late fourteenth, and in the fifteenth, century the miracle plays were supplemented by morality plays; a gild of the Lord's Prayer for such performances existed at York in 1389. The former had tended to deal with the whole range of the divine scheme for humanity, though the most popular themes were episodes in the life of Christ. The latter transferred the interest from Holy Writ to the behaviour and destiny of man, with characters representing abstract virtues such as the seven deadly sins and the seven cardinal virtues. They dealt abundantly with 'Dethe, Goddes mesangere'. *The Summoning of Everyman* in the late fifteenth century is one of the better plays. It deals with the final preparations Everyman made to meet his Maker. On the advice of Good deeds and Knowledge, he got the company of Strength, Discretion, Five Wits, and Beauty, on his last pilgrimage when summoned by Death. Most failed him, but Good Deeds remained faithful. Knowledge heard the angels sing, and Everyman was welcomed in Jesus's presence at the end. *Mankind*, dating from about 1475, is an example of the morality play showing decadence. The 'hero' is mankind, subjected to various temptations and surrounded by coarse language. The whole play evidently aimed at entertainment not edification. At all times the miracle and morality plays tended to degenerate into pure farce; at York, the actions of the midwives had to be deleted from the Nativity. On the other hand, they contained much homely wisdom. The Wakefield Master, about the only author whose name we know, was a satirist and humorist who had much to say of the wrongs suffered by the humble poor. He complained of the 'gentlery men' who taxed the poor, the behaviour of their wives and, in good English fashion, of the weather.

The mystery and morality plays show the man in the street laying claim to the great legacy of literature. They reveal the vitality and creativeness of the abundant 'fraternities' and groups which proliferated in the fourteenth and fifteenth centuries, and the warmth and liveliness that permeated humble men's lives. They contributed much to the broader development of secular drama. This obviously owed a good deal to both aristocratic and courtly influences; to jousts and processions, receptions of royalty and foreign ambassadors.[1] But it owed most to the gild, and to the emergence of a new England in which Everyman spoke the English language, a rich and flexible vehicle of English loyalties and hopes.

Finally, the century produced William Caxton, born about 1422 (nearly coincident with Henry VI), and printer of Malory's *Morte Darthur* in 1485. Before this, Caxton had been a very successful merchant and as such, in 1463, he became Governor of the English Nation of Merchants in the Low Countries. He relinquished this office about 1469 to begin work as a translator, putting into English a French *History of Troy*. This was published at Bruges in 1475 as the first printed book in the English tongue. In 1476 Caxton returned to England and opened shop as a pioneer printer, with the first printing press ever set up in England. He was highly intelligent and shrewd and printed for profit as well as pleasure. Hence, it is significant to find him publishing the *Canterbury Tales*, the *Confessio Amantis*, and *Morte Darthur*, as well as a long list of other works. He printed for aristocratic readers the kind of books to which they had long been accustomed, but he knew that he also had a more general public, much of which had grown up in the fifteenth century. He dedicated his efforts to rich patrons in the traditional

[1] Glynn Wickham, *Early English Stages 1300–1600*, vol. I (London 1959).

manner, but he received encouragement and support from London merchants and friends. Caxton was no great stylist. Nevertheless, when he died in 1491 he had begun a new period in English literature, a period when books became accessible to many people, when English became truly and beyond question the mother tongue, and when the old patronage with its manifold influences had begun perceptibly to decline.

10. ARCHITECTURE

In architecture, the fifteenth century conservatively continued the Perpendicular style. It has been claimed, indeed, that art and architecture now began to show some decadence, partly arising from the development of commercialism. It is true that there grew up a thriving trade with the continent in such things as small statues and retables, the raw material for which came from the alabaster quarries of Nottingham, Lincoln, and York. Contacts were established by which new techniques were imported, particularly from the Netherlands; but these were not developed; whilst manufacture for trade brought inevitable consequences of repetitive work and lack of originality. This affected the domestic art as well as that which was exported. At Malvern the same cartoons were used for different personages represented in the windows, sometimes reversed. Thus, it may be conceded that there were lapses and that no single artistic creation from this century equals the tragic beauty of Edward II's effigy at Gloucester. But the significance of these facts does not seem to outweigh that of the continued beauty and copious reproduction of a very great English architectural style.

There is, indeed, ample evidence of such a continuation. The great age of fan-vaulting, for example, may be said to have begun as early as 1357 in the cloisters at Gloucester; but it only culminated in the late fifteenth century. There was less building in cathedrals and collegiate churches but more in parish churches, colleges, and schools. It is very hard to see that there was any perceptible loss of beauty. For dignity and grace it would be hard to surpass the Divinity School at Oxford, built in the second and fourth quarters of the fifteenth century, or the quadrangle at Magdalen College in the same last quarter. The hammerbeam was utilized in stately and beautiful secular buildings like Ockwells Manor, Berkshire, erected about 1450, and the Great Hall at Eltham Palace, built about 1475. Similar architectural triumphs were achieved in the second quarter of the century at Hurstmonceux in Sussex and Tattershall in Lincoln-shire, both examples of the way in which beauty and comfort were transforming military architecture, in spite of civil wars and aristo-cratic feuds.[1]

Taking the art and architecture of the century as a whole, what we are faced with seems to be a cultural expression which was broadening its base and maintaining its self-confidence and mastery over material whilst suffering no significant loss. The architecture of the century, in particular, would be a credit to any age. Thus, we may sum up the development of late-medieval art and architec-ture, though very much has had to be omitted, as the continuing creation of a society that was inspired by its inner resources of strength to artistic creations of great beauty and serenity. Like other expressions of English society in the age, these steadily became more native whilst remaining also European; but this did not result in any diminution of achievement. On the contrary, it may be claimed that the development of architectural and artistic styles showed an almost uninterrupted advance. All periods contributed to this long evolution. The thirteenth, as in other matters, was the time of fruition; the fourteenth was that of the most exciting change. But nothing should be allowed to obscure the magnitude of what was accomplished at all times, with resources fantastically more limited than those of modern times.

[1] G. Webb, *Architecture in Britain in the Middle Ages*, Plates 154–78.

I I

THE FRAMEWORK OF SOCIETY 1216–1485

1. THE PROBLEM OF ORDER AND LIBERTY

THE three centuries which witnessed the emergence of the English nation also witnessed the creation of a new institutional framework. They saw the decline of the personal monarchy, the beginning of a greatly expanded machine of government, and the creation of the prototype of the modern parliament. They offered an outstanding contribution to the constitutional problem of liberty and authority. No one of the three centuries can claim a monopoly of achievement. Each had its own vicissitudes, but each added something to what was cumulatively a remarkable advance.

To equip her for a unique contribution to the problems of law and government, England, as suggested above, had several well-known assets. Her insularity protected her against complete involvement in European affairs, especially after 1204. Her limited size was a source of strength, though ultimately it would prove to be a weakness. Geography helped her, along with the Anglo-Saxon heritage and the Norman Conquest, to be a pioneer in the development of political unity. At no time after the Norman Conquest did the English magnates have much real chance of regional independence; hence they had an exceptional interest in the working of the central government. On the other hand, as a consequence of the comparative security from attack provided by the Channel, they could afford the luxury of limiting the power of their monarch rather than depending on his strength for defence. Their king was one of the most powerful in Europe, but only in co-operation with his subjects, not by his royal power alone.

The problem posed by the growth of this power was nevertheless urgent by the beginning of the thirteenth century. The most important single cause of this lay in the emergence of the territorial state with its centralization of administration and the extended powers and claims of its government. The danger inherent in such a development had already been made evident in the Angevin monarchy. This had been one of the most efficient in Europe, but its efficiency had included an element of arbitrariness against which Englishmen had as yet found no better remedy than the old-fashioned feudal revolt, opposing injustice by force.

This strengthening of government to a point where efficiency threatened to beget tyranny owed much to the beginnings of bureaucracy. The new 'civil servant' this produced was a man of special expertise, trained in the new universities, often learned in Civil and Common Law and zealous for the royal authority. Through his efforts, along with the general expansion of government, the legitimate claims of the ruler on his subjects took on new dimensions, and individual opposition to oppression became little more than a dangerous gesture of discontent.

In such circumstances more sophisticated attempts to define the relations between government and subject became inevitable. Magna Carta in 1215 was a beginning. It broke fresh ground in its restrictions on the ruler, but these were necessarily tentative and limited. It was in fact, if not in form, the first of a long series of statutes (it was actually enrolled as such in 1297) by which a new constitution was eventually worked out; but its importance lay rather in the way it was gained than in any novel political ideas. It was an agreement between the ruler and his magnates, and took the form of a royal boon; but it emanated from the subjects rather than from the ruler. It was wrested by force from one of the strongest rulers so far to sit upon the English throne, and it was only made possible by the development of a new political awareness in the magnates and a new sense of responsibility for the welfare of the realm. Thus the long and at times violent political dialogue of the thirteenth century was begun by a striking assertion of rights and claims not by the ruler but by the magnates, and this set the keynote of English politics for three centuries to come.

One or two clauses of Magna Carta were of permanent significance. It laid down that no free man was to be taken or imprisoned or disseised, or in any way destroyed, except by the lawful judgment of his peers or/and by the law of the land (clause 39), and that to no

one could the king sell, or deny, or delay, right or justice (clause 40).
Taxation beyond the traditional feudal 'aids' was to be through
common counsel to which all tenants-in-chief were to be summoned (clause 12). But the magnates could safeguard these claims
by nothing more satisfactory than a 'council' of twenty-five barons,
elected by all, charged to take care with all their might that the
provisions of the Charter were kept. If this was not done, the 'council'
together with the commonalty of the whole land (*communa totius
terrae*), were to distrain and distress the king in every possible way.
This provision was no solution to the problem of royal authority,
and was in fact omitted in the reissues of 1216 and 1225. The Charter
of 1215 itself was annulled by the king and the pope almost as soon
as it was sealed; but it remains the greatest constitutional document
of the thirteenth century, on which directly or indirectly much of
the progress of the century was ultimately to be based.

2. THE MONARCHY

Despite the beginnings of bureaucracy, the monarchy itself was
unmistakably the supreme institution of government. Kings
succeeded by hereditary right and by election; but the former need
only be based on the possession of royal blood, and the latter could
degenerate into mere acclamation. However he succeeded to his
office, the early medieval ruler encompassed within himself and his
attributes the welfare of the whole community. In consequence he
was a man set apart, so precious to his subjects that he might regard
himself, and be regarded, as an instrument of God. 'You are the
vicar of God in the kingdom' was said of him early in the thirteenth
century.[1] In well-known words, Shakespeare made Richard II
proclaim:

> Not all the water in the rough rude sea
> Can wash the balm from an anointed king;
> The breath of worldly men cannot depose
> The deputy elected by the Lord.

With the expansion of government the majesty of the royal office
steadily increased. From the reign of Henry I the king exercised
thaumaturgical powers. John Wyclif argued in the fourteenth
century that the king reflected in his office the divinity of Christ,
whilst the pope reflected only His humanity. Ordinary oil, of the

---

[1] In the tract 'What should be The Office of a King', translated in my *Constitutional
History of England 1216–1399*, vol. III, pp. 100–101.

catechumen or even the chrism, was not enough for later corona-
tions; a legend of the discovery of miraculous oil for this purpose
began to arise under Edward II and was officially proclaimed under
Henry IV. He was *Christus Domini*, the anointed of the Lord. 'As
a god on earth', a publicist said in the fifteenth century, 'the king
has right.'

There developed a cult of the monarch which culminated eventually
in the loyalties shown towards Elizabeth and Charles I. Such a
cult took many forms, but its conscious promotion is probably most
conspicuous in the realm of literature and the arts, and in the development of the court as an instrument of policy. Henry III's building
at Westminster Abbey served to express both his own piety and his
devotion to Edward the Confessor which had political overtones.
He was crowned in the Confessor's church on 17 May 1220, and
every year celebrated St. Edward the Confessor's day there on 13
October, gathering his household about him in new robes, knighting
young nobles, and holding a great feast. In all this he was believed
to be in rivalry with Louis IX of France, who built a palace chapel
at Paris and in other ways added to the majesty of the king.

Edward I, though himself no mean builder, added to the royal
attributes mainly by the cult of King Arthur. His 'round tables'
and famous jousts and feasts, linked up with Arthurian romance.[1]
Sir Maurice Powicke asks how far the king allowed himself to live
in this world of fancy[2]; but he also recognizes that the conqueror of
Wales and the Hammer of the Scots was a realist. Whether or not
Edward believed that the tomb he opened at Glastonbury was that
of King Arthur we shall never know; but the political value of this
romanticism is not seriously in doubt. It had its final home in the
royal court, even if that of Edward I has been described as being
still essentially only the centre of royal administration and socially
not much more than the household of a great lord.

A most significant aspect of the development of the royal majesty
came with the expansion of the court under Edward III. Its inspiration was the monarch himself whose charisma reflected a mixture of
shrewd politics and Arthurian chivalry. At different times, poets like
Froissart and Chaucer adorned Edward's court. Queen Philippa

[1] N. Denholm-Young in *Studies in Medieval History Presented to F. M. Powicke*, pp.
240–68; R. S. Loomis, 'Chivalric and Dramatic Imitations of Arthurian Romance', in
Medieval Studies in Memory of A. Kingsley Porter, edited by W. R. W. Koehler (Harvard
1939), vol. I, pp. 79–97.
[2] *The Thirteenth Century*, pp. 515–16.

began a new phase in the importance of women there. More than thirty painters worked there, or at least at Edward's expense.[1] Court patronage helped to create a new architectural style.

It has, indeed, been argued that it was not Edward III but Richard II who made a new era in the life of the court; and its style under him was certainly in many ways unprecedented. The association it portrayed, between a highly organized court life and new literary movements, was a phenomenon of great significance which is to be observed in many parts of Europe and which had an important source in the courtly life of King Robert of Anjou from 1309 to 1343 in Naples, where French traditions were strong.

By the 1390s Richard II's court had become larger than Edward III's had ever been. It had acquired what has been described as 'a certain civilian character'. Richard himself encouraged such a character by his interest in books and art; one of his personal volumes shows a deep interest in the planets and their influence on human affairs. He developed a formal and elaborate ceremonial, with a proliferation of new titles together with an accentuated hierarchical grading, and an inordinate interest in dress and even in cookery, again reflecting the personal preferences of the king. If Edward could boast of his patronage of the great Chaucer, Richard could boast of both Chaucer and Gower, at least until 1393.

But it is doubtful if the prestige of the medieval court ever fully recovered from the collapse of Richard's high ambition. Edward IV was the first ruler after him to have the time and opportunity to make a significant restoration, but even he lacked some of the qualities of Edward III. In a political poem of 1461 he was hailed as a king who offered a promise of military glory; but he never fulfilled his promise, at least by campaigning abroad. Perhaps in any case the days of the Arthurian knightly tradition were beginning to pass away.

Edward was not indifferent to the value of a brilliant court. In 1471 he caused a famous *Black Book* to be compiled which set forth the organization of the king's household in unprecedented detail. Its authors took as their model Edward III's organization, 'house of very polytye and the flowre of England'. The purpose of the costly and elaborate setting they described for the royal Court 'above stairs' was to produce magnificence and enhance the king's majesty. 'Below stairs' the dominant notes were frugality and efficiency.

---

[1] I owe this to Gervase Mathew's *Richard II*.

Edward's court, like that of the third Edward, was enlivened by 'masks', spectacles, jousts, and processions. In 1467, friendship between England and Burgundy was celebrated by a lavish display in which Antoine the Bastard of Burgundy jousted on successive days with Anthony Woodville, Lord Scales, brother of the Queen. In 1468 there was a similar spectacle when Edward's sister Margaret married the duke of Burgundy in Bruges. An Englishman who was present for the occasion likened the Burgundian court to that of King Arthur.

There is no doubt that the royal court, often misunderstood as a focal point of degenerate chivalry, was a great source of strength to the best medieval rulers even if it was a great source of weakness, by its rivalries and intrigue, to kings like Edward II and Henry VI. The same can be said of the royal coronation which inaugurated the reign of the monarch, and which in the later Middle Ages was a source of both weakness and strength.

The coronation was a time when the king and his subjects entered their solemn and enduring relationship, bound by oaths and symbolic actions. It was impressive and memorable, setting forth the king as the chosen of his people and his God. That of Edward II included some startling innovations and began a new period in the history of the ceremony.[1] It came close to reflecting the image of a king with a new dependence on his own subjects in the manner of his succession and the making of new laws. Richard II in 1377 promised to maintain only those laws which were justly and reasonably chosen by his people, and his subjects were asked to give him obedience, but the consequences of the coronation of 1308 could never be entirely undone.

Both the crowning and the unction in the age-long ceremony set the king apart and gave him a unique power and responsibility. In bearing his great responsibility, the ruler could not be answerable to any man. Nevertheless, he was not a tyrant. He was, as Bracton believed, subject not only to God but also to the law. Few Englishmen believed in tyrannicide, but they did believe that a ruler who became a tyrant destroyed the essence of his royal office. If this happened, many would argue that the king should be opposed. Both feudal law and Anglo-Saxon tradition combined to insist that

---

[1] Recent writing on this very debatable question is discussed in my *Constitutional History 1216–1399*, vol. II, pp. 85–109, and vol. III, pp. 72–94. See also 'Notes on the Coronation Records of the Fourteenth Century', in *E.H.R.*, vol. LXX (October 1955), pp. 581–600.

the king should listen to the counsel of his magnates and his wise men. Government had always been a matter for co-operation between the ruler and those who stood upon the steps of the throne, although the monarch was set apart by his responsibilities and by the blessing of the Church.

3. Personal Monarchy and the Rise of Bureaucracy

The personal monarchy thus symbolized was hallowed by tradition, but its whole basis was slowly undermined by the rise of the territorial state. The king's ministers were ceasing to be his personal servants and were becoming more and more officials of the state. Henry III could call his ministers his *domestici*, and as late as 1269 the chancellor could still be referred to as the king's domestic clerk; but such references were ceasing to correspond with the realities of government.

It is true that all administration grew out of the king's household. Ministers in both theory and fact continued to be answerable to the ruler alone. Far into the thirteenth century they were peripatetic along with the king and his court; the last great migration of the chancellor and his officials was as late as 1337. Such travels were elaborately organized, with pack-horses, chests, harbingers and purveyors; though even so they caused the king's clerks and officials much inconvenience and even downright suffering. By such incessant travelling and by unceasing activity, the king had long made his personal influence widely felt. But the extent to which he could do so diminished with every generation. With the increasing complexity of government, the personal control of the ruler over affairs was slowly transmitted into a system which gave the direction of affairs largely into other hands.

This development was both necessary and beneficial; but it created massive problems by the devolution of authority. The more bureaucracy enlarged the order and unity of the realm, the more the great officers interfered with the lives and property of the king's subjects. As a result they were less and less able to claim that they were only the king's *familia*. Moreover, their great power threatened to disturb the balance of politics: their zealous promotion of the king's interests seemed to point the way to despotism. Their extended duties give rise to attempts by Lords and Commons to control them; but this seemed to offer a direct challenge to the supremacy of the king. Such a problem was not new in history, and failure to answer it had, at different times, produced disastrous results. Bureaucracy has always been necessary for the achievement of a high civilization; but bureaucracy beyond control has in the end destroyed the vitality of the political life it was created originally to sustain.

One important reason for a great expansion in the machinery of government was a rapid increase in the use of writing and records. Written authorizations or warrants had long supplemented oral commands; now they tended to supersede them. Such warrants vastly expanded the scope of independent ministerial action and departmental authority. Through the use of precise written authorizations under the royal seal, the administration could expand almost indefinitely, but yet be kept under a central control. On the one hand this obviously contributed to the power of the central authority, but on the other it aided self-government in the localities. Above all, however, it made possible the transference of authority from the king to his ministers. The greatest of these until 1232 was the justiciar, who acted as the king's *alter ego*. Alongside him were the chancellor, who kept the great seal, and the treasurer who looked after finance. These great officers were supported and eventually eclipsed by the king's council. All were in close contact with the king's justices who administered his law. In the hands of such officials as these the welfare of the kingdom gradually began to reside.

4. The Chancery

After 1232, the most important single officer was the chancellor, who had begun as a royal servant responsible for writing the king's charters and writs. During the thirteenth century he acquired important functions not only in administration but also in justice. Already, under the Angevins, the chancery had greatly developed the practice of issuing 'original' writs by which suits in the king's courts were begun. During the thirteenth century the issue of such writs was greatly increased to meet a rapidly expanding jurisdiction. If no writ existed applicable to any particular case, a new one had to be devised. New writs had to be approved by the ruler and possibly by magnates but, by the Statute of Westminster II in 1285, the chancellor was empowered to issue new writs *in consimili casu*, by his own authority. As a result the chancellor's activities in the processes of law and justice were an important complement to a great extension of his activities in other fields including both central and local administration.

In consequence of its increased activities the chancery began to seek semi-permanent headquarters. Robert Burnell, Edward I's chancellor, left the king hunting in the New Forest and betook himself to London where, it was said, all could have access to him who wished to seek writs under the great seal or to prosecute their rights. At Westminster, we may glimpse the beginnings of a modern 'capital'. With its headquarters there, the chancery could develop as a great office of government. The chancellor became not only a leading minister of the king but also an important member, and often president, of the council. He frequently, in later years, expressed the king's wishes at the opening of parliament.

He had under him a hierarchy of clerks, headed by the Keeper of the Rolls. Beneath this important officer were twelve clerks of the first grade, twelve of the second grade, and *cursitors*—so called because they wrote writs *de cursu* ('of course') which were largely routine. Important letters by junior clerks were examined and approved by seniors before they were sent out. The officials of the chancery lived in a common 'household' where they took dinners together. Before 1341 they were clerics. After this date laymen appeared. The clerks were given robes from the king, and received certain perquisites of office and promotion in the Church. The chancellor himself could expect to become a bishop or even an archbishop. His office would compare in work and organization with any chancery in Europe.[1] Its clerks were in effect important under-secretaries of state.

The hey-day of the office was probably the time between the accession of Edward I and the deposition of Richard II. This was the age of the great medieval chancellors, men like Robert Burnell, John Stratford, and William of Wykeham. From the middle of the fourteenth century the department began to be adversely affected by the elaboration of government, in particular by the evolution of the council and the interposition of small seals between the chancellor and the king. The use of the privy seal had been politically important since the days of the Ordainers. The signet seal acquired a similar importance under Richard II. At the time of the Lords

[1] My *Chancery Under Edward III* (Manchester 1929), p. 87; 'The Chancery', in *The English Government at Work 1327–1336*, edited by J. F. Willard and W. A. Morris (Cambridge, Mass. 1940), pp. 162–205.

Appellant, Arundel had refused to recognize the signet seal as a sufficient warrant for the great seal; and the Merciless Parliament had prohibited its use 'to the disturbance of the law and the danger of the realm'.

In the fifteenth century these trends became more evident. The office of the chancery came to be far removed from direct contact with the ruler. The chain of command between it and the king may be seen in famous regulations of 1444, drawn up by the Lords of the Council to restrain the king's prodigality. The king, these said, might sign a bill asking for some favour by subscribing it with his own hand, or he might ask his chamberlain or secretary to sign. After this, warrants were to be made out by letters under the signet seal. These would authorize a letter from the office of the privy seal to the chancellor. The keeper of the privy seal might show such a letter to the Lords of the Council, 'if it seems to him that the matter contained in the same is one entailing great expenditure'.[1] Finally, the privy seal warrant would give rise to a formal expression of the king's will under his great seal.

By reason of such a process of authorization, those officials who controlled the early stages leading to royal enactments became very important, as did the seals they controlled. Henry IV in 1404 renewed an old royal promise that the Common Law should not be disturbed by letters under the secret or privy seal. When Henry VI urgently needed troops from Coventry in 1455 and 1470 he wrote to the town under his signet seal.[2] Even more important in some ways was the Sign Manual of household officers like the chamberlain—the king's Sign Manual was the supreme authentication of a warrant for the great seal. But the endorsement of a bill by Adam Moleyns, who was clerk of the council up to 1444 and keeper of the privy seal until 1450, was accepted as an authorization for both great and privy seals. Inevitably, the king's secretary also grew steadily in importance, and he often kept the secret seal. In 1402 Henry IV sent the Steward of his Household and his secretary to make a report to the Commons. Adam Moleyns acted as one of the king's principal secretaries in his notorious climb to power. In 1450 the Commons included Thomas Kent clerk of the council, and Gervays le Valore a secretary to the king, among the 'favourites' they attacked. When Henry VI recovered his sanity at Christmas 1454

---

[1] My *Constitutional History of England in the Fifteenth Century*, pp. 234–6.
[2] *Ibid.*, pp. 370–3.

he ordered his secretary to make an offering at the shrine of St. Edward. With such officials close to the king's side the chancellor's influence with the ruler could not fail to be greatly reduced.

The less important his care of the great seal became, the more he tended to leave his administrative work to subordinates and give his attention to politics. A good example is to be seen in Thomas Arundel, made chancellor of Richard II in 1386. He owed his promotion to family influence and political pressure. He flagrantly abused his office and betrayed his ministerial loyalty to the king during the crises of 1386 and 1388, yet he was eventually rewarded for his political intrigues by the highest position in the Church. He was disgraced and exiled by Richard in 1397, but became a pillar of the Lancastrians and a fervent persecutor of Lollards under Henry IV.[1]

Another example is to be found in the career of George Neville (1433 ?–76). He was brother of the Kingmaker and obtained rapid promotion in the Church; a prebend in York was granted to him when he was only fourteen. He studied at Balliol as a contemporary of John Tiptoft. When barely twenty-one he was made Chancellor of the University, a position he held from 1453 to 1457. He became bishop of Exeter in 1456 (he had been elected by the Chapter in November 1455), when he was already deeply involved in Yorkist politics. He was made the king's chancellor on 26 July 1460, immediately after the battle of Northampton, receiving the great seal which had been resigned by the Archbishop of Canterbury. He gave the strongest possible support to Edward IV at the time of his accession, and Edward as monarch re-granted him the great seal on 10 March.

At Edward's first parliament in 1461, Neville delivered a sermon on the theme 'Amend your ways' (Jeremiah, VII. 3). He subsequently took a prominent part in negotiations with France, Burgundy, and Scotland. In March 1465 he was made archbishop of York. But he fell victim to the deepening quarrel between Edward and Warwick, and in 1467 was dismissed from office. He was not asked to open the session of parliament which met on 3 June. On 8 June, Edward went in person to the chancellor's inn where Neville was lying sick, took possession of the great seal, and put it into the hands of keepers until a new chancellor should be appointed.

[1] Details, and a more favourable judgment on Arundel are in Margaret Aston's *Thomas Arundel: A Study of Church Life in the Reign of Richard II* (Oxford 1967).

George Neville subsequently joined in the insurrection of Warwick and Clarence and shared their vicissitudes. During the *Readepcio* he again became chancellor, this time for Henry VI, and organized that monarch's sorry procession through London. Neville surrendered Henry and himself to Edward when the victor of Barnet entered the city. He was apparently fully pardoned by the king; but shortly afterwards he was arrested on a charge of corresponding with the exiled earl of Oxford. He was imprisoned, his treasures were confiscated, and his administrative and political career came to an end. Though set free by Edward he did not long survive, dying at Blyth in Northumberland on 8 June 1476.

His career was exceptional, but it nevertheless illustrates the extent to which the chancellor's office was becoming political. The days when he had been the king's personal servant and keeper of the only royal seal were now far in the past. Outside politics, the chancellor's greatest claim to importance was provided by his place on the council and his work as the most important law officer of the Crown.

5. The Exchequer

Alongside the chancery, the exchequer expanded in a similar pattern. As early as Henry I's reign it had begun to move away from the king's side and to become an important office of finance. Its duties were shared by the household offices of Wardrobe and the Chamber which looked after the immediate needs of the ruler and his court, accompanied the ruler on his wars, and provided moneys for his campaigns. A nucleus of Chamber knights actually provided the core of the royal army. In times of great warfare, as in the reign of Edward I, the Wardrobe and Chamber were responsible for receiving and disbursing much of the 'national' income; and some historians have argued that this was partly, at least, the result of deliberate royal policy, since it prevented the magnates from exercising any check on the king's financial activities, because household officers were not subject to baronial influence or control. There may be some truth in this view, though it would seem to have been carried much too far. There was no distinction in the minds of contemporaries between the relationships of the treasurer on the one hand, and the 'household' officers on the other, to either the king or to the magnates.[1] Both served equally the purposes of the king and

[1] My *Studies in the Constitutional History of the Thirteenth and Fourteenth Centuries,* chapter ix.

owed the same loyalty and obedience. Edward I made more use of his Wardrobe than any ruler in history; but nevertheless, in 1290, the proceeds of the tax on movables were placed under the direct control of the exchequer, and it is probable that Edward intended to make the latter responsible for all the income of the Crown.[1]

The more complex and costly government became, the more the functions, importance, and organization of the exchequer expanded. In the thirteenth century, the office administered new 'national' taxation, tightened its control over an increasing hierarchy of local officials, and developed a jurisdiction of its own. It became zealous, probably over-zealous, in its assertion of the king's rights and the prosecution of his claims, an attitude which had been anticipated by Richard FitzNeal in the reign of Henry II. Under Henry III it began an extensive practice of sending out royal commissions to enquire into all encroachments on such rights; a practice which culminated in Edward I's famous *Quo Warranto* inquisitions.

The new forms of taxation, to meet the needs of the emerging territorial state, began as early as 1166 and 1188, in the form of an imposition on movable property. They may be said to have come of age in 1225, with the grant of a fifteenth of such property in return for a reissue of Magna Carta. They fell on all subjects above a certain wealth, rather than only on tenants-in-chief; and they soon became the main support of the English monarch. His 'modern' taxation helped him to become one of the richest rulers in Europe and persisted all through the later Middle Ages. The next important innovation came in 1275 with the levy of a permanent custom on wool. This, too, became an important prop of English royal finance. Both these impositions represented non-feudal taxation to support the needs of an increasingly non-feudal state.

The exchequer also helped to develop the great expansion of royal credit. By 1289, Edward I owed the Riccardi the enormous sum of £107,000. This was not simply a sign of his inability to finance his wars and other projects. The capacity to borrow was also a source of strength, enabling rulers to expand their activities and meet crises which their predecessors could not have survived.

To facilitate credit, the exchequer expanded the function of old aids to accounting which the office had long employed, in the shape of the tallies, or small sticks of wood on which was notched the amount which sheriffs and others owed to the king. The notches

[1] F. M. Powicke, *Thirteenth Century*, p. 524.

were a symbolic language which all could understand. After being marked, the tallies were slit in half, to provide identical records for both debtor and exchequer. Thousands of those preserved in the exchequer were destroyed by a great fire in the vaults of parliament in 1834.

Tallies could be used not only to record debts but also to act as receipts and a procedure gradually grew up whereby they were prepared as such, and issued to creditors who would then exchange them for cash at the hands of some sheriff or other royal official. The official would recoup himself from the royal revenue he collected and substitute the tally of receipt for the appropriate amount. The process now looks very primitive and clumsy, but it provided the king with an important source of credit. It was extended to other departments besides the exchequer, especially to the Wardrobe and Chamber. This was one reason why such offices seemed at times to be rivals of the exchequer. In the first year of Edward II, the receipts of the Wardrobe were greater, at least on parchment, than those of the exchequer.

Many officials connected with finance, and even some who apparently were not, were appointed in the exchequer. An enormous number of writs were issued from the office on an increasing variety of business, under a duplicate of the great seal. To cope with all its activities, the exchequer had a large staff of officials, rivalling in importance that of the chancery. It was headed by the treasurer and the barons of the exchequer. One such official, the chancellor of the exchequer was destined to become ultimately the chief financial officer of the Crown. According to the law book *Fleta*, of Edward I's reign, this officer sat on the lefthand of the treasurer in the exchequer court. Without his consent or counsel, an earlier description said 'nothing of importance is done or ought to be done'. Members of the exchequer court were known as barons of the exchequer. The treasurer himself, like the chancellor, was an important member of the king's council and a conspicuous member of the government. Walter Langton, bishop of Lichfield and treasurer from 1295 to 1307 was an outstanding personality of his age, as was William Edington, treasurer from 1344–56. A successful treasurer, like a good chancellor, might expect to be rewarded with a bishopric.

As the years went by the tax on movables lost some of its importance, as did even the custom on wool. The tax became fixed after 1334, yielding only about £37,000, a figure which was later diminished by exemptions. The landed gentry only paid on the movables on their demesne lands, and the merchants largely escaped. The merchants obviously contributed to the custom; but this tax also declined in value during the fourteenth century because of the diminution of wool exports; and it became very low early in the fifteenth. There was no compensation for this decline through an increase in the custom on cloth. Exports of cloth increased but did not pay customs like the wool. The royal income from other sources was added to in 1399 by revenues from the broad Lancastrian estates; but in spite of this the Lancastrian kings were normally heavily in debt. The result was that other taxes were devised after 1377, to fall on all the king's subjects who could pay.

In 1377 a poll tax of 4*d* a head was granted in parliament, to be paid by all lay persons over the age of fourteen; whilst the clergy granted 1*s* from every beneficed clerk and 4*d* from all other ecclesiastics. The exchequer did not devise the new taxation, but we may guess that it contributed in other ways. In 1379 the poll tax was repeated, graduated according to wealth; from 10 marks paid by the duke of Lancaster to a groat (4*d*) paid by the poorest individual. In 1380 the rate was three groats for every person over the age of fifteen. Each locality assessed its own tax. The idea was that the rich should assist the poor, though no married couple was to pay more than £1 or less than one groat. In spite of provisions for an equitable sharing of the burden, the tax of 1380 proved to be not much less unjust than that of 1377. All these taxes weighed heavily on the poor. There was much resentment and widespread evasion; but in fact the injustices reflected the feelings of the parliamentary Lords and Commons who thought that the poor were undertaxed. Despite grievous faults, the poll taxes showed a recognition of the need for new non-feudal impositions. If they had been made more equitable they might have led to a broadening of the whole financial system. This, in turn, might have brought about a wider representation in parliament, just as the tax on movables had earlier helped to extend the concept of the *universitas*.

Failing a successful expansion of taxation, royal borrowing reached unprecedented and ruinous heights. English financiers supplied Edward III, and many became bankrupt in the process. After 1399 the Lancastrians became notorious for their loans (at between 25 and 33⅓ per cent) and their debts. Henry VI's real revenue fell from an average of £54,000 a year to a little over £33,000. The

revenues were estimated in 1433 to leave a credit balance of only
£8000 after meeting the ordinary expenses of the king's household
and administration, the wages and pensions due at the Exchequer,
and the defence of England and the possessions abroad. Soon, the
expenses were increased by £6700 required for Margaret of Anjou,
whilst in 1440 the lieutenant-general appointed for the French war
was promised £20,000 a year. In 1449 the king's debts amounted to
the enormous sum of £372,000 which, to arrive at modern currency,
would have to be multiplied very many times.[1]

In face of this situation another device in taxation was tried in the
fifteenth century in the shape of an income tax, in 1404, 1411, 1431,
and 1435. In 1404 it was at the rate of 20s for all lay persons on each
£20 of income, beginning with incomes of 500 marks or more
from lands and rents. In 1411, the tax was 6s 8d for each £20
and began on incomes of £20. In 1431 it was levied at 5 per cent on
incomes as low as £5. In 1435 the tax again began on incomes of £5:
from £5 to £100 the rate was 6d in the £. Incomes from £100 to
£400 paid a graduated tax. Those of £400 or more paid 2s in the £.
The taxes were efficiently imposed; but in spite of this, though this
form of taxation was revived twice, in 1450 and in 1472, it did not
become permanent. Edward IV restored the solvency of the Crown
without it, by good business methods and by Benevolences and
Forced Loans, which were in effect a form of taxation on the well-
to-do.

In these last years, the exchequer responsibilities were diminished
by the extension of the work of the Chamber, a development
greatly furthered by Henry VII. The Chamber had always been
important, headed at times by 'familiars' like Peter de Rivaux and
Hugh Despenser the Younger, but it did not begin to supersede
the exchequer in its essential functions until early modern times.
The steps leading to this in Edward IV's reign are quite obscure,
partly because important records have perished. All we can be sure of
is that under Henry VII the treasurer of the Chamber became the
receiver-general of the king's revenue, and the Chamber in effect
took over the functions of the Exchequer of Receipt.

Meanwhile, however, the treasurer, like the chancellor, had come
to depend heavily on the council and on politics for his importance.

---

[1] Some figures and sources are given by R. L. Storey, *The End of the House of Lancaster*,
pp. 49, 246, and in my *Constitutional History of the Fifteenth Century*, pp. 259–61, with
reference to recent works.

Fifteenth-century treasurers included such prominent politicians as Henry Bourchier viscount and earl of Essex, and John Tiptoft earl of Worcester. Similar appointments were not uncommon throughout the struggles between Lancastrians and Yorkists. It is clear, indeed, that with the rise of political influences in both great offices of government a new era in the development of both politics and bureaucracy had begun.

6. Justice and Law

Many of these processes were equally apparent in the growth of the Common Law. Like administration in general, that of the king's law was affected by an unceasing process of localization, special-ization, and disintegration. The *Curia Regis* gradually split up during the thirteenth century into the Common Law courts of King's Bench and Common Pleas. Both entertained criminal and civil cases; though the court *Coram Rege* or King's Bench dealt particu-larly with those between the king and the subject, whilst the *Curia de Banco* or Common Pleas dealt particularly with cases between subject and subject. Both courts greatly extended their jurisdiction during the thirteenth century. The former became the usual court for important actions on the writ of Trespass in which it was alleged that the use of violence and arms had created a breach of the king's peace. In all cases in which such a breach was alleged no local court dared to proceed. Similarly the writ of Entry, which challenged the title to ownership of land, was also developed in a great variety of forms. In these and other ways, those who were responsible for the king's courts seem to have begun thinking in terms of a general jurisdiction over land, without the slightest reference to existing feudal courts. Similarly in *Fleta*, written in the reign of Edward I we come to the complete dogma that all judicial power is derived from the Crown.

During the same century the king's representatives greatly in-creased their activities in taking his justice to the local courts of the hundreds and the shires. Commissions were sent on eyre to hear all pleas (*omnia placita*) in the shire courts. They were empowered to dispose of all the legal business of the county which was pending in any of the king's courts, and in this way the litigants were saved the cost of going to Westminster or elsewhere to seek out the king. The justices could also empanel juries in the shire and hundred courts to secure information on oath about local maladministration.

Enquiries into robbery and murder were mixed with those regarding illegal profits by the sheriffs. Shires and hundreds were fined for neglect of their communal duties. These general eyres, as the commissions were called, were profitable to the Crown and often advantageous to the subject; but they were nevertheless unpopular. However, by the reign of Edward I new commissions had been established and some old ones expanded; and the general eyre fell into disuse.

One such expanded session was the commission of Assize. This had originated in Henry II's Possessory Assizes which, according to the reissue of Magna Carta in 1217, were to be held twice a year. A good number of civil cases came to be heard before the commissioners; and in 1285 the Statute of Westminster II provided that, in effect, all civil cases might be heard before them. It was decreed that, when a civil case had been begun at Westminster, the court would direct the sheriff of the county where the litigants lived to have jurors at Westminster on a certain date, unless before that date (*nisi prius*) justices of Assize should come to the county. However, the justices normally arrived before the stipulated date. Hence, the justices were in reality empowered to try all civil cases; though judgment was finally given by the court in which the action had begun. At first, the commissioners were four knights of the county; but under Henry III professional judges were appointed as well.

A further special commission was that of gaol delivery which heard criminal cases in which any prisoner in gaol was involved. It was limited in its action because gaols and prisoners (usually charged with homicide) were not numerous. But it was supplemented by a third commission, that of *Oyer and terminer*, which was developed under Edward I to hear and settle all cases of felonies and crimes in a county, and to receive indictments against individuals who were not actually in gaol. A commissioner of gaol delivery might be a royal justice or a local landowner, very likely a knight.

The growth of royal commissions took the king's justice effectively into the shires and greatly expanded its action. At first the expansion involved a greater participation of local men, especially the gentry; but in time the commission came to be dominated by the royal justices. The new procedures guaranteed one royal law common to all the kingdom; but this was a law administered mainly by the paid servants of the king. The increasing domination over justice by the central government was partly, but only partly, balanced by the development of trial by jury, which became firmly established by the end of the reign of Edward I.

The modern jury only slowly supplemented Henry II's jury of presentment which was supposed to know the facts. One action which helped this process was that which was based on a writ *de odio et atia*, by which a defendant asked that a jury should determine whether or not he had been accused out of spite and hate. The jury used in this case was usually smaller than that of presentment, and hence it came to be called a 'petty' jury. The two juries gradually came to be distinguished from each other, and the smaller began to be drawn from a considerable area in the countryside. As a result, it became obvious that some of its members could not possibly have a firsthand knowledge of the facts. This became even more apparent as the use of the petty jury was extended to other actions besides those based on the writ *de odio et atia*. When this extension had been effected, the jurors' lack of firsthand knowledge became very apparent, and the modern jury finally emerged. There was some uncertainty about it as late as 1352, but Sir John Fortescue in the fifteenth century praised it highly in modern terms. It did not bring about a flawless administration of justice; but it did give an important share of responsibility to the communities of the boroughs and shires.

This was all the more important since by the middle of the thirteenth century the administration of the king's law was falling into the hands not only of professional judges but also of professional pleaders. The change may have been speeded by the influence of Canon Law and of ecclesiastical courts. The coif appeared as the distinctive dress of the pleaders; and some of them became famous and influential. In 1292 Edward I ordered his judges to provide a certain number of such experts who should have the sole right of practising in his courts, and who should train apprentices in their profession. Those who pleaded the king's own cases were called serjeants-at-law. Litigants in civil cases also began to appoint attorneys, especially when they were about to journey abroad. Such attorneys became a specialized and important class of lawyer, recognized as such in the regulations of 1292.

The lawyers and their apprentices tended to congregate together. The apprentices listened to pleadings and discussed them afterwards in their lodgings. We have it on record that in 1305 a royal judge was baffled in a discussion by a case which had been invented by such students to illustrate a problem at law. Later, these lodgings grew into the famous Inns of Court. Lincoln's Inn and Gray's Inn were named after the owners of the property which was rented by the lawyers; the Inner and Middle Temple began in buildings owned by the Knights Templars. All were organized during the fourteenth century. Alongside them appeared in due course similar Inns of Chancery, in which gathered chancery clerks and junior aspirants to the legal profession who, as a preliminary training, had to master the different kinds of chancery writ.

Thus an important class of professionals emerged, who were to have a great influence. They not only strengthened and defended the law; they also provided a conspicuous ingredient in the new managerial class which now rapidly developed. Highly-educated and experienced men, they were able to give advice and service to the great lords as well as to the king; and they helped to introduce a new sophistication into English political life.

Another aspect of change in the administration of justice is to be found in the great statutes of Edward I. In his reign, statutes first superseded custom as the principal basis of law. The formulation of a statute was obviously an important public event in which the relative contributions of king and community were not easy to determine. On the whole, the lawyers were agreed that law-making should be a conjoint effort by the king and the 'community' of the realm. As Bracton said under Henry III:

> For the king has no other power in his lands, since he is a minister and vicar of God, save that alone which he has of right. Nor is that to the contrary where it is said *quod principi placuit legis habet vigorem*, for there follow after 'law' the words 'together with the *lex regia* which has been laid down concerning his authority'. Therefore it is not anything rashly presumed by will of the king, but what has been rightly defined with the king's authorization on the advice of his magnates after deliberation and *tractatus* concerning it.[1]

This is not a description of statute-making, but it portrays its proper spirit. Bracton's view was not always adhered to. For reasons of expediency, and maybe sometimes of set purpose, the king and council under Edward I often entirely dominated the making of statutes. But the Bractonian tradition was too strong to be set aside,

---

[1] Translated in my *Constitutional History 1216-1399*, vol. III, pp. 101-2. A *tractatus* may be defined as a discussion between parties with a view to agreement, though it had many variations of meaning.

and under Edward II the lords pressed strongly their claim to participate in legislation. Indeed, the king rather than the community now stood on the defensive. The monarch's right of initiative was strongly asserted in the Statute of York; but, in spite of this, that of the Lords and Commons also became firmly established, even though expressed in the humbler form of a petition rather than of a formal demand. When, as became frequent, a grant of supplies by Lords and Commons was made conditional on consent to a petition, the humble wording became largely a matter of form. Hence, during the fourteenth century the initiative in legislation steadily passed from the king to the Estates in parliament; though the government could always initiate a law if it wished, and the king could accept or refuse in the famous words *le roi le veult* or *le roi s'avisera*.

In any case, the ruler still had an immense influence on the administration of justice through his claim to the loyalty of his judges. Edward I revealed the inner relationship which existed by his famous proceedings against his justices and others in 1289. The judges were accused of misbehaviour during the king's absence in Gascony. They were tried by a royal tribunal and many of them were condemned. Thomas Wayland, chief justice of the bench of Common Pleas, was starved out of sanctuary and exiled. Henry Bray, justice of the Jews, twice tried to commit suicide when imprisoned in the Tower. The famous Ralph Hengham, chief justice of the King's Bench, was heavily fined. Contemporaries compared Edward with the lord of the parable who had gone into a far country and had returned to avenge himself on the defaulting labourers in his vineyard. The judges were the labourers of their royal master, even if sworn to uphold the law. In 1311 the Ordainers demanded that they should be appointed with the assent of the Lords and in parliament, but this radical notion did not prevail. Judges continued, in fact, to hold their office during the royal pleasure until as late as 1701.

Edward I's view of the judges as labourers in his vineyard was not exceptional. Three-quarters of a century later, Edward III deprived Sir William Thorp, chief justice of the King's Bench of his office. Sir William was imprisoned and even threatened with death for receiving bribes. It has been concluded[1] that in the fourteenth century the bench was still regarded as part of the government, if not of the civil service. Edward III seems to have regarded it as such

[1] T. F. T. Plucknett, *A Concise History of the Common Law* (2nd edition), p. 215.

when, in 1340-1, he dismissed judges as well as ministers on grounds which seem to have been mainly political. Richard II in 1387 brought heavy pressure to bear on a group of his judges, in order to have proceedings of the parliament of 1386 declared invalid and traitorous, and those who gave him the opinion he wanted were later impeached and banished by the king's political opponents. T. F. Tout believed that by the declaration of the judges a deep line of division was drawn between the upholders of prerogative and the friends of parliamentary supremacy and the rule of law.[1]

After 1388, however, the judges tended to be removed from the sphere of politics, and the royal pressure upon them diminished. The attitude of one justice, Sir William Gascoigne, at the beginning of the fifteenth century (if the famous story about him is true) perhaps indicates that lawyers were increasingly influenced by law rather than by politics. The young prince Henry was charged with misdemeanor and brought before the court. There, he showed defiance and perhaps uttered some threat of violence. Upon which, the chief justice committed him to prison for contempt.

Perhaps the same tendency is apparent in high politics. The courts were little involved in the fifteenth-century usurpations of the throne. Approval was sought not from the judges but from parliament, or at least the Estates. The justices were appealed to when Richard of York claimed the throne in 1460; but they did not give an opinion, claiming that their duty was to determine such matters as came before them in law between party and party. Such a question as that of succession to the throne, they said, pertained to the lords of the king's blood and to the peers. During the later century, the judges stood apart from the political conflict, and the changes of dynasty left the bench largely unaffected. Sir John Fortescue was unique in the part he played in politics; but he preached a doctrine of English constitutionalism which contained much that was acceptable to both sides. He was a prominent Lancastrian, present at both Barnet and Tewkesbury; yet was later accepted into the council of Edward IV. In him, the politician overcame the judge; but his career was the exception and not the rule.

During the last century and a half of the Middle Ages, the law and the lawyers both became strengthened in the shires, despite the

---

[1] T. F. Tout, *Chapters in the Administrative History of Medieval England*, vol. III (Manchester 1928), p. 424.

violence and intimidation of the age. Commissions into the shires continued and were expanded. Among the new ones were those *Ad omnia placita* and *Trailbastion*, the former to deal with all pleas that were pending, the latter empowering the punishment of all criminals. The dispensation of justice in the counties was further strengthened by the rise of the Justice of the Peace. In 1422 the Lords of the Council declared that the execution of the law and the keeping of the peace depended greatly on the Justices of the Peace, the sheriffs, and the escheators. In 1461 it was laid down that all indictments and presentments normally taken at the sheriff's tourn, by which offenders were arrested and imprisoned, should be taken before these Justices. In 1485 a chief justice was quoted as marvelling at the load of duties they carried. By this time the characteristic English institution of the Justice of the Peace was firmly established, linked with an ascendancy of the gentry in the shires which lasted into very modern times.

Another great development of justice, this time at the centre, was the growth of equity. Equity was justice freed from a rigid subordination to statute and custom. It was the product of reason, the action of the ruler who was *legibus solutus*, at least to the extent that he had the duty of remedying complaints of his subjects, even if this meant superseding the letter of the law. The subjects asked for, and expected, the exercise of the royal grace. Without equity, the law would have strangled itself by its own increasing rigidity.

Medieval equity was for many years a simple exercise of the king's grace without any basis of formulated theory; though it developed both form and content by the end of the fifteenth century. Its obscure origins went back as far as the thirteenth century. As the king's government and law became more complex, the justices of King's Bench and Common Pleas were given much wider duties but enjoyed less discretion. They were particularly bound by the new statute law of Edward I. Accordingly, in spite of the proliferation of original writs, there were more and more cases which they could not entertain.

The only way of dealing with these was by recourse to the king's grace and favour, and the most convenient time for obtaining this came to be at the meeting of parliament. The method was for the individual who desired a remedy to address an individual petition to the king. This would ultimately be dealt with by the ruler himself, or by the king and council, or by the council alone though the petitioner was frequently sent to the chancellor or some other minister or to the Common Law courts, with a directive that justice be done. In time, the petitioners developed a habit of addressing themselves directly to ministers or council, and many cases might be disposed of without reaching the king. In 1280 Edward I ordered that all petitions addressed to him in parliament were to be shared out to the appropriate justices or 'departments'. Only if what was asked was so great, he said, or involved so much grace that the chancellor or the justices could not act without the king, should the petitions be brought to the king to learn his will.

As a result of these developments, both the council and the chancery developed an important exercise of the king's grace in the answering of petitions. In 1349 it was decreed that all matters of grace were to be dealt with in the first instance by the chancellor or the keeper of the privy seal. Such matters were not necessarily all judicial. An example of a borderline petition is provided in 1337, when Thomas of York, 'worker for the science of Alchemy', had been cast into prison because his secrets had been apprised by unscrupulous individuals who wished to make a profit from them at their leisure. He begged to be freed and have his instruments restored, so that he could prove his science.[1] There were also petitions for grants of money or land, or for livings in the Church. But it seems safe to assume that by this date an extensive practice of equity in the council and the chancery had clearly taken shape.

Equity was important for many reasons. In law, it made the whole system of justice more sophisticated and elastic. In politics, it helped to promote views of the royal prerogative as an indefinable power which could not be limited by enactment, whose essence lay beyond all existing restrictions of law. This had long been recognized as an attribute of the monarch. In 1242 it was claimed in the King's Bench that the king was above all law. A counsel under Edward I claimed that the king was above every subject and above the law in his kingdom, a claim also made in the dispute about the succession to Scotland in 1291–92 and echoed by Justice Bereford under Edward II. The prerogative was for the common good of the realm, as Edward I told his magnates[2]; nor could this claim, dangerous though it might become, easily be denied.

---

[1] My article 'The Chancery', in *The English Government at Work 1327–1336*, edited by J. F. Willard and W. A. Morris (Medieval Academy of America, Cambridge, Mass. 1940), vol. I, p. 193.

[2] My *Constitutional History of Medieval England 1216–1399*, vol. III, p. 154, n. 13.

Equity and high royalist notions of the king's prerogatives went hand in hand, especially under Richard II. Richard had the proceedings of 1386 condemned by his judges as being against his prerogatives. He later got the Lords and Commons to declare that his prerogative was free and unimpaired by the acts of 1386–88; and in 1397 he condemned Thomas Haxey for attempting an invasion of the same. Similarly, Henry IV after his usurpation of the throne was careful, on more than one occasion, to keep the royal prerogative intact.[1]

Both equity and the idea of the royal prerogative continued to expand during the fifteenth century. Appeals to the chancellor multiplied in the king's absence abroad between 1417 and 1421. His court of equitable jurisdiction became a commonplace. Aided by a new legal device called Use, by which property was held by one person for the use of another, and which was very advantageous to landowners in days of perils and forfeitures, opposition of the king's subjects to equity largely disappeared. The chancellor's court was fully recognized: he himself formally declared that he held two jurisdictions, one in Common Law and one in Equity. Edward IV explicitly directed him to determine matters in the latter court according to conscience and to equity. The same is true of the associated exercise of prerogative in the person of the ruler. In the *Advice to Henry VI*, probably written by Sir John Fortescue in 1470, it was stated that the suggestions made were not in any way to limit the king's power, liberty, or prerogative. 'That which is a prerogative of the king', it was declared before all the justices in the exchequer chamber, 'he cannot dismember from the king's person.'[2]

One consequence of all these developments was the rising importance of both the law and of the lawyers. The training of the latter was an important development of the fifteenth century. The education received in the Inns of Court came to rival that of the universities and it had a greater relevance to the problems of the period. William Paston studied there, to become a justice of the Court of Common Pleas in 1429. Others who attended had no plan to practise law. Some may have felt like Margaret Paston, who told her son Walter that she would love him better as a good secular man than as an unworthy priest. The Inns of Court, as Sir John

---

[1] My *Constitutional History of England in the Fifteenth Century*, pp. 237, 264.
[2] *Ibid.*, pp. 211, 264; S. B. Chrimes, *English Constitutional Ideas in the Fifteenth Century* (Cambridge 1936), p. 58.

Fortescue testified, attracted many of the sons of the aristocracy. They also produced not a few great legal writers. Sir John himself was educated at both Oxford and Lincoln's Inn. Littleton, another eminent legal writer, went to the Inner Temple and later wrote a treatise on Tenures which Sir Edward Coke with much exaggeration called 'the ornament of the common law, and the most perfect and absolute work that ever was written in any humane science'.

7. THE KING'S COUNCIL

Important though this complex and impressive development was, it was overshadowed in some ways by that of the king's council, which was both an instrument of administration and law and also a nexus of political life. In origin it was probably not, as has often been assumed, heir to the undifferentiated Angevin *Curia*; it rather descended from a small section of the *Curia* whose essential function was advice. Its antecedents can be discerned, faintly and doubtfully under Henry II, more clearly and definitely during the reign of King John. By 1236 a sworn council had emerged, whose members were clearly distinguished by their oath. As such, it formed a central feature of the projected reforms of 1244 and of the Provisions of Oxford in 1258. For many years its duty continued to be, in the words of F. W. Maitland, 'to advise the king upon every exercise of the royal power', and this was reflected in the councillor's oath. It had no records and no seal of its own. The loyalty of the councillors was to the king, and there is little doubt that Henry III regarded them as his personal servants, existing to further his interests and busy on his work.

King Henry was accused in his early years of giving his councillors custody of his treasury and of the laws and justice of his country; but the weight of evidence suggests that at this date the councillors did not normally have executive powers. By 1307, however, it was assumed in the councillor's oath that they would both judge and enforce right. By 1341 they swore to perform the king's business, not merely to give counsel about it; and they were to act for the good of the realm as well as of the king. They had obviously by this time acquired far-reaching executive functions of their own. The council had, indeed, become an important office of administration and justice. It authorized a broad variety of actions by individual ministers. Its activities in justice were broad and flexible. To it, as to the chancellor, the king delegated some part of his royal prerogative.

As the council became an indispensable centre of government, the question of its personnel became of the greatest political importance. The more its activities expanded the less satisfactory it became that councillors should be chosen solely by the king, who showed a tendency to rely on familiars rather than magnates and to demand loyalty to his interests rather than to the common good. This led to strong opposition from the great lords, who claimed to be the king's 'natural' advisers, and believed that both the personnel and the business of the council were the concern of the community as well as of the king. The clash between this belief and the royal view could only very slowly be resolved through the creation of the medieval parliament, where a conjoint exercise of authority by king and subjects in such debatable areas could eventually be achieved.

During the fourteenth century the council in some areas diminished, but in others greatly increased, its functions and importance. It lost some personal contact with the ruler and obtained headquarters of its own, thus losing influence over some royal decisions; but it greatly expanded its independent activities. Its importance in parliament decreased, but outside parliament it added to its activities in administration, justice, and politics. Its stature was shown in the fourteenth century by the use of the privy seal, once the king's personal instrument, to authenticate its acts. By 1332 there was a chamber at the exchequer 'where the king's council is commonly held', and where an imposing volume of administration was carried out with no reference whatever to the king.

A similar development continued in the fifteenth century, complicated greatly by royal minority and the increasing pretensions of those councillors who were great lords, particularly lords of the royal blood. In 1453 the chancellor was empowered by Act of parliament to enforce the attendance before it of all persons who had been summoned there by writ of privy seal, in regard to all cases that could not be determined by Common Law. By this time, also, the foundations had been laid for special sessions which later came to be known as the Council of Wales, the Council of the North, and the Star Chamber, the last of which became a formidable instrument for taming overmighty subjects of the Crown.

These last were judicial sessions of the council. At the same time the more general sessions developed remarkable procedures and techniques. It was laid down for the special council of 1406 that those who were present were to keep those who were absent informed about important business, and that the council's secrets were to be shared only by councillors. The king was not to be prejudiced against any one councillor by charges of misconduct without proof. Every matter before the council was to be carefully considered, agreed to by members in their own person and as far as possible be passed with the consent of all.[1] Certain bills which were endorsed by the chamberlain, letters sent under the signet seal, and other commands sent to the chancellor, treasurer, or keeper of the privy seal, should be endorsed or drawn up by the advice of the council. In later years there were many regulations, as for example in 1422, regarding attendance, agreement, and the subscription of instruments by members, especially by Lords of the Council. The first surviving journal of the council dates from 1392.

There were many forms of the council, but it is clear that in one form it continued its ancient function of advising the ruler. In 1406, it was assumed that some of the special councillors to be appointed in parliament would remain 'about the king's person'. In 1437 the keeper of the privy seal and others swore:

> to counsel him [the king] well and truly in such matters as shall be opened to them by the king's council, and to keep the king's counsel secret. In brief, they shall counsel and do all that good councillors should counsel and do to the king their sovereign lord.[2]

Through all these activities the council remained the great focus of politics next to parliament. In some ways, it was more important than the parliament of the fifteenth century because it was in continuous session and controlled much of the process of government. J. E. A. Jolliffe has argued that it had now become 'a natural guardian of the interests of both king and nation'.[3] Such an advance in function, he believed, called less for constitutional change than for a new political type, almost a new political morality. Thus, the Commons petitioned for 'councillors who should understand the elements of their own function, loyalty to the Crown, to the parliament, to each other, disinterestedness, diligence, freedom from factions, secrecy and discretion. In short, solidarity in the interests of the king, the nation, and in their own—a new technique of

[1] Translated in my *Constitutional History of England in the Fifteenth Century*, pp. 239, 241.

[2] *Ibid.*, p. 252.

[3] *The Constitutional History of Medieval England* (2nd edition 1947), p. 458.

counsel.' This picture may be both idealistic and in part anachronistic, but it does give the flavour of the revolutionary changes in the
traditions of the council which were beginning to take place.

The changes included not only the council's functions and responsibilities, but also its personnel. There was a decline in the importance of non-magnate members and the beginning of a marked
ascendancy of Lords of the Council with special powers.[1] Edward I
was the last ruler whose council was overshadowed by the official
element. Under Edward II, Thomas of Lancaster made new precedents for the claims of princes of the royal blood. The place of the
lords in the council was steadily enhanced during both the minority
and the senility of Edward III. It was greatly strengthened by their
contribution to the French wars, and it was consolidated by their
successful opposition to Richard II. By the end of the fourteenth
century their position had been largely transformed.

In the minority of 1327 it was enacted that four bishops, four earls,
and six barons were to remain at the king's side to counsel him, and
four at least should always be there. In 1376, because of the king's
imbecillitas, nine lords were appointed for a similar purpose. They
promised to govern loyally both Edward and his realm. At least
six were always to be at the king's side. Greater business required
the assent of all. In 1377, 1386, and 1388, lords were appointed to
Richard II's council with similar powers; on the last occasions
without the pretext of minority or imbecility. In 1389 and 1390
Richard asserted his royal authority by changing his chancellor
and diminishing the status of the lords in his council, excepting
only those of the royal blood.

The place of the lords in the council was certainly not lessened
as a result of the usurpation of 1399; it was probably in the long run
considerably enhanced. Finally, the minority of Henry VI in 1422
began a long struggle for supremacy between the Lords of the
Council and Humphrey, Duke of Gloucester in which the latter
suffered a spectacular defeat. The result was a council dominated by
lords and overshadowed by the court between 1437 and 1461. Sir
John Fortescue probably had such a council in mind when he wrote:
'The kyngis counsell was wonned to be chosen off grete princes,
and off the gretteste lordes off þe lande, both spirituelles and tem-
porellis, and also off oþer men that were in greate auctorite and

---

[1] Modern debate on this question is referred to in my 'Fact and Fancy in Fifteenth-
Century English History', in *Speculum*, vol. XLII (October 1967), pp. 673–92.

offices.'[1] He wanted a change in the council; which should consist, he argued, of eight lords and twenty-four of the wisest and best disposed men in the realm, who should continually commune and deliberate on matters of difficulty which fell to the king.

The dominance of the council by the lords at this time was not merely a political accident. It was the result of the increasingly aristocratic nature of society and of the process of change from feudal baron to Renaissance courtier. It was also a reflection of the supreme importance of the council itself, and of the rich prize it offered to successful politicians. Hence the Yorkist dynasty, with or without the advice of Sir John Fortescue, preoccupied itself with its reform. Edward IV did, indeed, begin a process by which the council once more became the instrument of the king, not of the magnates, and his efforts helped to build a foundation for Tudor rule.

Such offices and officers helped to lay the foundations of a new political order; but they also immensely complicated the old problems of liberty and authority. These problems did, indeed, become so acute that a solution had to be found by developing a new and unprecedented institution.

8. PARLIAMENT

In spite of the great contribution of the council to medieval government, it was parliament and not the council which became the key institution. It was through parliament and not through the council that men found the most effective answers to the political problems of their age. The English parliament was descended, like all other governmental institutions, from the Angevin *Curia Regis*. If it had any one direct ancestor, this was the largest meeting of the *Curia*, when it gathered for solemn or important occasions, like the Crown-wearing of Norman and Angevin kings. Its traditions were derived mainly from these assemblies, when the king had communed with his great lords on matters of mutual concern.

But as part of the evolution from the *Curia*, a transformation was necessary. Many old traditions of the old assembly had to be discarded, and some revolutionary notions had to be accepted. The old *Curia* was summoned by the king, and responded to his questions and demands. Magnates who attended did so by virtue of their individual obligations and rights. They did not have any

[1] Sir John Fortescue, *The Governance of England*, edited by Charles Plummer (Oxford 1885), p. 145.

sense of collective responsibility for the kingdom as a whole. But when parliament emerged from the feudal *Curia* it had acquired a different set of attributes. The barons who attended had become a *universitas* with a sense of collective identity, and they stood for the interests of all the *regnum*, which were not necessarily identical with those of the king. They were not there merely to discuss the king's business, answer his questions, and reply to his demands. They were there to 'treat' about matters of common concern. In such matters the ruler could not simply accept or reject his magnates' views. His relations with those who attended his parliaments as 'representing' the *universitas* of his realm were thus probably fundamentally different from his relations with his councillors, and even from those between him and his magnates in the *Curia Regis* of Angevin kings.

The *universitas* of barons which emerged in the early thirteenth century was a typical medieval group composed of individuals with a common purpose and some capacity for common action. The stage had been set for its evolution by the political experiences of the magnates during Richard I's absence on the Third Crusade, the struggle for Magna Carta, and the Minority of Henry III. On a broader plane, the evolution was the product of the territorial state whose needs gave rise to taxation and demands for military service which fell outside the pattern of feudal relations. New legislation by statute, and a foreign policy which increasingly affected the whole community, helped to make the problems of government more and more 'national'. They were not to be disposed of satisfactorily by negotiations between the king and individual vassals, even when these were gathered together in his *Curia*. Similar problems arose as a result of the impact of the new order on the clergy. After the pontificate of Innocent III, the Church began to assume the form of a centralized monarchy supported by an efficient but costly bureaucracy. The clergy were exposed to new financial demands by the pope, and an extended exercise of papal authority; and, like the laity, they tended to establish a *universitas* to defend their collective interests and rights. They were even better equipped for such a development than the lay magnates, since their leaders were often university graduates, versed in Civil and Canon Law and familiar with the notions to be found there of a body corporate, of representation, and of consent.

These growing needs, at a time of remarkable creativeness, led in two short generations to a transformation of the larger sessions of the *Curia Regis*. There were formidable obstacles to be overcome. In 1242 Henry III still tried to rely on the individual consent of his magnates, interviewing them in his private chamber, as Matthew Paris observed 'in the manner of penitents before a priest'. As late as 1255 the king sought to gain his ends, at a gathering of magnates, by ignoring the idea of common action on their part and by binding some of the leading magnates individually to his side. Matthew censured the lords for going home the following Christmas, each man to take his own counsel 'in the manner of Englishmen'. Nevertheless, in spite of such lapses, the progress made was very remarkable.

As early as 1225 the reissue of Magna Carta in return for the concession of a subsidy clearly implied that taxation involved the interests of all the kingdom and thus involved agreement by the *universitas*. The wording of the grant tended to 'blow away the dust of centuries'[1]; it showed that the great council could, in the name of the people of the realm, grant a tax which every householder of the realm had to pay. The idea that consent to a tax was a personal affair, so that one man could agree and another refuse, began to be overcome by the conception of action by the community; and in 1237 a similar tax was granted by the magnates and freemen for themselves and their villeins, involving the idea of representation as well as consent. The tax was conceded only after 'treaty' concerning the state of the king and kingdom, and its proceeds were pledged by Henry for use to meet the needs of the latter. And it was accompanied by a reissue of the charter of 1225.

The need for common action was constantly urged and clearly accepted. 'Do not let us be divided from the common counsel', Robert Grosseteste urged the bishops in 1244, 'for it is written that, if we shall be divided, immediately we shall all perish.'[2] On one occasion the magnates took an oath to give a common reply, or to do nothing without the general *universitas*. The growth of the idea of common action is apparent also in legislation. According to Bracton, the law should be changed only with the authority of the prince and the common assent of the lords; and with such a notion authorities like Matthew Paris and Robert Grosseteste agreed. At the time of the Statute of Merton in 1236, the king and his mag-

[1] F. M. Powicke, *The Thirteenth Century*, pp. 28–9.
[2] Matthew Paris *Chronica Majora*, edited by H. R. Luard, vol. III (R.S. 1877), p. 366.

nates, with the help of the judges, got together to decide hard legal problems; and the statute itself was arrived at by 'treaty' for the common good. Other aspects of government show the same tendency. In 1237, besides helping to provide a landmark in taxation, the magnates strongly complained that Henry had put himself outside the counsels of his 'natural' men, so that little or nothing concerning the business of the kingdom was treated about or disposed of with their advice. In 1247 papal exactions were recognized as creating a danger to the 'republic' and therefore constituting common business of all the realm. It was believed, in consequence, that both the king and the *universitas* should take action; and letters were sent 'on behalf of all the clergy and people of the English realm'.

It was not simply that a *universitas* of barons took it upon themselves to speak for the great mass of Englishmen, sub-tenants and others. What made these ideas constitute the basis of a constitutional revolution was the development of a principle of representation by which such a *universitas* could in time be transformed into a gathering which stood for the whole of the community. Not only would knights and burgesses be summoned to it, but they would speak for those not present, with full power to treat on their behalf. The importance of this representation was the fact that it did not entrust the interests of the English people to the aristocracy alone. Hence, the danger of oligarchy was diminished, whilst the strength of those who treated on behalf of the kingdom was increased.

Such representation was from one point of view an obvious and commonsense solution to a problem which had often presented itself in the Middle Ages wherever there was an active community upon which some external demand was made.[1] Nevertheless, there was a world of difference between summoning representatives to give information and summoning them to 'treat'. The latter may have been derived in part from ideas in Roman law familiar to the clergy, but its most important roots were in feudal habits and ideas.

How far the king, and not the magnates, encouraged this development has indeed been debated; but on the whole it seems wrong to

[1] Cf. H. M. Cam, 'The Theory and Practice of Representation in Medieval England', in *History*, vol. XXXVIII (1953), pp. 11–26; my ' "Political Revolution" of the Thirteenth and Fourteenth Centuries in England', in *Speculum*, vol. XXIV (October 1949), pp. 502–9; G. D. Cuttino, 'Medieval Parliament Re-interpreted', in *ibid.*, vol. XLI (October 1966), p. 681. For a broader discussion of theory, see Walter Ullmann, *The Individual and Society in the Middle Ages* (Baltimore 1966).

regard representation as a royal boon. In 1254, knights were summoned to 'parliament' when Henry III was absent from England. They were asked 'to provide . . .what sort of aid they will give us in so great an emergency', not to treat and say 'yes' or 'no' to a proposal by the government. When they were summoned again in 1261, it was the magnates who invited them to treat; the king directed them to rival assembly, deliberately it would seem asking them only for advice.[1]

Such a development of the summons owed much to expediency as well as to ideas and principles. Those who helped to establish it were opponents of the ruler who needed support from the towns and the shires. In any case, the extension to humble freemen demanded a most enlightened broadening of the aristocratic notions of the age.

Out of all these various ingredients, parliament was evolved in the middle years of the thirteenth century. It represented the answer to urgent political needs and was to prove to be the key to the problem of continuing and expanding feudal limited monarchy in the conditions of the territorial state. Its acceptance into English political life, as a new instrument of co-operation between the king and the community of his subjects, was assured by the precedents established by Simon de Montfort in his great reforming assemblies of 1264 and 1265.

Needless to say, there has been an impressive debate on these questions. For many years, beginning with F. W. Maitland in 1893, Stubbs's view that parliament was in essence the forum of the nation has been strongly attacked. Maitland, though he professed not to depart strongly from Stubbs's views, believed that a meeting of the council was the core and essence of the parliamentary assembly. Richardson and Sayles have argued that its supreme purpose was the dispensing of justice; it was in effect a court set above other courts. Many variations of these theories have been developed; but on the whole the evidence seems to support a neo-Stubbsian interpretation of parliament's growth, though this is obviously still a matter for debate.[2] By 1269, we may venture to conclude, the institution of

---

[1] My *Constitutional History of Medieval England 1216–1399*, vol. III, pp. 271, 303–4, 272. Henry summoned them only to a *colloquium*, which often meant only a discussion.

[2] The modern debate is reflected in my *Constitutional History 1216–1399*, vol. III, pp. 233–375. To the contributions there listed a few more recent ones may be cited, out of many which have appeared: J. G. Edwards, *Historians and the Medieval English Parliament* (Glasgow 1960); E. Miller, *The Origins of Parliament* (Hist. Ass. Pamphlet, London 1960); G. P. Bodet, *Early English Parliaments* (Boston 1968). My own volume, *The Creation of the Medieval Parliament* is in the press.

parliament was firmly established. In that year it was recorded that the king and the magnates treated about the business of the king and the kingdom, 'as was their wont, in the manner of parliament'. We should aim at more parliaments, the archbishop of York wrote in 1271, to mitigate the anger of the times, to reconcile discords, and to procure matters of peace by ordinance of the realm.

Edward I both consolidated and at the same time tended to distort the institution. He was too wise a king to underestimate the importance of the parliamentary assembly. He was, indeed, the first English king to be a parliamentarian. He made use of the precept of Roman Law that 'what touches all shall be approved by all', and he was lavish in declaring the need for co-operation in parliament. But it was the help of his subjects even more than their agreement that he sought. And if he was the father of the Lords, he was only the stepfather of the Commons. He renounced his royal right to tallage the towns by which, in theory at least, he had the power to impose taxes on them at will; but he did not accept any principle of consent by the knights and burgesses to all the taxes he imposed. He got a general agreement for his new custom on wool in 1275, but he imposed further impositions of the custom by *tractatus* with the merchants alone. His evasions of the right of his subjects to agree to taxes contributed to the political crisis of 1297. Nor did he consult the magnates themselves in other important matters. His failure to get their agreement to demands for military service led to the opposition of Bohun and Bigod and contributed to the *Confirmatio Cartarum*. He allowed parliament to be dominated by his council, especially in legislation, though even his father had declared that the interpretation of laws and customs belonged to both the nobles and the king.

Thus Edward I, long famous as the architect of parliament, made a mixed contribution to its growth. Through his methods it developed regularity of summons, traditions of procedure, and the habit of 'treating' about affairs of the king and the realm; but it suffered from his high regard for the royal authority, his paternalism, and his constant appeals for loyalty and obedience. Arbitrary actions were justified by 'necessity', a plea which was made famous by Pope Boniface VIII. Edward's justification of his actions made a strong appeal by virtue of his integrity and good intentions, but it also challenged some deeply rooted political traditions. Hence it is not surprising that, despite all his achievement and the heroic quality of his kingship, Edward I bequeathed a formidable legacy of unsolved parliamentary problems to his son.

Parliament was becoming so transcendental that both the king and his subjects were tempted to bend it to their interests instead of using it for the common good. Though its main purpose had initially been to unite the king and community, it now on the contrary drove them apart. It provided a focal point of discord throughout Edward II's reign. The Ordainers attempted to use it for their reforming purposes and as a means of attacking the king's intimates. The *Modus Tenendi Parliamentum* advocated in it a 'virtual subordination' (the words are those of V. H. Galbraith) of the king to his own subjects.[1] Against such doctrines and policies the Statute of York focused on parliament in an attempt to reassert the impregnable supremacy of the ruler. In the bitter conflicts of the reign, the Commons discovered a new importance. Knights and burgesses gradually came together into one House, and this Lower House took its first faltering steps towards equality with the Lords, debating apart, and initiating Common Petitions to the ruler as a prelude to legislation. The first extant example of such a petition dates from 1309, but a parliamentary 'bill' had been presented in parliament by a knight of the shire on behalf of all the community as early as 1301. The first official reference to a separate session of the knights and burgesses occurred in 1332.

The emergence of a House of Commons had decisive consequences. Together in this parliamentary grouping, the knights and burgesses had an importance which they could never have had apart. Nor was such a union by any means inevitable. Socially, and to some extent politically, the knights seemed at first to have more in common with the great lords than with citizens. But fortunately England, unlike most countries of Europe, never developed a caste whose nobility was transmitted to all their descendents, for ever marking them off from commoners: the younger sons of peers were and are indistinguishable at law from any other citizen. Hence, notions of an inalienable nobility did not exist to prevent English gentry from discovering in the end that they had stronger links with the merchants than they had with the peers.

The greatest single link between the knights and the citizens lay in the fact that both were elected representatives who stood for

[1] 'The *Modus Tenendi Parliamentum*' in the *Journal of the Warburg and Courtauld Institutes*, vol. XVI (1953) p. 83.

communities of shire or borough. The author of the *Modus* actually claimed that two knights who came to parliament for the same shire had a greater voice in the granting of an aid to the king than had a very great earl. One important common interest shared by knights and burgesses was, in fact, that of taxation; though other interests, such as military service and foreign policy, were involved.

The unity of knights and burgesses in one House helped them to tip the scales in favour of the opposition to rulers like Edward II and Richard II. On the other hand, the fact that they formed part of the opposition prevented this from degenerating into a movement towards oligarchy. Its leaders had to broaden their programme so as to attract the support of the middle strata of the population, and aristocratic opposition to English kings never quite lost sight of the interests of all the realm.

It seems unwise to believe, with some historians, that the Commons, with little choice of action and no understanding of politics, were the unwitting pawns of the magnates.[1] Their initiative and their debates about policy in 1376 would not have discredited the Long Parliament. They had an enlightened fear of the unrestricted power of central government, however much they profited by it. They were often, like the magnates, selfish and shortsighted, especially in matters of taxation; but they also had a regard for the well-being of the kingdom. In any case, their alignment was decisive in its consequences for the development of parliament.

The consequences were not slow in appearing. Edward II was warned that 'a new law should not be made without parliament'. His son was advised at the beginning of his reign in almost identical terms. By 1386 it could be categorically asserted that 'the law of the land is made in parliament by the king and the lords spiritual and temporal and all the commonalty of the realm'. A landmark in taxation came with the Statute of 1340 which said that no charge should in future be laid on the king's subjects except by common assent of Lords and Commons in parliament. A similar assent was demanded for the summoning of the local levies, though a clear practice was never established. Further afield, the Commons acquired a voice in the determination of foreign policy. In 1339, for example, they were fully informed about the situation abroad. They did not always welcome their new burden and its implications. In 1348 they

---

[1] Cf. my 'English Politics and Politicians of the Thirteenth and Fourteenth Centuries in England' in *Speculum* vol. XXX (January 1955), pp. 37–48.

rejected any responsibility for the French war; and in 1354 they left discussions about peace to the king and the great men, though both Lords and Commons had been strongly pressed in 1352 to give advice about the conduct of the war.

Finally, the Lords and Commons together asserted a claim to exercise some control over the king's ministers. The beginning of such a claim is plainly to be discerned in 1311. In 1340 it was requested that the king's ministers and councillors should be elected in parliament and should reply there for their tenure of office; and Edward finally conceded in a statute of 1341 that any minister proceeding against Magna Carta should give answer there. This was a notable landmark, even though this statute was subsequently revoked.

Still another step was taken in the political crises of 1376–88, when the Lords and Commons worked out the important procedures of impeachment and appeal. It has been argued, on the whole convincingly, that they took versatile forms of legal action which existed before 1376 and translated them to parliament.[1] Individuals, including the king's ministers, were accused of wrong-doing either by the Commons through their Speaker in 1376 and 1386, or by a group of Lords Appellant in 1388. They were judged by the House of Lords. The participation of the king himself was largely formal, and the actions actually proceeded in his absence or against his wish. The procedures of 1386 and 1388 were backed by declarations enunciating the concept of a High Court of Parliament, notable for the fact that this court was said to be above the Common Law, and to have a law and procedure of its own. The greatest immediate consequence which flowed from all this was the establishment of a measure of responsibility of the king's ministers to Lords and Commons. As a more distant consequence, the balance of power in parliament was changed, even though Richard II in 1397 employed appeal for his own purposes, and in 1450 Henry VI evaded the condemnation of Suffolk by the Lords. The changes initiated in the parliaments of 1376, 1386 and 1388, could not be undone, and their implications were still being worked out in the reign of Charles I.

---

[1] Recent discussions of these much-debated questions are in my *Constitutional History 1216–1399*, vol. II, pp. 204–83; T. F. T. Plucknett, 'The Impeachments of 1376', in *T.R.H.S.*, 5th series, vol. I (1951), pp. 153–64; J. G. Bellamy, 'Appeal and Impeachment in the Good Parliament', *B.I.H.R.* vol. XXXIX (1966), pp. 35–46; G. Lambrick, 'The Impeachment of the Abbot of Abingdon in 1368', *E.H.R.*, vol. LXXXII (1967), pp. 250–76.

By impeachment and appeal, the Lords and Commons took a long step forward towards meeting the political challenge presented by the growth of bureaucracy. But in the process they threatened to make the great instrument of parliament an instrument to destroy the power of the ruler. The relative position of the king, the Lords and the Commons was drastically changed. The king retained his formal ascendancy; indeed, the irony of the situation was that the royal power which Richard led to defeat in 1399 was in some respects greater than it had ever been. But the events of these years brought the parliamentary Estates much nearer to equality with the ruler. Impeachment and Appeal, added to deposition in 1327 and 1399, laid the groundwork for a new sovereignty of the king-lords-and-commons in parliament.

In other directions the gains made by the Lords and Commons were important if not as spectacular. The two Estates gradually displaced the council from its preeminence in parliamentary procedure. The councillors ceased to sit in the assembly as a separate body. Members of the Upper House established their claims to be summoned by hereditary right and to enjoy the privilege of trial by their peers. Lords and Commons 'communed' together to arrive at a common policy on particular occasions. The Lords, with the co-operation of the Commons, accepted responsibility for the kingdom in the illness or minority of the king.

In these changes, the peers, the judges of the High Court of Parliament, appeared to have made the greater advance. They deeply influenced the Commons both inside parliament by procedure and prestige and outside through their influence in the constituencies. The first Speaker of the Commons to be recorded, in 1376, was the steward of the earl of March. In 1378 John of Gaunt could return to chancery a writ which had ordered an election of knights, with the endorsement, 'by virtue of this writ I send you . . . two knights'. Nevertheless, the advances made by the Commons were to prove in the long run to be more important. Representation became more clearly a privilege rather than a burden. Great magnates might still on some occasions simply command the election of representatives in shire and borough, but on others they probably had to make considerable efforts to this end. We are on the eve of the period when there would be strong competition in shires and boroughs for the privilege of making nominations. Altogether, the gains made by the Commons in the fourteenth century must have made the inflated claims of the *Modus Tenendi Parliamentum* on their behalf seem much less extravagant by 1399.

Through the progress achieved by both Lords and Commons, and through the beginnings of the conjoint rule of the king and the Estates in parliament, Englishmen were learning to make a unique contribution to the problem of government. They could both have their cake and eat it; they could enjoy strong government but yet preserve limited monarchy. Their ruler was powerful but only in co-operation with his subjects. The road to greater order and efficiency was left wide open, but the way was increasingly barred to the establishment of absolute rule.

The continuation of this process of integration in parliament was the great achievement of the fifteenth century. For this there were many reasons. There was an increase in the importance of gentry and bourgeoisie. The great lords had mixed gains and losses during the loss of France and the Wars of the Roses. There was a tendency in politics to appeal for the support of the *plebs* with some increase, as a result, in their importance. Nor can Englishmen have ever quite forgotten the memorable 'risings' of 1381 and 1450 or failed to recognize the political importance of Londoners and Kentishmen.

Whatever the causes, in 1399 the Commons could be designated only as petitioners and demanders in parliament; yet fifteen years later they could ask Henry V to recognize them also as assentors. In March 1401 the Speaker of the Commons could liken the Estates to the Trinity in which three equals were mystically united in one. Practice kept pace with theory. The custom grew whereby parliamentary Bills were 'read' before both Lords and Commons, and only then sent forward to the king. Thus in legislation the knights and burgesses achieved formal equality with the peers. Bills also began to be put forward which already contained within themselves the form of the Act that was desired, so as to prevent alterations by the crown against the intentions of the Commons and Lords. Without the assent of the Commons such bills could not go forward at all. Finally, Acts began to be issued 'by authority of parliament', and this formula included all the members of the assembly. In 1420 the knights and burgesses petitioned against its use unless they had consented to the Act.

Similar progress was made in taxation. From the end of Richard II's reign it became customary for money grants to be made by the Commons with the advice and consent of the Lords. When in 1407

Henry IV consulted the Lords first and, in effect, sought only the concurrence of the Commons, 'the commons were greatly disturbed'. Whereupon the king withdrew his suggestion and formally ruled that both Lords and Commons had the right to deliberate apart on this or any other matter, and that grants should be reported 'in the accustomed manner' through the Speaker of the Commons.[1] As a result of such clarification, Sir John Fortescue could claim later that the king did not by himself or by his ministers impose tallages, subsidies, or any other burdens whatever on his subjects, without the assent of his whole realm expressed in parliament. The progress of parliament was at times adversely affected by politics; but its survival, and its development on lines already established, were never seriously in doubt. Lancastrian neglect could not quench fires already burning, as was shown by the Impeachment of Suffolk; nor could Yorkist legitimism take away parliament's inner strength. It is perhaps unwise to estimate this strength either by the frequency of its meetings or by the paucity of attendance in the Upper House.[2]

Parliament was fast becoming in a new sense the community of all England gathered together as one body in head and members. As an unknown rhymer put it:

> When all the kingdom gathered is
> In God's law, and by one assent,
> For to amend what was amiss,
> Therefore is ordained a parliament.

Similarly Henry VIII said in the sixteenth century:

> We be informed by our judges that we at no time stand so high in our estate royal as in the time of parliament, when we as head and you as members are conjoined and knit together in one body politic.

This could well have been said at any moment in the fifteenth, but particularly after 1461.

9. THE RECONCILIATION OF ORDER AND LIBERTY

The long process of legal, institutional, and constitutional growth had created some formidable problems. It had destroyed the

---

[1] There are important differences of opinion about this episode; see my *Constitutional History of England in the Fifteenth Century*, pp. 281–2, 310.

[2] There is some discussion by J. S. Roskell, in 'The Problem of Attendance of the Lords in Medieval Parliaments', *B.I.H.R.*, vol. XXIX (1956), pp. 153–204, and in my 'Fact and Fancy in Fifteenth-Century English History' referred to above.

'personal' monarchy and rendered obsolete the ideas and processes of the Angevin *Curia Regis*; it had created new notions of royal prerogative; and it had produced a central government which was perhaps the strongest in Europe. In the process, it had precipitated violent political conflicts, the ultimate cause of which, outside the infirmities of men, lay in the problem of reconciling the authority thus created and the practice of liberty.

In their conflicts with the monarch, the concentration of early thirteenth-century reformers on counsellors and the council led them down a blind alley, for the council was by tradition pre-eminently an instrument of the ruler. The reforming proposals of 1244 show this preoccupation clearly. There was an understanding of the urgent need for change, but a failure to seek this in the whole *Curia Regis*, the keystone of the arch of Angevin rule.

The great exploitation of the traditions of the *Curia* came in the movement of baronial rebellion and reform between 1258 and 1265. At this time the convergence of many forces led to the emergence of a genuinely new institution. This was a great step forward. Nevertheless, in a society growing as fast as that of the thirteenth century there could be no final solution to the problem of government. Bureaucratic development rapidly undermined the personal monarchy around which the early parliament developed, and tended to render Simon de Montfort's parliamentary notions obsolete before they were ever fully applied.

Under Edward I, parliament continued to be the king sitting in his court in his Council, attended by his subjects; and in consequence the attainment of a true co-operation between him and them had still to surmount obstacles almost as formidable as those which had already been overcome. The king was tempted to deny the spirit of the parliamentary assembly by adopting methods of absolutism; the subjects made demands there which were incompatible with effective monarchical rule. Hence, instead of allaying discords as Walter Giffard had hoped, parliament gave rise to new problems which added fuel to the fire. The magnates were not only alarmed by the obvious growth of royal powers under an expanding government and by a loss of old intimacies with the ruler; they were also stimulated by an increase in their own powers and ambitions. Some of them who were fortunate by reason of marriage or royal favour acquired an accumulation of estates, like the five earldoms of Thomas of Lancaster, reinforced in his case by the claims of a prince of the royal blood; and such claims became formidable after the marriage policies of Edward III. Bastard feudalism expanded the horizons of the great lords. Confederacies became fashionable, like that which Thomas of Lancaster tried to create in 1321 and which the Appellants did create in 1387 and 1388. A 'confederacy' of the Marcher lords helped to destroy Edward II, and the northern magnates played a vital role in the overthrow of Richard II.

With recourse to such confederacies the magnates were slow to develop opposition in parliament. Parliamentary concessions were important in 1297 and they were much more obvious in 1311; but the movement of that year nevertheless had its origin in a promise extracted from Edward II at his coronation. As late as the fifteenth century baronial opposition was expressed in civil war. Nevertheless, parliament as the focus of political conflict gradually became more important. It was central in the settlement of 1322. Opposition to Edward III was essentially parliamentary, as in 1340–41 and in 1376; and the same is true even of the bitter opposition to Richard II. The deposition of 1327 was 'parliamentary' and the sanction for the Lancastrian accession in 1399 was by the Estates and *populus* who had gathered together for a meeting of parliament.

Impeachments and appeals from 1376 to 1397 were a landmark in this process, for though they led to 'political' trials and executions, they involved judgments by the Lords and the concept of the High Court of Parliament. Parliament was becoming the instrument through which king and community could exercise a conjoint control over the growing machine of government. It looked as if men were moving away from politics based on the feudal *Widerstandsrecht* to politics conducted mainly in the forum of parliament. It is not without significance that there was no actual civil war in England, except for the skirmishes at Boroughbridge and Radcote Bridge, between 1272 and 1399.

It is true that the fifteenth century witnessed a retrogression. The French war and the minority of Henry VI caused a deterioration in politics. The council gained in importance at the expense of parliament, and the magnates in the council gained power at the expense of other members. The king himself, in the person of Henry VI, lost effective control over the government. The result was a period of unprecedented quarrels within the council from 1422 to 1447 in which were sown the seeds of civil war. War, and conditions making for war, threatened the destruction of parliament. But the important fact is, not that it lost its vitality, but that its vitality was essentially preserved and possibly even enlarged.[1]

Thus, through three centuries of strife the English carried forward the essence of their primitive government into the institutional framework of the early modern state. In the process they became notorious for violence and instability: Froissart could represent the Londoners as boasting that they would slay half a hundred kings until they had one that suited them.[2] Englishmen made regicide a commonplace and the threat of civil war an instrument of policy, but they wrote a brilliant chapter in the long history of men's efforts to harmonize liberty and authority. They created a complicated institutional framework which sustained a continuing economic and social progress, without sacrificing the vitality of simple political notions which had been at the foundations of all the achievements of this spectacular age.

[1] This debatable question is briefly discussed in my 'Fact and Fancy in Fifteenth-Century English History', referred to above.

[2] *Chroniques*, edited by S. Luce and G. Raynaud (Soc. de l'histoire de France, Paris 1869–99), vol. I, p. 249; cf. Jusserand, *Piers Plowman*, p. 48.

EPILOGUE

1. The Thirteenth Century Age of Achievement

ENGLAND in the later Middle Ages presents no simple movement of change, but on the whole shows unmistakable signs of progress by a society which was inherently vigorous and strong. This is very evident in the thirteenth century, a period of great achievement; but it is also to be discerned in the fourteenth, marked by natural catastrophe and political strife; and it may even be said of the fifteenth, often still regarded as a period of sterility if not of outright decline. Taken together, the three centuries not only witnessed overall progress, but may also be regarded as the time when English society was revolutionized by the cumulative forces of change. The English people, like other peoples of Europe, were faced with immense and incalculable consequences of their own economic, intellectual, and political achievements, which presented them with new and intractable problems and profoundly modified the old and familiar patterns of their life.

The changes were comprehensive because all aspects of society at any given time were bound together, however tenuously, by a thread of common mood and purpose. There was an age of Simon de Montfort just as truly as there was an age of Wyclif or an age of Edward IV, and as in modern times we may talk of the age of Elizabeth or of Victoria. It is unwise to press the idea of a cultural and political complex too far; but it seems to be true that the broad changes which occurred in the last three centuries of medievalism were reflected, to a greater or less degree, in all the various aspects of life.

By and large, English society at the beginning of the thirteenth century belonged to the feudal past and looked to its traditions as providing norms and the basic ideals. It was still dominated by the effects of the Norman Conquest, which had imposed on England an alien and strongly militaristic aristocracy. Beyond that, it was part of a European world many of whose habits and assumptions went back to the early Middle Ages, and which seemed destined to last forever, part of God's universal design. The source of its dominant culture and language was not in England but in France. England herself was divided between two peoples, a division which had not greatly weakened even as late as 1216, one hundred and fifty years after the Conquest. This both strengthened and weakened the community, giving it a diversity of culture but denying it the fullness of a common heritage.

The thirteenth century saw the beginnings of a transformation by which the country finally became united, and when it also passed the point of no return in its long progress from feudalism and agrarian economy to the conditions of a money economy and a territorial state. This was the greatest change which occurred until the industrial revolution of the nineteenth century. Nevertheless, though the transformation of all aspects of life was strongly under way in the thirteenth century, its importance was as yet hardly apparent. The dominant note was that of the consummation of old processes rather than the beginning of new. The heritage of the past was too strong, and the sense of movement and change too weak, for any clear-cut departure from old and venerated customs and ideas.

Both the conservatism and the dynamism of the age are well illustrated in its politics. These still revolved around the old concept of personal monarchy, although statesmen of this period discovered the unique institution of parliament, and Edward I was in some respects both the last medieval ruler and the first of the 'modern' kings. The essence of the monarchical position was still, at the end of the period, provided by the coronation oath of King Edgar in 973. Edward himself cloaked his modernity in the robes of King Arthur and his knights of the Round Table. The more modern the king became the more he clung to chivalric notions derived from what was fast becoming a distant and elusive past.

There was the same mixture of old and new in the aristocracy. At the end of the century the magnates were still faithful, in spite of Simon de Montfort and the beginnings of parliament, to the spirit of Magna Carta and the defence of baronial liberties. Even the Provisions of Oxford were thought of as only a temporary infringement of the monarchical order of government. The magnates had, indeed, begun a long movement of transformation from the fighting baron to the Renaissance courtier, and they accepted new responsibilities in the kingdom; but they remained the same feudal landlords, whose primary interest was in the countryside and in agrarian affairs. They claimed their rightful share in the government of England, but they had no substitute for personal monarchy and no desire to revolutionize the political system. They followed French patterns of language and literature, admired the thoroughly feudal French monarch Louis IX, and had apparently no clear appreciation of the fundamental reorientation which had begun with the loss of Normandy in 1204. They still remained more French than English, their outlook fortified by the cosmopolitan cult of chivalry and war which had always been centred on France.

Despite the rise of a money economy and the rapid growth of towns, politics and society continued to be dominated by the feudal aristocracy. The whole hierarchic society still reflected the rhythms and limitations of an agricultural community, with its strength and endurance but also its weaknesses, both intellectual and material. The vast majority of Englishmen were peasants. The culture and the refinements of life were confined to the privileged few. The conditions of society were sanctioned by religion and experience, and commanded an almost universal acceptance. There was no Peasants' Revolt in thirteenth-century England, and no claim by the mass of Englishmen to participate in public affairs at a high political level. This is true, though London was always an exception, in spite of the fact that politics were beginning to be accepted as affecting all the community of the realm. Despite these foreshadowings of change, it is fair to say that a work like Langland's *Piers Plowman* reflecting a new interest in and a new importance of the common man was as yet almost unthinkable.

The same is true wherever we touch the complex development of the thirteenth century. Changes in warfare and military service contained revolutionary elements, but they were easily reconciled to established notions. They created new efficiencies without challenging existing feudal patterns. This was true even of the Bastard Feudalism which made its appearance towards the end of the century. Even in the explosive area of intellectual endeavour there was the same dominance of the known and tried and the avoidance of revolutionary conflict. Robert Grosseteste stands forth as the great embodiment of both an intellectual pioneer and a religious reformer, with his mind searching the secrets of heaven and earth, but with his loyalties and faith unimpaired. There was nobody comparable to Ockham in thirteenth-century England, even though he was anticipated by Duns Scotus, and there was no Albigensian heresy or even Wycliffite reform. There was anti-apapal feeling, but the most stubborn religious reformers were severely orthodox.

The pattern of religious life was, in fact, being transformed by the rise of two great monarchies. One was religious and papal, to which Innocent III had made a powerful contribution. The other was secular and ultimately national, contributed to by St Louis of France and by King Edward I. The church in England was still dominated by otherworldliness and still kept some Hildebrandine traditions of the relations of Church and State, but it was deeply enmeshed in affairs of state and its clergy were often servants of the laity. The two monarchies competed for revenues, loyalty and obedience, even whilst prelates like Grosseteste were busy reconciling their first obedience to the Vicar of Christ with that which they owed to the community of England and its king.

But the church was still in essence one indivisible *Respublica Christiana* whose heart lay outside England. Its vital new Orders in the thirteenth century were founded by an Italian and a Spaniard and were distinguished by their loyalty to the pope. It is true that English churchmen and reformers began to look more and more inwards, and that the century was distinguished by the first clear anti-papalism among the laity and the first collective opposition by the clergy to excessive papal demands. There were the beginnings of English movements of revolt. But the immense and all-pervading influence of old loyalties and beliefs was portrayed in memorable forms by the serenity and beauty of the universal Gothic architectural style which was reflected in churches all over England. It was essentially an importation from France. There was as yet no distinctively English form; there was only an expression of the whole Christian faith, symbolizing in its form and content the eternal city of God.

Dominated by French influence, and part of an apparently eternal *Respublica Christiana*, ruled by a militaristic but extraordinarily successful aristocracy which was similarly cosmopolitan, and supported by the timeless order and seasonal routines of an agrarian peasantry, the forms and spirit of the Anglo-French society seemed to be perfectly in balance with nature, deeply satisfying men's needs and aspirations, and destined indefinitely to endure. Supplementing this harmony was the hard fact that whilst England remained overwhelmingly agrarian, with technology primitive and a quantitative understanding of the world impossible, the conditions for revolutionary change might be emerging but the change itself was still beyond men's understanding or reach.

Nevertheless, the order which found such general acceptance was, in fact, being profoundly affected by the expansion of government, the creation of wealth, and the broadening of horizons. The way was being paved for change by such forces as individualism, patriotism, and secularism which would one day transform men's outlook as well as their social conditions. It is hard to measure the new forces at work in a society so governed by an agelong pattern and sacrosanct ideals; but it seems to be beyond question that a widespread revolution was in the making beneath the conservative exterior of life.

2. The Revolutionary Age of Wyclif

The inner harmony of society was not by any means destroyed in the fourteenth century. Nevertheless a note of conflict and discord arose touching many aspects of life. Men were not, as is sometimes thought, afflicted with a *crise de nerfs*, by doubts about their capacity to solve their problems or surmount their difficulties. They suffered more perhaps from over-confidence. There was nothing in their outlook comparable to that of a civilization in decline. However, the very progress of the past combined with natural calamities of the present to suggest to men the need for radical solutions to their problems and to create visions of change. It was an exciting and, for some, a dangerous age. But, contrary to what some writers have argued, it was also an age when great issues were debated, great ideals were upheld, and great decisions were made.

In politics, extremism gave the English an unenviable reputation and provided precedents for later opposition to the Stuarts. England, it may be argued, stood for the first time, despite the precedents of the anarchy of Stephen and of Angevin 'tyranny', at the crossroads between an overweak monarchy and the development of absolute rule. That this was no mere academic matter was shown conclusively by the constitutional development of France. But though there were extreme movements to put the king under baronial tutelage and corresponding reactions to make impregnable the royal powers, there was, in the end, the triumph of the golden mean, a reassertion of old political ideals adapted to the new needs of the emerging 'modern' state.

Extreme solutions were similarly offered in regard to social and economic problems. There was a loosening of the cohesion of society and the rise of individualism, the effects of which are obscure but which may have been considerable. The phenomena of the yeoman farmer and the bowman of Crécy could not fail to constitute a challenge to the feudal pattern. The dislocations of the Black Death added to the uncertainty and perhaps to the fluidity of agrarian life. Whatever the particular causes, an unprecedented discontent and challenge to existing conditions were reflected in the Peasants' Revolt of 1381. Nor was the tendency towards a radical departure from the past confined to the countryside. It was evident also in conflict between enfranchised and unenfranchised inhabitants of the towns. It may even be seen in parliament, in the new demands of the knights and burgesses and in the novel pretensions of the Commons in 1376.

The Good Parliament fell between the first and second redactions of Langland's *Piers Plowman*, and his poem reflects a new attitude towards the importance of the common man. And to this poetic radicalism we might well add that of Wyclif's Poor Preachers and of the Lollardy to which these gave rise. It is to the credit and not to the discredit of the fourteenth century that, in spite of this new radicalism, old notions of society in the main prevailed; though the new phenomena revealed a society no longer sure of its old foundations, questioning the eternal and divine nature of its way of life, and turning its face, however uncertainly and hesitatingly, towards far-reaching change.

Similar conflicts emerged in scholarship and religion. In the former, the efforts of thirteenth-century scholars to reconcile philosophy and religion had proved to be only the beginning, not the end, of an intellectual crisis. Here again, their successors were faced with extremism. The intellectual iconoclasm of Ockham was confronted with the unyielding traditionalism of Wyclif. The unqualified triumph of either school of thought might well have been disastrous. It was as important to preserve the Christian intellectual tradition which Ockham threatened as it was to open the door to the understanding of the universe which seemed to be promised by the methods Wyclif opposed. The bitter scholastic disputes of the

fourteenth century prolonged the worst aspects of scholastic speculation; but they were probably a necessary price to be paid for
balanced intellectual progress; and they ended with a compromise
which was, as it proved, only the prelude to further spectacular
advance.

In religious affairs there was the same clash of extremes. The
weaknesses of the Church which Wyclif denounced were not
created in the fourteenth century; they were inherited and aggravated. They could not be remedied, however logical and persuasive
the reformer, but they could be confronted and decried. There was a
real danger of bitter fratricidal strife between Christians, of the
heretic versus the orthodox, which would merely divide the country
rather than produce measures of reform. There was a danger that
reform would be identified with heresy and extremism and thus indefinitely deferred. The conflict engendered by Wyclif and the
Lollards was indeed bitter; but it did not prove to be disastrously
divisive. The Church was not reformed; but Wyclif's inspiration
was never entirely forgotten, and the changing relations of
Church and State paved the way for a peaceful Reformation in
1534.

These conflicts and changes nearly all ended in compromise, but
they nevertheless contributed to a broad process of transformation.
The revolution impending in the thirteenth century moved perceptibly closer. The old conservatism found a way to tolerate new
tendencies. The dynamism of society was increased rather than
diminished, and the links with the future begin to be almost as
clearly apparent as those with the past.

3. The Fifteenth Century Age of Transition to the Early Modern World

The fifteenth century had rightfully been regarded by historians
as preeminently one of transition, in which the cumulative changes
of progress and expansion brought England to the threshold of a
new age. In this process some old ideas were discarded and old
institutions finally transformed; but the process should not be
interpreted in terms of the decay and failure of an old order yielding
place to new. The feudal order was expanded and developed, not
simply superseded. It evolved to create the ideas and institutions of
the early modern territorial state.

The outstanding features of the century were the broadening

of the basis of the social hierarchy, the rise of the bourgeoisie, and the working out in detail of the concept of limited monarchy. This was not a spectacular achievement compared with those of both earlier and later periods. There were no outstanding contributions comparable to those of the age of Robert Grosseteste or Simon de Montfort or John Wyclif. There were no great intellectual or artistic innovations like the writings of Chaucer or the architectural 'miracle' of Gloucester. There were not even, in the opinion of most writers, great political struggles dignified by a clash of principles or ideas. The products of this society in process of transition were different, though perhaps no less admirable.

Though still aristocratic, society became less feudal. The royal court remained the centre of patronage and influence as well as of power, but it declined from the glories of Edward III's reign. The aristocracy were never more splendid and ostentatious, but they were in some ways at least, on the defensive. Their display and extravagance were less spontaneous and more calculated than those of Edward III's Round Table. Their traditions of chivalry could still make a strong appeal, witness the writings of Tiptoft, William of Worcester and Malory; but they could not dominate literature or inspire great artists like Chaucer and Gower. Nor could the clash of ideas produce a genius like Langland who expressed the glowing faith in Mother Church appropriate to the mystics of the fourteenth century but not to the Lollards and the age of domestic piety. The creative power of the fifteenth century writer was influenced by the tastes and preferences of a broader audience. Two things must not be forgotten. One was the vigour of popular writing such as ballads, songs, satires and mystery plays. The other was the brevity of this period of transition from the age of Chaucer and the royal court to that of William Shakespeare and the Globe. Perhaps its most significant figure was William Caxton with his printing press, making the treasures of both courtly verse and popular works of devotion accessible to a broad stratum of Englishmen.

In politics, the fifteenth century continued and expanded the lines of development established at the end of the fourteenth. Despite many vicissitudes, the ideal it bequeathed through the Yorkist kings was essentially that of the Tudors, of effective rule by kings who were true in essence to Sir John Fortescue's idea of *dominium regale et politicum*. The aristocratic Wars of the Roses made no small contribution to the rising importance of popular levies; and

the careers of Warwick the Kingmaker and Richard, duke of Gloucester, later Richard III, show the importance of popular support in
political affairs. It would be going too far to claim that this element
in politics and war had begun to rival that of the dominant aristocracy. This did not happen even in the sixteenth century. But it
seems probable that by the end of Richard III's short-lived and
spectacular failure to keep the throne after forfeiting the nation's
allegiance, a new political balance had been achieved in England,
fully revealed in the political methods of the Tudor Age. Already
the great lords 'worked' to have their supporters returned to parliament from shires and boroughs. Already there were signs of a new
'sovereignty' in parliament, of king-lords-and-commons, the mystic
unity which Sir Arnold Savage had somewhat fancifully presaged.

The new society which was emerging was reflected not only in
the Wars of the Roses but also in the *Libelle of English Polycye*, in
the Merchant Adventurers, in the rise of the cloth trade and the
expansion of English shipping, in the Celys and the Pastons. In the
end, despite all the persistence of old forms, the divided feudal
society of the early thirteenth century became the united English
nation of the early sixteenth, prepared for the Reformation, and
ready to change its ancient aspirations to revive an Anglo-French
monarchy for a broader vision of a new commercial expansion overseas. A many-sided transformation of society had occurred which
may not have been a revolution in the sense of a destruction of old
institutions and an old social order, but which nevertheless represented a successful transition from a feudal and agrarian society
to the beginnings of the modern age.

4

Thus there was no break at any point in the last three centuries
of English medieval history; there was a continuous process of
evolution, at whose heart was the successful creation of a territorial
state without recourse to absolutism, and the broadening and
strengthening, not the surrender, of individual liberty. The great
legacy which the fifteenth century handed on to Tudor England
was not only the government and law of a strong and unified state.
It was not only the beginnings of New Learning going back to the
days of Humphrey of Gloucester and soon to create a scholarship
which Erasmus said would not disgrace Italy herself. Nor was it
the beginnings of a new age of commercial expansion and a garnered

store of material wealth. It was not even the bourgeoisie and the broadened basis of the political society.

It was the happy combination of the old and the new, in which the traditions of the *Respublica Christiana* were as important as the potentialities for a new humanism and a new understanding of the universe; in which old loyalties mingled with new individualism, and traditions and standards of the old aristocracy survived a new equality under the levelling power of the state. The strength of the society of Tudor England was not created in the sixteenth century, but by centuries of evolution. Very many generations had made their contribution, but none perhaps more conspicuously than those of the years after 1216. Men of the early modern period were not very grateful to their predecessors in these centuries, and tended to despise the whole feudal order which had provided the foundations for their own prosperity; but perhaps we may now redress the balance a little. We may be grateful to the men of the later Middle Ages for what they preserved and transmitted as well as for what they destroyed.

NOTE ON BOOKS

1. BIBLIOGRAPHIES

A comprehensive bibliography, but now badly out of date, is that of C. Gross, *The Sources and Literature of English History to about 1485* (Second Edition, London 1915). More modern bibliographies are given in the *Oxford History of England*: Sir Maurice Powicke, *The Thirteenth Century* (Oxford, 1953); May McKisack, *The Fourteenth Century* (Oxford, 1959); and E. F. Jacob, *The Fifteenth Century* (Oxford, 1961). Additional references will appear shortly in the relevant volumes of *English Historical Documents*, edited by D. C. Douglas and G. W. Greenaway. Recent contributions to political and constitutional history are listed in my *Constitutional History of England 1216–1399* (3 vols. London, 1948–58) and the *Constitutional History of England in the Fifteenth Century* (London, 1964). A survey of contemporary writing is made by the Historical Association in its *Annual Bulletin of Historical Literature*.

2. STANDARD SECONDARY WORKS

All three volumes in the *Oxford History* are indispensable, and one or two chapters in the *Cambridge Medieval Hostory* are still valuable. Constitutional problems are dealt with in the volumes on this subject cited above. J. E. A. Jolliffe's, *The Constitutional History of Medieval England* (1937) is a scholarly but somewhat erratic individual interpretation. My *Studies in the Constitutional History of the Thirteenth and Fourteenth Centuries,* (Manchester, 1937) deals with some major problems. Administration is dealt with on a massive scale by T. F. Tout in *Chapters in the Administrative History of Medieval England* (Manchester, 1923–35). Architecture, art, and literature are dealt with in the *Oxford History of Art* (P. Brieger, *English Art 1216–1307* (1957), and Joan Evans, *English Art, 1307–1461* (1949)); the *Cambridge History of English Literature*, edited by A. W. Ward and A. R. Waller (1920–27); George Sampson, *The Concise Cambridge History of English Literature* (Cambridge, 1942); the *Oxford History of English Literature*

(H. S. Bennett, *Chaucer and the Fifteenth Century* (1947); E. K. Chambers, *English Literature at the close of the Middle Ages* (1945)). There is an excellent treatment of Anglo-Norman writing by M. Dominica Legge, *Anglo-Norman Literature and its Background* (Oxford, 1963). For intellectual history, the standard survey is still *The Universities of Europe in the Middle Ages,* by Hastings Rashdall, 2nd. ed., vol. III, edited by F. M. Powicke and A. B. Emden, (Oxford 1936). Economic history is dealt with in the *Cambridge Economic History of Europe* (vols. II, and III, edited by M. M. Postan and E. E. Rich, 1952, 1963), and social history in A. L. Poole's, *Medieval England* (2 vols. Oxford, 1958). There is no standard survey of the history of religion, but there are excellent volumes by M. D. Knowles, *The Religious Orders in England* (2 vols., Cambridge, 1955). Alongside these are more restricted works: J. R. H. Moorman, *Church Life in England in the Thirteenth Century* (Cambridge, 1945) and W. A. Pantin, *The English Church in the XIV century* (Cambridge, 1955). There are many good biographies of individual bishops, some of which are referred to in the footnotes above.

INDEX